P9-CKQ-825

Using Russian

A guide to contemporary usage

DEREK OFFORD
Reader in Russian, University of Bristol

CAMBRIDGE
UNIVERSITY PRESS

Published by the Press Syndicate of the University of Cambridge
The Pitt Building, Trumpington Street, Cambridge CB2 1RP
40 West 20th Street, New York, NY 10011-4211, USA
10 Stamford Road, Oakleigh, Melbourne 3166, Australia

First published 1996
Reprinted 1997

Printed in Great Britain at the University Press, Cambridge

A catalogue record for this book is available from the British Library

ISBN 0 521 45130 2 hardback
ISBN 0 521 45760 2 paperback

CE

To Catherine and Helen,
coevals of this book

Contents

Preface

This book, like the volumes already published in the series on contemporary usage in French, German and Spanish, is aimed at the advanced learner who has studied the basic grammar of the language and is now striving for a more comprehensive and sophisticated knowledge. To this end the book includes much material on register, vocabulary, verbal etiquette and word-formation, as well as material on the subjects of morphology, prepositions and syntax with which the post-A-level student should already have some familiarity. The book is not conceived as a comprehensive grammar, although the main grammatical topics that trouble the English-speaking student are quite fully covered in the later chapters. The approach adopted is not prescriptive. That is to say an attempt is made to show the range of linguistic phenomena that might be encountered in modern Russian and to define the limits within which they are used rather than to lay down rules for usage.

While offering, it is hoped, a multi-faceted view of the modern language, two purposes are kept in mind throughout the book.

Firstly, it is intended to demonstrate that Russian, like any other modern language with which the student may be familiar, is not a stable, uniform abstraction that is applied inflexibly in all situations. As a living language spoken by millions of individuals of different ages from different backgrounds and in different situations Russian exists in many varieties. Words, forms and constructions which are appropriate in one context may be quite out of place in another. Even apparently hard-and-fast grammatical rules may be relaxed, to the frustration of the foreign student who has laboriously mastered them. Chapter 1 therefore aims to make the student aware of the existence of variety in the Russian language, and this variety is borne in mind and examples of it indicated in all the chapters that follow.

Secondly, the book attempts to address problems that the English-speaking student of Russian may find especially taxing. Russian operates, of course, according to quite different grammatical principles from those to which the English-speaker is accustomed. (One thinks in particular of its system of declension of nouns, pronouns, adjectives, numerals and participles and of the aspectual distinction that runs through the Russian verbal system.) Moreover, in the field of vocabulary correspondences between Russian and English words are often limited or inexact and similarities can be misleading. Again, in certain situations Russians simply do not express themselves in the same way as English-speakers in a similar situation, or at least a direct translation of what an English-speaker would say in that situation would seem to a Russian to some degree unnatural. Much attention is therefore devoted in this book to problems of non-equivalence in the two languages in vocabulary, phraseology and verbal etiquette as well as grammar.

Beyond these purposes it is also hoped that the book, through its broad approach, will increase the student's general awareness of the structure and resources of the Russian language, and that his or her understanding and appreciation of the immense vitality and depth of experience of the Russian people may thus in some small way be enhanced.

Acknowledgements

Several colleagues have given help and advice during the compilation of this book. My greatest debt is to Natalia Gogolitsyna and Natalia Sergeeva, both of whom have read drafts of the whole work, made innumerable comments and helpfully answered my many questions. Among English-speaking colleagues I am especially grateful to Felicity Cave and Peter Mayo for their very numerous corrections and suggestions. My thanks are also due, for comment on matters of detail or for drawing my attention to useful material, to Natalia Beliak, Birgit Beumers, Mary MacRobert, Robert Porter and Rodney Sampson. I also acknowledge my dependence on the works already published in the current series on French usage (R.E. Batchelor and M.H. Offord), German usage (Martin Durrell), and Spanish usage (R.E. Batchelor and C.J. Pountain), all of which have provided models for me to follow. The discussion of register in the first two of these books has been of particular use to me. The magazine *Cosmopolitan, Russia* and the newspaper *Izvestiia* have kindly given me permission to reproduce the excerpts at 1.6.2 and 1.6.6 respectively. Finally I am most grateful to Kate Brett, Alison Gilderdale and Glennis Foote of Cambridge University Press, the former for encouraging me to undertake the project at the outset and for her perseverance with it and the latter two for their assistance in the later stages of work on it. For all the mistakes, misapprehensions and imperfections of presentation that no doubt remain in spite of the best efforts of all these colleagues and advisers I myself accept sole responsibility.

D.C.O.
Bristol

Sources

Dictionaries

Avanesov, R.I., ed., *Орфоэпический словарь русского языка*, Русский язык, Moscow, 1985

Chernyshev, V.I., *et al.*, ed., *Словарь современного русского литературного языка*, Академия наук СССР, 17 vols., Moscow, 1950–65

Evgen′eva, A.P., *Словарь синонимов русского языка*, Наука, 2 vols., Leningrad, 1970–1

Galperin, I.R., ed., *New English–Russian Dictionary*, 2 vols., Soviet Encyclopaedia Publishing House, Moscow, 1972

The Oxford Russian Dictionary (Russian–English, English–Russian), revised and updated by Colin Howlett, Oxford University Press, Oxford, New York, 1993

Ozhegov, S.I., *Словарь русского языка*, 20th edn, Русский язык, Moscow, 1988

Rozental′, D.E., ed., *Словарь ударений для работников радио и телевидения*, Советская энциклопедия, Moscow, 1970

Wheeler, Marcus, *The Oxford Russian–English Dictionary*, 2nd edn, Clarendon Press, Oxford, 1990

Grammars

Borras, F.M, and Christian, R.F., *Russian Syntax*, 2nd edn, Clarendon Press, Oxford, 1979

Forbes' Russian Grammar, 3rd edn, revised and enlarged by J.C. Dumbreck, Oxford University Press, 1964

Pulkina, I.M., *A Short Russian Reference Grammar*, translated from the Russian by V. Korotky, 7th edn, Русский язык, Moscow, 1984

Unbegaun, B.O., *Russian Grammar*, Oxford University Press, 1957

Vinogradov, V.V., *et al.*, *Грамматика русского языка*, Академия наук СССР, 2 vols. in 3 books, Moscow, 1960

Wade, Terence, *A Comprehensive Russian Grammar*, Blackwell, Oxford, Cambridge Mass., 1992

I have also made use, especially in Chapters 8–10, of material from my own work, *Modern Russian: An Advanced Coursebook*, Bristol Classical Press and Duckworth, London, 1993.

Specific references

Many sections in this book (indicated by the references in brackets after the titles below) draw on the works on particular areas of vocabulary or grammar in the following list or relate to areas more fully dealt with in those works.

Akulenko, V.V., ed., *Англо-русский и русско-английский словарь «ложных друзей переводчика»*, Советская энциклопедия, Moscow, 1969 (2.5)

Avanesov, R.I., and Orlova, V.G., eds., *Русская диалектология*, 2nd edn, Наука, Moscow, 1965 (1.4)

Bivon, R., *Element Order*, Cambridge University Press, 1971 (10.14)

Bratus, B.V., *The Formation and Expressive Use of Diminutives*, Cambridge University Press, 1969 (7.8)

Comrie, B., and Stone, G., *The Russian Language since the Revolution*, Clarendon Press, Oxford, 1978

Cooper, Brian, 'Problems with the In-Laws: The Terminology of Russian Family Relationships', *Journal of Russian Studies*, no 52, 1987, pp. 37–45 (5.7)

Davison, R.M., *The Use of the Genitive in Negative Constructions*, Cambridge University Press, 1967 (10.1.6)

Flegon, A., *За пределами русских словарей*, Flegon Press, London, 1973 (4.6)

Fomina, M.I., *Современный русский язык: лексикология*, 3rd edn, Высшая школа, Moscow, 1990 (2.1.1–2.4)

Foote, I.M., *Verbs of Motion*, Cambridge University Press, 1967 (10.7)

Formanovskaia, N.I., *Употребление русского речевого этикета,* Русский язык, Moscow, 1982 (6.1–2, 6.4–16)

Forsyth, James, *A Grammar of Aspect: Usage and Meaning in the Russian Verb*, Cambridge University Press, 1970 (10.5)

Harrison, W., *The Expression of the Passive Voice*, Cambridge University Press, 1967 (10.8, 10.11.4)

Kuz′min, S.S., Shchadrin, N.L., *Русско-английский словарь пословиц и поговорок*, Русский язык, Moscow, 1989 (4.7–8)

Maksimov, V.I., *et al.*, *Словарь перестройки*, Златоуст, St Petersburg, 1992 (4.1)

Mustajoki, Arto, *Падеж дополнения в русских отрицательных предложениях*, Slavica Helsingiensa, 2, Helsinki, 1985 (10.1.6)

Norbury, J.K.W., *Word Formation in the Noun and Adjective*, Cambridge University Press, 1967 (Chapter 7)

Rassudova, O.P., *Употребление видов глагола*, Moscow University Press, 1971 (10.5)

Room, Adrian, 'Russian Personal Names since the Revolution', *Journal of Russian Studies*, nos. 45, 1983, pp. 19–24 and 46, 1983, pp. 13–18 (6.3)

Rozental′, D.E., *Практическая стилистика русского языка*, 4th edn, Высшая школа, Moscow, 1977 (esp 1.3)

Rozental′, D.E., and Telenkova, M.A., *Словарь-справочник лингвистических терминов*, 3rd edn, Просвещение, Moscow, 1985 (Glossary)

Shansky, N.M., and Bystrova, E.A., *700 фразеологических оборотов русского языка, Русский язык*, Moscow, 1975 (4.7)

Suslova, A.P., and Superanskaia, A.V., *О русских именах*, 3rd revised edn, Лениздат, Leningrad, 1991 (6.3)

Valgina, N.S., *Синтаксис современного русского языка*, 3rd edn, Высшая школа, Moscow, 1991 (esp 10.14–15)

Vasil′eva, A.N., *Particles in Colloquial Russian*, translated by V. Korotky and K. Villiers, Progress Publishers, Moscow, 1972 (4.4)

Vlasto, A.P., *A Linguistic History of Russia to the End of the Eighteenth Century*, Clarendon Press, Oxford, 1988

Vsevolodova, M.V., 'Употребление кратких и полных прилагательных', *Русский язык за рубежом*, 1971, no. 3, pp. 65–8 and 1972, no. 1, pp. 59-64 (10.3)

Wade, Terence, *Prepositions in Modern Russian*, University of Durham, 1983 (Chapter 9)

Ward, Dennis, *The Russian Language Today: System and Anomaly*, Hutchinson University Library, London, 1965

Zemskaia, E.A., and Shmelev, D.N., eds., *Городское просторечие: Проблемы изучения*, Наука, Moscow, 1984 (1.3.2)

List of abbreviations

acc	accusative	math	mathematical
act	active	med	medical
adj	adjective	mil	military
adv	adverb	mus	musical
agric	agricultural	N	North
biol	biological	n	neuter
C	Central	NE	North-East
col	column	nom	nominative
collect	collective	non-refl	non-reflexive
conj	conjunction	NW	North-West
D	demotic	obs	obsolete
dat	dative	OCS	Old Church Slavonic
dimin	diminutive	offic	official
E	East	part	participle
econ	economic	pass	passive
Eng	English	pej	pejorative
esp	especially	pers	person
f	feminine	pf	perfective
fig	figurative	phil	philosophical
fin	financial	pl	plural
Fr	French	poet	poetic
fut	future	pol	political
gen	genitive	prep	prepositional
geog	geographical	pres	present
geol	geological	R	register
Ger	German	refl	reflexive
gram	grammatical	rhet	rhetorical
imp	imperative	Russ	Russian
impers	impersonal	sb	somebody
impf	imperfective	SE	South-East
incl	including	sg	singular
indecl	indeclinable	Sp	Spanish
infin	infinitive	sth	something
instr	instrumental	subst	substantivised
iron	ironical	SW	South-West
lit	literally	tech	technical
loc	locative	theat	theatrical
m	masculine	vulg	vulgar

The Russian particle -нибудь is frequently abbreviated to -н.

Note on transcription and transliteration

Where it has been necessary to indicate precisely how a Russian word is pronounced (eg in the sections on regional variation in 1.4) a standard system of phonetic transcription has been used, according to which the Cyrillic consonants have the following values:

б	в	г	д	ж	з	й	к	л	м	н	п	р	с	т	ф	х	ц	ч	ш	щ
b	*v*	*g*	*d*	*ž*	*z*	*j*	*k*	*l*	*m*	*n*	*p*	*r*	*s*	*t*	*f*	*x*	*c*	*č'*	*š*	*šš'*

The symbol ′ placed after a letter indicates that the preceding consonant is soft, eg *l'es* (лес). Since most consonants, when they precede the vowels represented by the Russian letters **е**, **ё**, **и**, **ю** and **я**, are soft, these letters will in effect be transcribed, within this phonetic system, as *'e, 'o, 'i, 'u, 'a* respectively, eg *i'ul'a* (июля). The symbol ′ may also indicate the presence of a soft sign in the Russian word, eg *noč'* (ночь). Stress is indicated by the use of an acute accent over the stressed vowel, eg *xl'éba* (хле́ба).

The system of transliteration used to render Russian names (eg *Petia*, ie Петя), place names and, occasionally, other Russian words (eg *perestroika*), in Roman script is that used in the *Slavonic and East European Review*.

Glossary of linguistic terms

Besides providing explanation of terms used in this book the following glossary should aid understanding of the linguistic concepts required for advanced study of Russian. It will in any case be found that many educated Russians have a high degree of awareness of the grammar of their language and that in talking about it they will use some of the terms defined here. Numbers in brackets refer to the section(s) in this book that deal(s) with the phenomenon in question.

accusative case (вини́тельный паде́ж): the case in which the direct object of a transitive verb is expressed, eg О́льга чита́ет **кни́гу**, *Olga is reading a book* (10.1.2).

acronym (звукова́я аббревиату́ра): word made up of the initial letters of other words, eg ***laser*** (***l****ight* ***a****mplification by the* ***s****timulated* ***e****mission of* ***r****adiation*) (5.10).

active voice (действи́тельный зало́г): construction in which the subject of the verb itself performs the action, eg *The boy* ***stroked*** *the cat*; cf **passive voice**.

adjective (и́мя прилага́тельное): word that qualifies a noun, eg *a* ***red*** *pen*.

adverb (наре́чие): word modifying the meaning of a verb, adjective or adverb, eg *Peter walks* ***slowly***, ***quite*** *big*, ***very*** *quickly* (8.4, 10.14(c)).

adversative conjunction (противи́тельный сою́з): conjunction expressing contrast, eg ***but***.

affix (а́ффикс): an element added to a root, stem or word to modify its meaning or use, eg ***un****willing*, *wonder****ful***. **Prefixes**, **infixes** and **suffixes** (qv) are all types of affix.

affricate (аффрика́та): consonant sound beginning as a **plosive** (qv) and passing into the corresponding **fricative** (qv), eg the initial and final sounds in ***church***, ie *t* + *š*. Standard Russian has two affricates, *c* (ц) and *č* (ч).

akan'e (а́канье): loss of distinction between the phonemes *a* and *o* in the pretonic syllable of a word (ie the syllable preceding the stress), eg *Maskvá* (Москва́; see 1.4.1). А́канье is a feature of pronunciation of Muscovite Russian, other C dialects and the S regional dialect.

alphabetism (бу́квенная аббревиату́ра): word consisting of initial capital letters of other words, eg *ОО́Н* (**О**рганиза́ция **О**бъединённых **Н**а́ций, *United Nations Organisation*) (5.10).

animacy (одушевлённость): grammatical category embracing nouns denoting living things; in Russian, inflection of the accusative singular of most masculine nouns and of the accusative plural of nouns of all genders is determined by whether they are classified as animate or inanimate (see 10.1.3).

attributive adjective (атрибути́вное прилага́тельное): a descriptive adjective which qualifies a noun or noun-equivalent directly, eg *the **new** car* (8.3.1); cf **predicative adjective**.

biaspectual verb (двувидово́й глаго́л): verb in which one form may function as either imperfective or perfective, eg **веле́ть, ра́нить**.

buffer vowel: vowel added for the sake of euphony in certain situations to some Russian prepositions and prefixes which end in a consonant, eg в**о** внима́ние, пе́ред**о** мной, с**о**жгу́.

calque (ка́лька): a loan translation, ie a compound word or phrase that is a literal translation of a foreign expression, eg Eng ***motorway*** from Ger Autobahn.

cardinal numeral (коли́чественное числи́тельное): numeral expressing *how many*, eg ***five*** (10.4); cf **ordinal numeral**.

case (паде́ж): morphological variant of a noun, pronoun, adjective, numeral or participle which expresses the relation of that word to other words in the clause.

clause (предложе́ние): word group containing a subject and predicate, eg ***I shall do it*** [main clause] ***as soon as I can*** [subordinate clause]. (An overt subject, however, is not always present, eg in the imperative ***Do it!***) See also **main clause**, **subordinate clause**.

cognates (однокоренны́е/однокорневы́е слова́): words that are etymologically related or derived from the same root, eg Eng *mother*, Fr *mère*, Ger *Mutter*, Russ мать, Sp *madre*; or, within Russian, **стар**и́к, **ста́р**ость, **стар**у́ха, **ста́р**ый, у**стар**е́лый, etc.

colloquial (разгово́рный): informal or familiar style, expression or form widely used in everyday speech (1.3.1).

complement (дополне́ние): word or group of words that completes the meaning of an utterance, esp a noun or noun phrase that directly defines the subject, eg *She is **a teacher*** (10.1.10(e)).

conditional mood (усло́вное наклоне́ние): verbal form expressing condition or hypothesis, eg *if it **rains***; *if it **were to rain*** (10.9).

conjugation (спряже́ние): system of verb inflections expressing tense, mood, voice, person and number.

conjunction (сою́з): word used to connect words, groups of words or sentences, indicating the relationship of the connected elements, eg *dogs **and*** cats (coordinating conjunction); *I had supper **after** they had gone* (subordinating temporal conjunction); *I like curry **although** it's hot* (subordinating concessive conjunction); *She drank some water **because** she was thirsty* (subordinating causal conjunction) (10.12.1–3).

consonant (согла́сный): any speech sound other than a vowel, ie sound produced by some obstruction of the airstream (see also **affricate**, **fricative**, **plosive**); also any letter representing such a sound.

coordinating conjunction (сочини́тельный сою́з): a conjunction connecting two words, groups of words or sentences and indicating that both are independent and have the same function and importance, eg ***and*** (10.12.1).

dative case (да́тельный паде́ж): the case used to denote the indirect object of a verb, eg *I gave it **to my father***; Она́ посла́ла **мне** письмо́, *She sent the letter **to me*** (see 8.1.2, 8.1.8, 10.1.7).

declension (склоне́ние): system of inflections of noun, pronoun, adjective, numeral or participle expressing gender, case and number.

defective verb (недоста́точный глаго́л): verb which for some reason lacks some personal form or forms, eg **победи́ть** which has no first-person singular form.

denominal preposition (отымённый предло́г): preposition derived from a noun, eg **по отноше́нию к**, ***with regard to*** (9.2).

devoicing (девокализа́ция, оглуше́ние): transformation of **voiced consonant** into a **voiceless consonant** (qv), eg pronunciation of final *b* of раб as ***p***.

dialect (диале́кт): a variety of language distinguished from others by features of its sound system, vocabulary, morphology and syntax. Dialects may be geographic (ie spoken by people of the same territory) or social (ie spoken by people of the same class, social or occupational group). In Russian the term **наре́чие** designates a regional dialect spoken over a very wide area, whilst the term **го́вор** designates a local dialect confined to a much smaller area (1.4).

direct object (прямо́е дополне́ние): the thing on which the action denoted by a transitive verb is directed, eg *I broke a **window***, *She bought a **newspaper*** (10.1.2–3, 10.1.6).

disjunctive conjunction (раздели́тельный сою́з): conjunction which unites clauses or sentences but separates meanings, eg ***or***.

dual number (двойственное число́): a grammatical form indicating duality; the form is obsolete in Russian but remnants of it survive, eg in plurals such as **глаза́**, **у́ши** and in the use of genitive singular forms of nouns after the numerals *2*, *3* and *4*.

ekan'e (е́канье): pronunciation of *'a* as ***'e*** after a soft consonant in the pretonic syllable, eg *p'**e**tak* (пята́к), *p'**e**t'í* (пяти́).

ellipsis (э́ллипсис): omission of a word or words whose meaning will be understood by the listener or reader, eg *after all [**that has been said**]*; Вы меня́ [**спра́шиваете**]? [***Are***] *you* [***asking***] *me?* (10.13).

ending (оконча́ние): in Russian, inflectional suffix added to a word to indicate its case, number, tense, mood, etc in a particular context.

faux ami (ло́жный друг): a word in a foreign language that does not mean what a foreigner, on the basis of his or her own language, might expect it to mean, eg Russian **трансля́ция** does not mean *translation* (2.5).

fricative (фрикати́вный): consonant sound produced by the breath being forced through a narrow opening, eg Eng ***f***, ***v***, ***s***, ***z*** and ***th*** in both ***th****at* and ***th****ink*.

genitive case (роди́тельный паде́ж): the case expressing possession, eg кни́га **бра́та**, *(my) brother's book* (8.1.2, 8.1.4, 8.1.7, 10.1.4).

gerund (деепричáстие): in Russian, verb form invariable in gender, case and number which may be derived from verbs of either aspect and which defines the relationship in time of one action to another action denoted by the main verb of the sentence, eg Она́ гуля́ла, **напева́я** мело́дию, *She strolled,* ***humming*** *a tune* (imperfective gerund denoting simultaneous action); **Прове́рив** рабо́ту, он закры́л тетра́дь, ***Having checked*** *his work he closed the exercise-book* (perfective gerund denoting prior action) (8.7.1–2, 10.11.1).

government (управле́ние): way in which a word controls the form of another word, eg the verb горди́ться governs an object in the instrumental case; the preposition о́коло governs a noun or noun-equivalent in the genitive case.

grammar (грамма́тика): rules of morphology and syntax of a language.

hard sign (твёрдый знак): the letter **ъ**, as in eg раз**ъ**е́хаться, the function of which is explained at 7.2.2.

homoform (омофо́рма): a word identical with another word only when it is in one of the several morphological forms it may adopt, eg **лечу́** (2.2).

homograph (омо́граф): a word written in the same way as another word but pronounced in a different way and having different meaning, eg **потом**, ie по́том and пото́м (2.3).

homonym (омо́ним): a word having the same sound as another word and written in the same way, but having a different meaning and possibly a different origin, eg ***bank*** (side of river and financial institution) (2.1.1–2).

homophone (омофо́н): a word which sounds the same as another word but is written differently, eg ***bare/bear***, ***right/write*** (2.2).

iakan'e (я́канье): pronunciation of *'e* as ***'a*** after a soft consonant in the pretonic syllable. In **strong** (си́льное) я́канье, pretonic *'a* replaces *'e* irrespective of the quality of the vowel in the stressed syllable, eg *n'aslá* (несла́), *s'alóm* (село́м), *n'asú* (несу́), *t'ap'ér'* (тепе́рь). In **moderate** (уме́ренное) я́канье, pretonic *'a* replaces *'e* only before hard consonants, eg *n'aslá* (несла́), *s'alóm* (село́м), *n'asú* (несу́), but *t'epér'* (тепе́рь) where *p* is soft.

idiom (идио́ма): expression peculiar to a language, group of words with a single meaning which cannot readily be derived from the meanings of the individual component words, eg Eng ***to spill the beans***, Russ **Ви́лами на/по воде́ пи́сано**, *It's still up in the air* (4.7).

ikan'e (и́канье): pronunciation of the vowels *'e* and *'a* in the pretonic syllable after a soft consonant as ***'i***, eg *d'**i**t'éj* (детей), *n'**i**slá* (несла́), *t'**i**p'ér'* (тепе́рь), *vz'**i**lá*, (взяла́), *r'**i**dý* (ряды́), *t'**i**nú* (тяну́).

imperative mood (повели́тельное наклоне́ние): verbal mood expressing command, invitation, suggestion, entreaty, request, etc, eg ***come in***, ***sit down*** (5.8, 8.6.11, 10.5.6).

imperfective aspect (несоверше́нный вид): describes an action without reference to its extent and thus presents it as incomplete, eg Она́ **пе́ла**, *She **was singing/used to sing*** (see 10.5); cf **perfective aspect**.

indicative mood (изъяви́тельное наклоне́ние): mood which affirms or denies that the action or state denoted by the verb in question is an actual fact, eg *I **read***, *she **went***, *they **were sitting***, *the sun **was** not **shining***.

indirect object (ко́свенное дополне́ние): a noun, pronoun or phrase denoting an object indirectly affected by an action, eg *He gave the book* [direct object] ***to his sister*** [indirect object]. See also **dative case**.

indirect speech (also called **reported speech**; ко́свенная речь): discourse in which the substance of sb's words or thoughts is related without being quoted verbatim, eg *He told me **that he would do it***, *She said **she was twenty*** (10.6(a)).

infinitive (инфинити́в): verb form expressing the idea of an action without reference to person or number, eg ***to speak***, **говори́ть**.

infix (и́нфикс): element inserted in the middle of a word to modify its meaning or use, eg запи́**сыва**ть (7.6); English has no infixes.

inflection (also **flexion**; оконча́ние): the grammatical ending that expresses relations of case, tense, number, gender, etc in nouns, pronouns, adjectives, numerals, verbs and participles, eg бра́т**а**, себ**е́**, но́в**ого**, тр**ёх**, чита́**ю** сидя́щ**ая**.

instrumental case (твори́тельный паде́ж): the case denoting the agent **by** which or the instrument **with** which sth is done, eg подпи́санный **им** догово́р, *the treaty signed **by him***, писа́ть **карандашо́м**, *to write **with a pen*** (8.1.2, 8.1.8, 10.1.9).

interjection (междоме́тие): an exclamatory word, invariable in form, which is thrown into an utterance to express emotion, eg ***oh!***, **ох!** (4.5).

intransitive verb (неперехо́дный глаго́л): a verb that does not require a direct object, eg *The sun **rises***, *A crowd **gathered*** (3.4, 10.8).

isogloss (изогло́сса): a line separating one region from another which differs from it in a feature of dialect. The isogloss may indicate eg the limits of distribution of a certain word or the boundary beyond which one phenomenon (eg о́канье) is replaced by another (а́канье).

lexical (лекси́ческий): relating to vocabulary (as opposed to grammar).

locative case (ме́стный паде́ж): the case which indicates location of an object; used after the prepositions в and на (8.1.5, 10.1.11).

long form (of adjective; по́лная фо́рма): full form that must be used when a Russian adjective is attributive, eg **ру́сский**, **но́вая**, **бе́лое**, **си́льные**, etc (8.3.1); cf **short form**, which may be used when the adjective is predicative.

main clause (гла́вное предложе́ние): a clause which can stand independently, eg ***I went home*** [main clause] *after I had spoken to you* [**subordinate clause**, qv].

mobile vowel (бе́глый гла́сный): one of the vowels **о**, **ё** or **е** when (a) they precede the final consonant of a masculine noun in its nominative singular form but disappear once an inflection is added, eg у́г**о**л (угла́, etc; see 8.1.3), or (b) are inserted in certain types of feminine or neuter noun which in the genitive plural have a **zero ending** (qv), eg доска́ (дос**о́**к), полоте́нце (полоте́н**е**ц; see 8.1.7).

modal particle (мода́льная части́ца): a short indeclinable word which emphasises, intensifies or in some other way expresses the speaker's emotion or attitude (4.4).

modal verb (мода́льный глаго́л): verb (eg Eng ***can***, ***could***, ***may***; Russ **мочь**) expressing possibility, permissibility, obligation, etc, and followed by another verb which it modifies (3.3).

monosyllable (односло́жное сло́во): word comprising one syllable, eg ***cat***, ***word***.

mood (наклоне́ние): form of the verb that indicates how the speaker views an action or state, ie whether it is seen as matter-of-fact, desirable, contingent on sth else, etc. See also **conditional**, **imperative**, **indicative**, **subjunctive**.

morphology (морфоло́гия): study of the forms of words. **Inflectional morphology** (see **inflection**) relates to the declension of nouns, pronouns, adjectives, numerals and participles and conjugation of verbs (see Chapter 8). **Lexical** (qv) **morphology** relates to **word-formation** (qv; see Chapter 7).

neologism (неологи́зм): a new word or phrase (eg **бомж**), or the use of an old word in a new sense (eg **я́стреб**) (4.1).

nominative case (имени́тельный паде́ж): the case in which the subject is expressed, eg **О́льга** чита́ет кни́гу, *Olga is reading a book* (10.1.1).

number (число́): the grammatical property of a word which indicates whether it is singular, **dual** (qv) or plural. The difference between *car/cars, mouse/mice, I am/we are* is in each instance a difference of number.

numeral (числи́тельное): a word denoting number, eg ***two***, ***five***; see also **cardinal numeral** and **ordinal numeral**.

object (дополне́ние): see **direct object** and **indirect object**.

oblique case (ко́свенный паде́ж): any case other than the nominative (and in other Slavonic languages, vocative), ie in Russian accusative, genitive, dative, instrumental, prepositional. In this book the term is used to embrace the last four of these cases, but not generally the accusative.

okan′e (о́канье): the phonemes *a* and *o* preserve their value in the pretonic syllable, eg *travá* (трава́), *sová* (сова́); cf **akan′e** above. In **full** (по́лное) о́канье *o* retains its value even in the syllable before the pretonic syllable, eg *molodój* (молодо́й). In **incomplete** (непо́лное) о́канье, *a* and *o* in the syllable preceding the pretonic syllable are reduced to ***ŭ***, eg *m**ŭ**lokó* (молоко́) (1.4).

Old Church Slavonic (церкòвнославя́нский язы́к): the language used by the early Slav missionaries, in the ninth and tenth centuries, for the transmission of Christian teaching; the language used in Russia for liturgical purposes and most literary forms before westernisation in the eighteenth century.

ordinal numeral (поря́дковое числи́тельное): numeral indicating place in order or sequence, eg ***second***, ***fifth***.

orthography (орфогра́фия): correct or accepted use of the written characters of a language.

paradigm (паради́гма): table setting out the system of inflection of a word.

paronym (паро́ним): a word which may be confused with another to which it is close in sound, written form and possibly meaning, and which may be of similar origin, eg ***principal/ principle***. In this book the term is used in a broad sense to include all easily confused words, even those of quite different origin, eg **бре́мя**, **вре́мя** (2.4).

participle (прича́стие): a verb form that combines both the qualities of a verb (eg transitiveness or intransitiveness, active or passive meaning, tense and aspect, but not person) and the qualities of a noun (eg gender, case and number). Russian has present and past active participles and present and past passive participles (8.7.3–6, 10.11.2–4).

passive voice (страда́тельный зало́г): the form of a verb which indicates that the subject suffered the action, ie was not itself the agent, eg *I **was hit** by a stone, They **were taught** French by their mother.*

perfective aspect (соверше́нный вид): describes an action restricted in its extent and thus presents it as complete; perfectives relate to the beginning of an action (eg **зазвене́ть**, *to start to ring*), the limited duration of an action (eg **посиде́ть**, *to sit for a while*), or the completion of an action (eg **вы́пить**, *to drink up*) (10.5); cf **imperfective aspect**.

periphrasis (перифра́за): complicated, round-about expression, use of more words than is strictly speaking necessary, eg ***in this day and age***.

person (лицо́): form of the verb which represents: (a) the person/persons or thing/things speaking (ie 1st pers, eg *I/we read*); (b) the person/persons or thing/things spoken to (ie 2nd pers, eg *you read*); or (c) the person/persons or thing/things spoken about (ie 3rd pers, eg *he/she reads, they read*).

phrase (фра́за): group of words lacking a finite verb but felt to express a single idea or to constitute a discrete element in a sentence.

plosive (взрывно́й): consonant sound produced by momentary stoppage of the air passage at some point, eg Russ ***b*** and ***p*** (labial plosives), ***d*** and ***t*** (dental plosives), ***g*** and ***k*** (velar plosives); also sometimes called an 'occlusive' (смы́чный) or 'stop'.

predicate (сказу́емое): word or group of words which says sth about the subject, eg *I am **studying languages***; *Cats **catch mice***. A verb is generally the chief part of the predicate.

predicative adjective (предикати́вное прилага́тельное): adjective that forms part of the predicate, ie which is separated from the noun it qualifies by some part of the verb *to be* or, in Russian, by part of the verb *to be* that is understood, eg *The film is **long***, Кни́га была́ **интере́сна**.

prefix (приста́вка): element added to the beginning of a word to modify its meaning, eg ***pre**determine*, **при**ходи́ть (7.3–5).

preposition (предло́г): word that defines the relation of a noun or pronoun to some other word, eg *The book is **on** the table; I went **across** the road; A plane flew **over** the houses* (Chapter 9).

prepositional case (предло́жный паде́ж): case used after certain prepositions when they have certain meanings (8.1.2, 8.1.8, 10.1.11); see also **locative case**.

present perfect continuous: the tense which in English indicates that an action begun in the past is still continuing, eg *I **have been living** here for three years*. In Russian this tense must be rendered by an imperfective verb in the present tense (10.6(b)).

pronoun (местоиме́ние): word used instead of a noun, eg ***he***, ***she*** (8.2, 10.2.1–6).

prosthetic (also **prothetic**; протети́ческий): sound inserted at the beginning of a word for ease of pronunciation, eg the sound *n* in на **н**его́ (8.2).

proverb (посло́вица): short familiar sentence expressing a supposed truth or moral lesson, eg ***Every cloud has a silver lining*** (4.8).

register (стиль): a variety of language determined by such factors as medium, subject-matter, purpose and situation (1.3, 1.6).

relative pronoun (относи́тельное местоиме́ние): a word which introduces a subordinate clause describing a preceding noun or pronoun (the antecedent), eg Eng ***who***, ***which***, Russ **кото́рый**, eg *The man* ***who*** *sells newspapers; The table* ***which*** *I bought yesterday* (10.2.1).

reported speech: see **indirect speech**.

root (ко́рень): the base of a word which bears its fundamental meaning, eg стол in **сто́лик, столо́вая, насто́льный**, etc.

secondary stress (второстепе́нное ударе́ние): in long words, especially compound words, a syllable other than the main stressed syllable which may also need to be pronounced with additional force. Secondary stress is marked in this book by a grave accent, eg церко̀внославя́нский.

semantic (семанти́ческий): relating to meaning.

sentence (предложе́ние): minimum complete utterance, eg *I told him; Come back!*

short form (of adjective; кра́ткая фо́рма): the truncated masculine, feminine, neuter and plural forms, eg **нов, нова́, но́во, но́вы**, which in modern Russian are indeclinable and which may only be used predicatively (8.3.2, 10.3); see also **predicative adjective**.

simile (сравне́ние): rhetorical likening of a thing to sth else, eg ***drunk as a lord, like a bolt from the blue*** (4.9).

Slavonicism (славяни́зм): a form borrowed at some time from **Old Church Slavonic** (qv). Many Slavonicisms exist in Russian alongide East Slav forms. They are characterised by (a) certain phonetic features, notably (with the Slavonicism first in each pair): **прах/по́рох, мла́дший/молодо́й, среда́/середи́на, расте́ние/рост, ладья́/ло́дка, граждани́н/горожа́нин, ночь/все́нощная, еди́ный/оди́н, юро́дивый/уро́д**); (b) certain prefixes, eg **избра́ть** (cf **вы́брать**), **низверга́ть, чрезме́рный** (cf **че́рез**), **предви́деть** (cf **пе́ред**), **преступле́ние** (cf **перехо́д**); (c) certain suffixes, eg **пе́рвенец, сочу́вствие, жизнь, моли́тва, святы́ня, творе́ние, горя́щий** (cf **горя́чий**), **богате́йший, широча́йший**. Slavonicisms tend to have a more bookish flavour than related Russian forms of East Slav origin and tend to occur in more elevated varieties of language.

soft sign (мя́гкий знак): the letter **ь**, the function of which is to indicate that the preceding consonant is soft.

stress (ударе́ние): in all Russian words of more than one syllable, as in such English words, one syllable is pronounced with more force than the other(s). This stress is marked in this book, as in most textbooks, by an acute accent, but it is not normally indicated in Russian publications. Russian stress patterns are numerous and complex.

stump-compound (аббревиату́ра): word compounded of segments of other words, eg **колхо́з** (коллекти́вное хозя́йство, *collective farm*).

subject (подлежа́щее): the agent performing the action expressed by the verb in an active sentence, or the person on whom or the thing on which the action of a passive sentence is performed, eg ***The priest** delivered a sermon, **We** saw the queen, **The man** was struck by lightning.*

subjunctive mood (сослага́тельное наклоне́ние): the verbal mood which indicates that the action or state denoted by the verb in question is regarded as hypothetical or subject to another action or state, eg *I wish he **were** right; I demand that it **be** done* (10.10).

subordinate clause (прида́точное предложе́ние): clause which cannot function as a sentence in its own right but is dependent on another clause which can, eg *I think* [main clause] ***that she is nice*** [subordinate clause]; *I like the house* [main clause] ***which you have bought*** [subordinate clause]; *I went to bed* [main clause] ***because it was late*** [subordinate clause].

subordinating conjunction (подчини́тельный сою́з): conjunction introducing a subordinate clause, eg ***although, after, because*** (10.12.2-3).

substantivised adjective (субстантиви́рованное прилага́тельное): word which has adjectival form but is used as a noun, eg **моро́женое**, *ice-cream.*

suffix (су́ффикс): element added to the end of a word to modify its use or meaning, eg *writ**er***, *happi**ness*** (7.7–11).

syntax (си́нтаксис): grammatical structure in a sentence, or study of that structure.

tense (вре́мя): verbal form indicating whether the action or state denoted by the verb is viewed as past, present or future.

transitive verb (перехо́дный глаго́л): verb that requires a direct object, eg *I **bought** a car* (3.4, 10.8).

tsokan′e (цо́канье): loss of distinction between the affricates (qv) *c* and *č′*. In **hard** (твёрдое) цо́канье the standard soft hushing affricate *č′* is replaced by a hard hissing affricate ***c***, eg ***c**údo* (чу́до). In **soft** (мя́гкое) цо́канье *č′* is replaced by a soft hissing ***c***, eg ***c′**údo.*

velar (задненёбный): consonant sound produced by raising the back of the top of the tongue against the soft palate (нёбо); in Russian the sounds ***g***, ***k***, ***x***.

vocative case (зва́тельный паде́ж): case used in direct personal address; now defunct in Russian, except in relics such as **Бо́же** and **го́споди** and in certain colloquial forms in the spoken language (see 6.3.1). (The vocative survives in other Slavonic languages, eg Czech, Polish, Serbo-Croat.)

voiced consonant (зво́нкий согла́сный): consonant produced with the vocal cords vibrating, eg Russian ***b***, ***v***, ***g***, ***d***, ***ž***, ***z***; see also **voiceless consonant**.

voiceless consonant (глухо́й согла́сный): consonant produced without vibration of the vocal cords, eg Russian ***p***, ***f***, ***k***, ***t***, ***š***, ***s***, ***x***, ***c***, ***č′***, ***šš′***.

vowel (гла́сный): sound produced by passage of air through mouth without obstruction of the airstream, eg ***a***, ***e***, ***i***, ***o***, ***u***.

word-formation (словообразова́ние): formation of new words by combining roots and affixes or by other means; also the study of the structure of words and the laws of their formation in a language (Chapter 7).

zero ending (нулево́е оконча́ние): ending of a Russian noun in an oblique case in which no inflection is present eg солда́т, *soldier* (which is genitive plural as well as nominative singular); жён (gen pl; nom sg жена́, *wife*); мест (gen pl; nom sg ме́сто, *place*).

1 Varieties of language and register

1.1 The Russian language and its distribution

The Russian language belongs to the East Slav group of languages, itself part of the Slavonic branch of the Indo-European family. The relationship of Russian to the other modern European languages may be illustrated by Fig. 1 (which includes only languages still used by a substantial number of speakers).

It is difficult to give accurate up-to-date figures for the number of Russian-speakers in the new Russian state and the Russian diaspora. For one thing there has been some movement of the population between regions and states following the collapse of the Soviet Union in 1991. For another, Russian is spoken as a native language not merely by ethnic Russians but also by many non-Russian inhabitants of Russia and the other former republics of the Soviet Union, some of whom (for example Ukrainians and Belorussians) are ethnically close to the Russians but many of whom (for example Latvians, Kazakhs, Koreans) belong to quite different ethnic groups, including non-European groups.

However, once these qualifications have been made it is useful to refer to the Soviet census of 1989, according to which there were some 120 million ethnic Russians in the Russian Federation and a further 25 million ethnic Russians living in the other republics of the Union (see 5.11.1 for a list of these republics), the majority of them in Ukraine. At least another 10 million inhabitants of the Soviet Union regarded Russian as their native language. Moreover, since Russian was used as a second language throughout the non-Russian areas of the Union, whose total population in 1989 was 287 million, one may assume that it was known well by perhaps a further 50 million Soviet citizens.

Russian is of course also spoken, with varying degrees of fluency, accuracy and proximity to the Russian now spoken in Russia itself, by many émigrés or their descendants. Russians have left the Soviet Union – or not returned to it – in four main waves (in the years immediately after the Bolshevik revolution; after the Second World War, following their displacement; in the Brezhnev period; and from the mid-80s, following the relaxation of emigration controls) and have at one time or another settled in particular in France, Germany, Britain, USA and, most recently, Israel. It should be added, finally, that Russian is known to many foreigners, especially from Africa, Asia, Latin America and Eastern Europe, who have studied in Russia since the Second World War,

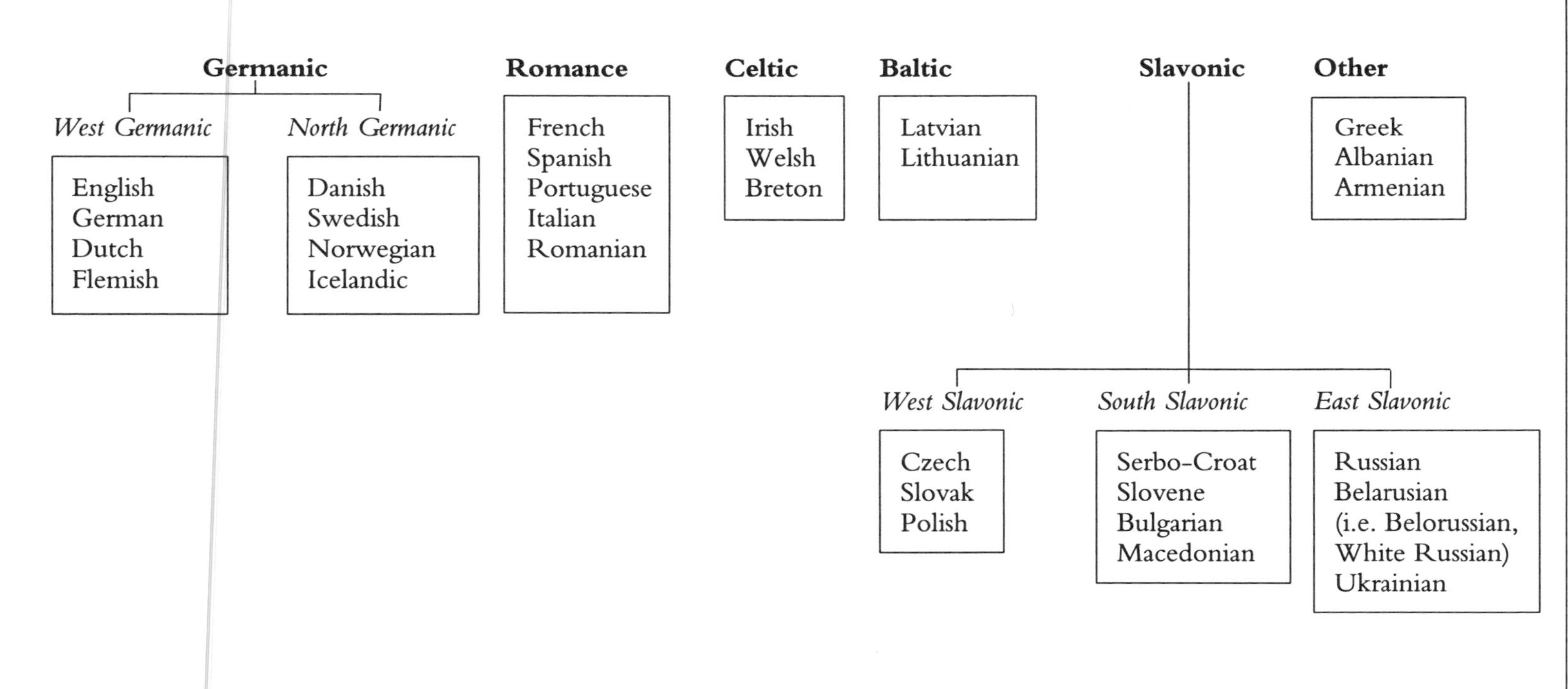

Fig. 1. The Indo-European Languages

particularly at the height of Soviet power from the 1960s to the 1980s. However, the number of foreigners learning Russian (some 20 million in 1979) has dwindled in the post-Soviet period following the end of Russian domination in the Eastern bloc countries (East Germany, Poland, Czechoslovakia, Hungary, Romania, Bulgaria) and the weakening of Russian influence in numerous states in other parts of the world (eg Cuba, Angola, Ethiopia, North Yemen, Vietnam).

Although Russian is thus widely distributed, and although it is also the language in which one of the world's great bodies of imaginative literature has been created over the last two centuries, it is with the Russian that is spoken by ethnic Russians in Russia today that this book is primarily concerned.

Note: many languages other than Russian (for the most part languages which are not Indo-European) are spoken by the numerous ethnic minorities in Russia itself, especially Finno-Ugric languages (Estonian, Finnish, Karelian; Komi, Mari, Mordvin, Udmurt), Caucasian languages (Abkhaz, Chechen, Ingush; Lezgi; Georgian), Turkic languages (Azerbaijani, Bashkir, Kazakh, Kirgiz, Tatar, Turkmen, Yakut), languages of the Mongolian group (Buriat, Kalmyk), and Tadzhik (a language of the Iranian branch of the Indo-European family).

1.2 Varieties of language

The student learning a foreign language in a systematic way will generally study a form of it, or the single form of it, which educated native speakers consider normative, eg 'BBC English', Parisian French, Tuscan Italian, Mandarin or Cantonese. In the case of Russian this normative form is what Russians refer to as the 'literary language' (литерату́рный язы́к). However, the term 'literary language' suggests to an English-speaker exclusively the written language, and the expression 'standard Russian' is therefore preferred in this book. Standard Russian embraces the spoken language of educated people as well as the written language, and its spoken form is based on educated Muscovite speech.

Study of the normative form of a language should inculcate a standard pronunciation and vocabulary and 'correct' grammatical rules. It is essential that the foreign student absorb such a norm both in order that he or she should be able to understand and communicate with educated speakers of the language in a way acceptable to the largest possible number of them, and in order to establish criteria in his or her own mind for judging correctness and error in the language.

However, there comes a point in one's study of a foreign language when it also becomes necessary to recognise that the concept of norms is to some extent theoretical and abstract. This is so because a living language is constantly evolving and because innumerable varieties of it exist both within what is regarded as the norm and beyond the limits of that norm.

For one thing, what people consider correct changes with the passage of time. For example, authoritative Russian dictionaries indicate end stress throughout the future tense in the verbs помести́ть and посели́ть (помести́шь, etc, посели́шь, etc), but many educated speakers now consider помéстишь, etc and посéлишь, etc normal and correct. As far as the historical evolution of Russian is concerned, the student needs to be aware that while the Russian of Pushkin, Turgenev and Tolstoy is easily comprehensible to Russians today it differs in some respects morphologically and especially lexically from the contemporary language. Moreover, Russian is undergoing rapid change at the present time. This change is due to some extent to the global technological and managerial revolution of the late twentieth century, with its large new vocabulary, but also to the quite sudden breakdown of the communist order in Russia and the political, economic, social and cultural innovations and dislocations which that breakdown has entailed.

More importantly from the point of view of this book, the language spoken in Russia today, while having a common core, has numerous varieties, as do modern English, French, German, Spanish and so on. For native users of a language do not all use their language in the same way. Nor as a rule does any individual use the language in the same way in all situations. People make linguistic choices, which are determined by the situation in which they find themselves, selecting certain lexical, morphological and syntactic forms from among the options available in their language. They may even vary their pronunciation according to the context. It is important for advanced learners of a language to be aware of this variety in the language's use, both in order that they may be sensitive to the nuances of what they hear and read and in order that they themselves might use language that is appropriate in a given situation and has the desired impact. After all, a sophisticated expression used in the wrong context may sound laughably pompous, while a coarse turn of phrase addressed to the wrong company may cause offence.

One needs therefore to reflect on the following factors. Who is using the language in a given instance, and with what intent? What form of communication is being used? What is its subject-matter? And what is the context? In other words one should consider the user, purpose, medium, field and situation.

Factors relating to the speaker himself or herself which help to determine the type of language he or she uses are the speaker's age, sex, place of origin (see 1.4), level of education and social position or status. These factors may impinge on language directly, by affecting a person's accent, way of addressing others, range of vocabulary and command of grammar, and indirectly, by shaping and delimiting a person's knowledge and experience.

The purpose of communication in a given instance also has a bearing on the form of language used. One may be using language merely to impart information, as is the case for example in a scholarly article or lecture, a textbook or a weather forecast; or to persuade, as is the case in a publicistic article, a lawyer's speech in court or a political broadcast; or merely for social intercourse, as is the case in a conversation with friends. Language used for the first purpose is likely to be logical, coherent, matter-of-fact, relatively sophisticated syntactically and shorn of emotional expressiveness. Language used for the last purpose, on the other hand, is likely to be less rational, less complex syntactically, and replete with the emotional and expressive resources of which the language is capable.

The medium used for communication also significantly affects the language used. One's choice of words, the constructions one uses, and even to some extent pronunciation (and in Russian stress and intonation too), may depend on the nature of the medium and its relative formality or informality. A learned article, a radio interview, a conversation over supper in the kitchen all involve differing levels of formality into which native speakers will unconsciously settle. Each medium has an appropriate sphere of grammatical usage and vocabulary and its own linguistic formulae. One does not consistently step outside those spheres, unless one is striving for particular effect – perhaps comic, facetious, offensive – without sounding a discordant note. Again, what one writes is not necessarily what one would say on the same subject and for the same purpose.

Language is affected by subject-matter in an obvious way, inasmuch as fields of activity and branches of knowledge have their special terminology, for example political, philosophical, scientific, medical, musical, literary, sporting, professional and so forth. However, the effect of field on language may go further than terminology. Groups have distinctive ways of expressing themselves: doctors, for example, are likely to describe patients' symptoms in language altogether different from that used by patients themselves.

Finally, one's mode of expression may be affected by the nature of the relationship which exists between the user and the person or people with whom he or she is communicating. Language is likely to vary according to such factors as whether one is speaking, for example, to one's elders (with any one of a range of nuances from respect, deference, sympathy or affection to condescension or intolerance) to children (lovingly, reproachfully, sternly), to a superior or junior at work, or to an intimate or a stranger.

1.3 Register

The varieties of language that result from the interaction of the factors described in 1.2 represent stylistic levels which may be termed registers. Although the number of registers that may be identified is quite large, for the purposes of this book a scale will be used on which three main registers are marked (low, neutral and high). These registers will be referred to throughout the book as R1, R2 and R3 respectively. Beyond the first of these registers lie demotic speech (1.3.2) and vulgar language (4.6) and within R3 lie various functional styles which will be classified here as scientific, official and publicistic (1.3.4).

These registers, which are examined in more detail below, broadly speaking reflect a spectrum ranging from informality, in the case of R1, to formality, in the case of R3. Insofar as this spectrum reveals a view of language as low (**сни́женный**), neutral (**нейтра́льный**) or high (**высо́кий**) it may be traced back in Russia to the work of the poet, scientist and student of language Lomonosov, who in his *Предисло́вие о по́льзе книг церко́вных в росси́йском языке́* (1758) famously defined three linguistic styles (**ни́зкий, посре́дственный, высо́кий**) and laid down the genres in which it seemed appropriate to use each of them. To a considerable extent this spectrum of register runs parallel to that which ranges from the colloquial form of spoken Russian at one end to a bookish form of the written language at the other. It should though be noted that while the written language tends to be more formal than the spoken language it is not necessarily so: the written language in the form of a letter to a friend or relation is likely to be less formal and therefore in a lower register than such examples of the spoken language as an academic lecture or a political speech.

1.3.1 The colloquial register (R1)

The principal function of this register is social intercourse. Its medium is dialogue or conversation and its field is one's personal relationships and practical everyday dealings with others. It is therefore distinguished by relative spontaneity, simplicity and the absence of forethought or technical or official tone. Non-lexical features, such as intonation, pauses, stress, rhythm and tempo, play an important part in it. Meaning is reinforced by non-linguistic resources such as facial expression and gesture. The function, medium and field of the register account for many of the factors which it tends to exhibit in the areas of pronunciation, vocabulary and phraseology, word-formation, morphology and syntax.

pronunciation

- Articulation is often careless and indistinct, and vowels may be reduced or consonants lost as a result of lazy or rapid delivery, eg *kŭdá* (когда́), *u t'e'á* (у тебя́), *tóko* (то́лько), *p'iis'át* (пятьдеся́т). Local accent is marked (eg with а́канье and associated phenomena or о́канье, treatment of *g* as occlusive or fricative; see 1.4). Stress may differ from the accepted norm (eg до́говор, при́говор, разви́лось, разви́лись instead of догово́р, пригово́р, развило́сь, развили́сь respectively).

vocabulary • This tends to be basic and concrete since the register is concerned with the practicalities of life. All parts of speech are represented in numerous colloquial forms, ie nouns (eg зади́ра, *bully*; карто́шка, *potato*; толкотня́, *crush, scrum*); adjectives (eg долговя́зый, *lanky*; дото́шный, *meticulous*; мудрёный, *odd*; работя́щий, *hard-working*; расхля́банный, *lax*); verbs (eg арта́читься, *to dig one's heels in* (fig); дры́хнуть (impf) and вздремну́ть (pf), *to have a nap*; вопи́ть, *to wail, howl*; впихну́ть, *to cram in*; гро́хнуть(ся), *to bang, crash*; ехи́дничать, *to gossip maliciously*; куроле́сить, *to play tricks*; ме́шкать, *to linger, loiter*; огоро́шить, *to take aback*; помере́ть, *to die*; прихворну́ть, *to be unwell*; секре́тничать, *to be secretive*; тарато́рить, *to jabber, natter*; тормоши́ть, *to pull about, pester*); adverbs (eg ба́ста, *enough*; вконе́ц, *completely*; втихомо́лку, *on the quiet*; давне́нько, *for quite some time now*; ми́гом, *in a flash*; многова́то, *a bit too much/many*; нагишо́м, *stark naked*; недосу́г, *lack of leisure*; помале́ньку, *gradually, gently, tolerably*; потихо́ньку, *slowly, softly, on the sly*; хороше́нько, *well and truly*; часте́нько, *quite often*; чу́точку, *a tiny bit*); and pronouns (э́такий, *what a/such a*). Some colloquial words are derived from the same root as non-colloquial words (eg карто́шка, помере́ть).

The speaker has frequent recourse to various types of filler words (eg зна́чит), hesitation markers (eg гм) and comment clauses (eg предста́вь себе́; see 4.3 on all of these). The language's means of expressing emotion, notably modal particles (eg ведь, же; 4.4) and interjections (eg ах, тсс; 4.5), may be exploited. Informal modes of address predominate (6.2–3). People conversing in this register are more likely to address each other as ты than as вы and to call each other by their first names, indeed by diminutive forms of them (6.3.1), than by the combined first name and patronymic.

phraseology • Idioms (4.7) and expressive turns of phrase are used, giving a variety of tones, for example ironic, scornful, jocular. Phraseology may be structurally distinctive, eg бе́з году неде́ля, *only a few days*; гляде́ть в о́ба, *to be on one's guard*; ждать не дожда́ться, *to be on tenterhooks*; из ко́жи вон лезть, *to do one's utmost*; танцева́ть от пе́чки, *to start again from the beginning*.

word-formation • Bookish suffixes, especially those of Old Church Slavonic origin, are relatively scarce, but many other noun suffixes (see 7.7) abound and indeed occur mainly in this register, eg -ак (проста́к, *simple-minded fellow*), -як (добря́к, *good-natured bloke*), -ан (старика́н, *old chap*), -ян (грубия́н, *boor*), -ач (борода́ч, *bloke with a beard*), -аш (алка́ш, *alcoholic*; торга́ш, *small trader, mercenary person*), -ака (зева́ка, *idler*), -яка (гуля́ка, *playboy*), -ёжка (зубрёжка, *cramming*, ie study), -ень (ба́ловень, *spoilt brat*), -ла (вороти́ла, *bigwig*), -лка (раздева́лка, *cloakroom*), -ня (возня́, *row, racket*), -отня (беготня́, *running about, bustle*), -тяй (лентя́й, *lazy person*), -ун (болту́н, *chatterbox*), -уха (толсту́ха, *fat woman*), -ыш (малы́ш, *kid*), -яга (бедня́га, *poor devil*). Diminutive and pejorative suffixes (7.8) indicate a speaker's attitudes, eg -ок (сыно́к, *dear son*), -ишка (лгуни́шка, *wretched liar*), -ишко (городи́шко, *ghastly town*), -ища (бороди́ща, *hideous beard*). The adjectival suffix -ущий (большу́щий, *whacking great*), the adjectival prefix пре- (преглу́пый, *really stupid*), and the verbal suffix -ничáть (бродя́жничать, *to be a tramp*) are also characteristic of the colloquial register.

morphology

- In some masculine nouns certain forms may be preferred to standard forms in some cases, eg prep sg in -у́ (в отпуску́ instead of в о́тпуске, *on leave*; 8.1.5); nom pl in -а́ (сектора́ instead of се́кторы, *sectors*; 8.1.6); gen pl in zero ending (грамм, помидо́р instead of гра́ммов, *of grammes*, помидо́ров, *of tomatoes*; 8.1.7). Diminutive forms of first names may be used in a truncated vocative form, eg Тань, *Tania* (6.3.1). The suffix -ей may be preferred in short comparatives (eg быстре́й instead of быстре́е, *quicker*) and the prefix по- is commonly attached to such comparatives (eg полу́чше, *a bit better*; 8.3.3). The infinitive forms вида́ть, слыха́ть may be preferred to ви́деть, *to see*, слы́шать, *to hear* (2.4). There is a tendency to simplification, which entails weakening of certain grammatical rules, eg a speaker may fail to decline all components of a numeral in an oblique case (10.4.3, note 2) or both parts of a compound word (eg полго́дом ра́ньше, *half a year earlier*, instead of полуго́дом). Forms may be used which strictly speaking are grammatically incorrect, eg Ты умне́е на́шего instead of Ты умне́е нас, *You're brighter than us*, and even к пе́рвому ма́рту instead of к пе́рвому ма́рта, *by 1 March*.

syntax

- The nature of the register makes for incomplete sentences, sentences consisting of only one word (eg да, *yes*; нет, *no*; вон, *get away*; марш, *forward*; как же, *of course* (iron); пожа́луйста, *please*), and simple sentences, or – in complex sentences – a prevalence of coordinating conjunctions, some of them exclusive to this register (10.12.1(b)). Syntax may be disjointed, with repetitions (eg да, да, да, *yes, yes, yes*), weak links, breaks in sentences and interpolations of various sorts (eg providing comment, clarification or correction). Questions and exclamations abound. Rules dictating the government of words may be relaxed, eg a preposition might govern an infinitive (насчёт поговори́ть, *about having a chat*) or might be combined with a word other than a noun, pronoun or adjective (Отло́жим разгово́р на по́сле обе́да, *Let's put off our conversation until after dinner*). Speakers frequently resort to ellipsis (eg Я к вам, *I'm coming to see you*; 10.13) and other distinctive constructions, which may involve various types of complex predicate, eg Стояла пела, *She was standing singing*; Он возьми́ да и кричи́, *He went and shouted*; она́ то́лько и де́лает, что, *she does nothing but*; Знай себе́ идёт, *He's walking along quite unconcerned* (10.13), including predicates containing particles, eg Написа́ть-то напишу́, но она́ не отве́тит, *Well, I'll write, but she won't reply* (4.4) and predicates consisting of interjections, eg стук, *banged* (4.5).

It is worth adding, finally, that the low style is notable for what it lacks as well as for what it contains. It eschews the complex subordinate clauses, gerunds, active participles and passive constructions involving reflexive verbs which are characteristic of the high style as well as much sophisticated or specialised vocabulary and many set phrases and formulae.

1.3.2 Demotic speech (D)

Beneath the normal colloquial register, which may be used by all social groups for informal and everyday matters, there are other linguistic strata whose elements, unlike much in R1, would sound more or less unacceptable and discordant in R2. These strata include what will here be termed 'demotic' (просторе́чие, which is sometimes also translated as 'popular speech'), as well as slang and vulgar language (4.6).

Demotic is the spontaneous, informal speech of the uneducated (or, if it is used by the educated, then it is used for special effect). It lies outside the bounds of what is considered the literary standard (though that standard is constantly shifting and continually admits elements which were recently considered unacceptable). It has been described (by Kapanadze in Zemskaia and Shmelev, eds., p. 8; see Sources) as the oral equivalent of an illiterate letter. Unlike the various registers embraced by the standard language, demotic speech observes no norms. It is distinguished to some extent, as illustrated by the following examples of features of mainly Muscovite просторе́чие, by stress and morphological and syntactic peculiarities, but above all by a layer of racy vocabulary.

stress

- Some words are stressed on a different syllable from that which bears stress in the standard language, eg доку́мент (докуме́нт, *document*); кило́метр (киломе́тр, *kilometre*); мага́зин (магази́н, *shop*); мо́лодежь (молодёжь, *youth*); по́ртфель (портфе́ль (m), *briefcase*); шо́фер (шофёр, *driver*). Stress variation also affects some verb forms, eg зво́нишь, etc (звони́шь, *you ring*); гна́ла (гнала́, *chased*); отда́ла (отдала́, *gave back*), and the short forms of past passive participles, eg приве́дено (приведено́, *brought*); приве́зено (привезено́, *brought (by transport)*); прине́сено (принесено́, *brought (by hand)*).

vocabulary
- Use of words considered unacceptable in standard usage, eg nouns such as балбе́с, *coarse, idle person*; башка́, *head, nut*; забулды́га, *debauched person*; образи́на, *ugly mug*; пу́зо, *belly, gut*; хапу́га, *thief, scrounger*; adjectives such as му́торный, *disagreeable and dreary*; нахра́пистый, *high-handed*; verbs such as барахли́ть (impf), *to stutter* (of engine, machine, heart); бреха́ть (брешу́, бре́шешь), *to bark, talk nonsense, tell lies*; дре́йфить/сдре́йфить, *to be a coward*; лимо́нить/слимо́нить, *to nick*; нали́зываться/нализа́ться, *to get pissed*; рехну́ться, *to go off one's head*; обалдева́ть/обалде́ть, *to become stupefied*; околпа́чивать/околпа́чить, *to fool, dupe*; спере́ть (pf; сопру́, сопрёшь), *to nick*; укоко́шить (pf), *to kill, knock off*; улепётывать/улепетну́ть, *to rush off*; ха́пать/ха́пнуть, *to pinch, scrounge*; and adverbs such as да́веча, *recently*; отродя́сь, *never in one's life*.

word-formation
- Use of the verbal suffix -ану́ть (see also 7.11), eg звездану́ть (pf), *to bash*; садану́ть (pf), *to hit hard, bash*.

morphology
- The nominative plural form in -а́ for masculine nouns is more widespread than in the standard language (eg шофера́, *drivers*) (8.1.6). Types of declension may be confused (eg use of -ов as a genitive plural flexion for nouns other than masculine nouns, as in место́в; see also 1.4.3 and 8.1.7). Confusion of verbal conjugation, eg маха́ю (машу́ (from маха́ть), *I wave*). Use of certain non-standard imperative forms, eg едь (ешь, *eat*), е́хай (поезжа́й, *go (by transport)*). Non-reflexive forms may be substituted for reflexive forms, especially in gerunds and active participles, eg сиде́л заду́мавши (сиде́л заду́мавшись, *sat thinking*); загоре́вший дом (загоре́вшийся дом, *the house which has caught fire*). Use of past passive participial forms in -тый where in the standard language the ending -нный would be used, eg по́рватый (по́рванный, *torn*).

syntax
- Loose and broad use of prepositions, eg че́рез in the sense of *because of* (из-за), eg Че́рез него́ опозда́л(а), *I was late because of him*. Non-standard use of prepositions after verbs, eg (standard forms in brackets) беспоко́иться про кого́-н (о ком-н), *to worry about sb*, ра́доваться о чём-н (ра́доваться чему́-н), *to be glad at sth*.

1.3.3 The neutral register (R2)

This is the norm of an educated speaker, the standard form of the language that is used for polite but not especially formal communication. It might be used in broadcasting, among colleagues at work, by educated people who do not know each other very well, by teachers to their pupils. It is the register that the foreign student as a rule first learns and which is most suitable for his or her first official or social contacts with natives. It is 'correct' without being fussy or pedantic. This register is perhaps best defined in negative terms, as lacking the distinctive colloquial features of R1 and the bookish features of R3, though it may to some extent contain elements of both without altogether taking on a colloquial or bookish colouring. Both forms of address, ты and вы, are possible in R2, depending on the degree of intimacy between the people speaking. First names and patronymics are likely to be used between acquaintances. On the other hand secondary diminutive forms of first names (eg Ната́шенька, Та́нечка; see 6.3.1) might seem overfamiliar.

1.3.4 The higher register (R3)

This register is most commonly the vehicle for ideas which have been thought out in advance and are expressed in uninterrupted monologue. The exposition of such ideas may follow established patterns. Language in the higher register is therefore relatively well organised and formal and may have recourse to set phrases and formulaic expressions. It eschews elements that can be identified as colloquial (1.3.1), including regional variation (1.4). Vocabulary may be sophisticated, specialised or terminological. Syntax is complex. Constructions containing reflexive verbs used in a passive sense (10.8), gerunds (10.11.1) and active participles (10.11.2) are used freely. Nouns in the same case, especially the genitive, may be 'threaded' together (so-called нани́зывание падеже́й), eg представи́тель Министе́рства вну́тренних дел Герма́нии, [lit] *a representative of the Ministry of the Interior of Germany*. Nouns may be preceded by adjectival phrases containing nouns, eg пе́рвое в ми́ре коммунисти́ческое госуда́рство, *the first communist state in the world*.

Within this register the following functional styles may be identified.

(a) Scientific/academic style (нау́чный стиль)

The purpose of this style is communication in the sense of reporting information. The style may be appropriate in any medium from a monograph, learned article or textbook to a lecture or seminar. The academic style may also be used in many fields, indeed in any academic discipline from the natural sciences (eg physics, chemistry and biology), through the social sciences (eg politics, sociology and economics) to the arts (eg philosophy, philology and the study of literature). (It should be noted that the Russian word нау́ка, like the German word *Wissenschaft*, has a much broader range than the English *science*, embracing all academic work, not merely the natural and social sciences.) The language of the academic style is characterised by logical and orderly development (hence the use of transition words (4.2)) and is carefully formulated with explanation of the relationships between things (hence the use of numerous subordinating conjunctions (10.12.2)). Choice of words is precise.

Much vocabulary is terminological and words are used in their literal meanings. Verbs which would occur in R1/R2 might be replaced by phrases consisting of verb + verbal noun (eg происхóдит рост instead of растёт, *grows*; имéет мéсто повышéние температýры instead of повышáется температýра, *the temperature rises*). Various means are used to express a copula for which English would use some form of the verb *to be*, eg состоúт из, заключáется в, представлЯет собóй, all meaning *is* (3.2). The style is shorn of artistry and lacks the expressive devices of the colloquial language (see 1.3.1).

(b) Official/business style (официáльно-деловóй стиль)

This style, which, like the academic style, has as its purpose communication in the sense of reporting, may be found in treaties, legislation, regulations, codes of practice, forms and certificates, official correspondence and even public notices. Its field spans diplomacy, law, administration and commerce and even some of the standard methods of address in letters (6.17). Whereas in other styles clichés may be a defect, here they are more or less *de rigueur*. The language of this style is therefore characterised by numerous formulae, eg в отвéт на Ваш запрóс, *in reply to your enquiry* (6.17). Material is arranged according to some generally accepted form. Terminology abounds together with set phrases (eg вступúть в сúлу, *to come into effect*; исполнЯть обЯзанности, *to fulfil obligations*), abbreviations (5.9) and verbal nouns (see eg 7.7.1), prepositional phrases based on a noun (eg в дéле, *in the matter of*; 9.2), complex conjunctions (ввидý тогó, что, *in view of the fact that*; в связú с тем, что, *in connection with the fact that*; see 10.12.3) and formulaic links (на слýчай, éсли, *in the event that*; с тем услóвием, что, *on condition that*). Word order tends to be straightforward. The official/business style is impersonal and eschews the expressive resources of the colloquial register. It is also relatively stable and resistant to change.

(c) Publicistic style (публицистúческий стиль)

This style has, or may have, as its purpose not only communication of information but also persuasion. Its medium may be a political speech or debate, propaganda, a pamphlet or polemical article or even a slogan. It is widespread in journalism, though it is not the sole style of journalism, in which it may be as important to present information as to influence opinion. The style is characterised by socio-political vocabulary and it easily absorbs neologisms (4.1). It resorts to certain stereotypes and clichés (дать зелёную ýлицу, *to give the green light*) and periphrasis (eg вЫразить надéжду, *to express the hope*; окáзывать пóмощь, *to render assistance*; питáть нéнависть, *to harbour hatred*; принимáть решéние, *to take a decision*; производúть осмóтр, *to carry out an inspection*). Introductory constructions indicate the source of information (eg как сообща́ет наш корреспонде́нт, *as our correspondent reports*; по да́нным, *according to information*). Unlike the academic and official styles, the publicistic style makes use of such graphic, emotive and expressive resources of the language as rhetorical devices, repetition, parallelism and exclamation. It is mainly bookish but elements of colloquial language are used to lend it vitality. Slogans commonly embody the ellipsis of colloquial speech (eg реше́ния съе́зда—в жизнь, *let us put into practice the decisions of the congress*).

1.3.5 Styles of belles-lettres (сти́ли худо́жественной литерату́ры)

Account must also be taken of the language used by the creative artist, although this language stands apart from the scale of register that stretches from the colloquial informality of R1 to the bookish formality of R3. Unlike the varieties of language dealt with in 1.3.1–4 inclusive, the literary language has an aesthetic function as well as a communicative one. It may be contrasted in particular with the academic style of R3, which expounds ideas in conceptual terms and literally, for the language of the work of art expresses ideas with the help of images and uses words in non-literal ways. The medium of the language of belles-lettres may be a poem, a play, a short story, a novel, or even a song. As for register, the language of belles-lettres may, according to the author's purpose and subject-matter, embrace all the registers and styles examined in 1.3.1–4, even the demotic and – nowadays – the vulgar. Unlike the impersonal objective styles of R3 (academic and official/business), it may be personal and subjective. It makes use of the resources of the language for expressing emotion and attitude (eg modal particles, interjections, diminutive and pejorative suffixes, the syntax of R1). It may deploy dialect words, jargon, professional or common parlance or archaisms to lend a particular colouring. Tone may be varied, from the elevated to the ironic or parodic.

1.4 Regional variation in Russian

Account must also be taken, when considering variety in a language, of the existence of geographic dialects. The higher and neutral registers of a language (R3 and R2) are subject to little, if any, regional variation, but the colloquial form (R1) does vary from one region to another, both when used by relatively uneducated speakers and even when used by educated speakers in informal situations. Regional features often reflect archaic usage that has died out in the standard language and infringe the grammatical norms of that standard language which the foreign learner is expected to observe.

Considering the enormous size of the territory in which Russian is the main language – Russia stretches over 7,000 miles from the border with Belarus in the west to the Bering Strait in the east and almost 2,000 miles from the Kola Peninsula in the north to the Caucasus in the south and covers in all an area of some 6½ million square miles – the Russian language is surprisingly uniform. The language spoken in Vladivostok is easily comprehensible to the Muscovite. This relative uniformity (compared for example to the greater phonological differences in a much smaller country such as Switzerland) results from the frequent migrations of populations and the lack of major geographical barriers within the country. Nevertheless there is regional variation in Russian, in pronunciation, vocabulary, morphology and syntax (though it should be emphasised that certain factors have tended to reduce such variation in post-revolutionary Russia; see 1.5).

The foreign student is not advised to use regional linguistic features, which do not belong in the standard language or higher registers and which may in any case seem out-of-place unless all the distinctive features of a particular dialect are deployed consistently and comprehensively. The following sections are therefore intended only to give a superficial impression of the extent of regional variation in Russian and to draw attention to a few of the salient regional features.

1.4.1 Standard pronunciation

The regional features listed in 1.4.3 below are deviations from the standard to which reference is made, unless otherwise indicated, elsewhere in this book. The lexical, morphological and syntactic features of standard Russian are examined in the following chapters, but since standard pronunciation is not dealt with elsewhere it is as well to list here a few of the phonological features of Muscovite speech on which, owing to the status of Moscow as the capital city, standard pronunciation is based.

- Non-dissimilative áканье: pretonic *a* and *o* (and also initial *a* and *o*) are both pronounced as *a*, irrespective of the quality of the vowel in the stressed syllable, eg *travá* (трава́), *savá* (сова́), *ablaká* (облака́). In other unstressed positions both vowels may be reduced to *ŭ*, eg *mŭlakó* (молоко́).

- и́канье: after soft consonants pretonic *'e* and *'a* are pronounced as *'i*, eg *n'islá* (несла́), *vz'ilá* (взяла́). This phenomenon is characteristic of many C dialects as well as the standard language.

- In the standard language, as in the N regional dialect and many C dialects (see 1.4.2), the voiced velar *g* is an occlusive sound (like Eng *g*). Voiceless *g* becomes *k*, eg *nok* (ног), *sn'ek* (снег).

- There are four labiodental fricatives, ie hard voiced *v* and soft voiced *v′* and hard unvoiced *f* and soft unvoiced *f′*. At the end of a word or before a voiceless consonant *v* and *v′* are devoiced, eg *drof* (дров), *láfka* (ла́вка), *gotóf′t′e* (гото́вьте).

- There are two distinct affricates, the hard hissing affricate *c*, as in *cygán* (цыга́н), and the soft hushing affricate *č′*, as in *č′aj* (чай). (This distinction is also observed in most S and C dialects.)

1.4.2 Classification of Russian dialects

Dialects are defined not by a single phenomenon but by a set of phenomena, on the basis of a so-called bundle of isoglosses (see Glossary). However, the isoglosses defining the territorial limits of the use of one phenomenon do not necessarily coincide neatly with isoglosses relating to another phenomenon. Identification and classification of Russian dialects is therefore a complex matter that will not be addressed here, except insofar as it is possible to make a broad distinction between the following regional forms of Russian that may be heard in European Russia.

(a) The N regional dialects (**се́верное наре́чие**), ie the Russian spoken north of a line running a little to the north of Novgorod, Tver′ and Nizhnii Novgorod (but excluding St Petersburg). This regional dialect embraces such groups of local dialects as the Ladoga-Tikhvin group, the Vologda group and the Kostroma group. The N regional dialect is characterised especially by **о́канье** and use of occlusive *g*.

(b) The S regional dialect (**ю́жное наре́чие**), ie the Russian spoken from the borders of Belarus and Ukraine in the west and south and up to a line passing through Kolomna, to the north of Kaluga and Riazan′. This regional dialect embraces a SW group of dialects around Smolensk (influenced by Belarusian features), an Upper Dnepr group, an Upper Desna group around Briansk, the Kursk and Oriol group, and a group including the Russian of Riazan′, Tambov and Voronezh. The S regional dialect is characterised especially by **а́канье** and use of fricative *γ*.

(c) The C dialects (**среднеру́сские го́воры**), ie the Russian spoken in the lateral strip of territory running from the border with Belarus in the west. This group of dialects embraces the Novgorod group and the Pskov group in the west, the group around Moscow, and the group around Vladimir to the east. These transitional dialects exhibit varying mixtures of N and S regional features such as **о́канье** and **а́канье**, occlusive *g* and fricative *γ*.

1.4.3 Regional features

This section lists some of the principal regional deviations from the standard form of the language which the foreign student will normally learn and indicates in which broad regions these variations from the norm might be encountered. It should be borne in mind that although these deviations may be found in the language of belles-lettres they will generally be altogether absent from the styles classified in 1.3.4 as R3a, R3b and R3c and may infrequently occur in R2. The degree to which they will occur in a person's speech will depend on such factors as the speaker's background, education, age and experience, the circumstances in which he or she is speaking and the identity of the person being addressed. In general one may expect such features to occur more markedly in the speech of the poorly educated rural or provincial dweller.

Note: letters in brackets in this section (eg N, S, C, NE, SW) indicate the region(s) in which the features in question may be encountered. However, they do not imply that the feature is exclusive to that area or universal in it, even among the sort of speakers whose speech may exhibit dialect features.

pronunciation (cf 1.4.1)

- я́канье (see Glossary), eg *t'ap'ér'* (тепе́рь), *n'as'í* (неси́), *s'aló* (село́), *n'asú* (несу́) (ie strong я́канье; SE), or before hard consonants only, eg *s'aló* (село́), *n'asú* (несу́) (ie moderate я́канье; SW).
- о́канье (see Glossary), eg *sová* (сова́). (N regional and some C dialects.)
- е́канье (see Glossary), eg *p'et'í* (пяти́). (Some C dialects.)
- Fricative *γ*, eg *naγá* (нога́). Correspondingly, devoiced *γ* becomes *x*, eg *nox* (ног), *sn'ex* (снег). (S regional dialect.) In some SW regions bordering on Belarus and Ukraine *g* becomes *h*.
- Labiodental *v* and *v'*, when they occur at the end of a word or syllable, are pronounced as bilabial *w*, eg *drow* (дров), *láwka* (ла́вка). (Most S and many W and NE dialects.)
- Initial *v* may become *u*, eg *uméste* (вме́сте), *u górŭd* (в го́род), and some homonyms may result, eg внёс, унёс (both pronounced *un'ós*). (Some S dialects.)
- цо́канье (see Glossary), eg *caj* (чай), *cýsto* (чи́сто), *cúdo* (чу́до), ie hard цо́канье (NW and also many C and SE dialects), or *c'aj*, *c'ísto*, *c'údo*, ie soft цо́канье (NE dialects).
- Assimilation producing the long consonant *m̄* from the combination *bm*, eg *om̄án* (обма́н) (some N dialects), or simplification of the group *st* to *s* in final position, eg *mos* (мост) (some N and a few S dialects).
- Occurrence in some words of the combination *mn* instead of standard *vn*, especially *damnó* (давно́) and *ramnó* (равно́). (Some N and S dialects.)

stress

- Tendency to more innovatory stress in the S dialects, eg

movement of stress from prefix to stem in the past tense of certain verbs (о́тдал → отда́л, *gave back*); shift of stress from preposition to noun in certain phrases (на́ берег → на бе́рег, *on to the bank*). The NE dialects are more conservative in stress. In this area S practice affects the evolution of the standard language.

vocabulary

- A dialect may have a word different from the standard word to denote a certain phenomenon or action, eg (standard forms in brackets):

  бере́мя (n) (оха́пка, *armful, bundle*)
  бирю́к (волк, *wolf*) (some S dialects)
  бура́к (свёкла, *beetroot*) (some S dialects)
  вёдро (хоро́шая пого́да, *fine weather*)
  до́бре (хорошо́, *well*) (some S dialects)
  дю́же (о́чень, *very much, awfully*) (also R1)
  ве́кша (бе́лка, *squirrel*)
  козю́ля (змея́, *snake*) (some S dialects)
  ко́чет (пету́х, *cock(erel)*) (some S dialects)
  мура́шка (мураве́й, *ant*) (some SW dialects)
  назём/позём (наво́з, *manure*) (some N dialects)
  ора́ть (паха́ть, *to plough*) (some N and WC dialects)

  Regional words may be used in particular to denote age-old features of rural life such as paths, fences, outhouses, animal sheds, vegetables, parts of a plough or certain implements and utensils.

- A word which in the standard language or in some regions has one meaning may in certain regions have another meaning or an additional meaning, eg жи́то (*corn*) may mean *rye* in SW dialects and *barley* in NW dialects; паха́ть (*to plough*) may in N dialects also mean *to sweep*; пого́да (*weather* in the standard language) may mean *bad weather* in some N dialects and *good weather* in some S dialects.

- Special words may be used in particular dialects to denote phenomena, especially flora, fauna, topography, climate, clothing or architecture, which are peculiar to the region in question, eg ла́хта, a bay or inlet in NW Russia; рёлка, raised ground in swampy district, islet in river; обе́дник, a type of sea wind; понёва, a homespun skirt in S Russia; ха́та, a peasant hut in S Russia.

morphology

- Treatment of many nouns in -о that in the standard language are neuter, especially nouns with stress on the stem (eg де́ло, се́но, ста́до), as feminine, eg плоха́я де́ла (плохо́е де́ло, *a bad business*). (Some S and C dialects.)

- Declension of the nouns мать, *mother*, and дочь, *daughter*, that differs from the standard declension, eg nom sg мати, acc sg ма́терь. (Some N dialects.) In some W dialects the nouns ма́тка and до́чка replace мать and дочь respectively.

- Use of the flexion -е for the genitive singular of nouns in -а after prepositions, eg без родне́ (без родни́, *without relations*), от жене́ (от жены́, *from [one's] wife*); у сестре́ (у сестры́, *at [one's] sister's*).

- Occurrence of fewer nouns than in the standard language with nominative plural form in -á, eg гла́зы́ (глаза́, *eyes*); до́мы́ (дома́, *houses*); лу́ги́ (луга́, *meadows*) (some N, W and SW dialects); or of more nouns with this nominative plural form than in the standard language, eg деревня́ (дере́вни, *villages*); лошадя́ (ло́шади, *horses*).
- Extension of the genitive plural ending -ов to neuter and even feminine nouns, eg дело́в (дел), место́в (мест), ба́бов (баб), я́годов (я́год). (Many S dialects.)
- Various deviations from standard flexions in dative, instrumental and prepositional plural forms, such as: coincidence of dative and instrumental plural forms, eg с рука́м (с рука́ми, *with hands*), с нам (с на́ми, *with us*) (many N dialects); use of dative and prepositional forms of the type гостём, гостёх; лошадём, лошадёх (some S dialects); use of instrumental plural endings such as -амы, -ама, eg рука́мы, рука́ма (рука́ми, *hands*).
- Use of accusative/genitive pronominal forms мене́, тебе́, себе́. (S dialects.)
- Use of soft *t'* in third-person singular forms, eg *id'ót'* (идёт). (Some S and C dialects.)
- Various paradigms of мочь, eg могу́, мо́гешь, etc; могу́, могёшь, etc; мо́жу, мо́жешь, etc. (Some S dialects.)
- Use of first-person singular forms of second-conjugation verbs without epenthetic л or consonant change, eg любю́ (люблю́), ходю́ (хожу́). (Some S and SW dialects.)

syntax

- Use of certain compound prepositions of the type по-над, по-под, which are not found in the standard language (used with instrumental to indicate the site of action and with accusative to indicate direction of movement), eg по-под горо́й, *under the hillside*; по-над ре́чкой, *over the river*. (Some N and S dialects.)
- Use of certain prepositions with a case different from the case they govern in the standard language, eg во́зле, ми́мо, по́дле + acc (cf genitive in the standard language), eg во́зле реку́ (во́зле реки́, *near the river*). (Some N dialects.)
- Use of с + gen in sense of *out of* (cf из in the standard language), eg вы́йти с ко́мнаты, *to go out of the room*; прие́хать с Москвы́, *to come from Moscow*.
- Use of nominative rather than distinctive accusative (or accusative/genitive) form of a noun which is the direct object of a transitive verb, eg принести́ вода́ (принести́ во́ду, *to bring water*); кача́ть ребёнок (кача́ть ребёнка, *to rock a baby*). (Some N dialects.)

- Use of за + acc after short comparative adjectives (cf genitive in the standard language), eg Он ста́рше за Са́шу (Он ста́рше Са́ши, *He's older than Sasha*). (Some S dialects.)
- Use of a pluperfect tense consisting of the past tense of быть + the past tense of the verb denoting the action in question, eg А в сентябре́ снег был вы́сыпал, а октя́брь был тёплый, *Snow had fallen in September, but October was warm*. (Some N dialects.)
- Predicative use of perfective gerunds, eg Де́рево упа́вши, *A tree is down*; Ка́ша пригоре́вши, *The porridge is burnt*. (Some NW dialects; however, the form вы́пивши, *drunk*, is used in this way in the standard language.)
- Various impersonal constructions involving the use of a short form of a past passive participle, eg Свои́ми рука́ми напи́лено, *I sawed it up with my own hands*; Мно́го бы́ло рабо́тано, *A lot of work has been done*; Си́жено бы́ло у меня́, *I've been sitting around/People have been sitting around at my place*; or use of a past passive participle that does not agree with the noun to which it relates, eg Оди́н солда́т похоро́нено здесь, *One soldier is buried here*; Молоко́ проли́т, *Some milk has been spilt*.
- Less differentiation than in the standard language of subordinating conjunctions (which in any case occur less in R1 than in R2 and especially R3; see 10.12.2); correspondingly broader use of certain conjunctions, especially: что in causal sense, eg Он хохо́чет над на́ми, что глу́пы дак, *He's laughing at us for being so stupid*; and как in (a) conditional sense (= е́сли, *if*), eg Как ти́хо пое́ду, а ве́тер—дак ни за что, *If it's calm I'll go, but if it's windy I certainly shan't*; (b) causal sense (= потому́ что, *because*), eg Ведь я-то не напишу́, как я негра́мотна, *I shan't write myself, because I can't write*; (c) temporal sense (= когда́, *when*), eg Как жа́рко бы́ло, дак ко́шки в траву́ ложи́лись, *When it was hot the cats would lie down in the grass*.
- Use of the emphatic post-positive particle -то (see 4.4 on use of this particle in the standard language). In some dialects (esp N and E) the article changes according to the gender and number of the noun, ie стол-от, кры́ша-та, окно́-то, столы́-те. In some C dialects the forms -ту and -ти or -ты may be used for the sake of harmony with the ending of the noun to which the particle is attached eg на берегу́-ту, без со́ли-ти.

1.5 The tendency to uniformity

Certain reservations might be made about the aforegoing classification of register and regional variation. Firstly, the distinctions which it is useful to make in theory may in practice be far from clear-cut (an example of language in any register or subdivision of a register may well contain traces of language from other registers). Secondly, there is not complete agreement even among Russian students of stylistics (стили́стика), as the study of register is known, as to where precisely the boundaries between one register and another should be drawn. Thirdly, these boundaries are in any case constantly changing as features which once belonged to one register become accepted in another. Lastly, and most importantly, various factors have tended since the beginning of the Soviet period somewhat to erode distinctions between registers. (These same factors have also tended to eliminate regional variation of the sort described in 1.4.) For example, the development of the mass media, mass literacy and the extension of education, the removal of class barriers, urbanisation and the conferment of equal status on women have all served to spread the standard language. At the same time the standard language has absorbed many colloquial features. This process has accelerated in recent years as a result of the collapse of the communist régime, the breakdown of old restraints and taboos, the influx of Western habits, a sharp relaxation of moral standards and an attendant celebration of informality. This lowering of the standard language is particularly noticeable in the media.

One should also note a tendency in the language towards economy. This tendency is reflected, for example, in preference for shorter forms of words over longer forms (eg сестро́й, *by (my) sister*, rather than сестро́ю; поня́в, *having understood*, rather than поня́вши; мок, *was getting wet*, rather than мо́кнул) and in the prevalence of composition and abbreviation as means of word-formation (eg вече́рник, *evening-class student*, derived from the phrase студе́нт вече́рнего факульте́та; вуз, *higher educational institution*, from вы́сшее учёбное заведе́ние; глазни́к, *oculist*, from глазно́й врач).

1.6 Passages illustrating register

1.6.1 R1: television interview with a teenager

— Нет, а твоё челове́ческое, вот, как сказа́ть, своеобра́зие… По хара́ктеру, у тебя́ есть каки́е-то свои́, таки́е вот ма[не́ры], мане́ры, привы́чки, кото́рые, вот, ну как сказа́ть, отлича́ют тебя́ от други́х ребя́т в шко́ле…

5 — Мане́ры и привы́чки… вообще́-то, отлича́ют, да… Меня́ счита́ют таки́м тихо́ней в шко́ле, потому́ что я… не обща́юсь осо́бо ни с ке́м. В шко́ле у меня́ друзе́й нет, как пра́вило, то есть, все внешко́льные.

— А тебя́ э́то не обижа́ет, что тихо́ней [счита́ют]?

10 — Так нет, я ж зна́ю, кто я на са́мом де́ле-то. То есть…

— А кто ты на са́мом де́ле?
— Ну я ж говорю́, что така́я разносторо́нне разви́тая ли́чность. То есть в шко́ле ду́мают, что я «бота́ник» тако́й весь. Есть кли́чка, то есть челове́к, кото́рый мно́го у́чится, всё тако́е... А
15 на са́мом де́ле, нет.
— А тебе́ плева́ть на чужо́е мне́ние, и́ли ты его́ учи́[тываешь]. Ну, как «плева́ть», я гру́бо сказа́ла. Но так сказа́ть, на тебя́ де́йствует чужо́е мне́ние, и́ли тебе́ э́то всё равно́?
— А-а вот так. Я на него́ плюю́, но оно́ на меня́ де́йствует,
20 вот так я скажу́. То есть я, мо́жет быть, для себя́ ничего́ не отмеча́ю, е́сли мне что-то сказа́ли. Но, подсозна́тельно, получа́ется, что де́йствует. Наве́рное у всех так.
— А к де́вушкам, как ты отно́сишься?
— К де́вушкам? Как сказа́л Шти́рлиц в анекдо́те: «Я к ним не
25 отношу́сь.»... Да ника́к. Де́вушки, э́то само́ по себе́, я сам по себе́.
— Ну дава́й с тобо́й тогда́ таку́ю ма́ленькую я ещё анке́ту проведу́. Мне э́то о́чень интере́сно. Вот твоё представле́ние о сча́стье.
30 — Сча́стье? Ну, сча́стье—э́то мо́жно определи́ть, исполне́ние всех жела́ний. Друго́е де́ло, каки́е жела́ния действи́тельно жела́ния, а каки́е сиюмину́тные.
— А твоё представле́ние о несча́стье?
— О несча́стье?... В смы́сле о несча́стье... Не зна́ю... Пока́ у
35 меня́ не́ было серьёзных таки́х несча́стий. Так, чего́ скрыва́ть?
— Скажи́, Жень, как ты ду́маешь, настоя́щая любо́вь, она́ с ка́ждым случа́ется в жи́зни, и́ли не с ка́ждым?
— Да нет, наве́рное, да́же... далеко́ не с ка́ждым. Я б так сказа́л.
40 — А с кем? Э́то соверше́нно случа́йно попада́ет, и́ли э́то, всё-таки, челове́к мо́жет как-то, э́то, наде́яться на то, что с ним э́то случи́тся, и́ли э́то от него́ не зави́сит?
— В шестна́дцать лет таки́е вопро́сы!

TV, May 1994

Q. *No, but your human, well, how can I put it, uniqueness. As far as character is concerned, have you got any of your own, well, like manners, habits which, well, how can I put it, make you different from other lads in the school...*
A. *Manners and habits... on the whole they make me different, yes... People think I'm such a quiet bloke at school, because I... don't particularly mix with anybody. I haven't got any friends at school, as a rule that's to say my friends are all outside school.*
Q. *But doesn't it offend you that people think you're such a quiet bloke?*
A. *Well no, I know who I really am. That's to say...*
Q. *So who are you in fact?*
A. *Well I'd say I was a rounded, developed personality. That's to say at school they think I'm a just a 'botanist'. That's a nickname for a person who studies a lot, and that... But in fact that's not so.*
Q. *Do you not give a damn about other people's opinions, or do you take account of them? Well, maybe not 'give a damn', that was a bit crude.*

But do other people's opinions have an effect on you, or is it all the same to you?

A. *Well, that's just it. I don't give a damn about them but they do have an effect on me, that's how I'd put it. That's to say perhaps I don't take much notice of it if somebody says something to me. But subconsciously it turns out that it does have an effect. I suppose it's the same with everybody.*

Q. *And girls, what's your attitude towards them?*

A. *Girls? As Shtirlits said in a joke 'I don't have any attitude towards them at all.'... None at all. Girls, they go their way, I go mine.*

Q. *Well may I do a little questionnaire with you then? This is very interesting for me. Let's take your view of happiness.*

A. *Happiness? Well, happiness... one can define it as the fulfilment of all desires. Which desires are really desires and which are just spur-of-the-moment things, that's another matter.*

Q. *And your view of unhappiness?*

A. *About unhappiness?... As regards unhappiness... I don't know... I haven't so far had any real unhappinesses. So, why conceal it?*

Q. *Tell me, Zhenia, what do you think, real love, does it happen to everyone in life or not?*

A. *Well no, I suppose, even... I'd even say not to everyone by any means at all. That's what I'd say.*

Q. *Who does it happen to then? Does it come to you absolutely by chance or can you still somehow expect it to happen to you, or does it not depend on you?*

A. *Questions like this at sixteen!*

This interview was conducted in a programme about Krasnoarmeisk in the South East Ukraine. The youth being interviewed is a good-natured, ingenuous, evidently sensitive and intelligent schoolboy who has the eccentric habit of wandering round his home town dressed in various costumes, including that of Charlie Chaplin. The interviewer, somewhat disingenuously, conducts the interview in the colloquial register in which she expects the youth to speak. She also has a habit of amplifying her questions to take account of the possibility of both a positive and a negative reply, eg или тебе́ э́то всё равно́ (18), или не с ка́ждым (37), или э́то от него́ не зави́сит (42).

delivery and pronunciation

The youth speaks unclearly, without careful enunciation, and the interviewer at times follows suit.

- Many words and phrases are very indistinctly pronounced.
- Sometimes the interviewer either breaks off a word which she has begun to utter, eg мане́ры (2), учи́тываешь (16), or leaves a word or phrase which may be understood more or less completely unuttered, eg счита́ют (9).

vocabulary

There are numerous highly colloquial features, including:

- an abundance of words and phrases which in themselves mean very little and whose function is mainly to allow speakers to pause for thought or change their line of thinking, eg вот (1), [ну] как сказа́ть (1, 3), вообще́-то (5), всё тако́е (14), так сказа́ть (17), в смы́сле (34);

- ubiquitous use of так (10, 35), тако́й (2, 6, 12, 13, 14, 27, 35, 43) and the phrase то есть (7–8, 10, 13, 14, 20);
- particles or expressions containing them: а (9, 11, 14, 16, 19, 23, 33, 40), вот так (19, 20), ж (10, 12), ну (3, 17, 27, 30), -то (5, 10);
- colloquial turns of phrase, eg всё равно́ (18), э́то само́ по себе́, я сам по себе́ (25–6), как ты ду́маешь (36), including constructions involving an infinitive predicate, eg тебе́ плева́ть (16), чего́ скрыва́ть (35);
- vagueness, exemplified in the use of indefinite pronominal phrases such as как-то (41) and каки́е-то (2).

forms of address — The interviewer addresses the youth as ты and as Жень, the vocative form of the diminutive of his first name (36); no disrespect is intended by this familiarity, though the interviewer does perhaps adopt a patronising tone at times.

syntax

- Utterances are fragmented and disjointed, with many false starts and pauses.
- Subordination is of a very simple kind, mainly with the use of что as a relative pronoun, eg обижа́ет, что (9), говорю́, что (12), ду́мают, что (13), получа́ется, что (22).
- Subordinating conjunctions are simple ones, ie потому́ что (6), and е́сли (21).
- Relative clauses are introduced by кото́рый (3, 14) and gerunds and participles are altogether absent.
- Frequent use of э́то as subject, eg э́то не обижа́ет (9), э́то всё равно́ (18), э́то само́ по себе́ (25), э́то о́чень интере́сно (28), э́то мо́жно определи́ть (30), Э́то соверше́нно случа́йно попада́ет (40), э́то от него́ не зави́сит (42).
- Ellipsis, eg Наве́рное у всех так (22); В шестна́дцать лет таки́е вопро́сы (43).
- Idiosyncratic word order, eg таку́ю ма́ленькую я ещё анке́ту проведу́ (27–8).

1.6.2 R2: magazine interview with a popular singer

— Е́сли бы ты не уме́л петь и́ли игра́ть, каку́ю профе́ссию ты бы вы́брал?

— Наве́рное, стал бы штанги́стом. Мне э́то о́чень нра́вится, си́льный спорт. Я сейча́с вообще́ о́чень мно́го вре́мени уделя́ю

5 спóрту.
— Чегó ты бóльше всегó боúшься в жúзни?
— Ничегó. Клянýсь. Вообщé. Для менá всё ужé пережúто рáньше, у менá всё бы́ло в жúзни.
— Кем ты хóчешь вúдеть своегó сы́на?
10 — Моú родúтели не заставлáли менá выбирáть профéссию. Я придéрживаюсь тогó же. Глáвное, чтóбы он был дóбрым, óчень дóбрым. Éсли у тебá есть добротá—ты универсáльный человéк. А всё остальнóе он вы́берет сам. Емý три гóда, и он óчень талáнтлив, я э́то ужé сейчáс вúжу.
15 — Каковы́ твоú сáмые рáнние воспоминáния дéтства?
— Прáздники. Рáньше их бы́ло мнóго. Кáжется, э́то бы́ло на мáйские. Веснá, сóлнце, ручéйки, всё распускáется. Я сижý на плечáх у дéда, мне лет пять. Ощущéние настоáщего прáздника, настоáщего счáстья, когдá всё впередú.
20 — Ты вéришь в Бóга?
— Да, óчень. Но к э́тому пришёл не срáзу, помоглá Áлла Пугачёва. В цéркви бывáю чáсто. Вéрую, не просá пóмощи. Бог не лю́бит, когдá у негó прóсят. Я прóсто вéрю, потомý что э́то бéлая сторонá, свет. А мне бóльше нрáвится свет. Но и тень не
25 отгоня́ю, э́то гармóния чёрного и бéлого, хорóшего и плохóго. Я принадлежý свéту, знáчит Бóгу.
— Ты пóмнишь свою́ пéрвую любóвь?
— Да, пóмню. Э́то бы́ло на рóдине, в Свердлóвске. Мне бы́ло лет вóсемь, ей стóлько же, а мóжет и мéньше. Э́то былá настоя́-
30 щая любóвь. Я ей носúл в подъéзд цветы́, засóвывал их в почтóвый я́щик, её пáпа менá гонáл. А когдá я её провожáл домóй, онá смотрéла на менá из окнá. Э́то былá чúстая любóвь. Потóм я её не встречáл.

From the first Russian edition of *Cosmopolitan*, May 1994

Q. *If you couldn't sing or play, what career would you have chosen?*
A. *I expect I'd have become a weight-lifter. I like weight-lifting a lot, it's a strong sport. I spend a lot of time on sport now.*
Q. *What are you most afraid of in life?*
A. *Nothing. I swear it. Nothing at all. I've already been through everything, I've seen everything.*
Q. *What would you like your son to be?*
A. *My parents didn't make me choose a career. I'm the same. The main thing is that he should be a kind person, very kind. If you're kind you're a universal man. Everything else he'll choose himself. He's three and he's very talented, I can see that already.*
Q. *What are your earliest recollections of childhood?*
A. *Holidays. There used to be a lot of them. It was the May holidays, I think. It was spring, there was sunshine, streams, everything was coming into bloom. I'm sitting on my grandad's shoulders, real happiness, when everything was in front of you. That sense of real holiday, real happiness, when everything is in front of you.*
Q. *Do you believe in God?*
A. *Yes, very much. But I didn't get there all of a sudden, Alla Pugachova was a help. I often go to church. I believe, without asking for help. God*

doesn't like it when people ask Him for things. I simply believe because that's the white side, the light. And I prefer the light. But I don't chase the darkness away either, that's the harmony of black and white, the good and the bad. I belong to the light, I mean to God.

Q. *Do you remember your first love?*

A. *Yes, I do. It was where I was born, in Sverdlovsk. I was eight, and she was the same, maybe even younger. It was real love. I used to take flowers to her door and shove them into the letter-box and her dad used to chase me away. And when I took her home she'd watch me from the window. That was real love. Then I stopped seeing her.*

Although this extract is an example of the written language it is at the lower end of R2 (unlike the following example, which is a verbal news report) and tends towards R1, since it is based on an interview. The familiar form of address (ты) is used by the interviewer. Syntax is simple, with little subordination. Some sentences consist of only one or two words, eg Ничего́. Кляну́сь. Вообще́. (7); Да, о́чень. (21); Да, по́мню. (28). There is frequent recourse to э́то as a subject, eg э́то о́чень нра́вится (3), э́то бы́ло на ма́йские (16–17), э́то гармо́ния (25), Э́то бы́ло на ро́дине (28) and in the construction э́то была́ настоя́щая/чи́стая любо́вь (29–30, 32). At the same time the vigour and spontaneity of speech have no doubt been lost to some extent in the transformation of the interview into the rather bland form required by the genre of the magazine feature. What is printed is, while simple, grammatically correct, fluent and coherent. The questions and answers are shorn of very colloquial vocabulary, although the use of вообще́ (4, 7) and засо́вывал (30) does have a colloquial flavour. With the exception of the form па́па (31) such expressive features of R1 as diminutives and other colloquial suffixes, particles and interjections are lacking. At certain points there is a sententious tone that is perhaps foreign to R1, eg Е́сли у тебя́ есть доброта́ . . . (12), Бог не лю́бит . . . (22–3).

1.6.3 R2: a television report on the war in Bosnia

Мусульма́нские войска́ продолжа́ют наступле́ние на пози́ции
се́рбов в за́падной Бо́снии. По да́нным из вое́нных исто́чников
они́ практи́чески окружи́ли го́род Боса́нска Кру́па в сорока́
киломе́трах от Би́хача. Из го́рода эвакуи́ровано всё гражда́нское
5 населе́ние, и хотя́ кольцо́ сжима́ется всё плотне́е, се́рбы
уде́рживают Боса́нску Кру́пу. Ожесточённые бои́ разгоре́лись и
на други́х фронта́х. В мину́вшие су́тки мусульма́нские войска́
атакова́ли пози́ции босни́йских се́рбов под Сара́ево, в райо́не
го́рных масси́вов И́гмен и Бела́шница. Коло́нны мусульма́н
10 дви́жутся из Ту́злы в направле́нии го́рода Бие́лина. Не стиха́ет
канона́да и на се́вере Бо́снии в го́рном райо́не Озре́н. В хо́де
ата́к мусульма́нских войск под Сара́ево был обстре́лян оди́н
из наблюда́тельных пу́нктов францу́зского батальо́на
миротво́рческих сил ООН внутри́ демилитаризи́рованной зо́ны.

15 И всё э́то происхо́дит на фо́не попусти́тельства со стороны́ всё тех же голубы́х ка́сок. Осужда́я де́йствия босни́йских се́рбов, миротво́рцы факти́чески закрыва́ют глаза́ на бесчи́нства мусульма́н. Бо́льше того́, босни́йское прави́тельство разверну́ла пропаганди́стскую кампа́нию про́тив сил ООН, обвиня́я их в
20 подде́ржке се́рбов. Соверше́нно очеви́дно, что сара́евские прави́тели по́лностью игнори́руют мне́ния междунаро́дного соо́бщества, добива́ясь сня́тия эмба́рго на поста́вки ору́жия. И е́сли э́то всё-таки произойдёт, война́ в Бо́снии вспы́хнет с но́вой си́лой.

Television news, November 1994

Muslim troops are continuing their attack on Serb positions in Western Bosnia. According to information from military sources they have virtually surrounded the town of Bosanska Krupa forty kilometres from Bihac. The entire civilian population has been evacuated from the town, and although the ring is tightening the Serbs are holding on to Bosanska Krupa. Fierce fighting has broken out on other fronts as well. In the last twenty-four hours Muslim troops have attacked Bosnian Serb positions around Sarajevo, in the region of Mt Igmen and Mt Belašnica. Columns of Muslims are moving from Tuzla in the direction of the town of Bijeljina. Nor is the bombardment abating in the north of Bosnia, in the mountain region of Ozren. In the course of attacks by Muslim troops around Sarajevo one of the observation posts of a French batallion of the UN peace-keeping forces inside the demilitarised zone was shelled. And all this is happening with the connivance of those same blue helmets. While condemning the actions of the Bosnian Serbs the peace-keepers are in fact turning a blind eye to the excesses of the Muslims. In addition the Bosnian government has started a propaganda campaign against the UN forces, accusing them of supporting the Serbs. It is perfectly obvious that the rulers of Sarajevo are completely ignoring the views of the international community in trying to bring about a lifting of the arms embargo. And if this does happen the war in Bosnia will flare up with new force.

This is for the most part a piece of factual reporting which stylistically is as notable for what it lacks as for what it contains. There are none of the particles, interjections, elliptical constructions or colloquial words or expressions of R1, nor any of the active participles of R3 (if one excludes the adjective of participial origin мину́вшие (7)). Word order is in the main direct and neutral. Since the passage is delivered orally the sentences are not long, nor is the syntax complicated, although relatively simple subordinate clauses do occur (the concessive clause introduced by хотя́ (5) and the conditional clause introduced by е́сли (23)). There are however hints of the higher publicistic register (R3c) in the use of imperfective gerunds, eg осужда́я (16), обвиня́я (19), добива́ясь (22), the rather literary turn of phrase Не стиха́ет канона́да (10–11), the journalistic phrase По да́нным из вое́нных исто́чников (2) and the metonymic phrase голубы́х ка́сок (16). There is also a faint element of emotional involvement on the part of the reporter, reflected in his choice of words such as попусти́тельство (15), бесчи́нства (17) and по́лностью игнори́руют (21). The hint of indignation towards the end of the report is introduced by the slightly colloquial use of the conjunction и to begin the sentence which starts in line 15.

1.6.4 R3a: scientific/academic style: from a paper on mathematics

Суще́ственно бо́лее сло́жный вариа́нт класси́ческой пробле́мы Ште́йнера получа́ется при увели́чении числа́ грани́чных то́чек. В э́том слу́чае реше́ние пробле́мы Ште́йнера ещё о́чень далеко́ от заверше́ния, хотя́ актуа́льность э́той зада́чи чрезвыча́йно
5 велика́. Де́ло в том, что пробле́ма Ште́йнера на пло́скости те́сно свя́зана с больши́м кла́ссом тра́нспортных зада́ч. А и́менно, к ней непосре́дственно сво́дятся зада́чи оптимиза́ции систе́м тра́нспортных коммуника́ций, свя́зывающих ряд поставщико́в-потреби́телей. Сюда́ отно́сится зада́ча оптима́-
10 льного расположе́ния систе́м доро́г, трубопрово́дов, телефо́нных ли́ний и т. п. Пробле́ма Ште́йнера име́ет и мно́го други́х приложе́ний (в тео́рии грани́ц разде́ла одноро́дных физи́ческих сред, в тео́рии минима́льных пове́рхностей, в тео́рии гра́фов, тео́рии групп, в биоло́гии, хи́мии и т. д.), причём число́
15 грани́чных то́чек, появля́ющееся в практи́чески зна́чимых зада́чах, мо́жет быть доста́точно велико́ (не́сколько со́тен).

Ока́зывается, лока́льная структу́ра минима́льных сете́й не зави́сит от коли́чества грани́чных то́чек (см. предложе́ние 1 ни́же). Одна́ко, о глоба́льном устро́йстве таки́х сете́й в о́бщем слу́чае
20 почти́ ничего́ не изве́стно, кро́ме, пожа́луй, того́, что минима́льная сеть представля́ет собо́й де́рево. Э́то де́рево называ́ется *минима́льным де́ревом Ште́йнера.* При иссле́довании же конкре́тного ви́да се́ти возника́ют серьёзные вычисли́тельные тру́дности.

25 Тако́е положе́ние веще́й привело́ к тому́, что, с одно́й стороны́, акти́вно развива́ются приближённые ме́тоды реше́ния пробле́мы Ште́йнера. С друго́й стороны́, веду́тся интенси́вные теорети́ческие иссле́дования э́той пробле́мы. Оди́н из подхо́дов состои́т в наложе́нии не́которых ограниче́ний на устро́йство
30 мно́жества M грани́чных то́чек.

Друго́й подхо́д состои́т в ослабле́нии поня́тия минима́льности и перехо́де к изуче́нию бо́лее широ́кого кла́сса лока́льно минима́льных сете́й. Так возника́ет обобщённая пробле́ма Ште́йнера. Интере́с к лока́льно минима́льным сетя́м
35 объясня́ется та́кже и тем, что се́ти тако́го ти́па ча́сто встреча́ются на пра́ктике.

Математи́ческий сбо́рник, a journal of the Mathematical Section of the Russian Academy of Sciences, December 1992

A substantially more complex variant of Steiner's classical problem is obtained when one increases the number of fixed nodes. In this case one is still very far from achieving a solution of Steiner's problem, although the problem has very great practical implications. The fact of the matter is that Steiner's problem in a plane is closely connected with a large class of transport problems. To be specific, the problems of optimisation of systems of transport communications which connect a series of suppliers and consumers are directly reducible to it. The problem of optimal distribution of road systems, pipe-lines, telephone lines and so forth has a bearing here. Steiner's problem also has many other applications (in the theory of interfaces of one-type physical environments, in the theory of minimal surfaces, graph theory, group theory, biology, chemistry, etc), the number of fixed nodes which appear in problems of practical significance perhaps being quite large (several hundred).

It turns out that the local structure of minimal nets does not depend on the number of fixed nodes (see proposition I below). However, virtually nothing is known about the global arrangement of such nets generally apart from the fact, perhaps, that the minimal net is a tree. This tree is called Steiner's minimal tree. But when one researches the concrete form of the net serious computing difficulties arise.

This state of affairs has led to the active development, on the one hand, of approximate methods of solving Steiner's problem. On the other hand intensive theoretical research into this problem is being carried out. One of the approaches consists in the imposition of certain limits on the arrangement of the sets S of fixed nodes.

Another approach consists in the relaxation of the concept of minimality and a shift to the study of a broader class of locally minimal nets. Thus there arises the generalised problem of Steiner. Interest in the locally minimal networks is explained also by the fact that networks of this type are often encountered in practice.

The passage is characterised by great precision, and the careful, logical development of ideas. Words are used unambiguously and in an impersonal way. There is no emotional content and such linguistic features as modal particles, interjections and diminutives are therefore altogether lacking, except for the use of the particle же for emphasis in line 22.

vocabulary

- Specialised vocabulary, much of which is of Western origin, either in the form of calques, eg грани́чная то́чка (2), тео́рия минима́льных пове́рхностей (13), минима́льные се́ти (17), or in the form of loanwords (вариа́нт, класси́ческий, пробле́ма (all line 1)), актуа́льность (4), оптимиза́ция (7), коммуника́ция (8), оптима́льный (9–10), тео́рия (12, etc), граф (14), серьёзный (23), интенси́вный (27), теорети́ческий (28).
- Abundance of verbal nouns, especially with the suffix -ение: реше́ние (3, 26), заверше́ние (4), оптимиза́ция (7), расположе́ние (10), приложе́ние (12), предложе́ние (18), устро́йство (19), наложе́ние, ограниче́ние (29), ослабле́ние (31), перехо́д, изуче́ние (32).
- Various means of expressing copula in definitions: представля́ет

собо́й (21), состои́т в (29, 31); the verb явля́ться is also used in a sentence not included here.

- Conventional abbreviations: и т. п. (11), и т. д. (14), см. (18).

phraseology

- Set phrases, including conventional predicate + object combinations: де́ло в том, что (5), те́сно свя́зана с (6), име́ть приложе́ние (11–12), тако́е положе́ние веще́й (25).

grammatical forms

- Participles of various sorts, viz: present active, свя́зывающих (8), появля́ющееся (15); past passive, обобщённая (33); the forms приведён and посвящённых also occur in a sentence not included here.
- Use of the short adjectival form велика́ (5).

syntax

- Frequent use of reflexive imperfectives in passive sense, giving an objective, impersonal air to the passage, eg получа́ется (2), сво́дятся (7), отно́сится (9), ока́зывается (17), называ́ется (21), развива́ются (26), веду́тся (27), объясня́ется (35), встреча́ются (36).
- 'Threading' of nouns in genitive case: зада́ча оптима́льного расположе́ния систе́м доро́г (9–10), ме́тоды реше́ния пробле́мы Ште́йнера (26–7), устро́йство мно́жества *М* грани́чных то́чек (29–30), в ослабле́нии поня́тия минима́льности (31–2).
- Verbal nouns combined with при: при увеличе́нии (2), при иссле́довании (22).
- Complex subordination, including use of то, что: clauses introduced by хотя́ (4), причём (14), кро́ме того́, что (20), привело́ к тому́, что (25), объясня́ется та́кже и тем, что (35).
- Inversion of subject and predicate: отно́сится зада́ча (9), возника́ют серьёзные... тру́дности (23–4), развива́ются приближённые ме́тоды (26), возника́ет обобщённая пробле́ма (33).
- Parenthetical explanations to support assertions: в тео́рии минима́льных пове́рхностей... (12–14), не́сколько со́тен (16), см. предложе́ние 1 ни́же (18).
- Use of transition words demonstrating logical connection between ideas: в э́том слу́чае (2–3), а и́менно (6–7), одна́ко (19), с одно́й стороны́... с друго́й стороны́ (25–7).

1.6.5 R3b: official/business style: example of a contract

Акционе́рное о́бщество... имену́емое в дальне́йшем «покупа́тель», с одно́й стороны́, и фи́рма... имену́емая в дальне́йшем «продаве́ц», с друго́й стороны́, договори́лись о нижесле́дующем:

5 Предме́т Контра́кта. Продаве́ц про́дал, а покупа́тель купи́л две ультразвуковы́е устано́вки с компле́ктом необходи́мых принадле́жностей и расхо́дуемых материа́лов в соотве́тствии с Приложе́нием к настоя́щему Контра́кту и явля́ющимся неотъе́млемой его́ ча́стью.

10 О́бщая су́мма Контра́кта. О́бщая су́мма настоя́щего Контра́кта составля́ет... до́лларов США. Це́ны явля́ются устано́вленными и не подлежа́т измене́нию в тече́ние всего́ сро́ка де́йствия Контра́кта.

Гара́нтия. Продаве́ц гаранти́рует, что поставля́емое обору́до-
15 вание соотве́тствует мирово́му техни́ческому у́ровню, сущест-ву́ющему для да́нного ви́да те́хники и его́ по́лное соотве́тствие со спецификáцией настоя́щего Контра́кта. Гара́нтия продавца́ де́йствует в тече́ние 12 ме́сяцев, счита́я с да́ты нача́ла эксплуата́ции обору́дования.

20 Реклама́ции. Реклама́ции мо́гут быть зая́влены в гаранти́йный срок в отноше́нии ка́чества поста́вленного това́ра в слу́чае несоотве́тствия его́ ка́честву, обусло́вленному в настоя́щем Контра́кте. В реклама́ции необходи́мо указа́ть коли́чество и наименова́ние реклами́руемого изде́лия, основа́ние реклама́ции.

25 Реклама́ция заявля́ется те́лексом и́ли телефа́ксом, и дуб-ли́руется заказны́м письмо́м с приложе́нием всех необходи́мых докуме́нтов, подтвержда́ющих реклама́цию.

Форс мажо́р. При наступле́нии обстоя́тельств невозмо́жности по́лного и́ли части́чного исполне́ния любо́й из сторо́н
30 обяза́тельств по настоя́щему Контра́кту, и́менно: пожа́ра, стихи́йных бе́дствий, блока́ды, запреще́ний э́кспорта и́ли и́мпорта, и́ли други́х незави́сящих от сторо́н обстоя́тельств, срок исполне́ния обяза́тельств отодвига́ется соразме́рно вре́мени, в тече́ние кото́рого бу́дут де́йствовать таки́е обстоя́тельства и их
35 после́дствия. Сторона́, для кото́рой создала́сь невозмо́жность исполне́ния обяза́тельств по Контра́кту, должна́ о наступле́нии и прекраще́нии обстоя́тельств, препя́тствующих исполне́нию обяза́тельств, неме́дленно извеща́ть другу́ю сто́рону.

Арбитра́ж. Все спо́ры, могу́щие возни́кнуть из настоя́щего
40 Контра́кта и́ли в связи́ с ним, подлежа́т рассмотре́нию в арбитра́жном поря́дке во Внешнеторго́вой Арбитра́жной Коми́ссии при Торго́во-Промы́шленной Пала́те Росси́и в соотве́тствии с пра́вилами о произво́дстве дел в э́той Коми́ссии.

Про́чие усло́вия. Все измене́ния и дополне́ния к настоя́щему
45 Контра́кту действи́тельны лишь в том слу́чае, е́сли они́ совершены́ в пи́сьменной фо́рме и подпи́саны обе́ими сторона́ми. По́сле подписа́ния настоя́щего Контра́кта, все предыду́щие перегово́ры и перепи́ска по нему́ теря́ют си́лу. Настоя́щий Контра́кт соста́влен на ру́сском и англи́йском
50 языка́х, причём о́ба те́кста име́ют одина́ковую си́лу.

The joint-stock company... hereafter The Purchaser, on the one hand, and the firm... hereafter The Vendor, on the other, have come to the following agreement:
Subject of the Contract. The Vendor has sold and the Purchaser has bought two ultrasound units with a set of the necessary accessories and

consumables in accordance with the Addendum to this Contract, which is an integral part of the Contract.
Sum Total of the Contract. The sum total of the present Contract is . . . US dollars. The prices are fixed and are not subject to alteration while the Contract is valid.
Guarantee. The Vendor guarantees that the equipment being delivered meets the international technical standard in existence for technology of the type in question and that it completely conforms to the specification of the present Contract. The Vendor's Guarantee is valid for twelve months from the date on which the equipment begins to be used.
Claims. Claims may be made during the period of the Guarantee in respect of the quality of the goods delivered in the event of their not being of the quality stipulated in the present Contract. In any claim the name of the article in respect of which the claim is being made and the grounds for the claim must be indicated. The claim should be made by telex or fax and a copy should be sent by registered letter together with all the necessary documents supporting the claim.
Force majeure. In the event of circumstances which make either party wholly or partially unable to fulfil its obligations under the present Contract, namely: fire, acts of God, blockades, export or import bans, or other circumstances over which the two parties have no control, the deadline by which they must fulfil their obligations is extended in accordance with the period of time during which such circumstances and their consequences obtain. The party which has been unable to fulfil its obligations under the terms of the Contract must notify the other party without delay of the onset and cessation of the circumstances which prevent it from fulfilling its obligations.
Arbitration. All disputes which may arise out of the present Contract or in connection with it are subject to arbitration by the Foreign Trade Arbitration Commission of the Russian Chamber of Commerce and Industry in accordance with the rules concerning the conduct of business in the Commission.
Other Conditions. All amendments and additions to the present Contract are valid only in the event of their being made in writing and signed by both parties. After the signing of the present Contract all preceding negotiations and correspondence relating to it become invalid. The present Contract is drawn up in Russian and in English, both texts having equal force.

The passage is an abridged form of a contract relating to the sale of technical equipment. As a business document seeking to describe an agreement in a legally binding way it is formal and precise and is carefully set out according to an established pattern. The register it exemplifies has features which are similar to those of the scientific/academic register illustrated above (1.6.4), notably profusion of verbal nouns, gerunds and participles, use of reflexive verbs in a passive sense, use of при with verbal nouns. However, its formulae and phraseology are distinctive.

vocabulary

- Legalistic or official formulae and turns of phrase, eg имену́емое/имену́емая в дальне́йшем (1, 2–3), договори́лись о нижесле́дующем (3–4), явля́ющимся неотъе́млемой его́ ча́стью

(8–9), не подлежа́т измене́нию (12), в тече́ние всего́ сро́ка де́йствия Контра́кта (12–13), извеща́ть другу́ю сто́рону (38), подлежа́т рассмотре́нию (40), в арбитра́жном поря́дке (40–1), о произво́дстве дел (43), теря́ют си́лу (48), име́ют одина́ковую си́лу (50).

- Use of явля́ться (8, 11) and составля́ть (11) in the sense of the verb *to be* (see 3.2).
- Numerous verbal nouns (given below in nominative form), with various suffixes, eg измене́ние (12, 44), эксплуата́ция (19), наименова́ние (24), основа́ние (24), приложе́ние (26), наступле́ние (28, 36), исполне́ние (29, 33, 36, 37), запреще́ние (31), прекраще́ние (37), рассмотре́ние (40), дополне́ние (44), подписа́ние (47).
- Use of prepositions and prepositional phrases based on nouns, viz в соотве́тствии с (7, 42–3), в тече́ние (12, 18, 33–4), в отноше́нии (21), в слу́чае (21), соразме́рно (33), в связи́ с (40), в том слу́чае, е́сли (45).

grammatical forms

- Use of the gerund счита́я (18) and active participles, viz существу́ющему (15–16), подтвержда́ющих (27), препя́тствующих (37), могу́щие (39).
- Use of present passive participles, viz поставля́емое (14), реклами́руемого (24), and the adjective расхо́дуемых (7) which is derived from a present passive participle.
- Use of past passive participles, viz устано́вленными (11), зая́влены (20), поста́вленного (21), обусло́вленному (22), совершены́ (46), подпи́саны (46), соста́влен (49).

syntax

- Reflexive verbs used in a passive sense, eg заявля́ется (25), дубли́руется (25–6), отодвига́ется (33).
- The present tense is used throughout, from line 11 on, to indicate obligation (cf use of Eng modal *shall*, 3.3).
- Verbal noun combined with при: при наступле́нии (28).
- The adjectival phrase placed before the noun, незави́сящих от сторо́н обстоя́тельств (32).
- The introduction of a subordinate clause by the conjunction при-чём (50).

1.6.6 R3c: publicistic style: a piece of political journalism

Возглавля́вший в Верхо́вном Сове́те комите́т по законода́тельству и вновь и́збранный в Госуда́рственную Ду́му М. Митюко́в суро́вому сво́ду процеду́р, до ме́лочей регули́рующих парла́ментскую жизнь и гаранти́рующих юриди́ческую
5 эффекти́вность рабо́ты Федера́льного собра́ния, придаёт насто́лько большо́е значе́ние, что называ́ет не ина́че, как «ма́лой Конститу́цией». В осно́ве прое́кта регла́мента—но́рмы но́вой Конститу́ции, го́рькие уро́ки росси́йского парламентари́зма. Одна́ко он во́все не обольща́ется: депута́ты

10 сде́лают всё, что́бы отве́ргнуть большинство́ положе́ний доку-
ме́нта и тем са́мым сбро́сить свои́ бу́дущие пу́ты.

Поско́льку гла́вной причи́ной неда́вней конфронта́ции власте́й с траги́ческой для страны́ развя́зкой ста́ло не то́лько полновла́стие сове́тов, съе́зда, Верхо́вного Сове́та, но и ниче́м
15 не ограни́ченная власть председа́теля ВС, его́ замести́телей, прези́диума, их беспардо́нное вмеша́тельство в компете́нцию президе́нта и прави́тельства, в но́вом регла́менте фу́нкции спи́керов обе́их пала́т прописаны с преде́льной юриди́ческой чёткостью: веде́ние заседа́ния и руково́дство вну́тренним
20 распоря́дком. И никаки́х покуше́ний на де́ятельность парла́ментских комите́тов, на свобо́ду фра́кций. Прези́диумы упраздня́ются.

Ещё оди́н суще́ственный моме́нт—в це́лях эконо́мии депута́тского вре́мени, повыше́ния ка́чества докуме́нтов и
25 ско́рости их прохожде́ния обсужде́ние законопрое́ктов перено́сится непосре́дственно в комите́ты.

С приня́тием но́вой Конститу́ции, поясни́л М. Митюко́в, ро́ли в госуда́рстве перераспредели́лись, и тепе́рь парла́менту отво́дится фу́нкция законотво́рчества и законода́тельства.
30 Президе́нт же осуществля́ет как вну́треннюю, так и вне́шнюю поли́тику, но на осно́ве Федера́льных зако́нов и Конститу́ции. В слу́чае приня́тия Федера́льным собра́нием зако́на, угрожа́ющего стаби́льности госуда́рства, президе́нт наделён пра́вом верну́ть его́ на дорабо́тку.

35 Федера́льное собра́ние—лишь усло́вное объедине́ние двух самостоя́тельных пала́т: Сове́та Федера́ции и Госуда́рственной ду́мы. На са́мом де́ле, как э́то и при́нято в развиты́х стра́нах, по отноше́нию друг к дру́гу они́ явля́ются страху́ющими инста́нциями. Основно́й «поставщи́к» законопрое́ктов—
40 Госуда́рственная ду́ма, а ве́рхняя пала́та—контролёр: ли́бо одобря́ет по́данные докуме́нты, ли́бо отверга́ет. Отсю́да ра́зные регла́менты для обе́их пала́т, незави́симые пра́вила игры́.

Изве́стия, 24 December 1993

M. Mitiukov, who heads the Committee on Legislation in the Supreme Soviet and who has again been elected to the State Duma, attributes such great significance to the strict code of procedures, which regulates parliamentary life down to the last detail and guarantees the legal effectiveness of the work of the Federal Assembly, that he calls it nothing less than a 'minor Constitution'. At the basis of the draft of the standing orders lie the norms of the new Constitution, the bitter lessons of Russian parliamentarism. However, he by no means deceives himself: the deputies will do everything they can to overturn the bulk of the document's regulations and thereby to throw off their future shackles.

Since the cause of the recent confrontation of authorities, which had such a tragic dénouement for the country, was not only the sovereignty of the soviets, the congress and the Supreme Soviet but also the unlimited power of the chairman of the Supreme Soviet, his deputies and the presidium and their unpardonable interference in the competence of the President and the government, in the new standing orders the functions of the speakers of both houses are prescribed with legal precision: the conduct of the meeting and the keeping of internal order. And no encroachment on the activity of the parliamentary committees or the freedom of factions. The presidiums are being abolished.

One other substantive factor: in the interests of saving the deputies' time and improving the quality of documents and speeding up their passage the discussion of draft legislation is being transferred directly to the committees.

With the acceptance of the new Constitution, Mr Mitiukov explained, roles in the state have been reallocated and the function of law-making and law-giving is now being assigned to parliament. Internal as well as foreign policy is being carried out by the President, but on the basis of the federal laws and the Constitution. In the event of the Federal Assembly accepting a law which threatens the stability of the state, the President is invested with the power to return it for further work.

The Federal Assembly is merely a conditional amalgamation of two independent chambers: the Soviet of the Federation and the State Duma. In fact, as is customary in developed countries, they act as safeguards in relation to one another. The State Duma is the basic 'provider' of laws, while the upper chamber is the check: either it approves the documents submitted to it or it rejects them. Hence the different standing orders for the two chambers, the independent rules of the game.

Political journalese is a variety of language which is extremely widespread. The student must therefore be able to identify and understand it, although he or she cannot be advised to emulate it.

The passage given here has much in common with the passages illustrating the scientific/academic and official/business varieties of the formal register (1.6.4 and 1.6.5 above), notably the prevalence of verbal nouns and participles, the use of reflexive verbs in a passive sense, the complex syntax, and some turns of phrase that would not be out of place in an official document (see below). However, the publicistic variety of R3 differs from the other varieties in that it has a more subjective tone, which is reflected here in the use of such adjectives as суро́вый (3), го́рький (8), траги́ческий (13), беспардо́нный (16) and in the striving for literary effect with the object of bringing readers to the author's point of view, namely that it is right to limit the powers of the Supreme Soviet.

vocabulary

- Abundance of political, legal and administrative terms borrowed from Western European languages (in this passage these words make up over 10 per cent of the whole): процеду́ра, парла́ментский, регули́ровать, гаранти́ровать, юриди́ческий, эффекти́вность, федера́льный, конститу́ция, прое́кт, регла́мент, но́рма, парламентари́зм, депута́т, докуме́нт, конфронта́ция, прези́диум, компете́нция, президе́нт, фу́нкция, спи́кер, фра́кция, эконо́мия, комите́т, парла́мент, поли́тика, стаби́льность, инста́нция, контролёр.

- Free use of verbal nouns: ведéние (19), повышéние (24), прохождéние (very formal; 25), обсуждéние (25), принятие (27, 32), дорабóтка (34), объединéние (35).
- The word поставщи́к (39) is used in a modish Western sense; similarly the phrase прáвила игры́ (42). The adjective беспардóнный (16) is preferred to a Russian synonym or near-synonym such as бессты́дный or непрости́тельный.
- The figurative noun пу́ты (11) has an archaic flavour and is used for rhetorical effect.

phraseology

- Bookish, formal or official turns of phrase, eg фу́нкции спи́керов обéих палáт прописаны с предéльной юриди́ческой чёткостью (17–19); президéнт наделён прáвом (33); the prepositional phrases в цéлях (23) and в слу́чае (31–2).

morphology

- Free use of present and past active participles in place of котóрый + indicative: возглавля́вший (1), регули́рующих (3–4), гаранти́рующих (4), угрожáющего (32), страху́ющими (38).
- Use of reflexive verbs to render passive voice: упраздня́ются (22), перенóсится (26), перераспредели́лись (28), отвóдится (29).

syntax

- Long and highly complex sentences: Возглавля́вший в Верхóвном Совéте ... «мáлой Конститу́цией» (1–7), Поскóльку глáвной причи́ной ... руковóдство вну́тренним распоря́дком (12–20).
- Subordination, eg the clause beginning Поскóльку... (12ff).
- Complex adjectival phrases preceding noun: Возглавля́вший в Верхóвном Совéте комитéт по законодáтельству и вновь и́збранный в Госудáрственную Ду́му М. Митюкóв (1–3); с траги́ческой для страны́ развя́зкой (13).
- Inversion, eg of indirect object and predicate: суpóвому свóду процеду́р ... придаёт настóлько большóе значéние, что... (3–6).
- Constructions involving surrogate of быть and instrumental complement: глáвной причи́ной... стáло не тóлько полновлáстие совéтов (12–14); они́ явля́ются страху́ющими инстáнциями (38–9).
- Balance: не тóлько полновлáстие совéтов, съéзда, Верхóвного Совéта, но и ничéм не ограни́ченная власть председáтеля ВС ... (13–15); Президéнт же осуществля́ет как вну́треннюю, так и внéшнюю поли́тику (30–1); ли́бо одобря́ет пóданные доку́мéнты, ли́бо отвергáет (40–1).

1.6.7 The language of belles-lettres: Valentin Rasputin

There follow two passages from Rasputin's novella Проща́ние с Матёрой (first published in 1976). The first is the opening passage of the novel, describing the Siberian village of Matiora, which is shortly to be flooded by the River Angara as a consequence of the building of a hydroelectric power-station further up the river. The second introduces the reader to a number of old women who have lived in the village all – or in one case most of – their lives and whose simple way of life is about to be ruined by this manifestation of technological progress. The first passage illustrates Rasputin's polished narrative style; the second contains elements of colloquial and local demotic speech in the old women's conversation.

И опя́ть наступи́ла весна́, своя́ в своём несконча́емом ряду́, но после́дняя для Матёры, для о́строва и дере́вни, нося́щих одно́ назва́ние. Опя́ть с гро́хотом и стра́стью пронесло́ лёд, нагромозди́в на берега́ торо́сы, и Ангара́ освобождённо откры́лась, вы́тянувшись в могу́чую сверка́ющую течь. Опя́ть на ве́рхнем мысу́ бо́йко зашуме́ла вода́, ска́тываясь по рёлке на две стороны́: опя́ть запыла́ла по земле́ и дере́вьям зе́лень, пролили́сь пе́рвые дожди́, прилете́ли стрижи́ и ла́сточки и любо́вно к жи́зни заква́кали по вечера́м в боло́тце просну́вшиеся лягу́шки. Всё э́то быва́ло мно́го раз, и мно́го раз Матёра была́ внутри́ происходя́щих в приро́де переме́н, не отстава́я и не забега́я вперёд ка́ждого дня. Вот и тепе́рь посади́ли огоро́ды—да не все: три семьи́ сняли́сь ещё с о́сени, разъе́хались по ра́зным города́м, а ещё три семьи́ вы́шли из дере́вни и того́ ра́ньше, в пе́рвые же го́ды, когда́ ста́ло я́сно, что слу́хи ве́рные. Как всегда́, посе́яли хлеба́—да не на всех поля́х: за реко́й па́шню не тро́гали, а то́лько здесь, на острову́, где побли́же. И карто́шку и морко́шку в огоро́дах ты́кали ны́нче не в одни́ сро́ки, а как пришло́сь, кто когда́ смог...

Стару́хи втроём сиде́ли за самова́ром и то умолка́ли, налива́я и прихлёбывая из блю́дца, то опя́ть как бы не́хотя и уста́ло принима́лись тяну́ть сла́бый, ре́дкий разгово́р. Сиде́ли у Да́рьи, са́мой ста́рой из стару́х; лет свои́х в то́чности никто́ из них не знал, потому́ что то́чность э́та оста́лась при креще́нии в церко́вных за́писях, кото́рые пото́м куда́-то увезли́—концо́в не сыска́ть. О во́зрасте стару́хи говори́ли так:—Я, де́вка, уж Ва́ську, бра́та, на загорбке таска́ла, когда́ ты на свет родила́сь.—Э́то Да́рья Наста́сье.—Я уж в па́мяти находи́лась, по́мню.

—Ты, одна́ко, и бу́дешь-то го́да на три меня́ поста́ре.—Но, на́ три! Я за́муж-то выходи́ла, ты кто была́—огляни́сь-ка! Ты ишо́ без рубашо́нки бе́гала. Как я выходи́ла, ты должна́, поди́-ка, по́мнить.

—Я по́мню.

—Ну дак от. Куды́ тебе́ равня́ться! Ты супроти́в меня́ совсе́м моло́денькая.

And again spring came round, in its never-ending cycle, but the last one for Matiora, for the island and the village bearing the same name. Again with a thunder and with passion the ice was swept away and the hummocks were piled up on the banks and the Angara opened up with a sense of liberation and stretched itself out in a mighty gleaming flow. Again on the upper promontory the sprightly waters began to roar, rolling past the mound of land on two sides; again the vegetation burst out in colour over the ground and over the trees, the first rains poured down, the swifts and swallows flew in, and in the marsh the awakening frogs began of an evening to croak amorously to life. All this had happened many times, and many times Matiora had been in step with the changes taking place in Nature, not lagging behind or running ahead of each day. And now again people planted the vegetable gardens – but not everybody: three families had moved off back in the autumn and had gone to different towns, while another three had left the village even before that, in the first years when it had become clear that the rumours were true. As always people sowed crops – but not in every field: the ploughed land over the river they did not touch, just the land here, on the island, where it was a bit nearer. And the potatoes and carrots in the vegetable gardens were not all put in at the same time now, but whenever, as each could. . .

The old women sat in a threesome at the samovar, now silent, pouring tea and sipping it out of their saucers, now again striking up a feeble, sparse conversation as if they were weary and reluctant. They were sitting at Dar'ia's place; she was the oldest of the old women; none of them knew their precise age because that precision was left at the time of their christening in the church records which had subsequently been taken off somewhere without trace. They spoke like this about the old woman's age:

'I, my girl, was already dragging my brother Vas'ka round on my back when you came into the world.' That's what Dar'ia said to Nastas'ia. 'I was old enough to remember things, I recall.'

'But you must be about three years older than me.'

'Go on, three! What were you when I was getting married, think back, why don't you! You were still running about without a blouse on. You must remember me getting married, come on!'

'Yes, I do.'

'Well, so then. How can you compare yourself? You're just a kid by comparison with me.'

The function of this excerpt may be contrasted with that of the other passages used to illustrate register, for it has not only an informative purpose (ie to set the scene for and to begin to tell a story) but also an aesthetic purpose which consists in broaching certain themes and producing an impression on the reader. In order to achieve this purpose words are arranged in such a way as to heighten their effect and are used not merely in their literal sense but also in order to evoke certain responses in the reader.

For example, in lines 1–12 the author builds up an impression of the eternally recurring cycle of Nature. The explicit meaning is underpinned by means of the regular repetition of опять (1, 3, 5, 7); the uniform word order of the opening sentences, with inversion of subject and predicate, eg наступи́ла весна́ (1), зашумéла водá (6), запылáла... зéлень (7), пролили́сь пéрвые дожди́, прилетéли стрижи́ (8), заквáкали... лягýшки (9–10); the use of the inchoative prefix за- in зашумéла (6), запылáла (7), заквáкали (9); and even by the use of и as the first word of the work, suggesting an unbroken connection with something that has gone before. The power, inevitability and majesty of Nature's cycle are conveyed by the syntactic measure, balance and harmony of the passage, exemplified by the pairing of nouns and adjectives, eg для óстрова и дерéвни (2), с грóхотом и стрáстью (3), могýчую сверкáющую течь (5), по землé и дерéвьям (7), стрижи́ и лáсточки (8), and by the depiction of Nature as a living force endowed with passion and ardour, most notable in the personification of the River Angara liberating itself from the ice which imprisons it through the Siberian winter.

However, in lines 12–19, against this background of Nature's annual renewal, the author develops the theme enigmatically broached in the first sentence of the work, to the effect that this is the last spring for the village of Matiora (2). Here a sense of disruption and change in the life of the villagers is conveyed: not everyone plants a vegetable garden as they always have done, nor are crops sown in the fields more distant from the village, and potatoes and carrots are not all put in at the same time but haphazardly. Moreover, various lexical and syntactic devices (see below) lend this part of the excerpt the subjective human perspective of the simple villagers.

Finally, in lines 20–36, through description of three old women who live in Matiora and in particular through a brief example of their conversation, the author gives an insight into the nature of the villagers whose lives are to be ruined as a result of the disruption of the forces of Nature by modern technology and the urban values which promote it.

pronunciation

- The flavour of peasant speech in the women's conversation is conveyed by the spellings ишó (ie ещё, 32) and дак от (ie так вот, 35).

vocabulary

- Numerous features of colloquial or demotic speech are reproduced in the conversation of the old women, eg
- familiar terms of address, viz ты, тебé (27–35);
- forms of words characteristic of the colloquial language, eg куды́, супроти́в (35) and the contracted adverb уж (26, 28);
- particles, viz -то (30, 31), -ка (31, 33), ну (35);
- the interjection но (30);
- the regional form рёлка in the opening description (6), which relates to a feature of local topography;
- the rather colloquial forms картóшку and моркóшку (18), which

are the forms the villagers themselves might use (as opposed to the neutral картóфель and моркóвь respectively).

morphology

- In the women's conversation the morphological features of colloquial speech prevail, eg the short comparative form постáре (30), the imperative form подú (32), the diminutives дéвка (26), Вáська (27), молóденькая (36), and the pejorative form рубашóнка (32).
- The prepositional singular form на островý (17), preferred to the neutral на óстрове, is perhaps the form the villagers themselves might use.

syntax

- Gerunds (both imperfective and perfective) and active participles (both present and past) are freely used in the passages of authorial description and narrative, eg скáтываясь (6), отставáя (11), забегáя (12); нагромоздúв (4), вы́тянувшись (5); нося́щих (2), сверкáющую (5), происходя́щих (11); проснýвшиеся (9–10). However, once the author turns from his description of Nature to the life of the villagers, such forms are used much more sparingly: only the forms наливáя (20) and прихлёбывая (21) occur in the author's preamble to the old women's reported conversation.
- In addition to the syntactic features of the opening description of Nature mentioned above, one should note the more colloquial flavour of lines 12–19, exemplified by the use of the conjunction да (13, 16), the constructions где поблúже (17) and кто когдá смог (19), and the expression как пришлóсь (19).
- The old women's conversation is characterised syntactically by fragmentation and by inversion of direct word order with placing of predicates at the end of a clause, eg таскáла (27), родилáсь (28), находúлась (28), выходúла (31), бéгала (32). The author mimics this tone with the idiomatic turn of phrase концóв не сыскáть (25–6) and his elliptical interpolation Э́то Дáрья Настáсье (28).

2 Problems of meaning: Russian words

This chapter lists some of the Russian words which may give difficulty to the English-speaking student because of their range of meaning, because of the possibility of confusing them with other Russian words, because they are deceptively similar to English words, or because they occur in a plural form whereas their English equivalents occur in a singular form or vice versa.

2.1 Homonyms

Homonyms arise in several ways. Firstly, as a result of phonological change a word may come to coincide in sound and form with another word of different origin (as is the case with the pair лук). Secondly, identical forms may develop as a result of the processes of word-formation, by the addition of distinct suffixes to a root (eg уда́рник). Thirdly, it very often happens that an existing word takes on quite a new meaning (eg свет).

Many of the examples given here are full homonyms (ie they have identical pronunciation and paradigms, eg ключ in its different meanings), while others are partial homonyms (ie they do not share all the forms which they both possess, eg мир, which does not have plural forms in its sense of *peace*).

2.1.1 Examples of homonyms

блок	*bloc* (esp pol) *pulley*
брак	*matrimony* *defective goods, rejects*
вид	*air, appearance* *shape, form, state* *view* (eg from room) *species* *aspect* (gram term)
вре́мя	*time* *tense* (gram term)
вяза́ть	*to tie* *to knit*

гла́дить/погла́дить	*to stroke* (eg animal) *to iron* (clothes; pf also вы́гладить)
гнать	*to chase, drive, pursue* *to distil*
го́лос	*voice* *vote*
го́рло	*throat* *neck of bottle* (though as a rule the dimin form го́рлышко is used in this sense, except in the phrase пить из горла́ (D), *to drink straight from the bottle*)
горн	*furnace, forge* *bugle*
губа́	*lip* *bay, inlet* (in northern Russia) *tree fungus*
дере́вня	*countryside* *village*
долг	*duty* *debt*
жать	(жму, жмёшь) *to press, squeeze* (жну, жнёшь) *to reap*
же́ртва	*victim* *sacrifice*
Земля́ **земля́**	*Earth* *land*
икра́	*caviar* *calf* (part of leg)
исто́рия	*history* *story* *affair*
ка́рта	*map* *playing card*
клуб	*club* (society) *puff, cloud* (eg of dust)
ключ	*key* (to door); also fig, *clue* *spring, source* (of water)

коло́да	*block* (of wood) *pack of cards*
коса́	*plait* *scythe* *spit* (of land)
кося́к	*door-post* *shoal* (of fish) *herd* (of mares with one stallion)
кула́к	*fist* *strike force* (mil) *wealthy peasant*
курс	*course* *year* (of course in educational institution) *rate of exchange* (fin)
ла́ска	*caress, kindness* *weasel* (gen pl ла́сок)
лёгкий	*light* *easy*
леса́ (pl; gen лесо́в)	*forests* *scaffolding*
лопа́тка	*shovel* *shoulder-blade*
лук	*onion* *bow* (for shooting arrows)
масси́ровать	*to mass* (mil) *to massage*
мате́рия	*matter* (as opposed to spirit; phil) *pus* (med) *cloth*
маши́на	*machine* *car*
мир	*peace* *world* *peasant commune* (in pre-revolutionary Russia)
моме́нт	*moment* *factor*
нау́ка	*science* *learning*

нау́чный	*scientific* *academic*
нача́ло	*beginning* *premiss* (ie *postulate*)
не́бо	*sky* *heaven*
носи́ть	*to carry* *to wear* (clothes)
о́пыт	*experience* *experiment*
пар	*steam* *fallow*
пе́тля	*loop* *stitch* *buttonhole* *noose*
плита́	*slab* (eg paving-stone) *stove* (for cooking)
пол	*floor* *sex*
по́ле **поля́** (pl)	*field* *margin* (of page) *brim* (of hat)
поли́тика	*policy* *politics*
по́лка	*shelf* *weeding*
по́лька	*Polish woman* *polka* (dance)
поро́ть	*to thrash* (pf вы́пороть) *to unstitch* (pf распоро́ть)
предме́т	*subject* (eg of study) *object* (thing, topic)
програ́мма	*programme* *channel* (on TV) *schedule*; учёбная програ́мма, *curriculum*

рома́н	*novel* *romance*
рысь(f)	*trot* *lynx*
свет	*light* *world* *society* (ie the fashionable world)
све́тлый	*bright, radiant* *light* (of colours)
ско́рость (f)	*speed* *gear*
сове́т	*advice* *soviet* (ie council)
среда́	*Wednesday* (acc sg сре́ду) *milieu, environment* (acc sg среду́)
тита́н	*titanium* (chemical element) *Titan* (in Greek mythology) *boiler* (old-fashioned bathroom water heater)
трава́	*grass* *herb*
туши́ть	*to extinguish, put out* (pf потуши́ть) *to braise, stew*
тяжёлый	*heavy* *difficult*
уда́рник	*member of strike force* (mil); *shock-worker* *firing-pin* (of gun) *drummer* (in pop group; R1)
учёный	*scientist* *scholar, learned person*
ша́шка	*draught* (in boardgame); игра́ть в ша́шки, *to play draughts* *sabre*
язы́к	*tongue* *language*

2.1.2 Homonyms with different plural forms

A number of nouns distinguish different meanings which they may have by means of different nominative plural forms (and, if they denote inanimate objects, this form is identical with the accusative plural form).

- In many such instances one plural form has the usual ending for masculine nouns in **-ы** or **-и** and the other has the stressed ending **-á** or **-я́** (see 8.1.6), eg

nom pl in **-ы/-и**		nom pl in **-á/-я́**	
бóровы	*hogs, fat men*	**боровá**	*flues*
кóрпусы	*torsos, hulls*	**корпусá**	*corps, blocks* (buildings)
лáгери	*(political) camps*	**лагеря́**	*holiday/prison camps*
мехи́ (pl only)	*bellows*	**мехá**	*furs*
óбразы	*images*	**образá**	*icons*
óрдены	*monastic orders*	**орденá**	*medals*
пóясы	*geographical belts*	**поясá**	*belts* (clothing)
прóводы	*send-off* (no sg)	**проводá**	*(electrical) leads*
прóпуски	*omissions*	**пропускá**	*passes, permits*
сóболи	*sables* (animals)	**соболя́**	*sables* (furs)
счёты	*abacus* (no sg)	**счетá**	*bills, accounts*
тóки	*(electric) currents*	**токá**	*threshing-floors*; also *birds' mating-places*
тóны	*tones* (sound)	**тонá**	*tones* (colour)
тóрмозы	*impediments*	**тормозá**	*brakes* (of vehicle)
хлéбы	*loaves*	**хлебá**	*crops, cereals*
цветы́	*flowers*	**цветá**	*colours*

Note: the sg form is цветóк in the meaning *flower* but цвет in the meaning *colour*.

- Some partial homonyms have other variant plural forms, eg

		nom/acc pl	gen pl
колéно	*knee*	**колéни**	**колéней**
	joint (in pipe)	**колéнья**	**колéньев**
	bend (in river)	**колéна**	**колéн**
	generation (obs)	**колéна**	**колéн**
кóрень	*root*	**кóрни**	**корнéй**
	roots (used for culinary or medicinal purposes; no sg form)	**корéнья**	**корéньев**
лист	*leaf*	**ли́стья**	**ли́стьев**
	sheet of paper	**листы́**	**листóв**

пóвод	*ground, cause (for)* *rein*	**пóводы** **повóдья**	**пóводов (к)** **повóдьев**
сýдно	*vessel, craft* *chamberpot*	**судá** **сýдна**	**судóв** **сýден**

2.2 Homophones and homoforms

Homophones, which may offer material for word-play and puns, are much more widespread in English than in Russian (eg *bare, bear; right, write*), but even in Russian they may occur as a result, for example, of the devoicing of final voiced consonants (see eg гриб), or even of the coincidence of a word and a phrase (eg немóй, *dumb* and не мой, *not my*). In a given context it is most unlikely that any confusion as to the meaning of a word which sounds the same as another will arise.

Homoforms (see eg вожý) arise quite frequently as a result of the morphological complexity of Russian.

A very small number of Russian examples is given here to illustrate both these phenomena.

вожý	*I take on foot* (from водúть) *I take by transport* (from возúть)
гриб	*mushroom*
грипп	*influenza*
груздь (m)	*milk-agaric* (type of mushroom)
грусть (f)	*sadness, melancholy*
дне	prep sg of день, *day* prep sg of дно, *bottom*
дог	*Great Dane*
док	*dock*
есть	(infin) *to eat* (3rd pers sg and pl) *there is/are* (3rd pers sg) *is* (see 3.2)
кампáния	*campaign*
компáния	*company* (in various senses)
лесá	nom/acc pl of лес, *forest*
лисá	*fox*
лечý	*I fly* (from летéть) *I cure* (from лечúть)

луг	*meadow*
лук	*onion, bow* (see 2.1.1)
печь	f noun, *stove* infin, *to bake*
пилá	*saw* (tool) f past tense of пить, *to drink*
плод	*fruit*
плот	*raft*
порóг	*threshold*
порóк	*vice* (fault, sin)
походи́ть	(impf) *to resemble* (pf) *to walk around for a bit*
пруд	*pond*
прут	*twig*
род	*kin, sort, kind, genus, gender*
рот	*mouth*
стáли	gen/dat/prep sg of сталь, *steel* pl past tense form of стать, *to become*
стих	*line of verse* m past tense form of сти́хнуть, *to abate, die down, subside*
столб	*post, pole, column, pillar*
столп	*pillar* (fig, eg столп óбщества, *a pillar of society*)
сходи́ть	(impf) *to come down* (pf) *to go (there and back)*
три	*three* 2nd pers imp of терéть, *to rub*
труд	*labour*
трут	*tinder*
туш	*flourish* (mus)
тушь (f)	*Indian ink*
шáгом	instr sg of шаг, *step, pace* adv, *at walking pace*

2.3 Homographs

Russian has many pairs of homographs, a large number of which result from morphological coincidence (see eg адреса, воды, below). Only a very small sample is given here to illustrate the phenomenon.

áдреса	gen sg of áдрес, *address*
адресá	nom pl of áдрес
áтлас	*atlas*
атлáс	*satin*
воды́	gen sg of водá, *water*
вóды	nom/acc pl of водá
зáмок	*castle*
замóк	*lock*
и́рис	*iris* (flower)
ири́с	*toffee*
мóря	gen sg of мóре, *sea*
моря́	nom/acc pl of мóре
мýка	*torment*
мукá	*flour*
нóшу	acc sg of нóша, *burden*
ношý	1st pers sg of носи́ть, *to carry*
óрган	*organ* (biol, pol)
оргáн	*organ* (mus)
пи́сать (vulg)	*to piss* (пи́саю, пи́саешь, etc)
писáть	*to write* (пишý, пи́шешь, etc)
плáчу	1st pers sg of плáкать, *to cry*
плачý	1st pers sg of плати́ть, *to pay*
пóра	*pore*
порá	*it is time (to)*
пóсле	preposition meaning *after*
послé	prep sg of посóл, *ambassador, envoy*

по́том	instr sg of пот, *sweat*
пото́м	adv, *then*
сбе́гать	pf, *to run (there and back)*
сбега́ть	impf, *to run down*
се́ло	n past tense of сесть, *to sit down*
село́	*village*
сло́ва	gen sg of сло́во, *word*
слова́	nom pl of сло́во
со́рок	*forty*
соро́к	gen pl of соро́ка, *magpie*
у́же	short comp form of у́зкий, *narrower*
уже́	*already*

2.4 Paronyms

There are in Russian, as in English, many words which may easily be confused with other words which are similar in sound and written form. The problem is compounded when, as is often the case, the two words have related or similar meaning.

This section provides a small sample of such words, including a few whose difference is mainly one of register rather than meaning. In many cases the difference between two forms consists in the fact that one is a Slavonicism and the other a Russian form (eg граждани́н, горожа́нин; see Glossary). In others the difference is merely one of gender (eg жар, жара́). Some of the less common meanings a Russian word may have are omitted. Not included are verbal clusters derived from the same root by the addition of various prefixes (on which see 7.3).

банк	*bank*	**ба́нка**	*jar, can*
бли́зкий	*near, close*	**бли́жний**	*neighbouring*; Бли́жний восто́к, *Middle East*
бре́мя	*burden*	**вре́мя**	*time, tense*
вида́ть* (R1)	*to see*	**ви́деть**	*to see*

* This verb is used mainly in the infinitive or the past tense and tends to have a frequentative sense.

во́дный	*relating to water*, eg во́дное по́ло, *water polo*	**водяно́й**	*aquatic, living in water*, eg водяна́я пти́ца, *water bird; operated by water*, eg водяна́я ме́льница, *water-mill*
во́рон	*raven*	**воро́на**	*crow*
воскресе́нье	*Sunday*	**воскресе́ние**	*resurrection*
высо́кий	*high, tall*	**высо́тный**	*high-rise*, eg of building
гла́вный	*main, principal*	**головно́й**	*relating to the head*, eg головна́я боль, *headache*

Note: in R1 the form головно́й may also be encountered in the sense *main*, eg in the phrase головно́е предприя́тие, *head office*.

горожа́нин	*town-dweller*	**граждани́н**	*citizen*
горя́чий	*hot*	**горя́щий**	*burning*
дальнови́дный	*far-sighted* (prescient)	**дальнозо́ркий**	*far-sighted* (not myopic)
дипломати́ческий	*relating to diplomacy*	**дипломати́чный**	*tactful, shrewd*
драмати́ческий	*relating to drama*	**драмати́чный**	*dramatic, sensational*
дух	*spirit*	**духи́** (pl; gen духо́в)	*scent, perfume*
душ	*shower*	**душа́**	*soul*
жа́лоба	*complaint*	**жа́лованье**	*salary*
жар	*heat* (heat of day, fervour, ardour)	**жара́**	*hot weather*
жесто́кий	*cruel*	**жёсткий**	*hard, tough*
замеча́тельный	*remarkable, splendid*	**значи́тельный**	*significant, considerable*
за́навес	*curtain* (large, eg in theatre)	**занаве́ска**	*curtain* (eg in house)
здоро́вый	*healthy*	**здра́вый**	*sensible*; здра́вый смысл, *common sense*
земе́льный	*relating to land*	**земляно́й**	*made of earth, earthen*
знамена́тельный	*important, momentous*	**знамени́тый**	*famous, renowned*
изме́на	*betrayal, treachery*	**измене́ние**	*change* (see 3.1)
карье́р	*career* (gallop), eg во весь карье́р, *at full speed*	**карье́ра**	*career* (progress in job, etc)

коро́ткий	*short* (physical)	**кра́ткий**	*brief* (abstract)
ледови́тый	in phrase Се́верный Ледови́тый океа́н, *the Arctic Ocean*		
ледо́вый	*taking place on/amid ice*, eg Ледо́вое побо́ище, *the Battle on the Ice* (1242); ледо́вые пла́вания, *Arctic voyages*		
ледяно́й	*consisting of ice*, eg ледяна́я ко́рка, *an ice layer*; *covered in ice*, eg ледяна́я верши́на, *an icy peak*; *very cold* (also fig), eg ледяно́й взгляд, *an icy look*		
мане́р (R1)	*manner* (way), eg на ру́сский мане́р, *in the Russian manner*	**мане́ра**	*manner* (style); мане́ры (pl), *manners*
матема́тик	*mathematician*	**матема́тика**	*mathematics*
материалисти́ческий	*materialistic* (relating to matter)	**материалисти́чный**	*materialist* (coveting goods)
мел	*chalk*	**мель** (f)	*shoal, bank, shallows*
мех	*fur*	**мох**	*moss*
ми́рный	*peaceful*		
мирово́й	*relating to the world*, eg мирова́я война́, *world war*		
всеми́рный	*world-wide*		
мол	*pier* also *he says, they say* (particle; see 4.4)	**моль** (f)	*(clothes-)moth*
молодо́й	*young*		
мла́дший	*younger, junior*		
молодёжный	*relating to the young*		
моложа́вый	*young-looking*		
му́ха	*fly*		
му́шка	dimin of му́ха; also *beauty-spot*		
мо́шка	*midge*		
надева́ть/наде́ть	*to put on* (clothing)	**одева́ть/оде́ть**	*to dress* (trans)
не́бо	*sky, heaven*	**нёбо**	*palate*
неве́жественный	*ignorant*	**неве́жливый**	*rude, impolite*
оби́дный	*offensive*	**оби́дчивый**	*touchy, easily offended*
осно́ва	*base, basis, foundation*	**основа́ние**	*founding; ground, reason*; also *foot* (of mountain, column)

остава́ться/оста́ться	*to remain, stay behind*
оставля́ть/оста́вить	*to leave behind*
остана́вливать(ся)/останови́ть(ся)	*to stop*; also *to stay*, eg в гости́нице, *in a hotel*
отстава́ть/отста́ть	*to lag behind*

оста́тки (pl; gen оста́тков)	*remains, leftovers*	**оста́нки** (pl; gen оста́нков)	*remains* (of dead person)
оте́чество	*fatherland*	**о́тчество**	*patronymic*
паде́ж	*case* (gram)	**падёж**	*cattle plague*
пар	*steam* *fallow*	**па́ра**	*pair, couple*
передава́ть/переда́ть	*to pass, transfer*	**предава́ть/преда́ть**	*to betray*
пла́мя	*flame* (see 8.1.10)	**пле́мя**	*tribe* (see 8.1.10)
поднима́ть	*to lift*	**подыма́ть** (R1)	*to lift* (esp with difficulty)
поли́тик	*politician*	**поли́тика**	*politics*
полити́ческий	*relating to politics*	**полити́чный**	*careful, tactful*
посту́пок	*act, deed*	**просту́пок**	*misbehaviour*
пра́здничный	*festive*	**пра́здный**	*idle, vain*
практи́ческий	*practical*, ie *relating to practice*, eg of help, work	**практи́чный**	*practical*, ie *having experience, expertise*
прах	*ashes, remains*; *dust* (rhet)	**по́рох**	*powder*
проводи́ть/провести́	*to conduct, carry out, trick*	**производи́ть/произвести́**	*to produce, promote*; but in the expression произвести́ о́пыт, *to conduct an experiment*
прохла́дный	*cool*	**холо́дный**	*cold*
проче́сть (pf; R1)	*to read*	**прочита́ть** (pf)	*to read*
ра́вный	*equal*	**ро́вный**	*flat, level, even, exact*
развито́й	*developed*, ie *mature, advanced*	**разви́тый**	*developed* (ie past pass part of разви́ть)
рот	*mouth*	**ро́та**	*company* (mil)
свиста́ть (impf; R1)	*to whistle*	**свисте́ть** (impf)	*to whistle*

середи́на	*middle*	**среда́**	*Wednesday* *milieu, environment* (see 2.1.1)
слу́шать/послу́шать	*to listen (to)*		
слы́шать/услы́шать	*to hear*		
слыха́ть* (R1)	*to hear*		

* This verb is used mainly in the infinitive or the past tense and tends to have a frequentative sense.

сосе́дний	*neighbouring*	**сосе́дский**	*belonging to one's neighbour*
состоя́ть (impf)	*to consist* (in some contexts *to be*; see 3.2)	**состоя́ться** (pf)	*to take place*
сто́ить	*to cost, be worth*	**стоя́ть**	*to stand*
сторона́	*side*	**страна́**	*country* (nation)
теку́чий	*fluid, unstable*	**теку́щий**	*current, present*
те́хник	*technician*	**те́хника**	*technique, technology*
уда́чливый	*lucky*	**уда́чный**	*successful, felicitous*
фи́зик	*physicist*	**фи́зика**	*physics*
хорони́ть (impf)	*to inter*	**храни́ть** (impf)	*to keep, preserve*
экономи́ческий	*relating to economics*	**экономи́чный**	*economical*
эле́ктрик	*electrician*	**электри́чка**	*suburban electric train*

2.5 *Faux amis*

There are in Russian many words of foreign origin which bring to mind an English word but in fact have or may have quite a different meaning from the English cognate. This section lists a few of these, together with the usual Russian equivalents of the English word with which confusion has arisen.

авантю́ра	*shady enterprise*	**adventure**	приключе́ние
агита́ция	*(political) agitation*	**agitation**	волне́ние (anxiety) трево́га (alarm)
аккомпани́ровать (impf) + dat	*to accompany* (musically only)	**to accompany**	провожа́ть/проводи́ть (go with), сопровожда́ть (go with)
аккура́тный	*punctual, neat, tidy, conscientious*	**accurate**	то́чный (precise) ме́ткий (of shooting)

акту́альный	*topical, pressing*	**actual**	действи́тельный (real) настоя́щий (genuine) существу́ющий (existing)
а́кция	*share* (ie equity), also political or diplomatic action	**action** (ie an act)	де́йствие, посту́пок
анги́на	*tonsillitis*	**angina**	грудна́я жа́ба
арти́кль (m)	*article* (gram term)	**article**	in other senses: see 3.1
арти́ст	*(performing) artist*	**artist**	in other sense: see 3.1
ассисте́нт	*junior teacher* (in higher educational institution)	**assistant**	помо́щник, замести́тель (m; deputy)
ата́ка	*attack* (mil)	**attack**	in other senses: see 3.1
аудие́нция	*audience* (with important person)	**audience**	зри́тели (pl; gen зри́телей; spectators)
афе́ра	*shady transaction*	**affair**	де́ло (matter) рома́н (love affair)
бала́нс	*balance* (econ, fin)	**balance**	равнове́сие (equilibrium)
бассе́йн	*swimming pool, river-basin*	**basin**	таз (washbasin) ми́ска (bowl)
бискви́т	*sponge-cake*	**biscuit**	пече́нье (sweet) суха́рь (m; rusk)
бланк	*form* (to be filled in)	**blank**	про́пуск (omission) пробе́л (in memory) холосто́й заря́д (bullet)
гениа́льный	*of genius*	**genial**	весёлый (jolly) доброду́шный (good-natured)
го́спиталь (m)	*(military) hospital*	**hospital**	больни́ца
гума́нный	*humane*	**human**	челове́ческий
дека́да	*ten-day period*	**decade**	десятиле́тие
инструкти́вный	*instructional*	**instructive**	поучи́тельный (edifying) поле́зный (useful)
ка́мера	*chamber, cell* *video camera* (R1)	**camera**	фотоаппара́т
капита́л	*capital* (fin)	**capital**	столи́ца (city)
капита́льный	*main, fundamental*, eg капита́льный ремо́нт, *major repair*	**capital**	прописна́я бу́ква (letter) Note: сме́ртная казнь, *capital punishment*
карто́н	*cardboard*	**carton**	коро́бка
кекс	*fruit-cake*	**cake**	торт
компози́тор	*composer*	**compositor**	набо́рщик
консервато́рия	*conservatoire*	**conservatory**	оранжере́я

контро́ль (m)	*supervision*	**control**	руково́дство (management) власть (f; power) влия́ние (influence)
конфу́з	*embarrassment*	**confusion**	беспоря́док (disorder) пу́таница (muddle) неразбери́ха (R1; muddle) толкотня́ (R1; pushing)
корре́ктный	*polite, proper*	**correct**	пра́вильный
кросс	*cross-country race*	**cross**	крест
луна́тик	*sleep-walker*	**lunatic**	сумасше́дший умалишённый
магази́н	*shop*	**magazine**	журна́л
майо́р	*major*	**mayor**	мэр
манифеста́ция	*demonstration*	**manifestation**	проявле́ние
момента́льный	*instantaneous*	**momentous**	знамена́тельный
мотори́ст	*mechanic*	**motorist**	автомобили́ст
моцио́н	*exercise* (physical)	**motion**	движе́ние
объекти́в	*lens* (of camera)	**objective**	цель (f)
патети́ческий	*having passion, pathos*	**pathetic**	тро́гательный (touching) печа́льный (sad) жа́лкий (pitiable)
поэ́ма	*narrative poem*	**poem** (short)	стихотворе́ние
принципиа́льный	*of principle*	**principal**	гла́вный (main) веду́щий (leading)
про́ба	*test, model* (ie *prototype*), *sample*	**probe**	зонд (med, geol) иссле́дование (exploration)
проспе́кт	*avenue*; also *prospectus, summary*	**prospect**	перспекти́ва
репети́ция	*rehearsal*	**repetition**	повторе́ние
ре́плика	*rejoinder*, *cue* (theat)	**replica**	то́чная ко́пия
реце́пт	*prescription* (med), *recipe*	**receipt**	получе́ние (receiving) распи́ска, квита́нция (written acknowledgement)
симпати́чный	*nice* (of person)	**sympathetic**	сочу́вствующий (compassionate) отзы́вчивый (responsive) одобря́ющий (approving)
сквер	*small public garden in town*	**square**	пло́щадь (f; place) квадра́т (shape)

стаж	*length of service, probation*	**stage**	сцéна (theat) этáп (of process)
стул	*chair*	**stool**	табурéтка
темперáментный	*spirited*	**temperamental**	капри́зный (capricious) с нóровом (obstinate, awkward)
трансля́ция	*transmission, relay*	**translation**	перевóд
фáбрика	*factory*	**fabric**	ткань (f)
фамилья́рный	*overfamiliar, offhand*	**familiar**	знакóмый (known) извéстный (well-known) привы́чный (customary)
фрáкция	*faction*	**fraction**	части́ца (small part) дробь (f; math)
характери́стика	*reference* (testimonial)	**characteristic**	характéрная чертá

2.6 Problems of number

2.6.1 Nouns with plural form only

Many nouns exist which in English have a singular form but in Russian have only a plural form, at least when they have certain meanings, eg the word for *a clock* is **часы́** (gen **часóв**). Such nouns may belong to any of the declension types. In the lists below genitive forms (which cannot be deduced from the nominative forms) are given in brackets.

ворóта (ворóт)	*gate*
вы́боры (вы́боров)	*election*
грáбли (грáблей)	*rake*
дéньги (дéнег)	*money*
джу́нгли (джу́нглей)	*jungle*
дровá (дров)	*firewood*
духи́ (духóв)	*scent, perfume*
носи́лки (носи́лок)	*stretcher*
обóи (обóев)	*wallpaper*
пери́ла (пери́л)	*handrail*
пóхороны (похорóн)	*funeral*
сáни (санéй)	*sledge*
сли́вки (сли́вок)	*cream*
су́мерки (су́мерек)	*twilight*
су́тки (су́ток)	*day* (24-hour period)
схóдни (схóдней)	*gangway, gangplank*

счёты (счётов)	*abacus*
черни́ла (черни́л)	*ink*
ша́хматы (ша́хмат)	*chess*
щи (щей)	*cabbage soup*
я́сли (я́слей; in R1 also яслéй)	*crèche*

Note: many Russian nouns which are generally used only in a plural form do correspond to English nouns which also have a plural form, eg

брю́ки (брюк)	*trousers*
весы́ (весо́в)	*scales*
за́морозки (за́морозков)	*light frosts*
кавы́чки (кавы́чек)	*quotation marks*
кани́кулы (кани́кул)	*holidays*
коньки́ (конько́в)	*skates*
ку́дри (кудре́й)	*curls*
лохмо́тья (лохмо́тьев)	*rags*
лю́ди (людéй)	*people*
но́жницы (но́жниц)	*scissors*
очки́ (очко́в)	*spectacles*
перегово́ры (перегово́ров)	*talks, negotiations*
стихи́ (стихо́в)	*verses*
хло́поты (хлопо́т)	*efforts, trouble*
хло́пья (хло́пьев)	*snowflakes*

2.6.2 Nouns with singular form only

Some Russian nouns denoting fruits or vegetables give particular difficulty to the English-speaking student because they are used collectively and, in R2-3 at least, have only a singular form, eg

брусни́ка	*red whortleberries, cowberries*
ви́шня	*cherries*
горо́х	*peas*
ежеви́ка	*blackberries*
земляни́ка	*(wild) strawberries*
капу́ста	*cabbage*
карто́фель (m)	*potatoes*
клубни́ка	*(cultivated) strawberries*
крыжо́вник	*gooseberries*
лук	*onions*
мали́на	*raspberries*

морко́вь (f)	*carrots*
кра́сная сморо́дина	*redcurrants*
чёрная сморо́дина	*blackcurrants*

If it is necessary to refer to one particular unit of the thing in question then one may in some instances use a related word with the suffix -ина (eg горо́шина, карто́фелина), or one may insert the word шту́ка, *item* (eg пять штук ви́шни, *five cherries*).

Note [1] In R1 plural forms of some of these nouns may be encountered, eg пять ви́шен, *five cherries*; де́сять ежеви́к, *ten blackberries*.

[2] There are also of course many nouns denoting fruit and vegetables that do have plural forms, eg апельси́н, *orange*; огуре́ц, *cucumber*; помидо́р, *tomato*; я́блоко, *apple* (nom/acc pl апельси́ны, огурцы́, помидо́ры, я́блоки respectively).

3 Problems of translation from English into Russian

3.1 English words difficult to render in Russian

This section lists in alphabetical order some of the more common English words which give difficulty for students learning Russian and defines some of the Russian equivalents they may have. The list is intended to encourage the student to think about the precise meaning of the English word in a given context and to consider which of the various possible Russian renderings is appropriate in that context. The lists of Russian equivalents for the English words are not intended to include all possible translations of the English word, merely to draw attention to the ways in which Russian deals with the main fields of meaning which the English word may have. Rendering of English prepositions is dealt with separately in 9.4.

English has many phrasal verbs (eg *to hold back, hold on, hold up*) in which the precise meaning of the verb is clarified by the following preposition. Translation of phrasal verbs is not considered here except in a very small number of cases. It should be noted that in many cases the function of the English preposition is fulfilled in Russian by a verbal prefix (see 7.3), as well as by a following preposition.

ACCIDENT	**несча́стный слу́чай**	emphasising effect on victim
	ава́рия	involving machinery, transport, etc, eg на электроста́нции, *at a power station*
	круше́ние	*crash*, eg по́езда, *train crash*; кораблекруше́ние, *shipwreck*
	катастро́фа	esp natural disaster; also fig
	случа́йность (f)	*chance, contingency*
ADVERTISEMENT	**рекла́ма**	with a view to selling
	объявле́ние	*announcement* (eg of job vacancy)
	ано́нс	short notice about coming event
AGAIN	**опя́ть**	*once more as before*
	сно́ва	= опя́ть (slightly more bookish)
	за́ново	*anew, afresh*
	ещё раз	*one more time*

	Note: the prefix пере-, used as a verbal or noun prefix, may also carry the meaning *again*, eg перепи́сывать/переписа́ть, *to rewrite*; перестро́йка, *rebuilding* (see 7.3)	
AGE	**во́зраст**	stage in one's life
	век	lit *century*
	пери́од	*period*
	эпо́ха	*epoch*
AGREE	**соглаша́ться/согласи́ться с** + instr	*to concur with*
	соглаша́ться/согласи́ться на + acc	*to consent to*
	сходи́ться/сойти́сь	*to tally* (of figures), *to come to an agreement about,* eg в цене́, *a price*
	согласо́вывать/согласова́ть что́-н с ке́м-н (trans)	*to agree sth with sb*
	согласова́ться (impf and pf) **с** + instr	gram term
	договори́ться (pf)	*to come to an arrangement*
APPEARANCE	**появле́ние**	*emergence, coming into view*
	нару́жность (f)	*outward appearance, exterior*
	выступле́ние	*public appearance* (eg on stage, television), *speech*
	вид	*air, look, aspect*
APPLICATION	**заявле́ние**	esp for abstract object, eg о приёме на рабо́ту, *for a job*
	зая́вка	esp for concrete object, eg на материа́лы, *for materials*
	про́сьба	*request*, eg о по́мощи, *for help*
	наложе́ние	placing on, eg повя́зки на ра́ну, eg *of a bandage to a wound*
	примене́ние	putting to use, eg си́лы, *of force*; но́вой тео́рии, *of a new theory*
	испо́льзование	*utilisation*
	прилежа́ние	*diligence*
ARGUMENT	**спор**	*controversy, debate, dispute* (legal)
	ссо́ра	*quarrel*
	раздо́р	*discord, dissension*

	до́вод	*evidence*
	аргумента́ция	*argumentation*
ARTICLE	**изде́лие**	*manufactured article*
	това́р	*commodity*
	статья́	in newspaper, journal, treaty
	арти́кль (m)	gram term
ARTIST	**худо́жник**	*creative artist* (eg writer, painter, composer)
	арти́ст	*performing artist, artiste*
ASK	**спра́шивать/спроси́ть**	*to enquire*
	проси́ть/попроси́ть	*to request*
	задава́ть/зада́ть вопро́с	*to pose a question*
	справля́ться/спра́виться	*to make inquiries*
	приглаша́ть/пригласи́ть	*to invite*
ATTACK	**нападе́ние**	*assault* (in most senses)
	наступле́ние	*offensive* (mil)
	набе́г	*raid*
	ата́ка	*military attack*
	припа́док	*fit* (med), eg эпилепти́ческий припа́док *epileptic fit*
	при́ступ	*fit, pang, bout*, eg гри́ппа, ка́шля, *of flu, coughing*
	инфа́ркт	*heart attack*
BAD	**плохо́й**	general word
	дурно́й	*nasty*, eg дурна́я привы́чка, *bad habit;* дурно́й сон, *bad dream*
	парши́вый (R1)	lit *mangy*; *nasty, lousy*, eg парши́вая пого́да, *bad weather*
	злой	*wicked*
	вре́дный	*harmful, detrimental, injurious*
	тяжёлый	*severe*, eg тяжёлая боле́знь, *bad illness;* тяжёлое ране́ние, *bad injury*
	гнило́й	*rotten*, eg of fruit
	ки́слый	*sour*, eg of milk
	ту́хлый	*putrefied*, eg of egg

	испо́рченный	*spoiled, off* (of food)
	неподходя́щий	*unsuitable*, eg неподходя́щий приме́р, *bad example*
	неблагоприя́тный	*unfavourable*
BALL(S)	**шар**	spherical object
	ша́рик	dimin of шар
	клубо́к	eg of wool
	мяч	for games, sport
	ядро́	*cannonball*
	вздор	*nonsense, rubbish*
	я́йца (pl; R1 vulg)	*testicles*
BIG	**большо́й**	*large*
	кру́пный	*major, large-scale*
	вели́к/а́/и́	*too big* (in size; see 10.3)
BLUE	**си́ний**	*dark blue*
	голубо́й	*light blue*
	лазу́рный (poet)	*sky-blue, azure*
BODY	**те́ло**	of human or animal; also solid object, eg star
	ту́ловище	*torso*
	труп	*corpse*
	ку́зов	of carriage, car, etc
	организа́ция	*organisation*
BOX	**я́щик**	*chest, container*; почто́вый я́щик, *post-box*
	коро́бка	smaller container than я́щик; коро́бка скоросте́й, *gear-box*
	коро́бочка	dimin of коро́бка
	шкату́лка	*casket, trinket box*
	сунду́к	*trunk*
	бу́дка	*booth, kiosk*
	ло́жа	at theatre
	Note: А ла́рчик про́сто открыва́лся, *The box just opened*, meaning *The explanation was quite simple* (a quotation from Krylov).	
BRANCH	**ветвь** (f)	*bough*

	о́трасль (f)	*section, subdivision*, eg промы́шленности, *of industry*
	филиа́л	subsidiary section of organisation, eg ло́ндонский филиа́л ба́нка, *the London branch of a bank*
BREAK	**лома́ть/слома́ть**	*to fracture*, eg но́гу, *a leg*; *to cause not to work*, eg механи́зм, *a mechanism*
	разбива́ть/разби́ть	*to smash* (into many pieces), eg посу́ду, *crockery*
	наруша́ть/наруши́ть	*to infringe*, eg зако́н, *a law*; пра́вило, *a rule*
	прерыва́ть/прерва́ть	*to break off, interrupt, sever*, eg дипломати́ческие отноше́ния, *diplomatic relations*
	превыша́ть/превы́сить	*to break* (ie *exceed*), eg дозво́ленную ско́рость, *a speed limit*
BRIGHT	**я́ркий**	*vivid*
	све́тлый	*light-coloured, radiant*
	у́мный	*clever*
BROWN	**бе́жевый**	*beige*
	бу́рый	*reddish brown*, eg бу́рый медве́дь, *brown bear*
	гря́зный ко́фе с молоко́м	colour of milky coffee
	кори́чневый	*cinnamon-coloured*
	теле́сного цве́та	*skin-coloured*
	шокола́дного цве́та	*chocolate-coloured*
	ка́рий	of eyes
	сму́глый	of skin
	загоре́лый	*sunburned*
	шате́н/шате́нка (nouns)	*brown-haired man/woman*
BRUSH	**щётка**	for cleaning, brushing hair
	кисть (f)	for painting, eg маля́рная кисть, *paintbrush*
	ки́сточка	dimin of кисть, eg ки́сточка для бритья́, *shaving brush*
	метла́	*broom*
BURN	**горе́ть/сгоре́ть** (intrans)	eg дом гори́т, *the house is on fire*

	жечь (trans)	eg му́сор, *rubbish*
	сжига́ть/сжечь (trans)	*to burn up, cremate*
	зажига́ть/зажёчь	*to set light to*
	поджига́ть/поджёчь	*to set on fire* (with criminal intent)
	пыла́ть	*to blaze, flame, glow*; also fig, eg стра́стью, *with passion*
CALL	**звать/позва́ть**	*to call, summon*; impf only also means *to name*, eg Как вас зову́т? *What is your name?* Меня́ зову́т А́нна, *My name is Anna*
	вызыва́ть/вы́звать	*to call out*, eg врача́, *the doctor*
	называ́ть/назва́ть	*to name*
	подзыва́ть/подозва́ть	*to beckon*
	призыва́ть/призва́ть	*to appeal to*
	созыва́ть/созва́ть	*to call together, convoke*
	звони́ть/позвони́ть + dat	*to ring, telephone*
	заходи́ть/зайти́ к + dat	*to call on, visit*
	загля́дывать/загляну́ть к + dat	*to look in on*
CAREFUL	**осторо́жный**	proceeding with caution
	тща́тельный	*thorough, painstaking*
	внима́тельный	*attentive, considerate*
CASE	**слу́чай**	*instance*
	де́ло	*legal case*
	до́воды (pl; gen до́водов)	set of arguments
	больно́й	*(medical) patient*
	паде́ж	gram term
= container (see also *box*)	**чемода́н**	*suitcase*
	футля́р	for spectacles, musical instrument
	витри́на	*glass case*
CATCH	**лови́ть/пойма́ть**	*to seize, ensnare*, eg ры́бу, *a fish*; слу́чай, *an opportunity*
	хвата́ть/хвати́ть or **схвати́ть**	*to grab*
	схва́тывать/схвати́ть	*to grasp*; also fig, eg смысл, *sense*; просту́ду (R1), *a cold*
	застига́ть/засти́гнуть	*to take unawares*

	застава́ть/заста́ть	*to find*, eg Я заста́л его́ до́ма, *I caught him at home*
	заража́ться/зарази́ться + instr	*to be infected with*, eg Она́ зарази́лась анги́ной, *She caught tonsillitis*
	ула́вливать/улови́ть	*to detect, perceive*, eg звук, *a sound*; нюа́нс, *a nuance*
	зацепля́ться/зацепи́ться	*to get caught up on*, eg Рука́в мое́й руба́шки зацепи́лся за иглу́, *The sleeve of my shirt got caught on a thorn*
	простужа́ться/простуди́ться	*to catch a cold*
CHANGE (verb)	**меня́ть**	basic verb
	изменя́ть/измени́ть (trans)	*to change, alter*
	изменя́ться/измени́ться (intrans)	*to change, alter*
	меня́ть or **обме́нивать/обменя́ть**	*to exchange for*, eg Я обменя́л ста́рую маши́ну на но́вую, *I exchanged my old car for a new one*; Сейча́с обменя́ем валю́ту на рубли́, *We shall now change our currency into roubles*
	обме́нивать/обмени́ть	*to exchange accidentally, swop*
	переменя́ть/перемени́ть	*to shift* (from one position to another), eg перемени́ть пози́цию, тон, *to change one's position, tone*
	переменя́ться/перемени́ться	intrans of переменя́ть/перемени́ть
	разме́нивать/разменя́ть	a coin or note into smaller denominations
	сменя́ть/смени́ть	*to replace*, eg бельё, карау́л, ши́ну, *linen, a sentry, a tyre*
	преобразо́вывать/ преобразова́ть (R3)	*to transform, reform, reorganise*
	превраща́ть/преврати́ть (trans)	*to turn* (sth into sth else), eg преврати́ть во́ду в лёд, *to turn water into ice*
	превраща́ться/преврати́ться	intrans of превраща́ть/преврати́ть
	видоизменя́ть/видоизмени́ть (trans; R3)	*to alter, modify*
	переса́живаться/пересе́сть	*to change transport*, eg Здесь на́до пересе́сть на другу́ю ли́нию, *We must change to another line here*
	переодева́ться/переоде́ться	*to change one's clothes*
	переходи́ть/перейти́ на + acc	*to go over* (to sth different), eg Она́ перешла́ на другу́ю рабо́ту, *She changed her job*

	передýмать (pf)	*to change one's mind* (and think better of it)
	раздýмать (pf)	*to change one's mind* (and decide not to do sth)
	одýматься (pf)	*to change one's mind* (think again, perhaps in response to warning)
CHANGE (noun)	**изменéние**	*alteration*
	обмéн	*exchange*, eg of money into different currency, information, opinions
	перемéна	*shift* (from one thing to another)
	размéн	of note, coin, for money in smaller denomination
	сдáча	money handed back after purchase, eg сдáча с фýнта, *change out of a pound*
	мéлочь (f)	coins of small denominations
	смéна	*replacement*, eg белья́, караýла, *change of linen, guard*
	преобразовáние	*transformation, reorganisation*
	превращéние	*conversion* (into sth else)
	видоизменéние	*modification*
	пересáдка	from one vehicle or form of transport to another
CHARACTER	**харáктер**	*nature, personality*
	óбраз	in work of literature
	дéйствующее лицó	in play
	тип	*type*
	нрав	*disposition*
	осóба (f)	*person, individual*
CLEVER	**ýмный**	*intelligent*
	талáнтливый	*talented*
	спосóбный	*capable, able*
	даровúтый	*gifted*
	одарённый	*gifted*
	лóвкий	*adroit, dexterous*
	искýсный	*skilful*
	умéлый	*able, astute*

CLOUD	**о́блако**	in sky
	ту́ча	*rain-cloud, storm-cloud*
	клубы́ (pl; gen клубо́в)	ды́ма, пы́ли, *of smoke, dust*
COACH	**авто́бус**	*bus*
	ваго́н	part of train
	каре́та	*horse-drawn carriage*
COAT	**пальто́** (indecl)	*overcoat*
	шу́ба	*fur coat*
	дублёнка (R1)	*sheepskin coat*
	ку́ртка	short outdoor jacket
	ветро́вка (R1)	*anorak*
	па́рка	*parka*
	аля́ска (R1)	*winter coat with fur lining*
	плащ	*raincoat, waterproof cape*
	дождеви́к (R1)	*plastic raincoat*
	шине́ль (f)	*(military) greatcoat*
	шерсть (f)	animal's fur
	слой	*layer* (of paint)
	герб	*coat of arms*
COMPETITION	**ко́нкурс**	organised contest, eg ко́нкурс красоты́, *beauty contest*; also competition to get in somewhere
	состяза́ние	*contest, match*, eg по бо́ксу, пла́ванию, фехтова́нию, *boxing, swimming, fencing competition*; also unorganised competition
	соревнова́ние	sporting event; also *emulation*, eg социалисти́ческое соревнова́ние, *socialist emulation*
	сопе́рничество	*rivalry*
	конкуре́нция	*(economic) competition*
COPY	**ко́пия**	*reproduction*
	экземпля́р	*specimen, example*, eg У меня́ два экземпля́ра э́той кни́ги, *I have two copies of this book*
	ксе́рокс	*(photo)copy*
COUNTRY	**страна́**	*state*
	ро́дина	*native land*

	оте́чество	*fatherland*
	дере́вня	*countryside*
	ме́стность (f)	*terrain*
CUT (verb)	**ре́зать**	basic verb
	нареза́ть/наре́зать	*to cut into pieces, carve, slice*
	отреза́ть/отре́зать	*to cut off*
	среза́ть/сре́зать	*to cut off*; also fig, eg сре́зать у́гол, *to cut a corner*
	уреза́ть or **уре́зывать/уре́зать** (R3, offic)	*to reduce by cutting*, eg Прави́тельство уре́зало расхо́дования на обще́ственные ну́жды, *The government has cut public expenditure*
	сокраща́ть/сократи́ть	*to cut down, curtail*, eg расхо́ды, *expenses*
	прекраща́ть/прекрати́ть	*to cut short, stop*, eg Прекрати́ли пода́чу га́за, *They have cut off the gas supply*
	кро́ить/скро́ить	*to cut out* (a pattern)
CUT (noun)	**уре́з**	*reduction*, eg ассигнова́ний, *of (financial) allocations*
	сокраще́ние	*cutting down, curtailment*
	прекраще́ние	*cutting off, cessation*
	ски́дка	*reduction, discount*
DEVELOPMENT(S)	**разви́тие**	*growth, unfolding, evolution*
	разви́тие собы́тий	*development of events*
	разрабо́тка	*working out/up, elaboration*
	проявле́ние	photographic
DIE	**умира́ть/умере́ть**	*to pass away* (of natural causes, disease, starvation)
	погиба́ть/поги́бнуть	*to perish, be killed* (in accident, war, natural disaster)
	сконча́ться (pf; R3)	*to pass away*
	ложи́ться/лечь костьми́ (R3, rhet)	*to lay down one's life* (in battle)
DIFFERENCE	**ра́зница**	extent of disparity
	разли́чие	*distinction* (individual point of difference)
	разногла́сие	intellectual disagreement
	размо́лвка	*tiff*

	расхожде́ние	*divergence*; во мне́ниях, *difference of opinion*
DIFFERENT	**ра́зный**	*various, diverse*
	разли́чный	*divergent*
	отли́чный от + gen	*different from*
	не похо́жий на + acc	*dissimilar to*
	несхо́дный с + instr	*dissimilar to*
	отлича́ться от (impf only)	*to be different from*, eg Чем отлича́ется Москва́ от Са̀нкт-Петербу́рга? *In what way is Moscow different from St Petersburg?*
	друго́й	not the same as before, eg По́сле войны́ он был други́м челове́ком, *He was a different person after the war*
	ино́й	= друго́й
	по-ра́зному	*in different ways*
DREAM	**сон**	in sleep
	сновиде́ние (R3)	in sleep
	кошма́р	*nightmare*
	мечта́	*daydream, ambition*
	мечта́ние	*reverie*
EDGE	**край**	*brim, brink*
	кро́мка (not common)	in various senses, esp physical, eg кро́мка крыла́, *edge of a wing*, кро́мка мате́рии, *edge of material*
	остриё	*cutting edge*, eg ножа́, *of a knife*
	поля́ (pl)	*margin* (of paper)
	опу́шка	of forest
	грань (f)	*facet*; also *brink* (fig), eg на гра́ни войны́, *on the brink of war*
	переве́с	*superiority, advantage*
EDUCATION	**образова́ние**	general instruction
	обуче́ние	*tuition*, eg совме́стное обуче́ние лиц обо́его по́ла, *co-education*
	воспита́ние	*upbringing*
	просвеще́ние	*enlightenment*
END	**коне́ц**	general word

	окончáние	*ending, conclusion*; also gram term
	кóнчик	*tip, point*, eg карандашá, языкá, *of a pencil, of one's tongue*
	кончи́на (R3; rhet)	*demise*
	край	*edge, limit*, eg на краю́ свéта, *at the world's end*
	цель (f)	*aim, goal*
ENJOY	**люби́ть**	*to like* (sth/doing sth), eg Онá лю́бит му́зыку, игрáть в тéннис, *She enjoys music, playing tennis*
	нрáвиться/понрáвиться (impers)	*to like*, eg Мне понрáвилась пьéса, *I enjoyed the play*
	наслаждáться/наслади́ться + instr	*to take delight in*, eg прирóдой, *nature*
	хорошó проводи́ть/провести́ (врéмя)	*to spend (time) pleasantly*, eg Вы хорошó провели́ óтпуск? *Did you enjoy your holiday?*
	весели́ться/повесели́ться	*to enjoy oneself, have a good time*
	пóльзоваться (impf; + instr)	*to have*, eg довéрием, репутáцией, уважéнием, *to enjoy confidence, a reputation, respect*
	обладáть + instr	*to possess*, eg правáми, хорóшим здорóвьем, *rights, good health*
EVIDENCE	**свидéтельство**	*indication, testimony*
	доказáтельство	*proof*; пи́сьменные доказáтельства, *written evidence*
	ули́ка	*piece of (legal) evidence*; неоспори́мая ули́ка, *indisputable evidence*
	при́знак	*sign, indication*
	дáнные (pl; subst adj)	*data*
	основáния (pl; gen основáний) (ду́мать)	*grounds (for thinking)*
	показáние	*(legal) deposition*
EXAMINE	**рассмáтривать/рассмотрéть**	*to consider*, eg вопрóс, *a question*
	осмáтривать/осмотрéть	*to inspect, look over*, eg багáж, больнóго, *baggage, a patient*
	обслéдовать (impf and pf)	*to inspect*, eg больнóго, *a patient*
	проверя́ть/провéрить	*to check, mark* (pupil's or student's work)
	экзаменовáть/проэкзаменовáть + acc	*to conduct an examination of*

	опра́шивать/опроси́ть	*to cross-examine*, eg свиде́теля, *a witness*
EXERCISE	**упражне́ние**	exertion of body or mind, task
	заря́дка	physical activity, *drill*
	трениро́вка	*training*
	моцио́н	*exertion* (of the body for good health), eg де́лать моцио́н, *to take exercise*
	уче́ния (pl; gen уче́ний)	*military exercise*
	манёвры (pl; gen манёвров)	*military manoeuvres*
EXPERIENCE	**о́пыт**	what one has learnt
	пережива́ния (pl; gen пережива́ний)	what one has lived through
	слу́чай	*incident*, eg неприя́тный слу́чай, *unpleasant experience*
FACE	**лицо́**	front part of head; also *exterior*
	ли́чико	dimin of лицо́, eg ли́чико ребёнка, *a child's face*
	выраже́ние	*expression*
	ро́жа (R1)	*mug*
	циферблá́т	*dial* (of clock, watch, gauge)
FALL	**па́дать/(у)па́сть**	basic verb
	выпада́ть/вы́пасть	of rain, snow, in the phrases вы́пал снег, *it snowed*; вы́пали оса́дки (eg in weather report), *it rained*
	опада́ть/опа́сть	of leaves
	распада́ться/распа́сться	*to fall to pieces, disintegrate*
	попада́ть/попа́сть кому́-н в ру́ки	*to fall into sb's hands*
	стиха́ть/сти́хнуть	of wind
	снижа́ться/сни́зиться	*to get lower*, eg у́ровень, цена́ снижа́ется, *the standard, price is falling*
	влюбля́ться/влюби́ться в + acc	*to fall in love with*
	замолча́ть (pf)	*to fall silent*
FAT	**то́лстый**	*thick, stout, corpulent*
	по́лный	*portly* (polite)
	жи́рный	*plump* (of people), *greasy, rich, fatty* (of food)

	ту́чный	*corpulent, obese*
FEAR	**боя́знь** (f)	*dread*, eg боя́знь темноты́, *fear of darkness*
	страх	*terror*
	испу́г	*fright*
	опасе́ние	*apprehension, misgiving*
FEEL	**чу́вствовать/почу́вствовать**	*to be aware of*
	чу́вствовать себя́ (intrans)	eg Как ты чу́вствуешь себя́? *How do you feel?*
	ощуща́ть/ощути́ть	*to sense*
	щу́пать/пощу́пать	*to explore by touch*, eg щу́пать кому́-н пульс, *to feel sb's pulse*
	тро́гать/потро́гать	*to run one's hand over*
	пробира́ться/пробра́ться о́щупью	*to feel one's way*
	испы́тывать/испыта́ть	*to experience*
	пережива́ть/пережи́ть	*to endure, suffer, go through*
FIGHT	**дра́ться/подра́ться с** + instr	*to scrap, brawl*
	сража́ться/срази́ться с + instr	*to do battle with*, eg of armies
	боро́ться	*to wrestle, struggle* (also fig)
	воева́ть (impf)	*to wage war*
FIND	**находи́ть/найти́**	*to find* (as result of search)
	застава́ть/заста́ть	*to come across, encounter*, eg заста́ть кого́-н до́ма, *to find sb at home*
	счита́ть/счесть	*to consider*, eg Они́ счита́ют ру́сский язы́к тру́дным, *They find Russian difficult*
	встреча́ть/встре́тить	*to encounter*
	открыва́ть/откры́ть	*to discover*
	обнару́живать/обнару́жить	*to bring to light*, eg Меха́ник обнару́жил непола́дку в мото́ре, *The mechanic found a fault in the engine*
	признава́ть/призна́ть	legal term, eg Призна́ли его́ вино́вным, *They found him guilty*
FIRE	**ого́нь** (m)	general word
	пожа́р	*conflagration*, eg лесно́й пожа́р, *forest fire*
	костёр	*bonfire*
	ками́н	*open fire, fireplace*

	пыл	*ardour*
(AT) FIRST	**снача́ла**	*at the beginning*
	сперва́ (R1)	= снача́ла
	пре́жде сего́	*first of all, first and foremost*
	впервы́е	*for the first time*
	во-пе́рвых	*in the first place*
	на пе́рвых пора́х	*in the first instance*
	с пе́рвого взгля́да	*at first sight*
FOLLOW	**идти́/пойти́ за** + instr	*to go after*
	сле́довать/после́довать за + instr	*to go after*
	сле́довать/после́довать + dat	*to emulate*
	следи́ть за + instr	*to watch, track, keep up with*, eg ЦРУ следи́т за ни́ми, *The CIA is following them*; следи́ть за полити́ческими собы́тиями, *to follow political developments*
	соблюда́ть/соблюсти́	*to observe*, eg дие́ту, пра́вила, *a diet, rules*
	понима́ть/поня́ть	*to understand*
FOOD	**пи́ща**	general word
	еда́	what is eaten; еда́ и питьё, *food and drink*
	(пищевы́е) проду́кты	*food products*
	продово́льствие (sg)	*foodstuffs, provisions*
	прови́зия (sg only)	*provisions, victuals*
	консе́рвы (pl; gen консе́рвов)	*canned food*
	ку́хня	*cuisine*
	блю́до	*a dish*
	пита́ние	*nourishment, feeding*
	корм	*animal fodder*
FOREIGN	**иностра́нный**	general word; Министе́рство иностра́нных дел, *Ministry of Foreign Affairs*
	зарубе́жный	= иностра́нный; зарубе́жная пре́сса, *the foreign press*
	вне́шний	*external*; вне́шняя поли́тика, торго́вля, *foreign policy, trade*
	чужо́й	*alien*
FREE	**свобо́дный**	*at liberty, unconstrained*

	непринуждённый	*relaxed, at ease*
	бесплáтный	*free of charge*, eg бесплáтное образовáние, *free education*
FREEZE	**морóзит**	*it is freezing*, ie *there is a frost*
	мёрзнуть/замёрзнуть (intrans)	eg Óзеро замёрзло, *The lake has frozen*
	заморáживать/заморóзить (trans)	eg заморóженное мя́со, *frozen meat*; also fig, eg Прави́тельство заморáживает цéны, *The government is freezing prices*
	покры́ться льдом	*to be covered with ice*, as of river, road
	зя́бнуть/озя́бнуть (intrans)	*to suffer from/feel the cold*
	леденéть/оледенéть (intrans)	*to turn to ice, become numb with cold*
FRIEND	**друг**	general word
	подрýга	*female friend*
	дружóк	dimin of друг
	приятель(ница)	not so close as **друг/подрýга**
	товáрищ	*comrade, pal*
	знакóмый/знакóмая (subst adj)	*acquaintance*
	сторóнник	*supporter*
	доброжелáтель (m)	*well-wisher*
FUNNY	**смешнóй**	*laughable*
	забáвный	*amusing*
	стрáнный	*strange*
	непоня́тный	*incomprehensible*
	подозри́тельный	*suspicious*
GIRL	**дéвочка**	*little girl*
	дéвушка	*girl* (after puberty); also as term of address to woman (see 6.4)
	дéвка (R1)	affectionate or pej
	деви́ца	*maiden*
	продавщи́ца	female shop assistant
GLASS	**стеклó**	*glass* (as material), *window-pane, windscreen* (of vehicle)
	стакáн	*tumbler*
	рю́мка	*small glass* (for drink)

	рю́мочка	dimin of рю́мка, eg *vodka glass*
	фуже́р	*tall glass*, for water, juice (at formal dinner)
	бока́л	*wine glass, goblet, chalice*
	очки́ (pl; gen очко́в)	*spectacles*
GOAL	**цель** (f)	*aim, purpose*
	воро́та (pl)	(sport) goalposts and net
	гол	what is scored in sport
GOOD	**хоро́ший**	general word; хоро́ш собо́й, *good-looking*
	до́брый	in various senses, *kind*
	поле́зный	*useful*
	интере́сный	*interesting*
	весёлый	*cheerful*, eg весёлое настрое́ние, *good mood*
	прия́тный	*pleasant, agreeable*
	спосо́бный	*able, capable*
	послу́шный	*obedient*
	гора́зд (short forms only)	*skilful, clever*, eg Он на всё гора́зд, *He's good at everything*
GOVERNMENT	**прави́тельство**	ruling body
	правле́ние	system of government
	управле́ние + instr	act of governing; also gram term
GREET	**здоро́ваться/поздоро́ваться с** + instr	*to say hello to*
	приве́тствовать	*to welcome* (also fig, eg приве́тствовать предложе́ние, *to welcome a proposal*)
	встреча́ть/встре́тить	*to meet, receive*
	принима́ть/приня́ть	*to receive*
GROW	**расти́/вы́расти** (intrans)	*to get bigger*
	возраста́ть/возрасти́ (intrans)	*to get bigger, increase*
	нараста́ть/нарасти́ (intrans)	*to accumulate*
	подраста́ть/подрасти́ (intrans)	*to get a little bigger*
	выра́щивать/вы́растить (trans)	*to cultivate*, eg о́вощи, *vegetables*; *to bring up*, eg детей, *children*
	увели́чиваться/увели́читься	*to increase*, eg Проце́нт сме́ртности

	(intrans)	увели́чивается, *The mortality rate is growing*
	отпуска́ть/отпусти́ть	*to let grow*, eg во́лосы, бо́роду, *hair, beard*
GUN	**ружьё**	*rifle*
	обре́з	*sawn-off shot-gun*
	пистоле́т	*pistol*
	револьве́р	*revolver*
	пулемёт	*machine-gun*
	пу́шка	*cannon*
HARD	**твёрдый**	*firm, solid*, eg твёрдый грунт, *hard ground*; твёрдый знак, *hard sign*
	тру́дный	*difficult*
	тяжёлый	fig, eg тяжёлая рабо́та, *hard work,* тяжёлые усло́вия, *hard conditions,* тяжёлые времена́, *hard times*
	си́льный	*forceful*, eg си́льный уда́р, *a hard blow*
	суро́вый	*severe*, eg суро́вая зима́, *a hard winter*
	стро́гий	*strict*
	чёрствый	*stale*, eg чёрствый хлеб, *hard bread*
(adverb)	**приле́жно** or **мно́го**	*diligently, with application*, eg приле́жно/мно́го рабо́тать, *to work hard*
	усе́рдно	= приле́жно
HARVEST	**урожа́й**	*crop, yield*
	жа́тва	*reaping*
	убо́рка	*gathering in*, eg пшени́цы, карто́шки, *of wheat, potatoes*
	сбор	*gathering*, eg фру́ктов, овоще́й, *of fruit, vegetables*
HAT	**шля́па**	*hat with brim*
	ша́пка	*fur hat*; вя́заная ша́пка, *knitted hat*
	ке́пка	*peaked cap*
	фура́жка	*peaked cap*, esp mil
	цили́ндр	*top hat*
HAVE	**у** (with noun or pronoun in gen)	*to have* (esp concrete objects, eg У нас чёрная соба́ка, *We have a black dog*)

	имéть	*to have* (with abstract object, eg прáво, возмóжность, *a right, an opportunity*)
	обладáть + instr	*to possess* (esp qualities, eg талáнтом, хладнокрóвием, *talent, presence of mind*)
HEAD	**головá**	part of the body
	главá	fig, eg главá делегáции, администрáции, *head of delegation, administration*
	начáльник	*chief, superior, boss*
	руководи́тель (m)	*leader, manager*
HEAVY	**тяжёлый**	general word
	высóкий	eg высóкая ценá, *a heavy price*
	си́льный	eg си́льный дождь, нáсморк, удáр, *heavy rain, a heavy cold, blow;* си́льное движéние, *heavy traffic*
	проливнóй	in slightly bookish phrase проливнóй дождь, *heavy rain*
	интенси́вный	in slightly bookish phrase интенси́вное движéние, *heavy traffic*
	жи́рный	in phrase жи́рный шрифт, *heavy type,* ie *bold print*
HERE	**тут**	*here*; also *at this point* (not necessarily spatial)
	здесь	*here*
	сюдá	*to here*
	вот	*here is*
HOLE	**дырá**	general word
	ды́рка	*small hole*, eg in clothing
	щель (f)	*tear, slit, crack*
	отвéрстие	*opening, aperture*
	я́ма	*pit, hole* (in road); воздýшная я́ма, *air pocket*
	лýнка	in sport, eg on golf course; in ice (for fishing)
HOLIDAY	**óтпуск**	time off work
	прáздник	*festival*, eg Christmas, Easter
	кани́кулы (pl; gen кани́кул)	*school holidays, university vacations*

	свобо́дный день	*free day, day off*
	выходно́й день	day when shop, institution is not working; but **Я сего́дня выходно́й**, *It's my day off*; выходны́е may mean *weekend*
	о́тдых	*rest, recreation, leisure*
HOT	**жа́ркий**	eg жа́ркая пого́да, *hot weather*
	горя́чий	*hot* (to the touch), eg горя́чая вода́, *hot water*; горя́чий суп, *hot soup*
	о́стрый	*spicy, piquant*, eg о́стрый со́ус, *a hot sauce*
IDEA	**иде́я**	general word
	мысль (f)	*thought*
	ду́ма (R3)	*a thought*
	ду́мка	dimin of ду́ма
	поня́тие	*concept, understanding*
	представле́ние	*notion*; представле́ния не име́ю *I've no idea*
	план	*plan*
	за́мысел	*scheme, project*
	наме́рение	*intention*
INFORM	**информи́ровать/про-информи́ровать** + acc	*to notify*
	сообща́ть/сообщи́ть + dat	*to report to*
	извеща́ть/извести́ть + acc (R3b)	*to notify*
	осведомля́ть/осве́домить + acc (R3b, negative overtone)	*to notify*
	ста́вить/поста́вить кого́-н **в изве́стность** (R3b)	*to notify*
	доноси́ть/донести́ на + acc	*to denounce, inform against*
INTEREST	**интере́с**	*attention, pursuit*
	заинтересо́ванность (f)	*concern, stake (in)*, eg заинтересо́ванность в результа́те, *an interest in the outcome*
	проце́нты (pl; gen проце́нтов)	premium paid for use of money
	до́ля	*financial share*
INTRODUCE	**представля́ть/предста́вить**	*to present, introduce* (a person), eg Она́

		представила мне Иванова, *She introduced Ivanov to me*
	вводить/ввести	*to bring in*, eg новый закон, *a new law*
	вносить/внести	*to incorporate*, eg поправку в документ, *a correction in a document*
JOB	**работа**	*work, employment*
	задача	*task*
	поручение	*mission, assignment*
	должность (f)	position held
	место	*post*
	пост	*post*, eg высокий пост, *good job*
	обязанность (f)	*duty, responsibility*
LAST	**последний**	last in series, eg последнее имя в списке, *the last name in a list*
	прошлый	most recently past, eg на прошлой неделе, *last week*
LAW	**закон**	*rule, statute*; also scientific formula
	право	the subject or its study
	правопорядок	*law and order*
	правило	*rule, regulation*
	профессия юриста	*the legal profession*
	юридический	in expressions such as юридическая школа, *law school;* юридический факультет, *law faculty*
LEADER	**лидер**	*(political) leader*; лидер соревнования, *leader in a competition*
	руководитель (m)	*director, manager*
	вождь (m; R3, rhet)	*chief*
	передовая статья	*leading article* (in newspaper)
LEARN	**учиться/научиться** + dat of subject learned	*to learn, study*, eg учиться математике, *to learn mathematics*
	учить/выучить + acc	*to learn, memorise*
	изучать/изучить + acc	*to study*, eg изучать математику, *to learn mathematics*; pf изучить implies mastery
	заниматься/заняться + instr	*to study*, eg заниматься русским языком, *to learn Russian*
	узнавать/узнать	*to find out*

LEAVE	**выходи́ть/вы́йти**	*to go out*
	выезжа́ть/вы́ехать	*to go out* (by transport)
	уходи́ть/уйти́	*to go away*
	уезжа́ть/уе́хать	*to go away* (by transport)
	улета́ть/улете́ть	*to go away by plane, fly off*
	отправля́ться/отпра́виться	*to set off*
	отходи́ть/отойти́	*to depart* (of transport), eg По́езд отхо́дит в по́лдень, *The train leaves at midday*
	вылета́ть/вы́лететь	*to depart* (of plane)
	удаля́ться/удали́ться	*to withdraw*
	оставля́ть/оста́вить	*to leave behind*; also *to bequeath*
	покида́ть/поки́нуть	*to abandon, forsake*
	броса́ть/бро́сить	*to abandon, forsake*, eg жену́, *one's wife*
	забыва́ть/забы́ть	to forget to take, eg Я забы́л зо́нтик в авто́бусе, *I left my umbrella on the bus*
LIGHT	**свет**	general word
	освеще́ние	*lighting, illumination*
	просве́т	*shaft of light, patch of light*
	ого́нь (m)	on plane, ship; огни́ (pl), *lights* (in buildings)
	ла́мпа	*lamp*
	фа́ра	*headlight* (on vehicle)
	светофо́р	*traffic light*
	проже́ктор	*searchlight*
	ра́мпа	*spotlight* (in theatre)
LINE	**ли́ния**	in various senses
	ряд	*row, series*
	верёвка	*cord, rope*
	леса́ (pl лёсы, gen лёс)	*fishing-line*
	строка́	on page
	стих	of poetry
LONG	**дли́нный**	spatial, eg дли́нная у́лица, *a long street*
	до́лгий	temporal, eg до́лгое вре́мя, *a long time*

(A) LONG TIME	**до́лго**	*a long time*
	задо́лго до + gen	*long before*, eg задо́лго до конца́, *long before the end*
	надо́лго	*for a long time*, eg Он уе́хал надо́лго, *He went away for a long time*
	давно́	*long ago*; *for a long time*, in the sense of *long since*, eg Я давно́ изуча́ю ру́сский язы́к, *I have been studying Russian for a long time*
LOOK	**смотре́ть/посмотре́ть на** + acc	*to look at, watch*
	гляде́ть/погляде́ть на + acc	*to look/peer/gaze at*
	вы́глядеть (impf)	to have a certain appearance, eg Он вы́глядит не́мцем, *He looks like a German*
	похо́же на дождь	*it looks like rain*
	взгля́дывать/взгляну́ть на + acc	*to glance at*
	Слу́шай(те)!	*Look!* ie *Listen!*
	уха́живать за + instr	*to look after* (care for)
	присма́тривать/присмотре́ть за + instr	*to look after* (keep an eye on)
LOSE	**теря́ть/потеря́ть**	in various senses
	утра́чивать/утра́тить (R3)	eg иллю́зии, *one's illusions*
	лиша́ться/лиши́ться + gen	*to be deprived of*, eg лиша́ться води́тельских прав, *to lose one's driving licence*
	прои́грывать/проигра́ть	game, bet, etc
	заблужда́ться/заблуди́ться	*to lose one's way, get lost*
	отстава́ть/отста́ть	of timepiece, eg Мои́ часы́ отстаю́т на де́сять мину́т в день, *My watch loses ten minutes a day*
MAKE	**де́лать/сде́лать**	in various senses
	производи́ть/произвести́	*to produce*
	изготовля́ть/изгото́вить	*to manufacture*
	выраба́тывать/вы́работать	*to manufacture, produce, work out, draw up*
	выде́лывать/вы́делать	*to manufacture, process*
	гото́вить/пригото́вить	*to cook, prepare*
	вари́ть/свари́ть	*to cook* (by boiling)

	заставля́ть/заста́вить + infin	*to compel* (sb to do sth)
	зараба́тывать/зарабо́тать	*to earn*
	вы́йти (pf)	in construction Из неё вы́йдет хоро́шая учи́тельница, *She will make a good teacher*
MARRIAGE	**сва́дьба**	*wedding*
	жени́тьба	process of getting married (from point of view of man)
	заму́жество	*married state* (for woman)
	брак	*matrimony*
	супру́жество (R3)	*wedlock*
	сою́з	fig: *union, alliance*
MARRY	**жени́ться** (impf and pf) **на** + prep	*to get married* (of man to woman)
	выходи́ть/вы́йти за́муж за + acc	*to get married* (of woman to man)
	жени́ться/пожени́ться	*to get married* (of couple)
	венча́ться/обвенча́ться	*to get married* (of couple)
	венча́ть/обвенча́ть (trans)	*to marry* (ie what the officiating priest does)
MEAN	**хоте́ть сказа́ть**	*to intend to say*
	зна́чить	*to signify, have significance*
	означа́ть	*to signify, stand for*, eg Что означа́ют бу́квы США? *What do the letters USA mean?*
	намерева́ться	*to intend to*
	наме́рен/наме́рена/наме́рены (m/f/pl forms used as predicate) + infin	*intend(s)* (to do sth)
MEET	**встреча́ть/встре́тить** + acc	*to meet* (by chance), *go to meet*, eg Мы встре́тили их в аэропорту́, *We met them at the airport*
	встреча́ться/встре́титься с + instr	*to meet with* (by arrangement) *encounter*, eg встре́титься с затрудне́ниями, *to meet difficulties*
	знако́миться/познако́миться с + instr	*to make the acquaintance of*, eg Он познако́мился с ней в Ри́ме, *He met her in Rome*
MEETING	**встре́ча**	*encounter*

	свида́ние	*appointment, rendezvous*
	собра́ние	*gathering* (formal, eg party meeting)
	заседа́ние	formal session (people sitting and discussing)
	совеща́ние	*(high-level) conference* (people consulted, decisions made)
	ми́тинг	*political rally*
	слёт	*gathering, get-together*
	состяза́ние	sporting event
	ска́чки (pl; gen ска́чек)	*race meeting*
MISS	**тоскова́ть по** + dat	*to long for, yearn for,* eg тоскова́ть по ро́дине, *to miss one's country*
	скуча́ть по + dat	similar to тоскова́ть but not so strong
	опа́здывать/опозда́ть на + acc	*to be late for,* eg опозда́ть на по́езд, *to miss a train*
	не попада́ть/попа́сть в + acc	*to fail to hit,* eg Пу́ля не попа́ла в цель, *The bullet missed the target*
	пропуска́ть/пропусти́ть	*to fail to attend,* eg пропусти́ть заня́тия, *to miss classes*
	проходи́ть/пройти́ ми́мо + gen	*to go past,* eg Она́ прошла́ ми́мо поворо́та, *She missed the turning*
	оступа́ться/оступи́ться	*to miss one's footing, stumble*
MOVE	**дви́гать/дви́нуть** (trans)	to change the position of sth, set in motion
	дви́гать/дви́нуть + instr	to move part of one's body, eg дви́нуть па́льцем, *to move one's finger*
	подвига́ть/подви́нуть (trans)	to move sth a bit
	отодвига́ть/отодви́нуть (trans)	*to move aside*
	отодвига́ться/отодви́нуться (intrans)	*to move aside*
	передвига́ть/передви́нуть	*to shift* (from one place to another), eg передви́нуть стре́лки часо́в наза́д, *to move the clock back*
	сдвига́ть/сдви́нуть (trans)	*to shift, budge* (from some point), eg сдви́нуть крова́ть с её ме́ста, *to move the bed from its place*
	сдвига́ться/сдви́нуться (intrans)	*to shift, budge* (from some point)
	шевели́ться/шевельну́ться	*to stir*
	переезжа́ть/перее́хать	to move to new accommodation,

		eg переéхать на нóвую квартиру, *to move to a new flat*
	перебирáться/перебрáться	= переезжáть/переéхать in the sense above
	переходить/перейти	*to go across, transfer*, eg на нóвую рабóту, *to a new job*
	трóгать/трóнуть	*to touch, affect* (emotionally), eg Егó любéзность трóнула меня до слёз, *His kindness moved me to tears*
	идти	*to go*
	идти + instr	to move piece in board game, eg Он идёт пéшкой, *He is moving a pawn*
	развивáться/развиться (intrans)	*to develop* (of events, action), eg Собы́тия бы́стро развивáются, *Events are moving quickly*
MUCH	**мнóго**	*a lot*
	намнóго	*by a large margin*
	горáздо	with short comp adj, eg горáздо лýчше, *much better*
	кудá (R1)	= горáздо
	сли́шком (мнóго)	*too much*
	óчень	with verbs, *very much*, eg Э́та пьéса мне óчень нрáвится, *I like this play very much*
NAME	**и́мя** (n)	in various sense, incl *given name*
	óтчество	*patronymic*
	фами́лия	*surname*
	кли́чка	*nickname*, name of pet
	прóзвище	*nickname, sobriquet*
	назвáние	*designation, appellation*
	репутáция	*reputation*
NEED	**нуждá**	*need, necessity, want*
	необходи́мость (f)	*necessity, inevitability*
	потрéбность (f)	*requirement*
	нищетá	*poverty, indigence*
NICE	**прия́тный**	*pleasant, agreeable*
	симпати́чный	*likeable* (of person)
	дóбрый	*kind, good*
	любéзный	*kind, courteous*

	ми́лый	*sweet, lovable*
	обая́тельный	*charming* (of person)
	преле́стный	*delightful, charming* (of thing)
	ую́тный	*comfortable, cosy*
	вку́сный	of food, *tasty*
NIGHT	**ночь** (f)	general word
	ве́чер	*evening*, time of day up until bedtime, eg сего́дня ве́чером, *tonight*
NOTE	**запи́ска**	written message or memorandum
	заме́тка	a mark, eg заме́тки на поля́х, *notes in the margin*
	замеча́ние	*observation, remark*
	примеча́ние	additional observation, *footnote*
	но́та	musical note
	банкно́т	*bank-note*
NOW	**сейча́с**	*at the present moment; just now* (in the past); *presently, soon* (in the future)
	тепе́рь	*now, nowadays, today*
	ны́не	*nowadays*
	то... то	*now... now*, eg то дождь, то снег, *now rain, now snow*
NUMBER	**число́**	in various senses; also *date*
	но́мер	of bus, journal, etc; also *hotel room*
	телефо́н	*telephone number*
	ци́фра	*figure, numeral*
	коли́чество	*quantity*
OLD	**ста́рый**	in various senses
	пожило́й	*middle-aged* (showing signs of ageing)
	пре́жний	*previous*
	бы́вший	*former, ex-*, eg бы́вший президе́нт, *the ex-President*
	стари́нный	*ancient*, eg стари́нный го́род, *an old city*
	дре́вний	*ancient* (even older than стари́нный), eg дре́вняя исто́рия, *ancient history*

	ве́тхий	*dilapidated*; also in phrase Ве́тхий заве́т, *the Old Testament*
	устаре́лый	*obsolete, out-of-date*
ORDER	**веле́ть** (impf and pf) + dat + infin or что́бы	*to order* (sb to do sth), eg Я веле́л ему́ вы́йти, *I ordered him to leave*
	прика́зывать/приказа́ть + dat + infin or что́бы	*to order* (sb to do sth)
	зака́зывать/заказа́ть	*to book, reserve*, eg заказа́ть стол в рестора́не, *to order a table in a restaurant*
PART	**часть** (f)	*portion, component*
	до́ля	*share*
	уча́стие	*participation*, eg принима́ть/приня́ть уча́стие в чём-н, *to take part in sth*
	роль (f)	*role*, eg in play; игра́ть роль, *to play a part* (also fig)
	па́ртия	musical part
	край	of country, *region*
PAY	**плати́ть/заплати́ть** кому́-н **за** что́-н	*to pay sb for sth*
	опла́чивать/оплати́ть что́-н	*to pay for sth*, eg оплати́ть расхо́ды, счёт, *to pay the expenses, the bill*
	Note: Russians themselves may say оплати́ть за что́-н, but this usage is considered incorrect.	
	отпла́чивать/отплати́ть кому́-н	*to repay sb, pay sb back*
	выпла́чивать/вы́платить	*to pay out*, eg вы́платить зарпла́ты, *to pay wages*
	упла́чивать/уплати́ть что́-н	*to pay sth* (which is due), eg уплати́ть взнос, нало́г, *to pay a subscription, tax*
	распла́чиваться/расплати́ться с + instr	*to settle accounts with*
	поплати́ться (pf) **жи́знью за** что́-н	*to pay with one's life for sth*
	окупа́ться/окупи́ться	*to be rewarding*, eg преступле́ние окупа́ется, *crime pays*
	свиде́тельствовать/ посвиде́тельствовать своё почте́ние (R3b)	*to pay one's respects*
	обраща́ть/обрати́ть внима́ние на + acc	*to pay attention to*
	навеща́ть/навести́ть кого́-н	*to pay a visit to sb*

PAY(MENT)	**платёж**	in various senses; платёж в рассрóчку, *payment in instalments*; платёж нали́чными, *cash payment*
	плáта	eg за газ, обучéние, *for gas, tuition*
	оплáта	of costs, eg оплáта кварти́ры, питáния, проéзда, *payment for a flat, food, travel*
	уплáта	of sum due, eg уплáта пóшлины, *payment of duty*
	зарплáта	*wages, salary*
	полу́чка (R1)	= зарплáта
	жáлованье	*salary*
	взнос	*subscription*
PEOPLE	**лю́ди**	individuals, persons
	нарóд	*a people* (ethnic group)
POUR	**лить** (trans and intrans)	basic verb
	наливáть/нали́ть (trans)	eg напи́ток, *a drink*
	разливáть/разли́ть	*to pour out* (to several people)
	сы́пать (impf; trans)	basic verb, of solids, eg кóфе, рис, *coffee, rice*
	сы́паться (impf; intrans)	of solids, eg Песóк сы́плется из мешкá, *Sand is pouring from the sack*
	вали́ть (impf)	fig, eg Дым вали́л из дóма, *Smoke was pouring from the house*
	хлы́нуть (pf; intrans)	*to gush* (of blood, water); also fig, eg На у́лицу хлы́нула толпá, *A crowd poured into the street*
POWER	**власть** (f)	*authority*
	си́ла	*strength, force*; лошади́ная си́ла, *horse power*
	энéргия	*energy*, eg я́дерная энéргия, *nuclear power*
	мощь (f)	*might*
	мóщность (f)	esp tech, eg дви́гателя, *of an engine*
	держáва	an influential state; сверхдержáва, *a superpower*
	спосóбность (f)	*ability, capacity*
	стéпень (f)	math term

PRESENT (adj)	**настоящий**	now existing; настоящее время, *the present tense*
	современный	*modern, contemporary*
	нынешний	*today's*, eg нынешнее правительство, *the present government*
	присутствующий	in the place in question
PREVENT	**мешать/помешать** + dat + infin	*to hinder, impede, stop* (sb from doing sth)
	предотвращать/предотвратить	*to avert, stave off, forestall*
	препятствовать/ воспрепятствовать + dat	*to obstruct, impede*
PUT	**класть/положить**	into lying position
	ставить/поставить	into standing position
	сажать/посадить	into sitting position; посадить кого-н в тюрьму, *to put sb in prison*
	укладывать/уложить	*to lay*, eg уложить ребёнка в постель, *to put a child to bed*
	вставлять/вставить	*to insert*, eg, ключ в замок, *a key in a lock*
	вешать/повесить	*to hang*, eg бельё на верёвку, *washing on a line*
	помещать/поместить	*to place, accommodate*, eg поместить гостей в свободную комнату, *to put guests in a spare room;* поместить деньги в сберкассу, *to put money in a savings bank*
	девать/деть (in past tense девать = деть)	*to do with*, eg Куда ты девал/дел книгу? *Where have you put the book?*
	засовывать/засунуть	*to shove in*, eg засунуть руку в карман, *to put one's hand in one's pocket*
	высовывать/высунуть	*to stick out*, eg высунуть язык, *to put one's tongue out*
	задавать/задать	in the phrase задать вопрос, *to put a question*
	выдвигать/выдвинуть	*to put forward*, eg теорию, *a theory*
	надевать/надеть	*to put on*, eg шляпу, *a hat*
	откладывать/отложить	*to put off, defer*
	убирать/убрать	*to put away, clear up*
QUEEN	**королева**	monarch
	дама	playing card

	ферзь (m)	chess piece
	ма́тка	of insect, eg bee, ant
	гомосексуали́ст	*homosexual*
	голубо́й (subst adj; R1)	*gay*
QUIET	**ти́хий**	not loud, *tranquil, calm*
	бесшу́мный	*noiseless*, eg бесшу́мная маши́на, *a quiet car*
	споко́йный	*tranquil, calm, peaceful*
	молчали́вый	*taciturn*
REACH	**доходи́ть/дойти́ до** + gen	*to get as far as* (on foot)
	доезжа́ть/дое́хать до + gen	*to get as far as* (by transport)
	добира́ться/добра́ться до + gen	= доходи́ть/дойти́ and доезжа́ть/дое́хать, but implies some difficulty
	доноси́ться/донести́сь до + gen	*to carry* (of eg news, sounds, smells), eg До неё донёсся слух, *A rumour reached her*
	дотя́гиваться/дотяну́ться до + gen	by touching, eg **Я** могу́ дотяну́ться до потолка́, *I can reach the ceiling*
	достава́ть/доста́ть до + gen	*to stretch as far as* (of things and people)
	достига́ть/дости́гнуть + gen	*to attain*, eg це́ли, *a goal*
REALISE	**понима́ть/поня́ть**	*to understand*
	осознава́ть/осозна́ть	*to acknowledge*, eg осозна́ть оши́бку, *to realise one's mistake*
	отдава́ть/отда́ть себе́ отчёт в чём-н (R3)	*to be/become aware of sth* (esp a difficulty)
	осуществля́ть/осуществи́ть	*to bring into being, accomplish*
	реализова́ть (impf and pf)	*to convert into money*; also *to implement*, eg план, *a plan*
REMEMBER	**по́мнить** (impf)	basic verb
	вспомина́ть/вспо́мнить	*to recall, recollect*
	запомина́ть/запо́мнить	*to memorise*
	помина́ть	in phrase Не помина́й(те) меня́ ли́хом, *Remember me kindly*
	Note also the phrase **переда́й(те) приве́т** + dat, *remember (me) to*, ie *give my regards to.*	
RESPONSIBILITY	**отве́тственность** (f)	*answerability*
	обя́занность (f)	*obligation*

RICH	**богáтый**	in various senses
	зажи́точный	*well-to-do, prosperous*
	обеспéченный	*well provided-for*
	роскóшный	*luxurious, sumptuous*
	изоби́лующий + instr	*abounding in*, eg райóн изоби́лующий прирóдными ресýрсами, *a region rich in natural resources*
	тýчный	*fertile*, eg тýчная пóчва, *rich soil*
	жи́рный	*fatty* (of food)
	пря́ный	*spicy* (of food)
	слáдкий	*sweet* (of food)
RISE	**восходи́ть/взойти́**	*to mount, ascend*, eg Сóлнце восхóдит в шесть часóв, *The sun rises at six o'clock*
	вставáть/встать	*to get up*
	поднимáться/подня́ться	*to go up*
	повышáться/повы́ситься	*to get higher*, eg Цéны повышáются, *Prices are rising*
	увели́чиваться/увели́читься	*to increase*
	возрастáть/возрасти́	*to grow*
	возвышáться/возвы́ситься над + instr	*to tower over*
	продвигáться/продви́нуться	*to be promoted, gain advancement*
	восставáть/восстáть на + acc	*to rebel against*
	воскресáть/воскрéснуть	*to be resurrected*, eg Христóс воскрéс из мёртвых, *Christ rose from the dead*
ROOM	**кóмната**	general word
	нóмер	*hotel room*
	аудитóрия	*auditorium, classroom*
	зал	*hall, assembly room*; зал ожидáния, *waiting-room*
	мéсто	*space*
RUBBISH	**мýсор**	*refuse*
	сор	*litter, dust*
	дрянь (f)	*trash*
	рýхлядь (f)	*junk* (old and broken things)
	хлам	*junk* (things no longer needed)

	ерундá	*nonsense*
	чепухá	= ерундá
	вздор (more bookish)	*nonsense*
	нести́ ахинéю (R1)	*to talk rubbish*
SAVE	**спасáть/спасти́**	*to rescue*
	берéчь (impf)	*to put by, preserve*, eg берéчь свои́ си́лы, *to save one's strength*
	сберегáть/сберéчь	*to put money by*
	оставля́ть/остáвить	*to put aside* (for future use), eg остáвить буты́лку молокá на зáвтра, *to save a bottle of milk for tomorrow*
	избавля́ть/избáвить кого́-н **от** чего́-н	*to spare sb sth*, eg Э́то избáвило меня́ от мно́гих хлопо́т, *This saved me a lot of trouble*
	эконо́мить/сэконо́мить (**на** + prep)	*to use sparingly, economise (on)*, eg эконо́мить врéмя, труд, *to save time, labour*
	выгáдывать/вы́гадать	*to gain*, eg врéмя, *time*
SCENE	**сцéна**	in various senses
	зрéлище	*spectacle*
	явлéние	part of drama
	декорáция	*set, décor*
	скандáл	*scandalous event, row*
	пейзáж	*landscape*
	мéсто	*place*, eg мéсто преступлéния, *the scene of the crime*
SERIOUS	**серьёзный**	in various senses
	тяжёлый	*grave*, eg тяжёлая болéзнь, *a serious illness*
	о́стрый	*acute*, eg о́страя проблéма, *a serious problem*
SERVICE	**слу́жба**	in various senses
	услу́га	*assistance, good turn*, eg окáзывать/оказáть комý-н услу́гу, *to do sb a service*; also *facility*, eg коммунáльные услу́ги, *public services*
	служéние (R3)	act, process of serving, eg служéние му́зе, *serving one's muse*

	обслу́живание	*attention*, eg in shop, restaurant; also *servicing, maintenance*, eg маши́ны, *of a car*
	самообслу́живание	*self-service*
	се́рвис	*attention* (from waiter, etc)
	серви́з	set of crockery
	обря́д	*rite, ceremony*
	пода́ча	at tennis, etc
SHAKE	**трясти́** (impf; trans)	basic verb
	трясти́сь (impf; intrans)	basic verb
	потряса́ть/потрясти́ (trans)	*to rock, stagger* (fig), eg Она́ была́ потрясена́ э́тим собы́тием, *She was shaken by this event*
	встря́хивать/встряхну́ть	*to shake up, rouse*; встряхну́ть ко́сти, *to shake dice*
	встря́хиваться/встряхну́ться	*to shake oneself*
	вытря́хивать/вы́тряхнуть	*to shake out*, eg вы́тряхнуть ска́терть, *to shake out the table-cloth*
	стря́хивать/стряхну́ть	*to shake off*
	дрожа́ть (impf; intrans)	*to tremble, shiver*, eg Она́ дрожи́т от хо́лода, *She is shaking with cold*
	подрыва́ть/подорва́ть	*to undermine*, eg подорва́ть чью-н ве́ру, *to shake sb's faith*
	грози́ть/погрози́ть + instr	*to make a threatening gesture with*, eg грози́ть кому́-н кулако́м, па́льцем, *to shake one's fist, finger at sb*
	кача́ть/покача́ть голово́й	*to shake one's head*
	пожима́ть/пожа́ть кому́-н **ру́ку**	*to shake hands with sb*
SHINE	**блесте́ть** (impf)	*to glitter, sparkle*, eg Его́ глаза́ блесте́ли ра́достью, *His eyes shone with joy*
	блесну́ть (pf)	*to sparkle, glint*
	блиста́ть (impf)	*to shine* (esp fig), eg блиста́ть на сце́не, *to shine on the stage*
	сверка́ть (impf)	*to sparkle, glitter, gleam*
	сверкну́ть (pf)	*to flash*
	сия́ть	*to beam*, eg Со́лнце сия́ет, *The sun is shining* (viewer's subjective impression)
	свети́ть	of source of light, eg Свеча́ све́тит, *A candle is shining* (objective statement)

	свети́ться	*to gleam, glint*, esp when giving light is not the primary purpose of the subject, eg Бока́л свети́лась при све́те свечи́, *The glass was shining in the candlelight*
	горе́ть (impf)	*to be on* (of light)
	мерца́ть (impf)	*to twinkle, flicker*, eg Звезда́ мерца́ет, *A star is shining*
SHOE	**ту́фля**	*outdoor shoe*
	та́почка	*slipper, flipflop*
	босоно́жка	*sandal*
	башма́к	*clog*
	боти́нок (pl боти́нки, боти́нок)	*ankle-high boot, army boot*
	сапо́г (pl сапоги́, сапо́г)	*high boot*
	ва́ленок (pl ва́ленки, ва́ленок)	*felt boots*
	бу́тсы (pl; gen бутс)	*football boot*
	ке́ды (pl; gen ке́дов; obs)	*tennis shoes*
	кроссо́вки (pl; gen кроссо́вок)	*trainers*
	о́бувь (f)	*footwear*
SHOOT	**стреля́ть** (impf)	basic verb
	застре́ливать/застрели́ть	*to shoot dead*
	обстре́ливать/обстреля́ть	*to bombard*
	расстре́ливать/расстреля́ть	*to execute by shooting*
	подстре́ливать/подстрели́ть	*to wound by shooting*
	мча́ться (impf)	*to tear along*
	проноси́ться/пронести́сь ми́мо + gen	*to rush past*
	бить по воро́там	*to shoot at goal*
	снима́ть/снять фильм	*to shoot a film*
SHOP	**магази́н**	general word
	ла́вка	*small shop, store*
	универма́г	*department store*
	гастроно́м	*food shop*
SHOW	**пока́зывать/показа́ть**	general word
	проявля́ть/прояви́ть	*to manifest*, eg прояви́ть интере́с к му́зыке, *to show an interest in music*

SIDE	**сторона́**	in various senses
	бок	of body or physical object
	склон	*slope*, eg холма́, горы́, *of a hill, mountain*
	бе́рег	*bank, shore*, eg реки́, о́зера, *of a river, lake*
	край	*edge*, eg сиде́ть на краю́ крова́ти, *to sit on the side of the bed*
	обо́чина	of road
	борт	of ship
	кома́нда	*team*
	нару́жность (f)	*outside, exterior*
	изна́нка	*inside, wrong side*, eg оде́жды, *of clothing*
SIGHT	**зре́ние**	*vision*
	вид	*aspect*
	взгля́д	*glance, opinion*, eg на пе́рвый взгляд, *at first sight*
	зре́лище	*spectacle*
	достопримеча́тельность (f)	touristic attraction
	прице́л	aiming device
	Note also the phrase **знать** кого́-н **в лицо́**, *to know sb by sight.*	
SIT	**сиде́ть**	*to be seated*
	сади́ться/сесть	*to sit down*
	приса́живаться/присе́сть	*to take a seat*
	проси́живать/просиде́ть	*to sit* (for a defined time)
	заседа́ть (intrans)	*to be in session*, eg Парла́мент заседа́ет, *Parliament is sitting*
	быть чле́ном	*to be a member of*, ie *to sit on* (a committee)
	держа́ть экза́мен	*to sit an exam*
	сдава́ть экза́мен	= держа́ть экза́мен
SKIN	**ко́жа**	in various senses
	шку́ра	*hide, pelt* (of animal)
	ко́жица	*thin skin*, eg помидо́ра, *of a tomato*
	кожура́	*peel* (of fruit), eg я́блока, *of an apple*
	ко́рка	*thick skin, rind*, eg апельси́на, сы́ра, *of an orange, cheese*
	шелуха́	crackly dry skin, eg лу́ка, *of an onion*

	пе́нка	on milk, etc
SMALL	**ма́ленький**	in various senses
	небольшо́й	= ма́ленький
	ма́л (short form predominates)	*little, too small*, eg Э́та ша́пка мне мала́, *This hat is too small for me*
	немногочи́сленный	*not numerous*, eg немногочи́сленная гру́ппа, *a small group*
	ме́лкий	*petty, unimportant, trivial,* of small calibre, status or denomination, etc, eg ме́лкий шрифт, *small print*; ме́лкая со́шка, *small fry*; ме́лкие де́ньги, *small change*
	ме́лочный	*small-minded*
	незначи́тельный	*insignificant*, eg игра́ть незначи́тельную роль, *to play a small part*
	второстепе́нный	*second-rate*
	плохо́й	*bad, poor*, eg плохо́й аппети́т, урожа́й, *a small appetite, harvest*
	скро́мный	*modest*, eg скро́мный дохо́д, *a small income*
SMELL (verb)	**па́хнуть** (intrans; impers) + instr	to have the odour (of), eg Здесь па́хнет га́рью, табако́м, *It smells of burning, tobacco here*
	попа́хивать (intrans; impers; R1) + instr	*to smell slightly of*
	ду́рно па́хнуть (intrans)	*to emit a bad smell*
	воня́ть (impf; intrans) + instr	*to stink, reek (of)*, eg В ку́хне воня́ет ры́бой, *It reeks of fish in the kitchen*
	чу́ять/почу́ять (trans)	of animals, to perceive by smelling, eg Волк почу́ял за́йца, *The wolf smelt a hare*
	чу́вствовать/почу́вствовать	of humans, to perceive by smelling
	слы́шать/услы́шать (за́пах)	= чу́вствовать
	ню́хать/поню́хать	*to sniff*
	проню́хивать/проню́хать	*to smell out, get wind of* (also fig)
	обоня́ть (impf)	to have a sense of smell
SMELL (noun)	**за́пах**	*odour*
	обоня́ние	*sense of smell*
	арома́т	*aroma*
	благоуха́ние	*fragrance*

	вонь (f)	*stink, stench*
SOUND	**звук**	general word
	шум	*noise*, eg ве́тра, дождя́, мо́ря, *of the wind, rain, sea*
	визг	*scream, squeal, yelp, screech*
	го́мон	*hubbub* (not harmonious)
	гро́хот	*crash, din, thunder*
	гул	*rumble, hum*, eg движе́ния, *of traffic*
	жужжа́ние	*buzz, drone, humming*, eg пчёл, *of bees*
	журча́ние	*babbling*, eg воды́, *of water*
	звон	*chinking, clinking*, eg моне́т, стака́нов, *of coins, glasses*
	звоно́к	*ring* (sound of bell)
	ле́пет	*babble*, eg младе́нца, *of a baby*
	раска́т	*roll, peal*, eg гро́ма, *of thunder*
	свист	*whistling, warbling, hissing*
	скрип	*squeak, scraping*
	стук	*knock, thump, thud, tap*
	то́пот	*treading, tramping*; ко́нский то́пот, *the clatter of hoofs*
	треск	*crackle*, eg поле́ньев, костра́, *of logs, a bonfire*
	уда́р	*clap*, eg гро́ма, *of thunder*
	ше́лест	*rustle*, eg бума́г, камыше́й, *of papers, rushes*
	шо́рох	*rustle* (soft, indistinct, perhaps of animal)
SPEND	**тра́тить/истра́тить**	*to pay out*, eg де́ньги, *money*
	расхо́довать/израсхо́довать (R3b)	*to expend*, eg де́ньги, боеприпа́сы, *money, ammunition*
	проводи́ть/провести́	*to pass*, eg вре́мя, *time*
STAND	**стоя́ть**	*to be standing*
	проста́ивать/простоя́ть	*to stand* (for a specified time); *to stand idle*, eg Станки́ проста́ивают, *The machines stand idle*
	ста́вить/поста́вить	to put into standing position
	станови́ться/стать	to move into certain positions, eg стать на цы́почки, *to stand on tiptoe*

	вставáть/встать	*to get up*
	выноси́ть/вы́нести	*to endure*
	терпéть/потерпéть	*to endure*
	выдéрживать/вы́держать	*to withstand, stand up to*, eg Её кни́га не вы́держит кри́тики, *Her book will not stand up to criticism*
	оставáться/остáться в си́ле	*to remain in force*, eg Решéние остаётся в си́ле, *The decision stands*
	обстоя́ть (impf)	in expression Как обстои́т дéло, *How do things stand?*
STATE	**состоя́ние**	*condition*
	положéние	*position, state of affairs*
	настроéние	*mood, state of mind*
	госудáрство	body politic
STATION	**стáнция**	general word, eg радиостáнция, *radio station*; электростáнция, *power station*; also small railway station, underground station
	вокзáл	*railway terminus, mainline station*
	учáсток	in phrases избирáтельный учáсток, *polling station* and полицéйский учáсток, *police station*
	заправочный пункт/ запрáвочная стáнция	*filling station*
STEP	**шаг**	*pace*
	ступéнь (f)	on flight of stairs
	ступéнька	= ступéнь; also *step* on ladder
	лéстница	*ladder, staircase*
	стремя́нка	*step-ladder*
	поднóжка	*footboard* (of vehicle)
	крыльцó	steps into building, *porch*
	пóступь (f)	*tread*, eg тяжёлая пóступь, *heavy tread*
	похóдка	*gait, way of walking*
	мéра	*measure*, eg принимáть/приня́ть мéры, *to take steps*
	па (n, indecl)	*dance step*

	стопа́	in phrase идти́ по чьи-н стопа́м, *to follow in sb's footsteps*
	Note the expression **идти́ в но́гу с** + instr, *to be in step with.*	
STOP	**остана́вливать/останови́ть** (trans)	*to bring to a halt*
	остана́вливаться/останови́ться (intrans)	*to come to a halt*
	приостана́вливать/приостанови́ть (trans)	*to suspend*, eg приостанови́ть платежи́, *to stop payments*
	прекраща́ть/прекрати́ть (trans)	to arrest progress, eg прекрати́ть я́дерные испыта́ния, *to stop nuclear tests*
	прекраща́ться/прекрати́ться (intrans)	*to come to an end*
	перестава́ть/переста́ть + impf infin	*to cease* (doing sth), eg Он переста́л писа́ть, *He stopped writing*
	броса́ть/бро́сить + impf infin	*to give up* (doing sth), eg Она́ бро́сила кури́ть, *She has stopped smoking*
	меша́ть/помеша́ть + dat + infin	*to prevent* sb from doing sth, eg Ра́дио меша́ет мне рабо́тать, *The radio is stopping me working*
	прерыва́ть/прерва́ть	*to interrupt*, ie stop (sb) talking
	заде́рживать/задержа́ть	*to detain*, eg Он был заде́ржан полице́йским, *He was stopped by a policeman*
	уде́рживать/удержа́ть от + gen of verbal noun	*to restrain* (sb from doing sth)
	затыка́ть/заткну́ть	*to plug, seal*
STORM	**бу́ря**	*rainstorm, tempest*
	гроза́	*thunderstorm*
	мете́ль (f)	*snowstorm*
	вью́га	*blizzard* (snow swirling)
	пурга́	= вью́га
	бура́н	*snowstorm* (in steppes)
	урага́н	*hurricane*
	шквал	*squall* (at sea); also *barrage* (mil and fig)
	шторм	*gale* (at sea)
	вихрь (m)	*whirlwind*; also fig, eg революцио́нный вихрь, *the revolutionary storm*

	град	*hail*; also fig, eg пуль, оскорблéний, *of bullets, insults*
	штýрм	military assault
STORY	**расскáз**	*tale*
	пóвесть (f)	*novella*
	скáзка	*fairy tale*
	истóрия	series of events
	анекдóт	*anecdote, joke*
	фáбула	*plot* (literary term)
	вы́думка	*fabrication, invention*
	небыли́ца	*cock-and-bull story*
	статья́	in newspaper
STRING	**верёвка**	*cord, rope*
	бечёвка	*twine*
	ни́тка	*thread*, eg ни́тка жéмчуга, *a string of pearls*
	струнá	of musical instrument
	ряд	*row, series*
	верени́ца	line of people, animals or vehicles
	цепь (f)	*chain*
STRONG	**си́льный**	in various senses
	крéпкий	*sturdy, robust*, eg крéпкий чай, *strong tea*; крéпкое винó, *strong wine*
	прóчный	*stout, durable*, eg прóчный фундáмент, *a strong foundation*
	твёрдый	*firm*, eg твёрдая вéра, *strong faith*
	убеди́тельный	*convincing*, eg убеди́тельный дóвод, *a strong argument*
TEACH	**учи́ть/научи́ть** когó-н + dat of subject taught or + infin	to give instruction, eg Я учý егó испáнскому языкý, *I am teaching him Spanish*; Онá научи́ла меня́ игрáть на скри́пке, *She taught me to play the violin*
	обучáть/обучи́ть	= учи́ть/научи́ть
	проýчивать/проучи́ть когó-н (R1)	*to give sb a good lesson*
	преподавáть (impf)	to give instruction in higher educational institution

TEACHER	**учи́тель(ница)**	*schoolteacher*
	преподава́тель(ница)	in higher education
	воспита́тель(ница)	sb responsible for general, including moral, upbringing
	наста́вник	*mentor*
THEN	**тогда́**	*at that time*; also *in that case* in conditional sentences (see 10.9)
	пото́м	*afterwards, next*
	зате́м	*afterwards, next*
THICK	**то́лстый**	*fat*, eg то́лстый ломо́ть, *a thick slice*
	густо́й	*dense*, eg густо́й тума́н, *a thick fog;* густо́й суп, *thick soup*
	тупо́й (R1)	*dull-witted*
THIN	**то́нкий**	not fat or thick, eg то́нкий ломо́ть, *a thin slice*
	худо́й	*slender*, eg худо́е лицо́, *a thin face*
	худоща́вый	*lean*
	исхуда́лый	*emaciated*
	исхуда́вший	= исхуда́лый
	жи́дкий	of liquid, eg жи́дкий суп, *thin soup*
	ре́дкий	*sparse*, eg ре́дкие во́лосы, *thin hair*
	неубеди́тельный	*unconvincing*, eg неубеди́тельный до́вод, *a thin argument*
THINK	**ду́мать/поду́мать**	basic verb
	выду́мывать/вы́думать	*to think up, invent, fabricate*
	обду́мывать/обду́мать	*to think over, ponder*, eg Он обду́мал план, *He thought over the plan*
	приду́мывать/приду́мать	*to think up, devise*, eg Они́ приду́мали отгово́рку, *They thought up an excuse*
	проду́мывать/проду́мать	= обду́мывать/обду́мать
	мы́слить	to engage in thinking, eg Она́ мы́слит я́сно, *She thinks clearly*
	счита́ть/счесть + acc + instr	*to consider*, eg Я счита́ю сестру́ спосо́бной же́нщиной, *I think my sister is a capable woman*
	мне/тебе́/нам ка́жется	*I/you/we think*
	мне/тебе́/нам ду́мается	= мне/тебе́/нам ка́жется

	быть хоро́шего/высо́кого/ дурно́го мне́ния о ко́м-н	*to think well/highly/badly of sb*
TIME	**вре́мя**	in various senses; also *tense*
	раз	*occasion*
	эпо́ха	*epoch*
	пери́од	*period*
	век	*age, century*
	срок	*fixed period, term*
	моме́нт	*moment*, eg в подходя́щий моме́нт, *at the right time*
	сезо́н	*season*
	слу́чай	*instance*, eg в девяти́ слу́чаях из десяти́, *nine times out of ten*
	час	*hour, time of day*, eg Кото́рый час? *What time is it?* В кото́ром часу́? *At what time?*
	такт	mus term, eg отбива́ть/отби́ть такт, *to keep time*
	пора́ + infin	*it is time* (to do sth)
	досу́г	*spare time, leisure*, eg на досу́ге, *in one's spare time*
	в два счёта (R1)	*in no time, in a jiffy*
	Note also **во́время**, *on time*; **впервы́е**, *for the first time*; **заблаговре́менно** (R3), *in good time.*	
TOP	**верх**	in various senses
	верши́на	*summit*, eg горы́, *of a mountain*
	верху́шка	*apex*, eg де́рева, *of a tree*
	маку́шка	*top of the head*
	пове́рхность (f)	*surface*
	колпачо́к	of a pen
	кры́шка	*lid*, eg коро́бки, *of a box*
	нача́ло	*beginning*, eg страни́цы, *of a page*
	пе́рвое ме́сто	*first place, pre-eminence*
	во весь го́лос	*at the top of one's voice*
	на седьмо́м не́бе	*on top of the world*
	наверху́	*on top*
	све́рху	*from the top*

TOUCH	**тро́гать/тро́нуть**	basic verb, eg тро́нуть что-н рука́ми, *to touch sth with one's hands*; also fig, eg Её слова́ глубоко́ тро́нули меня́, *Her words touched me deeply*
	дотра́гиваться/дотро́нуться до + gen	*to make contact with*, eg Не дотро́нься до горя́чего утюга́, *Don't touch the hot iron*
	затра́гивать/затро́нуть	*to affect, touch on*, eg затро́нуть те́му, *to touch on a theme*
	каса́ться/косну́ться + gen	*to make contact with*, eg косну́ться мяча́, *to touch the ball; to touch on*, eg косну́ться сло́жного вопро́са, *to touch on a difficult question*
	прикаса́ться/прикосну́ться к + dat	*to touch lightly, brush against*
	достава́ть/доста́ть до + gen	*to reach*, eg доста́ть до дна, *to touch the bottom*
	дотя́гиваться/дотяну́ться до + gen	*to stretch as far as*, eg Он дотяну́лся до потолка́, *He touched the ceiling*
	равня́ться/сравни́ться с + instr	to compare in quality with, eg В матема́тике никто́ не мо́жет равни́ться с ней, *No one can touch her in mathematics*
	стрельну́ть (R1)	*to cadge*, eg Он стрельну́л у меня́ пятёрку, *He touched me for a fiver*
	не есть	*not to touch food*
	не пить	*not to touch alcohol*
	Note the expression **задева́ть/заде́ть** кого́-н **за живо́е**, *to touch sb to the quick.*	
TRY	**пыта́ться/попыта́ться**	*to attempt*
	про́бовать/попро́бовать	= пыта́ться in R1/2; also *to sample, taste* (food)
	стара́ться/постара́ться	*to attempt* (more effort than пыта́ться)
	стреми́ться (impf) + infin	*to strive* (to do sth)
	ме́рить/поме́рить	*to try on* (shoes, clothing)
TURN	**повёртывать*/поверну́ть** (trans)	basic verb, eg поверну́ть ключ, руль, го́лову, *to turn a key, steering wheel, one's head*
	повёртываться*/поверну́ться (intrans)	basic verb
	вывёртывать*/вы́вернуть	*to turn (inside) out*, eg вы́вернуть карма́н, *to turn out one's pocket*
	завёртывать*/заверну́ть	*to turn* (a corner), eg заверну́ть за́ угол, *to turn a corner*; also *to tighten* or *to shut off*

	by turning, eg заверну́ть га́йку, кран, *to tighten a nut, turn off a tap*
обёртываться*/оберну́ться	*to turn one's head; to turn out*, eg Собы́тия оберну́лись ина́че, *Events turned out differently*
перевёртывать*/переверну́ть	*to turn over, invert*, eg переверну́ть страни́цу, *to turn a page*
подвёртываться/подверну́ться	*to turn up, appear, crop up*
развора́чиваться/разверну́ться (intrans)	*to swing round, do a U-turn*
свёртывать*/сверну́ть	*to turn off* (in a new direction), eg сверну́ть с доро́ги, *to turn off the road*
крути́ть/покрути́ть	*to twist, wind*, eg крути́ть ру́чку, *to turn a handle*
верте́ть (impf; trans) + acc or instr	*to rotate, twirl*, eg Он ве́ртит зо́нтиком, *He is twirling his umbrella*
верте́ться (intrans)	*to rotate, revolve*
враща́ть (trans)	*to rotate, revolve*
враща́ться (intrans)	*to rotate, revolve*, eg Колесо́ ме́дленно враща́ется, *The wheel is slowly turning*
кружи́ться/закружи́ться	*to whirl, spin round*
направля́ть/напра́вить что-н **на** + acc	*to direct sth at/towards*, eg напра́вить своё внима́ние на очередну́ю зада́чу, *to turn one's attention to the next task*
превраща́ть/преврати́ть что-н **в** + acc	*to change sth into (sth)*
превраща́ться/преврати́ться в + acc (intrans)	*to change into (sth)*
станови́ться/стать + instr	*to turn into, become*, eg Он стал пья́ницей, *He has turned into a drunkard*
обраща́ться/обрати́ться к кому́-н	*to address oneself to sb*
переходи́ть/перейти́ к + dat	*to switch over to*, eg Она́ перешла́ к друго́му вопро́су, *She turned to another question*
включа́ть/включи́ть	*to turn on* (switch, tap)
выключа́ть/вы́ключить	*to turn off* (switch, tap)
гаси́ть/погаси́ть	*to turn out, extinguish*, eg погаси́ть свет, *to turn out the light*
выгоня́ть/вы́гнать	*to turn out, drive out*, eg Оте́ц вы́гнал

		сы́на и́з дому, *The father turned his son out of the house*
	прогоня́ть/прогна́ть	*to turn away, banish*
	восстава́ть/восста́ть про́тив + gen	*to turn against*, eg Толпа́ восста́ла про́тив мили́ции, *The crowd turned against the police*
	ока́зываться/оказа́ться + instr	*to turn out/prove to be*, eg Она́ оказа́лась прекра́сным адвока́том, *She turned out to be an excellent lawyer*
	закрыва́ть/закры́ть глаза́ на + acc	*to turn a blind eye to*
	бледне́ть/побледне́ть	*to turn pale*
	красне́ть/покрасне́ть	*to turn red, blush*

* Note: the impf forms in **-вёртывать** marked with an asterisk have alternative forms in **-вора́чивать (повора́чивать, повора́чиваться, вывора́чивать, завора́чиать, обора́чиваться, перевора́чивать, свора́чивать** respectively).

USE	**употребля́ть/употреби́ть** + acc	in various senses
	по́льзоваться/воспо́льзоваться + instr	*to make use of*, eg по́льзоваться услу́гами, *to make use of services*
	испо́льзовать (impf and pf) + acc	*to utilise*
	применя́ть/примени́ть	*to apply*, eg примени́ть я́дерную эне́ргию, *to use nuclear energy*
	эксплуати́ровать	*to exploit*
	прибега́ть/прибе́гнуть к + dat	*to resort to*
VIEW	**вид**	what can be seen, eg вид на о́зеро, *view of the lake*; вид с пти́чьего полёта, *bird's-eye view*
	взгляд	*opinion*, eg на мой взгляд, *in my view*
	мне́ние	*opinion*
	убежде́ние	*conviction*
	то́чка зре́ния	*point of view*
VILLAGE	**село́**	community with a church
	дере́вня	smaller community than село́; also means *country(side)*
	посёлок	*settlement*
VISIT	**навеща́ть/навести́ть**	*to call on*, esp people
	посеща́ть/посети́ть	*to call on, go to*, esp places
	наноси́ть/нанести́ визи́т (R3b)	*to pay a visit*

	быть у кого́-н **в гостя́х**	*to be a guest at sb's place*
	идти́/пойти́ в го́сти к + dat	*to go to* (as a guest)
	гости́ть/погости́ть у + gen	*to stay with* (as a guest)
	заходи́ть/зайти́ к + dat	*to call on*
	быва́ть/побыва́ть в + prep	*to spend some time in* (town, country)
	осма́тривать/осмотре́ть	*to inspect*, eg осмотре́ть достопримеча́тельности, *to visit the sights*
	сове́товаться/посове́товаться с + instr	*to consult* (eg doctor)
WAY	**путь** (m)	*road, path*, esp in abstract sense, eg на обра́тном пути́, *on the way back;* на полпути́, *halfway*
	доро́га	*road*
	направле́ние	*direction*
	спо́соб	*means, method*
	сре́дство	*means, method*
	о́браз	*manner, fashion*, eg таки́м о́бразом, *in this way*
	вход	*way in*
	вы́ход	*way out*
	перехо́д	*way across*
	расстоя́ние	*distance, way off*
	Note: *way* is often not directly translated in adverbial phrases, eg **по-дру́жески**, *in a friendly way*.	
WIN	**выи́грывать/вы́играть**	*to be the victor*; also trans, eg вы́играть приз, *to win a prize*
	побежда́ть/победи́ть	*to triumph, prevail*, eg Она́ победи́ла в бе́ге, *She won the race*
	завоёвывать/завоева́ть (trans)	*to gain, secure*, eg завоева́ть золоту́ю меда́ль, *to win a gold medal*
	одержа́ть (pf) **побе́ду** (R3)	*to triumph*
WINDOW	**окно́**	general word; also *free period* for teacher
	око́шко	dimin of окно́; eg of ticket-office
	фо́рточка	small window within window which can be opened for ventilation
	витри́на	*shop window*
	витра́ж	*stained-glass window*

WORK	**рабо́та**	in various senses
	труд	*labour*
	слу́жба	official/professional service
	ме́сто	position at work
	заня́тия (pl; gen заня́тий)	*studies, classes* (at school, university)
	зада́ча	*task*
	де́ятельность (f)	*activity*
	произведе́ние	creation produced by artist
	сочине́ние	= произведе́ние; собра́ние сочине́ний Пу́шкина, *collection of Pushkin's works*
	тво́рчество	corpus of works by writer, *œuvre*
WORKER	**рабо́тник**	sb who does work
	слу́жащий	*white-collar worker*
	рабо́чий	*manual worker*
	трудя́щийся	= рабо́чий, but more respectful
	пролета́рий	*proletarian*
	тру́женик (R3, rhet)	*toiler*
	работя́га (m and f; R1, slightly pej)	*hard worker*
WORLD	**мир**	in most senses, esp abstract including eg spheres of existence or activity, civilisations
	во всём ми́ре	*all over the world*
	живо́тный мир	*the animal world*
	расти́тельный мир	*the vegetable world*
	нау́чный мир	*the scientific world*
	дре́вний мир	*the ancient world*
	свет	narrower use, tends to be more concrete, eg Ста́рый свет, *the Old World*; Но́вый свет, *the New World*; путеше́ствие вокру́г све́та, *journey round the world*
	земно́й шар	*the Earth, globe*
	вселе́нная	*universe*
	о́бщество	*society*
	круги́ (pl; gen круго́в)	*circles*

	жизнь (f)	*life*
WRONG	**не тот/та/то**	not the right thing
	не тогда́	not at the right time
	не там	not in the right place
	не туда́	not to the right place
	не по а́дресу	*to the wrong address*
	непра́вый	of person, eg Он непра́в, *He is wrong*
	непра́вильный	*incorrect*, eg непра́вильное реше́ние, *incorrect decision*
	оши́бочный	*mistaken, erroneous*
	ошиба́ться/ошиби́ться	*to be mistaken*
	фальши́вый	*false*, eg фальши́вая но́та, *wrong note*
	неподходя́щий	*unsuitable*
	не на́до* + impf infin	*it is wrong to/one should not*
	не ну́жно*	= не на́до
	не сле́дует*	= не на́до
	не рабо́тает	*is not functioning*
	поша́ливает (R1)	*plays up from time to time*, eg of mechanism

* Stylistically these synonymous forms may be arranged in the following ascending order of formality: не на́до, не ну́жно, не сле́дует.

3.2 Translation of the verb *to be*

Translation of the verb *to be* into Russian gives rise to much difficulty, for it is rendered by some form of its most obvious equivalent, быть, in only a small proportion of instances. The following list gives some indication of the numerous verbs to which Russian resorts in contexts in which an English-speaker might comfortably use some part of the verb *to be*.

- **быть**, which is omitted altogether in the present tense (the omission sometimes being indicated by a dash; see 10.15) may be used when the complement offers a simple definition of the subject, eg

Вес ребёнка—о́коло четырёх килогра́ммов.
The child's weight is about four kilogrammes.
Э́то **была́** коро́ткая война́.
It was a short war.

Note: on use of case in the complement of быть see 10.1.10.

- **бывáть** = *to be* in habitual or frequentative meaning, eg

  Её муж рабóтает в Москвé, но **бывáет** дóма на все прáздники.
  Her husband works in Moscow but is home for all holidays.
  Егó инострáнные друзья́ чáсто у негó **бывáли**.
  His foreign friends often came to see him.

- **явля́ться/яви́ться** may be used when the complement defines the subject, eg

  Основны́ми истóчниками облучéния персонáла на я́дерных реáкторах **явля́ются** продýкты коррóзии металли́ческих повéрхностей труб.
  The products of corrosion of the metallic surfaces of the pipes are the fundamental sources of the irradiation of personnel at nuclear reactors.
  Состоя́вшиеся в Дамáске переговóры **яви́лись** очереднóй попы́ткой найти́ «арáбское решéние» конфли́кта в Зали́ве.
  The talks which took place in Damascus were the latest attempt to find an 'Arab solution' to the Gulf conflict.

Note 1 As is clear from the flavour of the above examples, явля́ться/яви́ться belongs mainly in R3.

2 The complement of явля́ться/яви́ться must be in the instrumental case. The complement is the noun which denotes the broader of the two concepts, whilst the subject, which is in the nominative case, denotes the more specific concept, the precise thing on which the speaker or writer wishes to concentrate.

3 It follows from what is said in note 2 that such relatively vague words as **истóчник**, *source*; **перспекти́ва**, *prospect*; **попы́тка**, *attempt*; **причи́на**, *cause*; **проблéма**, *problem*; **результáт**, *result*; **слéдствие**, *consequence*; **часть**, *part*, will usually be found in the instrumental case when явля́ться/яви́ться is used.

4 In practice the subject (ie the noun in the nominative) often follows явля́ться/яви́ться (see the first example above) because the phrase at the end of the sentence carries special weight and it is on this phrase that the speaker or writer wishes to concentrate (see 10.14 on word order). However, the choice as to which noun should be put in which case does not actually hinge on word order.

- **представля́ть собóй** (impf) is much less common than явля́ться/яви́ться but fulfils the same function of bookish substitute for быть, eg

  Э́ти материáлы **представля́ют собóй** обы́чные при́меси леги́рующих элемéнтов стáли.
  These materials are the usual admixtures in the alloying elements of steel.

Note: the complement of представля́ть собóй is in the accusative case.

- **стать** (pf) is now frequently used as an apparent synonym for явля́ться/яви́ться, eg

  Причи́ной катастрóфы **стáли** техни́ческие неполáдки.
  Technical malfunctions were the cause of the disaster.

Закры́тие ба́зы **ста́ло** одно́й из составны́х часте́й програ́ммы по сокраще́нию ассигнова́ний на оборо́ну.
The closure of the base was one of the components of a programme of defence cuts.

Note: all the points made in notes 1–4 on явля́ться/яви́ться will apply also to стать when it has this function.

- **заключа́ться в** + prep is frequently used in R2/R3 in the sense *to consist in*, eg

Одна́ из гла́вных причи́н недово́льства лицеи́стов **заключа́ется в** том, что они́ обеспоко́ены свои́м бу́дущим.
One of the main causes of the lycée pupils' discontent is that they are worried about their future.

- **состоя́ть в** + prep = заключа́ться in this sense, eg

Преиму́щество хлорфторуглеро́дов пе́ред други́ми вещества́ми **состои́т в** том, что они́ нетокси́чны.
The advantage of CFCs over other substances is that they are not toxic.

- **составля́ть/соста́вить** = *to constitute, to amount to*; it is followed by the accusative case and is particularly common in statistical contexts, eg

В э́том райо́не армя́не **составля́ют** меньшинство́.
Armenians are a minority in this region.
Температу́ра реа́ктора к моме́нту ги́бели подло́дки **составля́ла** се́мьдесят гра́дусов.
The temperature of the reactor at the moment the submarine was destroyed was 70 degrees.

Note: this verb is particularly common in the phrases **составля́ть/соста́вить часть**, *to be a part (of)* and **составля́ть/соста́вить исключе́ние**, *to be an exception.*

- **находи́ться** (impf) may be used when *to be* defines the position or location of people, places or things, and also when state or condition is being described, eg

Президе́нт находи́лся в Крыму́ на о́тдыхе.
The President was on holiday in the Crimea.
Черно́быль **нахо́дится** бли́зко от грани́цы с Белару́сью.
Chernobyl is close to the border with Belarus.
Аэропо́рт **нахо́дится** под контро́лем повста́нцев.
The airport is under the control of the rebels.
Обору́дование **нахо́дится** в отли́чном состоя́нии.
The equipment is in excellent condition.

- **располо́жен** (f **располо́жена**, n **располо́жено**, pl **располо́жены**) may also be used when location is being described, eg

Кипр **располо́жен** киломе́трах в шести́десяти к ю́гу от Ту́рции.
Cyprus is about 60 kilometres south of Turkey.

- **стоя́ть, лежа́ть, сиде́ть** = *to stand, to lie, to be sitting* respectively, eg

  Он **стои́т** в фойе́.
  He's in the foyer.
  Письмо́ **лежи́т** на столе́.
  The letter is on the desk.
  Они́ **сидя́т** в за́ле ожида́ния.
  They're in the waiting room.

- **сто́ить** = *to be worth, to cost*, eg

  Ско́лько **сто́ит** цветно́й телеви́зор?
  How much is a colour television set?

- **прису́тствовать** = *to be present*, eg

  Она́ **прису́тствовала** на заседа́нии.
  She was at the meeting.

- **рабо́тать** = *to work (as)*, eg

  Он **рабо́тает** по́варом.
  He is a cook.

- **служи́ть**, *to serve*, is more or less synonymous with рабо́тать but slightly more formal, eg

  Он **слу́жит** в а́рмии.
  He is in the army.

- **приходи́ться** = *to fall* (of dates), *to stand* in a certain relationship to, eg

  Правосла́вное Рождество́ **прихо́дится** на седьмо́е января́.
  The Orthodox Christmas is on 7 January.
  Он мне **прихо́дится** пра́дедом.
  He is my great-grandfather.

- **есть** is the copula when the subject and complement are the same, eg

  Я начина́ю узнава́ть, кто **есть** кто.
  I am beginning to find out who is who.
  Оши́бка **есть** оши́бка.
  A mistake is a mistake.

Note: есть also occurs in R3, in the scientific/academic or official/business styles, in definitions, eg Квадра́т **есть** прямоуго́льник, у кото́рого все сто́роны равны́, *A square is a rectangle all of whose sides are equal.*

- **существова́ть**, *to exist*, may translate *there is/there are*, eg

  Я ве́рю, что **существу́ет** Бог.
  I believe there is a God.
  В таки́х ситуа́циях **существу́ет** риск возникнове́ния войны́.
  There is a risk of war breaking out in such situations.

- **иметься** may also translate *there is/there are* in the sense of *to be available*, eg

  В го́роде **име́ется** музе́й.
  There is a museum in the town.
  Име́ются интере́сные да́нные об э́том.
  There is interesting information about this.

- **состоя́ться** (pf) may translate *there was/will be* in the sense of *to take place*, eg

  В де́сять часо́в **состои́тся** пресс-конфере́нция.
  There will be a press conference at ten o'clock.

Note: the verb *to be* may be used in English purely for emphasis, eg *It **was** only then that he realised what had happened.* When it has this purely emphatic function *to be* is not rendered in Russian by any verbal equivalent or substitute; the emphasis is conveyed instead by word order or by the manner of the speaker's delivery. Thus the above sentence might be translated: Он то́лько тогда́ по́нял, что случи́лось.

3.3 Translation of English modal auxiliary verbs

Modal verbs express the mood or attitude of the speaker towards an action. The English modals give rise to much difficulty for the English-speaking student trying to render their meaning in a foreign language, as they do for the foreign student of English, because each modal is used in various ways and is more or less interchangeable with one or more other modals in some meanings (eg *can/could, can/may, may/might*). Moreover, the differences of meaning between certain modals (eg *must, should, ought, may, might*) may be so subtle that English-speakers themselves will not agree on their precise nuances.

Not all the possible translations of each English modal are given in this section, but most of their important functions are covered.

CAN

(a) expressing ability or possibility: **мо́жно, мочь**, or (in the sense *to know how* to do sth) **уме́ть**, eg

This can be done at once.	Э́то **мо́жно** сде́лать сра́зу.
I can't lift this box.	Не **могу́** подня́ть э́тот я́щик.
He can swim.	Он **уме́ет** пла́вать.

(b) expressing request or permission (*can* is synonymous in this sense with *may* except in very formal English): **мо́жно, мочь**, eg

Can/May I come in?	**Мо́жно** войти́?
Can I go to the park, mum?	Мам, **мо́жно** пойду́ в парк? (R1)
You can/may smoke.	Вы **мо́жете** кури́ть.

(c) expressing right, entitlement: **мочь, име́ть пра́во**, eg

We can vote at eighteen.
Мы **имéем прáво** голосовáть в восемнáдцать лет.

(d) with verbs of perception, when *can* bears little meaning: auxiliary omitted, eg

I can see a dog.	Я **вúжу** собáку.
Can you hear?	**Слы́шно**?

(e) expressing doubt: **неужéли**, eg

Can this be right?	**Неужéли** э́то прáвда?

(f) in negative (*cannot*), synonymous with *may not, must not*, expressing prohibition: **нельзя́** + impf infin; **не** + 3rd person plural verb; also **не разрешáется, воспрещáется** (R3; formal, eg in notices):

You can't go in.	**Нельзя́** входúть.
You can't smoke here.	Здесь **не кýрят**.
	Здесь курúть **не разрешáется**. (R3)
You can't run up and down the escalators	Бéгать по эскалáторам **воспрещáется**.

(g) *cannot help*: **не мочь не** + infin, eg

I can't help laughing	**Я не могý не** смея́ться.

COULD

(a) past tense of *can*, ie = *was/were able to*: use past tense forms of the translations given under *can* above;

(b) polite request: **не мóжете ли вы; не моглú бы вы; пожáлуйста**, eg

Could you help me?	**Не мóжете ли** вы помóчь мне?
	Не моглú бы вы помóчь мне?
Could you pass the salt?	Передáйте, **пожáлуйста**, соль.

(c) *could have* (also *might have*), expressing unfulfilled possibility in past: **мог/моглá/моглó/моглú бы**, eg

She could/might have done it [but did not].
Онá **моглá бы** э́то сдéлать.

(d) *could have* (also *may have, might have*), expressing uncertainty as to whether action took place: **мóжет быть**, eg

She could/might have done it [and may have done].
Мóжет быть онá и сдéлала э́то.

(e) expressing emotion, wish: various translations, eg

She could have wept for joy.
Онá **готóва былá** заплáкать от рáдости.
I could have killed him.
Мне хотéлось убúть его́.

MAY

(a) expressing request or permission: see *can* (b);

(b) expressing possibility: **мочь, мóжет быть, мóжет** (= мóжет быть in R1), **пожáлуй** (*perhaps*), **возмóжно**, eg

	He may lose his way.	Он **мóжет** заблудиться.
	They may have gone home.	Они́, **мóжет (быть)**, пошли́ домóй.
	She may be right.	Oнá, **пожáлуй**, правá.
	It may be snowing there.	**Возмóжно**, там идёт снег.

(c) after verbs of hoping and fearing and in concessive clauses (see 10.10) *may* is not directly translated, a future or subjunctive form of the Russian verb being used instead, eg

I hope he may recover.	Надéюсь, что он **вы́здоровеет**.
I fear he may die.	Я боюсь, **как бы** он **не у́мер**.
I shall find you wherever you may be.	Я найду́ вас, **где бы** вы **ни́ были**.

(d) expressing wish in certain phrases:

May the best man win.	**Да победи́т сильнéйший**!
May he rest in peace.	**Мир прáху его**!

(e) *may not*, expressing prohibition: see *can* (f).

MIGHT

(a) expressing possibility: synonymous with *may* (b) (though *might* is perhaps more colloquial);

(b) *might have* in the sense *could have, may have*: see *could* (c) and (d);

(c) after verbs of hoping and fearing and in concessive clauses: synonymous with *may* (c);

(d) expressing formal polite request in interrogative sentences: various formulae, eg

Might I suggest that. . .
Позвóльте мне предложи́ть, чтóбы. . .
Might I discuss this matter with you tomorrow?
Мóжет быть, вы зáвтра разреши́те мне обсуди́ть э́то дéло с вáми?

(e) *might have*, expressing reproach: **мог/моглá/моглó/могли́ бы**, eg

You might have told me that.
Вы **могли́ бы** мне сказáть э́то.

MUST

(a) expressing obligation, necessity: **дóлжен/должнá/должны́, нáдо, ну́жно, слéдует** (see also note on 'wrong' in 3.1), eg

She must work.	Oнá **должнá** рабóтать.
We must get up early.	Мы **должны́** встать рáно.
You must come at once.	Тебé **нáдо** прийти́ срáзу же.
(We) must hurry.	**Ну́жно** торопи́ться.
One must observe the rules.	**Слéдует** соблюдáть прáвила.

(b) expressing certainty: **должнó быть**, surrounded by commas, eg

She must have gone.	Oнá, **должнó быть**, ушлá.
He must know this.	Он, **должнó быть**, знáет э́то.

(c) *must not*, expressing prohibition: see *can* (f).

OUGHT

(a) expressing advisability, recommendation, obligation (more or less synonymous with *should*): **слéдовало бы, дóлжен/должнá/должны́**, eg

He ought to drink less.
Ему́ **сле́довало бы** поме́ньше пить.
She ought [is obliged] to be at work today.
Она́ **должна́** быть на рабо́те сего́дня.

(b) *ought not*, expressing inadvisability, prohibition: **не сле́довало бы**, eg

You ought not to laugh at him.
(Вам) **не сле́довало бы** смея́ться над ним.

(c) *ought to have*, expressing reproach, regret at omission: **сле́довало бы, до́лжен был/должна́ была́/должны́ бы́ли бы**, eg

She ought to have passed her examination.
Она́ **должна́ была́ бы** сдать экза́мен.
You ought to have helped us.
Вам **сле́довало бы** помо́чь нам.

(d) expressing probability (less certain than *must* (b) but more certain than *may* (b) and *might* (a)): **наве́рно(е), вероя́тно**, eg

He ought to be [probably is] at work today.
Он **наве́рное** на рабо́те сего́дня.
She ought to be [probably is] home by now.
Она́ **вероя́тно** уже́ до́ма.

SHALL

(a) expressing 1st person singular and 1st person plural of future tense: future tense, eg

I shall write to him. — **Я напишу́** ему́.

(b) expressing promise or threat (synonymous with *will*): perfective future, eg

You shall receive the money tomorrow. — **Полу́чишь** де́ньги за́втра.
You shall pay for this. — Ты за э́то **заплатишь**.

(c) in questions asking whether sth is desirable or obligatory: impersonal construction with dative subject (or with no subject stated) and infinitive, eg

Shall I call in tomorrow? — **Мне зайти́** за́втра?
Shall I bring you some more vodka? — **Принести́** вам ещё во́дки?

(d) in R3b, in legal and diplomatic parlance, expressing obligation (synonymous with *will*): present tense, eg

The Russian side shall meet all these costs.
Росси́йская сторона́ **берёт** на себя́ все э́ти расхо́ды.

SHOULD

(a) synonymous in ordinary English speech with *would* (a), (b) and (c);

(b) expressing advisability, recommendation, obligation: more or less synonymous with *ought* (a);

(c) *should have*, expressing reproach or regret at omission: more or less synonymous with *ought* (c);

(d) expressing probability: more or less synonymous with *ought* (d);

(e) expressing modest assertion: various formulae, eg

		I should think that...	**Мне ка́жется**, что...
		I should say that...	**Я бы сказа́л(а)**, что...

(f) expressing surprise, indignation: various formulae, eg

Why should you suspect me?
С како́й э́то ста́ти вы меня́ подозрева́ете?
How should I know?
Отку́да мне **знать**?
You should see him!
Посмотре́ли бы вы на него́!

(g) as a subjunctive form in certain subordinate clauses: **что́бы** + past tense, eg

Everybody demanded that he should be punished.
Все потре́бовали, **что́бы** он **был** нака́зан.
I proposed that they should return the money.
Я предложи́л(а), **что́бы** они́ **возврати́ли** де́ньги.

WILL

(a) as auxiliary forming 2nd and 3rd person singular and plural of future tense (and in ordinary English speech also 1st person singular and plural forms): future tense, eg

She will arrive tomorrow. Она́ **прие́дет** за́втра.

(b) expressing probability, eg *She'll be home by now*: more or less synonymous with *ought* (d).

(c) expressing habitual action: imperfective verb, eg

He'll sit for hours in front of the television.
Он **сиди́т** це́лыми часа́ми пе́ред телеви́зором.

Note: *Boys will be boys*, **Ма́льчики остаю́тся ма́льчиками**.

(d) expressing polite invitation, exhortation or proposal in the form of a question: see *would* (d);

(e) *will not*, expressing refusal or disinclination: various renderings, eg

I will not do it.
Э́того я **не сде́лаю**.
Я не наме́рен(а) э́того де́лать.
Я не хочу́ э́того де́лать.

WOULD

(a) as 2nd and 3rd person singular and plural auxiliary (and in ordinary speech also 1st person singular and plural), expressing conditional mood: past tense form + **бы**, eg

They would go out if it stopped raining.
Они́ **вы́шли бы**, е́сли бы прекрати́лся дождь.

(b) as 2nd and 3rd person singular and plural auxiliary (and in ordinary speech also 1st person singular and plural) indicating future in indirect speech (see 10.6(a)): perfective future, eg

I told you I would come.	Я тебе́ сказа́л, что **приду́**.
He said he would ring me.	Он сказа́л, что **позвони́т** мне.

(c) with *like*, expressing wish: **хоте́л/хоте́ла/хоте́ли бы**, **хоте́лось бы**, eg

They would like to leave.
Они́ **хоте́ли бы** уйти́.
I would like to thank you warmly.
Мне **хоте́лось бы** тепло́ поблагодари́ть вас.

(d) expressing polite invitation, exhortation or proposal in the form of a question (more or less synonymous with *will*): various formulae or a modified imperative, eg

Would you close the window please?
Вам не тру́дно } закры́ть окно́?
Вас не затрудни́т } закры́ть окно́?
Не хоти́те ли вы } закры́ть окно́?
Will you wait a moment?
Подожди́те мину́точку, **пожа́луйста**.

(e) expressing frequent action in the past: imperfective past, possibly with a suitable adverb or adverbial phrase, eg

They would often pick mushrooms in the wood.
Они́, **быва́ло, ча́сто собира́ли** грибы́ в лесу́.
As a rule she would read in the evenings.
Она́, **как пра́вило, чита́ла** по вечера́м.

3.4 Transitive and intransitive verbs

A particular problem that confronts the English-speaking student of Russian is the morphological or lexical distinction which Russian makes more widely and clearly than English between transitive and intransitive verbs. Many English verbs which may function as either transitive or intransitive forms (eg *to improve, to hang*) must be rendered in different ways in Russian depending on whether or not they have a direct object. The student needs to be aware of two types of distinction.

- The distinction between transitive and intransitive usage may be made by the use of non-reflexive and reflexive forms respectively, eg Э́та ме́ра **улу́чшит** ситуа́цию, *This measure will improve* [trans] *the situation* and Ситуа́ция **улу́чшится**, *The situation will improve* [intrans]. This type of distinction applies to a very large number of common verbs (see 10.8).

- Other English verbs must be rendered in Russian by different verbs depending on whether they are used transitively or intransitively, eg Она́ **ве́шает** карти́ну на сте́ну, *She is hanging* [trans] *a picture on the wall*, but Карти́на **виси́т** на стене́, *A picture is hanging* [intrans] *on the wall.*

Common English verbs which must be rendered in Russian by distinct transitive or intransitive forms include the following:

	trans	intrans
to boil	**кипяти́ть/вскипяти́ть**	**кипе́ть/вскипе́ть**
to burn	**жечь/сжечь**	**горе́ть/сгоре́ть**
to drown	**топи́ть/утопи́ть**	**тону́ть/утону́ть**
to grow	**выра́щивать/вы́растить**	**расти́/вы́расти**
to hang	**ве́шать/пове́сить**	**висе́ть**
to hurt	**причиня́ть/причини́ть боль**	**боле́ть**
to rot	**гнои́ть/сгнои́ть**	**гнить/сгнить**
to sink	**топи́ть/потопи́ть** or **затопля́ть/затопи́ть**	**тону́ть/потону́ть** (R1) **тону́ть/затону́ть**
to sit (down)	**сажа́ть/посади́ть**	**сади́ться/сесть**
to smell	**чу́вствовать** or **ню́хать/поню́хать**	**па́хнуть**
to stand	**ста́вить/поста́вить**	**стоя́ть**
to taste	**различа́ть/различи́ть** or **чу́вствова́ть**	**име́ть при́вкус**

Note: in some cases the Russian transitive and intransitive verbs contain the same root, but in others they are derived from quite distinct roots (eg **жечь/сжечь** and **горе́ть/сгоре́ть**).

3.5 Translation of English forms ending in *-ing*

This English form has many functions, and Russian renders these functions in various ways.

(a) English progressive tenses: an imperfective verb, eg

I am going home.	**Я иду́** домо́й.
She was writing a letter.	Она́ **писа́ла** письмо́.
They'll be watching TV tonight.	Они́ **бу́дут смотре́ть** телеви́зор сего́дня ве́чером.

(b) attendant action, or lack of it: a separate clause, which in R3 might contain a gerund (see 8.7.1–2, 10.11.1), eg

He broke his leg while playing football.
Пока́ он игра́л/Игра́я в футбо́л, он слома́л себе́ но́гу.
You can find out about this by listening to the radio.
Е́сли слу́шать/Слу́шая ра́дио, мо́жно узна́ть об э́том.
She left the room without answering a single question.
Она́ вы́шла из ко́мнаты, **не отве́тив ни на оди́н вопро́с**.

(c) action prior to that denoted by the main verb: a subordinate clause, which in R3 may contain a perfective gerund, eg

I telephoned him on finding out about this.
Узна́в об э́том, я позвони́л(а) ему́.

After discussing the matter they came to a decision.
Обсуди́в де́ло, они́ пришли́ к реше́нию.

(d) in an English phrase describing a noun (equivalent to a relative clause): either a relative clause with **кото́рый** or, in R3, an active participle (see 8.7.3–4, 10.11.2), eg

a factory producing lorries
заво́д, **кото́рый произво́дит/производя́щий** грузовики́
for a firm specialising in trade with Russia
для фи́рмы, **кото́рая специализи́руется/специализи́рующейся** в торго́вле с Росси́ей

(e) English verbal noun describing some action or process, result or place of action, material, inner state or abstract concept: a Russian verbal noun (possibly with the suffix **-ние**, see 7.7.1), eg

reading	**чте́ние**
teaching	**обуче́ние**
building	**зда́ние**
lodging	**жили́ще**
lining	**подкла́дка**
feeling	**чу́вство**
hearing	**слух**

(f) English gerund, denoting some activity: verbal noun or infinitive, eg

His favourite subject is drawing.
Его́ люби́мый предме́т—**рисова́ние**.
I like playing chess.
Я люблю́ **игра́ть** в ша́хматы.

(g) after verbs of perception: subordinate clause introduced by **как**, eg

I heard you singing.	Я **слы́шал(а), как** ты пе́ла.
We saw him getting on a bus.	Мы **ви́дели, как** он сади́лся в авто́бус.

(h) after the verb *to keep*: **всё** + imperfective verb or **не перестава́ть** + imperfective infinitive, eg

Она́ **всё повторя́ла** те же слова́/Она́ **не перестава́ла повторя́ть** те же слова́.
She kept (on) repeating the same words.

(i) after *from* used with verbs such as *prevent, stop*: Russian infinitive, eg

You are preventing/stopping me from working.
Ты меша́ешь мне **рабо́тать**.

(j) often a construction containing **то** in the case appropriate in the context followed by **что́бы** + infinitive may be used, eg

We all have an interest in taking the best decisions.
Все мы заинтересо́ваны **в том, что́бы** приня́ть наилу́чшие реше́ния.

3.6 Translation of *too, also, as well*

The distinction between **та́кже** and **то́же** gives rise to problems for English-speakers. Та́кже may be used in most circumstances, but то́же is more restricted in its use. The following distinction can be made.

- **то́же** may be used when an additional subject is performing an action, eg

  Ты идёшь в кино́? Я **то́же** пойду́.
  Are you going to the cinema? I'll come too.
  Жена́ лю́бит му́зыку. Я **то́же** люблю́ му́зыку.
  My wife likes music. I like music too.

- **та́кже** (often in the phrase **а та́кже**) is used when a single subject is performing an additional action or performing an action that affects an additional object, eg

  Я сего́дня был(а́) на вы́ставке, **а та́кже** порабо́тал(а).
  I went to an exhibition today and did a bit of work too.
  Я интересу́юсь литерату́рой, **а та́кже** те́атром.
  I'm interested in literature and also in the theatre.

- **и** is very often used in the sense of *also, too, as well*, eg

  Экономи́ческий кри́зис приведёт к безрабо́тице. Возни́кнут **и** социа́льные пробле́мы.
  The economic crisis will lead to unemployment. Social problems will also arise.
  Над Антаркти́дой обнару́жена огро́мная дыра́. Наблюда́ется уменьше́ние озо́нового сло́я **и** над мно́гими гу́сто населёнными райо́нами плане́ты.
  A huge hole has been discovered over Antarctica. A reduction in the ozone layer is being observed over many densely populated regions of the planet as well.

Note: in clauses with a negative verb и may have the meaning *either*, eg Премьер-мини́стр не объясни́л, почему́ инфля́ция подняла́сь до тако́го у́ровня. В его́ ре́чи не нашли́ ме́ста **и** други́е о́стрые пробле́мы, *The prime minister did not explain why inflation had risen to such a level. Other serious problems found no place either in his speech.*

4 Vocabulary and idiom

4.1 Neologisms

The radical changes in Russian life, the sudden greatly increased exposure to Western influence, and the introduction of large numbers of new institutions, habits and concepts have led to the flooding of the Russian language with neologisms. These neologisms relate in particular to the ideology of *perestroika*, the economy and its management, social problems, scientific and technological progress, education and culture, law and order, and international and inter-ethnic relations.

Many of the neologisms are loanwords from other languages. Neologisms of this type, which are exemplified in 4.1.1, may be absorbed into Russian without morphological adaptation, if they are nouns (eg **бри́финг**, **хо́спис**), but the adjectives, verbs and also many nouns among them require the addition of Russian affixes to the foreign root (eg **вертика́льный**, **митингова́ть**, **самофинанси́рование**).

Many other neologisms, however, are derived from existing Russian resources by various means (see 4.1.2). These means include composition of acronyms (eg **бич**, **бомж**); affixation (eg **выводи́ловка**, **теневи́к**); and polysemanticisation (eg **вымыва́ть**), perhaps on the basis of some foreign model (eg **я́стреб**, *hawk*, used in a figurative sense).

The following lists contain only a small proportion of the neologisms which now occur in the Russian press and may therefore be felt to have some currency. These words belong in R2, and may therefore be used in most contexts, unless otherwise indicated.

4.1.1 Loanwords

A large number of words have entered Russian from non-Slavonic peoples and languages at various times in its history, for example from the Varangians who established the Riurikid dynasty in the ninth century (eg **я́корь**, *anchor*); from the Turkic nomads who inhabited the southern steppes in the early Middle Ages (eg **ло́шадь**, *horse*); from Greek around the time of the conversion of Russia to Christianity in the tenth century (eg **а́нгел**, *angel*; **ева́нгелие**, *the Gospels*); from the Tatars who ruled over Russia from the thirteenth to the fifteenth centuries (eg **де́ньги**, *money*; **тамо́жня**, *customs*; **ярлы́к**, *label*); from German, from the time of Peter the Great at the beginning of the eighteenth century (eg

банк, *bank*; **университе́т**, *university*); from French, from the middle of the eighteenth century on (eg **пьеса**, *play*; **те́атр**, *theatre*).

In the twentieth century a huge number of words of foreign, especially English, origin have entered Russian, eg **автостра́да**, *motorway*; **грейпфру́т**, *grapefruit*; **джаз**, *jazz*; **кокте́йль** (m), *cocktail*; **комба́йн**, *combine (harvester)*; **та́нкер**, *tanker*; **тра́улер**, *trawler*; **тролле́йбус**, *trolleybus* (all borrowed in the 1930s); **аквала́нг**, *aqualung*; **бадминто́н**, *badminton*; **бики́ни** (n, indecl), *bikini*; **хо́бби** (n, indecl), *hobby* (all in the post-Stalinist period when Zhdanovism abated and attitudes towards things Western again relaxed). The influx of such words has been particularly rapid since the introduction of *glasnost'* (the word is itself an example of the much smaller number of words that are loanwords from Russian in English and other Western European languages) and the breakdown of the Soviet Union.

It should be borne in mind that the position of many loanwords in the language must be very unstable. The foreign student might try to distinguish between (a) those for which there seems a genuine need, inasmuch as they denote a new concept which an existing Russian word does not convey, or at least does not convey with the necessary flavour, and (b) those which seem modish and are used, one suspects, more for the sake of their aura as up-to-date and alien than because they convey essentially new meaning. Examples of words in the first category might be **импи́чмент**, *impeachment* (which in application to Russian political life only became possible with the establishment of a bicameral parliament) and **ме́неджер**, *manager* (which conveys the sense of an executive in a commercial enterprise of a sort not found in a planned economy). An example of a word in the second category might be **крайм**, *crime* as a social phenomenon (which surely hardly adds to the sense of the long-established **престу́пность**). Loanwords in the latter category may in due course prove unnecessary and may therefore be discarded. Moreover, their introduction in such large numbers, and their association with alien – and to many Russians therefore unwelcome – influences may provoke a reaction from linguistic purists (as has happened at other times of relatively intensive linguistic borrowing, for instance at the beginning of the nineteenth century).

Given their probable provenance, loanwords may of course be particularly easy for the foreign speaker of Russian to grasp and deploy. However, the extent to which it is judicious for a foreigner to resort to them may be limited, and will depend on such factors as the nature of the circles in which he or she is moving and the degree to which it is hoped Russians will think the speaker modish or cosmopolitan. It should also be remembered that many neologisms may be incomprehensible to large numbers of Russians themselves, particularly to older people, who find it hard to keep abreast of the changes that are taking place, and to the poorly educated, who are unfamiliar with the Western languages and societies from which the new words and concepts are drawn.

The following list of loanwords contains some pre-revolutionary and early Soviet borrowings which have achieved a new currency in the conditions of the post-communist period (eg **а́кция**, **би́ржа**) as well as many recent borrowings.

Note [1] A loanword may be used in a much narrower sense than its equivalent in the language from which it is borrowed (eg **и́мидж**). Moreover, once accommodated by a language the loanword takes on a life of its own, and may come to acquire new meaning (eg **вивисе́кция**).

[2] Stress in a loanword may not be on the syllable where an English-speaker would expect to find it, eg марке́тинг, монито́ринг, пена́льти.

авторитари́зм	*authoritarianism*
авторита́рный	*authoritarian*
ажиота́ж	*stock-jobbing*; in R1, *flurry, kerfuffle*
ажиота́жный спрос на что́-н	sharply increased demand for scarce product
акционе́р	*shareholder*
акциони́рование	*corporatisation*
а́кция	*share, equity*
альтернати́ва	*alternative* (noun)
альтернати́вный	*alternative* (adj), presupposing choice
анде(р)гра́унд	*underground* (of groups or culture)
апока́липсис	*apocalypse*, ie end of the world as a result of war, natural disaster, spiritual degeneration, etc
аре́нда	*leasing*
аренда́тор	*lessee*
арендиза́ция	*introduction of leasing*
ба́ксы (pl, gen ба́ксов)	*bucks*, ie *dollars*
безальтернати́вность (f)	*lack of alternative*
бенефи́с	*benefit*, ie performance, match whose proceeds go to one performer or player
бестсе́ллер	*bestseller*
би́знес (tone now neutral)	*business* (activity)
би́ржа	*exchange* (eg stock exchange)
биржеви́к	person who works or operates on an exchange

бри́финг	*briefing*
бро́кер	*broker*
вертика́льный	*top-down* (eg of style of management)
вивисе́кция	*violent destruction*
геноци́д	*genocide*
гиперинфля́ция	*hyperinflation*
глобализа́ция	*globalisation*
горбима́ния	*gorbymania*
деидеологиза́ция	*weakening of ideology*
деканониза́ция	*decanonisation*
декоммуниза́ция	*decommunisation*
департиза́ция	removal of influence of a political party in the life of the nation
деполитиза́ция	*depoliticisation*
десоветиза́ция	*desovietisation*
десталиниза́ция	*destalinisation*
деструкти́вный	*destructive*
дефля́ция	*deflation*
децентрализа́ция	*decentralisation*
диа́спора	*diaspora*
дивиде́нд	*dividend*
ди́лер	*dealer* (on stock exchange)
диспле́й	*VDU*, ie *visual display unit*
до́нор	*donor*
жето́н	*token* (eg for metro, telephone)
и́мидж	*image* (ie character as perceived by the public)
импи́чмент	*impeachment*
инвести́ция	*investment*
инве́стор	*investor*
индекса́ция	*indexation*
иннова́ция	*innovation*
инфраструкту́ра	*infrastructure*
исте́блишмент	*establishment*, ie ruling or influential group
катализи́ровать (impf and pf) что-н	*to act as a catalyst to sth*

ка́тарсис	*catharsis*
клан	*clan* (in fig sense)
клип	*clip* (ie short TV item)
колла́пс	*collapse*
коммерциализа́ция	*commercialisation*
конве́рсия	*conversion* (ie of factories producing arms into factories producing consumer goods)
консе́нсус (R3)	*consensus*
консо́рциум	*consortium*
кооперати́в	*(economic) cooperative*
корру́пция	*corruption*
ло́бби (n, indecl)	*lobby*, ie pressure group
лобби́рование	*lobbying*
лобби́ст	*lobbyist*
ма́клер	*broker*
марафо́н	*marathon* (in fig sense)
маргина́л	person who has lost former social links and not adapted to new way of life
маргинализа́ция	*marginalisation*
марке́тинг	*marketing*
мафио́зи (m, indecl)	*member of the mafia*
ма́фия	*mafia*
ме́неджер	*manager*
ме́неджмент	*management*
менталите́т	*mentality*
митингова́ть (R1, pej)	*to take part in meetings*
монито́ринг	*monitoring*
наркоби́знес	*(illegal) drugs business*
наркома́ния	*drug addiction*
наркома́фия	*drugs mafia*
нонконформи́ст	*nonconformist*
но́у-ха́у (pl, indecl)	*know-how*
ортодо́кс	person incapable of changing views or looking at them critically
охлокра́тия	*ochlocracy*, ie mob-rule

паблисити (n, indecl)	*publicity*
платфо́рма	*platform*, ie political position
плексигла́совый щит	*glass shield* (for riot police)
плюрали́зм	*pluralism*
попули́стский	*populist*
порноби́знес	*pornography business*
приватиза́ция	*privatisation*
приватизи́ровать (impf and pf)	*to privatise*
приорите́т	*priority*
приорите́тный	*having priority*
путч	the putsch of August 1991
путчи́сты	those involved in the putsch
резерва́ция	*reservation*, ie land allocated to ethnic group
ре́йтинг	*rating*
ректифика́ция	*rectification* (of error)
респонде́нт	*respondent*, eg to questionnaire
ро́кер	*rocker*, ie youth with motor-bike
рок-му́зыка	*rock music*
русофо́б	*Russophobe*
русофо́бия	*Russophobia*
русофо́н	*Russian-speaker*
рэ́кет	*racket*, ie crime
рэкети́р	*racketeer*, ie criminal
самореализова́ться (impf and pf)	*to realise one's potential*
самофинанси́рование	*self-financing*
самофинанси́роваться (impf and pf; 3rd pers forms only)	*to be self-financing*
секс	*sex*, ie sexual activity
сексуа́льное воспита́ние	*sex education*
со́циум	*society*
спо́нсор	*sponsor*; also *sugar-daddy* (R1)
спо́нсорство	*sponsorship*
суици́д	*suicide* (the phenomenon)
тало́ны (pl; gen тало́нов)	*rationing tickets*

телефа́кс	*fax*
тинэ́йджер	*teenager*
толера́нтность (f)	*tolerance*
толера́нтный	*tolerant* (of others' views, etc)
тоталитари́зм	*totalitarianism*
тоталита́рный	*totalitarian*
трансфе́р	*transfer* (transformation of discontent into hostility towards national enemies); also sportsman's move
три́ллер	*thriller*
фундаментали́ст	*fundamentalist*
функционе́р (pej)	*functionary*
хари́зма	*charisma*
харизмати́ческий	*charismatic*
хо́лдинг-компа́ния	*holding company*
хо́мо-сове́тикус (iron)	*homo sovieticus*
хо́спис	*hospice* (for people dying of cancer)
цивилиза́ция	model of highly industrialised society with free market, democratic form of government and observance of human rights
ча́ртерный рейс	*charter flight*
шо́ковая терапи́я	*shock therapy* (esp in relation to economy)
электора́т	*electorate*

4.1.2 Neologisms derived from existing Russian words

This section includes words coined to denote new phenomena (eg **антиперестро́ечник**) and words which have been coined to denote phenomena that may now be discussed openly (eg **дедовщи́на**), or which in the new climate in Russia have found their way into the media (eg **ста́линщина**). Also included are some modish words and phrases which imitate foreign usage (eg **кома́нда**, **раска́чивание ло́дки**), and a few new expressions and phrases (eg **антизатра́тный механи́зм**, **доро́га к хра́му**) which it is impossible to understand without reference to some aspect of Russian life to which they relate.

антизатра́тный механи́зм	financial or economic measures designed to reduce waste

антиперестро́ечник	opponent of *perestroika*
антиреклáма	lit *anti-advertisement*, ie notice warning consumers that a product is defective
антиры́ночник	opponent of market economy
аппарáтные и́гры	manoeuvres by members of the state apparatus which appear to enhance democracy but have no real impact
арáльский синдрóм	*Aral syndrome*, ie set of factors leading to ecological ruin of the Aral Sea region
афгáнец (R1)	veteran of war in Afghanistan (in which Soviet forces participated from 1979–89)
афгáнский синдрóм	alienation among Russian veterans disillusioned by critical reappraisal of Soviet role in Afghan war
бандокрáтия	upper echelons of the Russian mafia
бéлые пя́тна	*blank spots*, ie facts, esp historical, which have been suppressed or distorted
бич (= бы́вший интеллигéнтный человéк)	cultured person who has hit hard times
боеви́к	member of illegal armed group, *paramilitary*
бомж (= без определённого мéста жи́тельства)	*homeless person, down-and-out*
буксовáть	*to be stuck on one spot/move forward very slowly*
васьки́зм	conduct of officials who take no account of public opinion or the new ethos (the word is based on Вáська, the name of the cat in a Krylov fable who goes on eating things in the kitchen despite the cook's reprimands)
взвéшенный	*well thought-out*
восьмидеся́тник	member of the generation whose outlook took shape in the 80s
вóтум довéрия/недовéрия	*vote of confidence/no confidence*
выводи́ловка (R1, pej)	*unearned salary increase*
вымывáть/вы́мыть	to discontinue output of unprofitable cheap goods
граждáнское неповиновéние	*civil disobedience*

гуманита́рная по́мощь	*humanitarian aid*
гэкачепи́ст	member of the committee which attempted the putsch of August 1991
дедовщи́на (R1)	bullying of new recruits by older soldiers (деды́)
деревя́нные рубли́	non-convertible Soviet/Russian money
доро́га к хра́му	the path to moral regeneration (from the film «Покая́ние»)
ельцини́ст	supporter of Yeltsin
жа́реные фа́кты	sensational negative information about sth
за бугро́м (D)	*abroad*
запрети́тельный синдро́м	prohibitive cast of mind characteristic of authoritarian régime
засто́й	*stagnation*, ie state of USSR under Brezhnev in 70s and early 80s
зато́птывание	drowning words of speaker by stamping
захло́пывание	drowning words of speaker by clapping
зелёные	*greens*, ie people concerned with care of the environment as a political issue; also *dollars*
зряпла́та (R1)	wasteful payment of money to sb who has not earned it
иждиве́нчество	*dependency*
индивидуа́льщик (R1)	*self-employed person*
интерде́вочка (R1; also валю́тная проститу́тка)	prostitute who demands hard currency for her services
кагеби́ст (also гэби́ст, кагебе́шник; all pej)	*member of the KGB*
ката́ла (R1, slang)	*card-sharper*
катра́н (R1, slang)	*illegal gambling den*
кома́нда	*team*, eg of advisers
конверти́руемая валю́та	*convertible currency*
крёстный оте́ц	*godfather*, ie leader of criminal group
ма́лый би́знес	*small business*
манку́рт	person who has lost historical memory,

moral bearings, contact with his or her people

многопарти́йная систе́ма — *multi-party system*

нало́г на доба́вленную сто́имость (НДС) — *VAT*

наме́стник (R1) — president's representative in the provinces

напряжёнка — difficult situation arising from shortage of sth

недоноси́тельство (R1) — failure to report crime

незавершёнка (R1) — incomplete building work

Не могу́ поступи́ться при́нципами — lit *I cannot waive my principles*; phrase used in polemical article defending the Soviet order; later used as ironic allusion to opponents of *perestroika*

несу́н (R1) — petty thief who steals things from place of work

нетрудовы́е дохо́ды — *illegal earnings*

нефтедо́ллары — *petrodollars*, ie foreign currency earned by export of Russian oil

номенклату́ра — *nomenclature*, ie set of posts filled by people whose appointment is approved at highest level; also refers to such an appointee

оборо́нщик (R1) — person high in the defence industry

о́бщество с ограни́ченной отве́тственностью — *limited liability company*

ОМО́Н (отря́д мили́ции осо́бого назначе́ния) — special police force of Ministry of the Interior

омо́новцы (pl) — members of ОМО́Н

оте́ц наро́дов (iron) — Stalin

отмыва́ние де́нег — *money-laundering*

охо́та за ве́дьмами — *witch hunt*

потоло́чный — *not properly thought-out* (ie derived from gazing at the ceiling)

правово́е госуда́рство — state operating on basis of legal principles (Ger *Rechtsstaat*)

при́нцип разу́мной доста́точности — military doctrine according to which country should have only the armed forces needed for self-defence

пробуксо́вка (R1) — work that does not get anywhere

пятизвёздник	*five-star hotel*
разблоки́рование	removal of obstacles blocking solution of a problem
разгосуда́рствление	transfer of state property to individual or collective ownership; liberation from excessive state control
расказёнить (pf)	*to free from excessive bureaucracy*
раска́чивание ло́дки	*rocking the boat*
ры́ночная эконо́мика	*market economy*
свобо́дное предпринима́тельство	*free enterprise*
сме́шанная эконо́мика	*mixed economy*
совме́стное предприя́тие	*joint venture*
ста́линщина (= сталини́зм)	*Stalinism*
таба́чный бунт	protest at shortage of tobacco
тамизда́т	literature published abroad
теа́тр абсу́рда	*theatre of the absurd*, ie Soviet reality
тенева́я эконо́мика	*shadow economy*
теневи́к	person who operates in the shadow economy
у́зник со́вести	*prisoner of conscience*
уравни́ловка (R1)	*(unjustifiable) levelling*, eg materially, socially
уте́чка мозго́в	*brain drain*
хозрасчёт	self-funding operation of organisation, ie without state subsidy
ча́стник/ча́стный со́бственник	*owner of private property*
челове́к го́да	*man of the year*
челове́ческий фа́ктор	*the human factor*
черёмуха	type of tear gas (lit *bird-cherry tree*)
чёрная дыра́	*black hole*
черну́ха (R1)	the negative side of life or its depiction
чёрные бере́ты	*black berets*, ie омо́новцы
четвёртая власть	*the fourth estate*, ie the media
ярлы́к	*label* (in fig sense)
я́стреб	*hawk* (in fig sense)

4.2 Transition words

The words or phrases in the following list are frequently used to link points and give coherence to an argument. Many of them (eg **во-пéрвых**, etc) are by their nature more likely to feature in the written language and the more formal speech of R3 than in the colloquial language of R1, and may therefore be contrasted with some of the fillers given in 4.3.

без (вся́кого) сомнéния	*without (any) doubt*
в концé концóв	*in the end, after all*
в сáмом дéле	*indeed* (confirms preceding idea)
на сáмом дéле	*in fact* (contradicts preceding idea)
во вся́ком слу́чае	*in any case*
во-пéрвых	*firstly*
во-вторы́х	*secondly*
в-трéтьих	*thirdly*
ведь	*you see, you know*
вкрáтце (R3)	*briefly, succinctly*
и́бо (R3)	*for,* ie *because*
итáк	*thus, so*
к моему́/нáшему прискóрбию (R3)	*to my/our regret*
к тому́ же	*besides*
корóче говоря́	*in short*
крóме тогó	*moreover*
наконéц	*lastly*
наоборóт	*on the contrary*
напримéр	*for example*
несомнéнно	*undoubtedly*
однáко	*however*
одни́м слóвом	*in a word, in short*
поэ́тому	*consequently*
прéжде всегó	*first of all, above all*
с однóй стороны́. . .с другóй стороны́	*on the one hand. . .on the other hand*
сáмо собóй разумéется	*it goes without saying*
сверх тогó	*moreover*

сле́довательно	*consequently*
сле́дует отме́тить (R3)	*it must be noted*
таки́м о́бразом	*in this way*
тем не ме́нее	*nevertheless*
то есть	*that is*

4.3 Fillers

Alongside transitional expressions of the sort exemplified in 4.2, which give coherence to a line of thought, languages have a stock of words or phrases that may be inserted in an utterance for various purposes. Such interpolations might represent a speaker's comment on the reliability of information (eg **ка́жется**), indicate the source or status of the information (eg **по-мо́ему**), describe the way an idea is expressed (**ины́ми слова́ми**), make some sort of appeal by a speaker to his or her interlocutor (**понима́ешь**), or express a speaker's attitude to what is said (**на беду́**). Often interpolations mean very little, serving mainly to fill out an utterance, perhaps in order to give the speaker time to marshal further thoughts. Unlike the transition words given in 4.2 many of the fillers given in this section belong primarily in the more informal spoken register (R1).

ви́дите ли	*do you see*
ви́дно	*evidently, obviously*
вообрази́(те) (себе́)	*fancy, just imagine*
вот	*so there we are*
гм	*er...*
говоря́т	*they say*
гру́бо выража́ясь	*roughly speaking*
действи́тельно	*really*
допу́стим	*let's suppose, say*
други́ми слова́ми	*in other words*
зна́ешь/зна́ете	*you know*
знать	*evidently, it seems*
зна́чит	*so, then*
извини́(те)	*excuse (me for saying so)*
ины́ми слова́ми	= други́ми слова́ми
к сожале́нию	*unfortunately*

к сча́стью	*fortunately*
коне́чно	*of course*
кста́ти (сказа́ть)	*by the way*
ме́жду на́ми	*between ourselves*
ме́жду про́чим	*incidentally*
на беду́	*unfortunately*
не пове́ришь/пове́рите	*you won't believe it*
ну	*well*
по всей вероя́тности	*in all probability*
по кра́йней ме́ре	*at least*
по пра́вде сказа́ть	*to tell the truth*
позво́ль(те)	*allow (me to say it)*
поми́луй(те)	*pardon (me)* (as expression of objection)
понима́ешь/понима́ете	*(do) you understand*
по́просту говоря́	*to put it simply*
предста́вь(те) себе́	*imagine*
прости́(те)	*forgive (me for saying it)*
пря́мо ска́жем	*let's be frank*
са́мое гла́вное	*the main thing*
скажи́(те) на ми́лость	*you don't say* (iron)
слу́шай(те)	*listen*
согласи́тесь	*you'll agree*
так	*so*
так сказа́ть	*so to speak*
чего́ до́брого	*who knows* (anticipating sth unpleasant)
что называ́ется	*as they say*

4.4 Modal particles

Modal particles are not often encountered in the relatively objective varieties of the formal written language (esp R3a/R3b) but in the spoken language, and in particular in colloquial conversation, where subjective utterances abound, they are extremely important. However, they are not easy for the English-speaking student to master, since English often achieves the nuances which particles convey by means of tone of voice or intonation rather than by lexical means. Moreover, the precise meaning or function of the Russian particles is elusive, partly because they are in most cases polysemantic and also because they interact with word order, phrasal stress and intonation to produce complex and variable nuances.

This section lists a number of the less elusive functions of the most important modal particles. At the end of the section a list is given of other particles which have a lexical or morphological function rather than a modal one.

а

(a) placed at the end of an utterance, exhorts the hearer to give an answer or agree to sth, eg

Моро́женое дать, **а**?
Want an ice-cream?
Всё в поря́дке, **а**?
Is everything all right then?
Ты гото́в(а)? Поéдем, **а**?
Are you ready? Shall we go then?

(b) occurs in vocative expressions (see 6.3.1) when a diminutive name is repeated, in which case the particle is placed between the two words in the vocative, eg

Тань, а Тань! Как ты ду́маешь, мне на ве́чер пойти́?
Tania, what do you think, should I go to the party?
Мам, а мам! Ты помо́жешь мне?
Mum! Will you help me?

(c) placed at the beginning of an utterance, gives a spontaneous link with what has been said or assumed, eg

— Отку́да э́то у тебя́ тако́й краси́вый шарф?
— **А** муж подари́л.
'Where did you get such a lovely scarf?'
'My husband gave it to me as a present.'
— Ми́тю мо́жно?
— **А** он на рабо́те.
— **А** когда́ бу́дет?
— В шесть. **А** кто его́ спра́шивает?
'Can I speak to Mitia?'
'He's at work.'
'When will he get home?'
'At six. Who's that asking for him?'

ведь

(a) expresses mild assertion of sth which the speaker considers obvious; sometimes this assertion constitutes an objection to another point of view, eg

Ведь ина́че и быть не мо́жет.
For it just couldn't be otherwise.
Пора́ у́жинать. Мы **ведь** с утра́ ничего́ не е́ли.
It's time to have supper. After all, we haven't eaten since this morning.
— То́ля, наде́нь ша́пку.
— Не хочу́.
— **Ведь** де́сять гра́дусов ни́же нуля́.

'Tolia, put your hat on.'
'I don't want to.'
'But it's minus 10.'
— Не бу́ду чита́ть э́ти кни́ги.
— **Ведь** прова́лишься на экза́мене.
'I'm not going to read these books.'
'Then you'll fail your exam.'

(b) expresses gentle reproach or warning, eg

Ну, хва́тит! Я **ведь** сказа́л(а), что не на́до шуме́ть.
That's enough. I told you not to make a noise.
Ты **ведь** совсе́м не обраща́ешь внима́ния на мои́ слова́.
You just don't pay any attention to what I say.

(c) expresses surprise at an unexpected discovery, eg

— Где моя́ ша́пка?
— Я её на ве́шалку пове́сил.
— А **ведь** её там нет.
'Where's my hat?'
'I hung it on the peg.'
'But it isn't there.'
Я **ведь** не по́нял(а́), что она́ уже́ аспира́нтка.
I hadn't realised that she was already a postgraduate.

(d) in questions, encourages sb to give the answer the speaker wants to hear; in this sense fulfils the same role as the English tail question, as in the following examples:

Ты **ведь** побу́дешь у нас?
You will come and stay with us for a bit, won't you?
Ведь не опозда́ете?
You won't be late, will you?

вот

(a) expresses demonstrative meaning, which may be rendered in English by *this* or *here*, eg

Они́ живу́т **вот** в э́том до́ме.
They live in this house here.
Попро́буй **вот** э́тот сала́тик. Он о́чень вку́сный.
Try this salad here. It's very nice.

(b) with interrogative pronouns and adverbs, lends emphasis of the sort rendered in English by the verb *to be*, eg

Вот где он упа́л.
This is where he fell over.
Вот почему́ я посове́товал(а) тебе́ не выходи́ть.
That is why I advised you not to go out.
Вот что я име́ю в виду́.
This is what I have in mind.

(c) with the future tense, may express promise, resolution, warning or threat, eg

Я бро́шу пить. **Вот** уви́дишь.
I'll give up drinking. You'll see.

Здесь ско́льзко. **Вот** упадёшь сейча́с!
It's slippery. You'll fall.
Ты разби́л(а) окно́. **Вот** расскажу́ роди́телям о твои́х проде́лках.
You've broken the window. I'll tell your parents about your pranks.

(d) in exclamations, may express such sentiments as surprise or indignation, in which case the particle itself is stressed, eg

— Президе́нт у́мер.
— **Во́т** как?
'The president has died.'
'Really?'
Во́т как ты тепе́рь живёшь!
So that's the way you live now, is it?
Во́т что ты де́лаешь по вечера́м! Пья́нствуешь.
So that's what you do in the evenings. You get drunk.

(e) in exclamations, may also intensify the speaker's emotional response to sth, eg

Вот хорошо́, что нас не забы́ли!
It's so nice that you haven't forgotten us.

да

(a) expresses objection or remonstration in a very familiar tone, eg

— Ты пока́ никому́ не говори́.
— **Да** я молчу́!
'Don't you tell anybody yet.'
'I wasn't going to anyway.
Да я бы на твоём ме́сте э́того не сде́лал(а).
I wouldn't have done that if I'd been in your place.

(b) expresses agreement or concession (see also ну (d), уж (c)), eg
— Мо́жно, я сейча́с вы́йду?
— **Да** выходи́, мне всё равно́.
'Can I leave now?'
'Go ahead, it's all the same to me.'
— Я, пожа́луй, спрошу́ О́лю.
— **Да** спроси́. То́лько вряд ли она́ тебе́ ска́жет.
'I might ask Olia.'
'Go ahead and ask her. But I don't suppose she'll tell you.'

(c) expresses insistent suggestion, friendly advice or reassurance, eg

Да не шуми́те. Я рабо́таю.
Don't make a racket. I'm working.
Да не беспоко́йся, па́па сейча́с подойдёт.
Don't worry, daddy'll come back in a minute.

(d) in a vague answer, carries a casual, indifferent tone, eg

— Куда́ она́ уе́хала?
— **Да** не зна́ю. Говоря́т в Сиби́рь.
'Where's she gone off to?'
'Oh, I don't know. Siberia I think.'

(e) with an indefinite pronoun containing the particle **-нибудь**, expresses certainty against a background of vagueness, eg

Чтó-нибудь да кýпим.
We're sure to buy something or other.
Когó-нибудь да застáнешь дóма.
You're bound to find someone in.

(f) in exclamatory questions, expresses the impossibility of a different state of affairs, eg

Да рáзве ты не знáл(а), что он женáт?
Surely you knew he was married.
Да заблудѝться средѝ бéла дня! Не мóжет быть.
What! Get lost in broad daylight? That's not possible.

ещё (a) expresses a feeling on the speaker's part that sth is unreasonable or does not correspond to reality, eg

А **ещё** мехáник!
And you call yourself a mechanic!
А **ещё** говорѝшь, что неспосóбен/неспосóбна к мýзыке.
And you still say you've no aptitude for music!

(b) expresses emphatic affirmation or denial, eg

Ещё бы!	*I'll say!*
— Ну, наéлся? — **Ещё как** наéлся! — Ты, мóжет, не наéлся. — **Ещё как** наéлся!	*'Have you had enough to eat?'* *'I'll say.'*

же (a) categoric emphasis on what the speaker considers a compelling point or an indisputable fact, eg

Рáзве ты идёшь на рабóту? У тебя́ **же** температýра.
Surely you're not going to work? You've got a temperature after all.
Я не умéю игрáть в шáхматы. Вы **же** сáми знáете, что не умéю.
I can't play chess. You yourself know very well that I can't.

(b) with imperatives, expresses insistence on the part of the speaker together with impatience or irritation, feigned at least, that the order has to be given or repeated, eg

Алёша! **Идѝ же** скорéе сюдá.
Aliosha, come here at once.

(c) in questions, may indicate that the speaker cannot envisage or accept any answer other than the one he or she invites, eg

Вы **же** не солжёте?
You surely wouldn't tell a lie, would you?
Ты же не бýдешь утверждáть, что не знáешь?
You're surely not going to say you don't know, are you?

(d) in questions framed with an interrogative pronoun or adverb, may express incredulity or perplexity on the speaker's part, in which case it may correspond to the English suffix *-ever*, eg

Где же ты был(á)?
Wherever have you been?
Почемý же вы возражáете на э́то?

Why on earth do you object to this?
Что же емý подарúть на Рождествó?
Whatever can we give him for Christmas?

(e) may also be used in questions in which the speaker is asking for precise information, eg

Вы говорúте, что ктó-то погúб. **Кто же** погúб?
You say that somebody was killed. Who exactly was killed?
Вы тóже живёте в цéнтре гóрода? На **какóй же** ýлице?
So you live in the centre as well? Which street do you live in?

Note 1 же may be shortened to **ж**.
2 же is generally placed immediately after the word or phrase which it highlights.

и

(a) expresses emphasis when sth follows naturally from what has been said, eg

— Не открывáй oкнó.
— **Я и** не открывáю.
'Don't open the window.'
'I'm not opening it.'
Онá былá на конферéнции. Мы там **и** познакóмились.
She was at the conference. That's where we met.
Мы подошлú к кафé. «Вот тут **и** пообéдаем», сказáла онá.
We approached a café. 'This is where we're going to eat,' she said.

Note: и is synonymous in this use with úменно and may render the English verb *to be* when it is used for emphasis only.

(b) may correspond to **дáже**, *even*, eg

Кáжется, нáша комáнда вы́играла, а я **и** не слы́шал(а) об э́том.
Apparently our side won, and I didn't even hear about it.

(c) may correspond to **хотя́**, *although*, eg

И теплó на ýлице, а я не хочý выходúть.
I don't want to go out, although it's warm outside.

(d) may increase uncertainty, eg

— Мóжет быть, вы читáли э́ту кнúгу?
— Мóжет быть, **и** читáл(а).
'You may have read this book.'
'I may have done.'

(e) with an interjection, may intensify an exclamation, eg

Ох, и обóрвыш ты!
God, you're scruffy!
Он умéет игрáть на скрúпке. **Ох и** игрáет!
He can play the violin. Oh and how he plays.

-ка

(a) attached to imperative forms, produces gentle informal exhortation or friendly advice, eg

Лéночка, **вы́йди-ка** сюдá на минýтку.
Lenochka, come out here for a moment would you.
Посмотрúте-ка, как онá похорошéла.

Just look how pretty she's become.
Подите-ка вы отдыхать. Вы наработались.
Go and have a rest. You've worn yourself out with work.

(b) attached to an imperative used in a conditional sense (see 10.9, note 3), expresses a challenge to sb to do sth perceived as difficult, eg

Поговорите-ка с этим парнем—увидите, какой он трудный.
You try speaking to this lad and you'll see how difficult he is.
Постой-ка на морозе без перчаток!
You just try standing out in the frost without gloves on.

(c) attached to the 1st person singular form of a perfective verb, indicates irresolution in the speaker, eg

А **пойду-ка** я на работу пешком.
I think I might walk to work.
Куплю-ка дочке новую юбку.
Perhaps I'll buy my daughter a new skirt.

ли (a) with a perfective infinitive, expresses vague intention or hesitancy on the part of the speaker, eg

В театр **ли** сходить?
Shall we go to the theatre? [I don't know].
Предупредить **ли** мне их?
Should I perhaps warn them?
Не купить **ли** конфет?
Shouldn't we buy some sweets?

(b) combined with **не**, expresses a very polite request or suggestion (which may be ironical), eg

Не скажете ли вы мне, как пройти на Красную площадь?
Could you possibly tell me the way to Red Square?
Не можешь ли ты помолчать?
You couldn't possibly be quiet for a bit, could you?
Не потрудитесь ли вы выйти? (iron)
Would you be so kind as to leave?

ну (a) exhorts sb to say or do sth, eg

Ну, как дела?
Well, how are things?
Ну говори, где ты побывал(а).
Come on, tell us where you've been.
Ну, пойдёмте.
Well, let's be going.

(b) reinforces the expression of attitudes such as objection, bewilderment, annoyance, frustration, eg

Ну, что мне с тобой делать. Совсем не слушаешься.
What on earth am I to do with you? You just don't do what I say.
Ну, сколько раз тебе говорить, что снять туфли надо.
However many times have I got to tell you to take your shoes off?

(c) introduces expressive exclamations, eg

Ну, какóе счáстье! *Well what a stroke of luck!*
Ну, конéчно! *But of course!*
Ну, ýжас! *But that's terrible!*

(d) expresses qualified permission or acceptance, eg

— Я устáл(а).
— **Ну**, передохнём.
'I'm tired.'
'Let's take a breather then.'
— Мóжно, я посмотрю́ на ваш мотоци́кл?
— **Ну**, посмотри́те.
'Can I have a look at your motor-bike?'
'All right.'

(e) in D, precedes a verb in the infinitive to stress the intensity of an action, eg

Начался́ спор, а он **ну кричáть**!
An argument broke out, and did he shout.

(f) in D, with the accusative form of a personal pronoun, expresses strong disapproval, eg

А нý тебя́!
To hell with you!
— Принимáй лекáрство.
— **Нý егó!**
'Take the medicine.'
'Give over!'

(g) also acts as a filler when the speaker is trying to collect his or her thoughts, eg

Не знáю. **Ну...** Что сказáть? Попытáюсь узнáть.
I don't know. Well... What can I say? I'll try to find out.

так (a) introduces suggestion in response to setback, in which case так often corresponds to English *then*, eg

— Здесь нет мы́ла.
— **Так** принеси́!
'There's no soap here.'
'Then bring some'.
Егó не бýдет? **Так** мы обойдёмся без негó.
He won't be there? Then we'll get by without him.

(b) with the same word used twice (так being placed between the word or words used twice), indicates concession on the part of the speaker, or acceptance of a suggestion, or that some property is fully manifested, eg

— Давáйте встрéтимся в кинó. Соглáсны?
— **В кинó так в кинó**.
'Let's meet in the cinema. Is that OK?'
'The cinema it is then.'
— Как поéдем домóй? Давáй на такси́?
— **На такси́ так на такси́**.
'How shall we get home? Shall we get a taxi?'

'All right then, we'll get a taxi.'
В Сиби́ри зимо́й уж **хо́лодно так хо́лодно**.
God, it's cold in Siberia in winter.

(c) expresses approximation with time, distance, quantity, etc, eg

— Когда́ прие́дешь?
— Часо́в **так** в шесть.
'When will you get here?'
'About six o'clock.'
— Далеко́ до це́нтра?
— **Так**, киломе́тра два.
'Is it far to the centre?'
'About 2 kilometres or so.'
— Ско́лько ве́сит ры́ба?
— Килогра́мм **так** пять.
'How much does the fish weigh?'
'About 5 kilos.'

-то (a) stresses sth, eg

В то́м-то и де́ло.
That's just it.
Зо́нтик-то не забу́дь. Идёт дождь.
Don't forget your umbrella. It's raining.

(b) in stressing part of an utterance, may reinforce a contrast, eg

Сте́ны-то уже́ постро́ены, но кры́ши ещё нет.
The walls are built but there isn't a roof yet.
Я-то вы́полнил(а) своё обеща́ние, а вы ме́длите.
I've fulfilled my promise, but you're procrastinating.

(c) in constructions in which a word is repeated and in which -то stands after the word when it is first used, expresses concession, eg

Писа́ть-то пишу́, а она́ не чита́ет мои́ пи́сьма.
She doesn't read my letters, although I make a point of writing to her.
Занима́ться-то занима́лся/занима́лась, а на экза́мене провали́лся/провали́лась.
I failed the exam, although I worked all right.

(d) in certain phrases expressing strong negation, has a euphemistic nuance, eg

Кни́га **не осо́бенно-то** интере́сна.
The book's pretty dull.
Мне **не о́чень-то** хоте́лось говори́ть с ней.
I really didn't want to talk to her.
Не та́к-то про́сто бы́ло его́ успоко́ить.
It wasn't all that easy to calm him down.

(e) in exclamations with a tone of admiration or wonder, eg

Она́ краса́вица. **Каки́е глаза́-то**!
She's beautiful. What wonderful eyes!
Наро́ду-то на ры́нке! Что там продаю́т?
What a lot of people in the market! What are they selling there?

(f) lends intimacy or informality to an utterance, eg

Теа́тр-то ходи́л(а) вчера́?
Did you go to the theatre yesterday then?
«Как тебя́ **звать-то**?»—спроси́л врач ребёнка.
'What should we call you then?' the doctor asked the child.

Note: used as a particle -то is always attached to the word it is intended to emphasise; it cannot stand on its own and never bears the stress.

уж

(a) expresses certainty about sth the speaker considers incontestable, eg

— Как ты ду́маешь, не опозда́ем?
— **Уж** не опозда́ем! То́лько шесть часо́в.
'Do you think we'll be late?'
'Of course we won't. It's only six o'clock.'
По-мо́ему, **уж** я́сно, что нас подвели́.
I think it's absolutely clear they've let us down.

(b) intensifies some word denoting affirmation, negation or degree, eg

— Ты уста́л(а)?
— **Да уж**. Пло́хо спало́сь.
'Are you tired?'
'I certainly am. I slept badly.'
Он **уж совсе́м** переста́л заходи́ть к нам.
He's completely given up calling on us.

(c) expresses acceptance or concession, perhaps reluctant, eg

— Дай мне свой зо́нтик на́ день.
— Бери́ **уж**, то́лько не забу́дь его́ в по́езде.
'Will you lend me your umbrella for the day?'
'All right, but don't leave it on the train.'
— Сигаре́ты тебе́ меша́ют? Мо́жет, попроси́ть, чтоб не кури́ли?
— **Уж** пусть они́ ку́рят.
'Are the cigarettes bothering you? Shall we ask them to stop smoking?'
'Oh let them smoke.'

(d) with an imperative, lends the order a blunt but good-natured tone, an air of camaraderie, eg

Молчи́ уж об э́том. Тебе́ не́чем горди́ться.
You'd better keep quiet about that. You've got nothing to be proud of.
Иди́ уж.
Get a move on.

хоть (бы)
хотя́ (бы)

(a) may mean *if only* or *at least*, or may have the same meaning as **да́же**, *even*, or **да́же е́сли**, *even if*, especially in set phrases, eg

Приезжа́й **хоть** на оди́н день.
Do come, if only just for a day.
Ах, **хоть бы** одно́ письмо́ от неё!
Oh, if only there were just one letter from her!
Хоть убе́й, не скажу́.
I couldn't tell you to save my life.

(b) introduces an example which readily springs to the speaker's mind; in this use it may be translated by *for example, to take only*, eg

Лю́ди лени́вы. Взять **хоть** тебя́.
People are lazy. Take you for example.

что (a) may introduce a question, perhaps with a tone of surprise, disapproval or indignation, eg

Что, боли́т желу́док?
So you've got stomach-ache have you?
Что, он говори́т, что не зна́ет меня́?
What! He says he doesn't know me?
Ты, **что** ничего́ не слы́шал(а) об э́том?
Are you serious? You haven't heard about this?

(b) combines with a personal pronoun in the nominative to form elliptical exclamations in which some verb such as говори́ть is understood, eg

— Мо́жет быть, ску́шаешь ещё что́-нибудь?
— **Что ты!** я сыт(а́).
'Would you like to have something else to eat?'
'What are you saying? I'm full.'
— Я тебе́ заплачу́ за пи́во.
— **Что ты!** Не на́до!
'I'll pay you for the beer.'
'For goodness sake. It's not necessary.'

Miscellaneous particles

-то **-нибудь** **-либо**	form indefinite pronouns (see 10.2.5)
де́скать	indicates reported speech, eg Он, де́скать, не слы́шал, *He said he hadn't heard.*
мол	contraction of мо́лвил; = де́скать
-с (obs)	(= су́дарь or суда́рыня) form of address to a social superior, eg serf to lord; also used ironically; widely encountered in classical literature
-ся (-сь)	forms reflexive verbs (10.8)
я́кобы	*allegedly, ostensibly, supposedly*, eg я́кобы невозмо́жная зада́ча, *a supposedly impossible task* (but the speaker does not believe it to be so)

4.5 Interjections

Interjections by their nature belong to the colloquial speech of R1. The following list gives some common interjections with translations that attempt to capture their flavour rather than the literal meaning of the words.

admiration	**ах**!	*wow!*
	замеча́тельно!	*wonderful!*
	здо́рово!	*great!*
	изуми́тельно!	*super!*
	чуде́сно!	*marvellous!*
agreement	**договори́лись**	*OK, agreed*
	замётано	*OK, agreed*
	есть (mil)	*yes, sir/aye-aye*
	идёт	*all right*
	ла́дно	*OK, fine*
	хорошо́	*good*
annoyance	**к чёрту его́**!	*to hell with him/it*
	пошёл к чёрту!	*go to hell*
	тьфу надое́л/а/о/и	*oh damn, I'm fed up with it/you*
	тьфу, про́пасть!	*confound it*
	наплева́ть на + acc	*to hell with, damn*
	прова́ливай!	*clear off, get lost*
	убира́йся!	*clear off, get lost*
	чёрта с два!	*like hell*
	чёрт возьми́! **чёрт побери́**!	*to hell with it*
	хрен с + instr (vulg)	*to hell with*
	Note: see also 4.6 on vulgar language.	
disbelief, surprise	**ах**!	*oh!*
	Бо́же мой!	*my God!*
	го́споди!	*good heavens, good gracious!*
	вот ещё!	*whatever next!*
	во́т как!	*really?*
	во́т что!	*really?*
	вот так та́к!	*well, I never!*
	ну и ну!	*well, well!*
fright, pain	**ай**!	*oh! ouch*
	ах!	*ah! oh!*
	ой!	*ouch!*

	ох!	*ah! oh!*
objection	**ни в ко́ем слу́чае**!	*no way!*
	ни за что на све́те!	*not for anything*
	ничего́ подо́бного!	*nothing of the sort*
warning	**внима́ние**!	*attention!*
	осторо́жно!	*careful!*
	смотри́(те)!	*look out!*
miscellaneous	**Бог (его́) зна́ет**!	*God knows*
	брысь!	*shoo* (to cat)
	будь здоро́в! **будь здоро́ва**! **бу́дьте здоро́вы**!	*God bless* (when sb sneezes)
	вот-во́т!	*that's it!* (expressing approval)
	вот так!	= вот-вот
	во́т тебе!	*take that!* (accompanying blow)
	вот тебе́ и + nom	*so much for*
	во́т тебе на́!	*well how do you like that*
	ещё бы!	*I'll say!* (expressing confirmation)
	лёгок/легка́ на поми́не	*talk of the devil* (on appearance of sb one has been talking about)
	на́	*here you are/here, take it*, eg На́ кни́гу, *Here, take the book.*
	подело́м тебе́/вам!	*it serves you right*
	ра́ди Бо́га	*for God's sake*
	тсс!	*shh! hush!*
	фу!	*ugh* (expressing revulsion)
	чего́ до́брого!	*who knows* (anticipating sth unpleasant)
	что́бы не сгла́зить!	*touch wood*

interjectional predicate

Some interjectional forms, most of them derived from verbs, may serve as a predicate in R1, eg

Айда́ в го́род.	*They set off and were in town in no time.*
Я бах/бац **Я трах** **Я хлоп** } его́ по спине́.	*I banged/slapped him on the back.*
Он — **прыг** на кры́шу.	*He leapt on to the roof.*
Он — **стук** в стекло́.	*He knocked on the window.*

Она́ — **шасть** в ко́мнату.	*She wandered into the room.*
Они́ — **шмыг** в тень.	*They nipped into the shadow.*

4.6 Vulgar language

This section must be prefaced by a triple warning. Firstly, the foreign student should be aware that no matter how good one's command of another people's language one may strike a discordant note or even give offence to a native speaker if one falls into very familiar registers in general and the vulgar register in particular. Secondly, it cannot be overemphasised that a vulgar word may have a greater impact in the Russian context than does its English lexical equivalent (even though the same anatomical features and sentiments are involved), since the English word occurs in a society that uses such vocabulary, for better or for worse, with relative freedom. Thirdly, it should be understood that whereas in Britain vulgar language may nowadays be used as freely by women as by men, in Russia the use of such language by a woman is likely to shock both men and women more than the use of that language by a man. The foreign student of Russian should therefore avoid using vulgar language if he, or especially she, wishes to win acceptance in any sort of 'polite' Russian society.

On the other hand, with the sudden influx into Russia of things Western, including pornography, vulgar language is a reality of Russian life which the foreign student is much more likely than before to encounter. It has also found its way on a large scale into serious literature, including works published in Russia as well as those published abroad by émigrés. The introduction of vulgar language into works of art may be traced to the brief thaw under Khrushchev (obscenities abound in Solzhenitsyn's *Оди́н день Ива́на Дени́совича*). In the age of *glasnost'* and the post-Soviet era such language has come to be widely used with great freedom in the works of writers such as Aleshkovsky, Venedikt Erofeev, Limonov, Narbikova, Petrushevskaia, Evgenii Popov and Zinik, some of whom it should be noted, are women, and many of whom are writers of literary note. The foreign student may therefore usefully acquire a passive knowledge of this area of language. A small selection of the very numerous obscenities available to the native-speaker is given below.

мат **ма́терный язы́к** **матерщи́на**	*foul language*
матери́ться	*to use foul language*
матюка́ться	*to eff and blind*

блева́ть (блюю́, блюёшь)	*to puke*
его́ вы́рвало (not vulg)	*he was sick*
пое́хать (pf) в Ри́гу	*to spew*
еба́ть or **еть** (ебу́, ебёшь; past tense ёб, ебли́)/**уе́ть**	*to fuck*; also *to curse, discipline severely*
отъеби́сь от меня́	*fuck off*
взъёбка	*a bollocking*
ёбаный	*fucking*
еба́ться or **е́ться с** чем-н	*to fuck about with sth*
заёба (m and f)	*pain-in-the-arse*
ёб твою́ мать	*fucking* (as epithet)
тра́хать/тра́хнуть (less vulg than еба́ть)	*to screw, bonk*
пи́сать (пи́саю, пи́саешь)/**попи́сать**	*to piss*
ссать (ссу, ссёшь)/**посса́ть**	*to piss*
отлива́ть/отли́ть	*to have a piss, take a leak*
жо́па (dimin **жо́пка**)	*arse*
жополи́з	*arse-licker*
бздеть (бзжу, бздишь)	*to fart (silently), foul the air, bullshit*
бздун	*fart* (weak person)
перде́ть (перди́т)/**пёрнуть**	*to fart*
пердёж	*farting*
перду́н	*farter, old fart*
срать (сру, срёшь)/**насра́ть**	*to shit*
ему́ насра́ть	*he doesn't give a shit*
засра́нец	*arse-hole* (ie person)
обсира́ть/обосра́ть кого́-н	*to shit all over sb* (fig)
дерьмо́	*crap, dung* (also person)
говно́	*shit*
говню́к	*shit(bag)* (ie person)
пизда́	*cunt*
пи́здить/спи́здить	*to swipe, nick, steal*
хуй (dimin **хуёк**)	*prick* (also person)
ни хуя́	*fuck all*
пошёл на́ хуй	*fuck off*

нахуйник	*condom*
хер	= хуй
ни хера́	= ни хуя́
хуйня́	*shit* (nonsense, rubbish)
херня́	= хуйня́
хуёвый	*lousy, fucking awful*
херо́вый	= хуёвый
муде́ (n, indecl; nom pl му́ди, gen pl муде́й)	*balls*
муда́к	*arsehole* (person)
мудня́	*bollocks* (nonsense)
дрочи́ла (m and f)	*wanker*
сво́лочь (f)	*swine, bastard*
блядь (f)	*whore*; also used as exclamation: *sod it!*
ку́рва	*tart*

4.7 Idioms

An idiom is an expression peculiar to a particular language. It may have a rough equivalent in another language, but its meaning may not be readily apparent to a foreigner or even logically explicable. Idioms lend colour to a language and authority to a speaker who is able to use them appropriately. While many of the idioms given here are colloquial, they may well be used in the literary language and in R3c as well to add force and vividness. They are much less likely to be encountered in the formal R3a and R3b.

The idioms given below, all of which are widely used in the modern language, are arranged in alphabetical order according to the letter with which the key word, usually a noun, begins. Where only one member of an aspectual pair is given either that member predominates or only that member may be used in the idiom in question. The English versions given are idiomatic or rough equivalents of the Russian rather than literal translations.

А

нача́ть с азо́в	*to begin at the beginning*
открыва́ть/откры́ть Аме́рику	*to say sth well-known*

Б

бить баклу́ши	*to fritter away one's time*
И бро́вью не повёл.	*He didn't turn a hair.*

броса́ться/бро́ситься в глаза́	*to be striking*
как ни в чём не быва́ло	*as if nothing had happened*

В

(У него́) всё ва́лится и́з рук.	*(He) is all fingers and thumbs.*
(знать что́-н) вдоль и поперёк	*(to know sth) inside out*
Ви́лами по воде́ пи́сано.	*It's still up in the air.*
И концы́ в во́ду.	*None will be the wiser.*
как в во́ду ка́нуть	*to vanish into thin air*
выводи́ть/вы́вести на чи́стую во́ду	*to expose, show up in true colours*
Водо́й не разолье́шь.	*(They're) thick as thieves.*
стре́ляный воробе́й	*an old hand*
держа́ть у́хо востро́	*to be on one's guard*

Г

говори́ть с гла́зу на́ глаз	*to talk tête-à-tête*
гла́зом не моргну́в	*without batting an eyelid*
закрыва́ть/закры́ть глаза́ на что́-н	*to turn a blind eye to sth*
лома́ть го́лову над че́м-н	*to rack one's brains over sth*
идти́/пойти́ в го́ру	*to go up in the world*
с грехо́м попола́м	*only just, with difficulty*

Д

неро́бкого деся́тка	*no coward*
петь дифира́мбы кому́-н	*to sing sb's praises*
(У него́) душа́ нараспа́шку.	*(He wears) his heart upon his sleeve.*

Е

держа́ть в ежо́вых рукави́цах	*to rule with a rod of iron*
моло́ть ерунду́	*to talk nonsense*

З

заблуди́ться в трёх со́снах	*to get lost in broad daylight*
е́хать за́йцем	*to travel without paying the fare*
Заруби́ э́то себе́ на носу́.	*Put that in your pipe and smoke it.*
Ни зги не ви́дно.	*It's pitch dark.*
положи́ть зу́бы на по́лку	*to tighten one's belt*
держа́ть язы́к за зуба́ми	*to hold one's tongue*

И

крича́ть во всю ива́новскую	*to shout at the top of one's voice*

К	
тёртый кала́ч	*person who has knocked about the world*
держа́ть ка́мень за па́зухой на кого́-н	*to bear a grudge against sb*
ка́мень преткнове́ния	*a stumbling block*
(Он) за сло́вом в карма́н не ле́зет.	*(He's) not at a loss for a word.*
завари́ть ка́шу	*to stir up trouble*
расхлеба́ть ка́шу	*to put things right*
входи́ть/войти́ в колею́	*to settle down again* (of life, situation)
выбива́ть/вы́бить из колеи́	*to unsettle*
Кома́р но́са не подто́чит.	*Not a thing can be said against it.*
своди́ть/свести́ концы́ с конца́ми	*to make ends meet*
оста́ться у разби́того коры́та	*to be back where one started*
Л	
(У него́) лёгкая рука́.	*(He has) good luck.*
Кто в лес, кто по дрова́.	*(They're) at sixes and sevens.*
сесть в лу́жу	*to get into a mess*
М	
идти́ как по ма́слу	*to go swimmingly*
Мура́шки по спине́ бе́гают.	*It gives one the creeps.*
Он му́хи не оби́дит.	*He wouldn't harm a fly.*
де́лать из му́хи слона́	*to make a mountain out of a mole-hill*
Н	
уйти́ несо́лоно хлеба́вши	*to go away empty-handed*
проходи́ть кра́сной ни́тью че́рез что́-н (R3)	*to stand out* (of theme, motif)
жить на широ́кую но́гу	*to live in grand style*
встать с ле́вой ноги́	*to get out of bed on the wrong side*
быть на коро́ткой ноге́ с ке́м-н	*to be on close terms with sb*
ног под собо́й не чу́вствовать	*to be dropping (from tiredness)*
води́ть кого́-н за́ нос	*to lead sb a dance*
ве́шать/пове́сить нос	*to be crestfallen*
задира́ть/задра́ть нос	*to put on airs*
клева́ть но́сом	*to nod off*
оста́вить кого́-н с но́сом	*to dupe sb*
оста́ться с но́сом	*to be duped*

О

говори́ть без обиняко́в	*to speak plainly*
пройти́ ого́нь, во́ду и ме́дные тру́бы	*to go through fire and water*
из огня́ да в по́лымя	*out of the frying-pan into the fire*
меж(ду) двух огне́й	*between the devil and the deep blue sea*

П

па́лец о па́лец не уда́рить	*not to raise a finger*
кому́-н па́льца в рот не клади́	*sb is not to be trusted*
попа́сть па́льцем в не́бо	*to be wide of the mark*
смотре́ть сквозь па́льцы на что́-н	*to shut one's eyes to sth*
вставля́ть/вста́вить па́лки кому́-н в колёса	*to put a spoke in sb's wheel*
перелива́ть из пусто́го в поро́жнее	*to beat the air*
Гора́ с плеч свали́лась.	*(It's) a weight off (my) mind.*
ждать у мо́ря пого́ды	*to wait for sth to turn up*
знать всю подного́тную	*to know the whole truth*
попада́ть/попа́сть в то́чку	*to hit the nail on the head*
стере́ть кого́-н в порошо́к	*to make mincemeat of sb*
всё кро́ме пти́чьего молока́	said when every possible dish is served at a meal
разби́ть в пух и прах	*to put to rout*
стреля́ть из пу́шек по воробья́м	*to use a sledgehammer to crack a nut*
(У него́) семь пя́тниц на неде́ле.	*(He) keeps chopping and changing.*

Р

показа́ть кому́-н где ра́ки зиму́ют	*to tear a strip off sb*
у кого́-н хлопо́т по́лон рот	*sb has his/her hands full*
махну́ть руко́й на что́-н	*to give up sth as lost*
сиде́ть сложа́ ру́ки	*to twiddle one's thumbs*
из рук вон пло́хо	*dreadfully, wretchedly*
рабо́тать засучи́в рукава́	*to work with zeal*
рабо́тать спустя́ рукава́	*to work in a slipshod manner*
ни ры́ба ни мя́со	*neither one thing nor the other*

С

Два сапога́ па́ра.	*They make a pair.*
подложи́ть кому́-н свинью́	*to play a dirty trick on sb*
ни слу́ху ни ду́ху (о ко́м-н)	*not a word has been heard (of sb)*
Вот где соба́ка зары́та.	*That's the crux of the matter.*

соба́ку съесть на чём-н	*to know sth inside out*
выноси́ть/вы́нести сор из избы́	*to wash one's dirty linen in public*
роди́ться в соро́чке	*to be born with a silver spoon in one's mouth*
держа́ть что́-н под спу́дом	*to hide sth under a bushel*
выходи́ть/вы́йти сухи́м из воды́	*to emerge unscathed*
без сучка́, без задо́ринки	*without a hitch*
в два счёта	*in a jiffy*

Т

быть не в свое́й таре́лке	*to be not quite oneself*
В теснотé, да не в оби́де.	*The more the merrier.*
сбива́ть/сбить кого́-н с то́лку	*to confuse sb*
за три́девять земе́ль	*at the other end of the world*
в Ту́лу со свои́м самова́ром	*coals to Newcastle*
заходи́ть/зайти́ в тупи́к	*to come to a dead end, reach deadlock*

У

заки́дывать/заки́нуть у́дочку	*to put out feelers*
попада́ться/попа́сться на у́дочку	*to swallow the bait*
бра́ться/взя́ться за ум	*to come to one's senses*
мота́ть/намота́ть что́-н себе́ на ус	*to take good note of sth*
из уст в уста́	*by word of mouth*
пропуска́ть/пропусти́ть что́-н ми́мо ушей	*to turn a deaf ear to sth*

Ф

кури́ть фимиа́м кому́-н	*to praise sb to the skies*

Ч

замори́ть червячка́	*to have a bite to eat*
у чёрта на кули́чках	*the back of beyond*

Ш

Де́ло в шля́пе.	*It's in the bag.*

Щ

по щу́чьему веле́нию	*as if by magic*

Я

Я́блоку не́где упа́сть.	*There isn't room to swing a cat.*
я́блоко раздо́ра	*bone of contention*
Язы́к прогло́тишь.	*It makes one's mouth water.*
откла́дывать/отложи́ть что́-н в до́лгий я́щик	*to shelve sth, put sth off*

4.8 Proverbs and sayings (посло́вицы и поогово́рки)

A proverb is a short statement expressing a supposed truth or moral lesson. Russian is rich in such colourful utterances, many of which are felt to express folk wisdom. A foreigner's knowledge of the more common among them is likely to impress a native-speaker, provided that they are used correctly and sparingly.

The following list contains many of the best-known Russian proverbs. Proverbs that are distinctively Russian and proverbs that differ in their terms from their English equivalents have been given preference in the selection. In most cases it is the English equivalent rather than a literal translation that has been given, but where there is no close equivalent a literal translation is offered, together, if possible, with an approximate English equivalent. In a few cases (eg **Незва́ный гость ху́же тата́рина**) the literal meaning makes the sense of the saying obvious.

Б	
Друзья́ познаю́тся в беде́.	*A friend in need is a friend indeed.*
Пришла́ беда́—отворя́й ворота́.	*It never rains but it pours.*
Семь бед—оди́н отве́т.	*One may as well be hanged for a sheep as a lamb.*
Бе́дность не поро́к.	*Poverty is no sin.*
Пе́рвый блин ко́мом.	lit *The first pancake is like a lump*, ie *The first step is always troublesome.*
В	
Век живи́—век учи́сь.	*Live and learn!*
С волка́ми жить—по-во́лчьи выть.	lit *If one is to live with wolves one has to howl like a wolf*, ie *When in Rome do as the Romans do.*
Ста́рого воробья́ на мяки́не не проведёшь.	*An old bird is not caught with chaff.*
Пу́ганая воро́на куста́ бои́тся.	lit *A frightened crow is afraid of a bush*, ie *Once bitten twice shy.*
Г	
В гостя́х хорошо́, а до́ма лу́чше.	*There's no place like home.*
Незва́ный гость ху́же тата́рина.	*An uninvited guest is worse than a Tatar.*
Д	
Дурака́м зако́н не пи́сан.	*Fools rush in where angels fear to tread.*
Ж	
Куй желе́зо пока́ горячо́.	*Strike while the iron is hot.*
Жизнь прожи́ть—не по́ле перейти́.	lit *Living through one's life is not like going through a field*, ie *Life is not a bed of roses.*

З	
За двумя́ за́йцами пого́нишься, ни одного́ не пойма́ешь.	lit *If you run after two hares you will catch neither.*
К	
Не плюй в коло́дец; случи́тся воды́ напи́ться.	lit *Don't spit in the well, you may need to drink out of it,* ie *Do not antagonise people whose help you may need later.*
Коси́ коса́ пока́ роса́.	*Make hay while the sun shines.*
Не всё коту́ ма́сленица, придёт и вели́кий пост.	*After the dinner comes the reckoning.*
Всяк кули́к своё боло́то хва́лит.	lit *Every sandpiper praises its own bog,* ie *People praise what is dear to them.*
Л	
Одна́ ла́сточка весны́ не де́лает.	*One swallow does not make a summer.*
Лес ру́бят—ще́пки летя́т.	lit *You cut down the forest and the bits of wood fly,* ie *You cannot make an omelette without breaking eggs.*
М	
Мир те́сен.	*It's a small world.*
В чужо́й монасты́рь со свои́м уста́вом не хо́дят.	lit *You don't go into sb else's monastery with your own* set of rules, ie *When in Rome do as the Romans do.*
Москва́ не сра́зу стро́илась.	*Rome was not built in a day.*
Н	
У семи́ ня́нек дитя́ без гла́зу.	lit *Where there are seven nannies the child is not watched,* ie *Too many cooks spoil the broth.*
П	
Всё переме́лется, мука́ бу́дет.	*It will all come right in the end.*
Плётью о́буха не перешибёшь.	lit *You can't break the head of an axe with a whip,* ie *The weakest goes to the wall.*
Поживём—уви́дим.	*Time will tell.*
Что посе́ешь, то и пожнёшь.	*As a man sows so shall he reap.*
Пра́вда глаза́ ко́лет.	*Home truths are hard to swallow.*
Р	
Своя́ руба́шка бли́же к те́лу.	lit *One's own shirt is nearer to the body,* ie *Charity begins at home.*
Ру́сский челове́к за́дним умо́м кре́пок.	*The Russian is wise after the event.*
Рыба́к рыбака́ ви́дит издалека́.	lit *The fisherman spots a fisherman from afar,* ie *Birds of a feather flock together.*
С	
Сде́ланного не воро́тишь.	*What's done can't be undone.*

Сме́лость города́ берёт.	lit *Boldness takes cities*, ie *Nothing ventured nothing gained.*
Соловья́ ба́снями не ко́рмят.	lit *You can't feed a nightingale with fables,* ie *Fine words butter no parsnips.*
Сы́тый голо́дного не разуме́ет.	lit *The well-fed cannot understand the hungry.*
Т	
Там хорошо́, где нас нет.	*The grass is always greener on the other side of the fence.*
Ти́ше е́дешь, да́льше бу́дешь.	*More haste less speed.*
У	
Ум хорошо́, а два лу́чше.	*Two heads are better than one.*
Х	
Хрен ре́дьки не сла́ще.	lit *Horseradish is no sweeter than ordinary radish,* ie *There is little to choose between two unpleasant things.*
Нет худа́ без добра́.	*Every cloud has a silver lining.*
Ц	
Цыпля́т по о́сени счита́ют.	*Don't count your chickens before they are hatched.*
Ч	
Не так стра́шен чёрт, как его́ малю́ют.	*The devil is not so terrible as he is painted.*
В ти́хом о́муте че́рти во́дятся.	*Still waters run deep.*
Я	
Язы́к до Ки́ева доведёт.	lit *Your tongue will get you to Kiev,* ie *Don't hesitate to ask people.*

4.9 Similes

A simile is an explicit likening of one thing to another. Languages have a stock of such comparisons, some of which are distinctive to that language. While the foreign student should take care not to use similes excessively or ostentatiously, their occasional use in the right context adds colour and authenticity to one's language, both oral and written. The following list gives some of the commonest Russian similes. It is arranged in alphabetical order of the key word in the comparison. As elsewhere in this chapter the translation offered gives the English equivalent of the Russian, where one exists, rather than a literal rendering.

(кружи́ться) как бе́лка в колесе́	*(to whirl around) like a squirrel in a wheel* (said of sb frantically busy)
дождь льёт как из ведра́	*it is raining cats and dogs* (lit *it is raining as out of a bucket*)

как с гу́ся вода́	*like water off a duck's back* (lit *like water off a goose*)
как в во́ду опу́щенный	*downcast, crestfallen*
как горо́х об сте́ну	*like a pea against a wall* (said of action that is futile)
(быть, сиде́ть) как на иго́лках	*(to be) on tenterhooks*
как две ка́пли воды́ похо́жи	*alike as two peas* (lit *like two drops of water*)
(жить) как ко́шка с соба́кой	*(to live) a cat and dog life*
холо́дный как лёд	*cold as ice*
(знать что́-н) как свои́ пять па́льцев	*(to know sth) like the back of one's hand*
как ры́ба в воде́	*in one's element/like a duck to water*
(би́ться) как ры́ба об лёд	*(to fight) like a fish against ice* (said about futile struggle)
как снег на́ голову	*like a bolt from the blue* (lit *like snow on one's head*)
как соба́ка на се́не	*like a dog in the manger*
гол как со́кол	*poor as a church mouse* (lit *naked like a falcon*)
как на раскалённых у́глях	*as on hot coals*
как чёрт от ла́дана	*like the devil from incense* (said of sb shunning sth)

5 Language and everyday life

5.1 Measurement

The metric system has been used in Russia since it was introduced on an obligatory basis by the Bolshevik government in 1918. The British Imperial system will not be understood by Russians, although some of the words denoting units of measure in that system may be familiar to them. Comparisons of units of different systems in the following sections are approximate.

5.1.1 Length, distance, height

Approximate metric equivalents of imperial units of measure of length:

1 inch = 25 millimetres
1 foot = 0.3 metres
1 yard = 0.9 metres
1 mile = 1.6 kilometres

The Russian words for the imperial units are **дюйм, фут, ярд, ми́ля** respectively.

The Russian words for the basic metric units of measure of length are:

миллиме́тр	*millimetre*
сантиме́тр	*centimetre*
метр	*metre*
киломе́тр	*kilometre*

Some rough equivalents:

10 сантиме́тров	4 inches
1 метр	just over a yard
100 ме́тров	110 yards
1 киломе́тр	five-eighths of a mile
100 киломе́тров	62 miles

мужчи́на ро́стом (в) метр во́семьдесят три (1,83)	a man 6′ tall
мужчи́на ро́стом (в) метр се́мьдесят пять (1,75)	a man 5′ 9″ tall
мужчи́на ро́стом (в) метр шестьдеся́т во́семь (1,68)	a man 5′ 6″ tall

де́вочка ро́стом (в) девяно́сто санти́ме́тров (0,90)	a girl nearly 3′ tall

Note: the versions of the above phrases without the preposition **в** are more colloquial.

A plane might fly at an altitude of 30,000 feet, ie **на высоте́ де́сять** [R3: **десяти́**] **ты́сяч ме́тров**.

The highest mountain in the world, Everest, has a height of roughly 29,000 feet, ie **во́семь ты́сяч восемьсо́т пятьдеся́т ме́тров.**

5.1.2 Area

Approximate metric equivalents of imperial units of measure of area:

1 square inch = 6.45 square centimetres
1 square foot = 0.09 square metres
1 square yard = 0.84 square metres
1 acre = 0.4 hectares
1 square mile = 259 hectares

The Russian adjective for *square* is **квадра́тный**. The metric unit of measure for large areas is the *hectare*, **гекта́р** (= 10,000 square metres).

Some rough equivalents with imperial measurements:

оди́н квадра́тный метр	just over 1 square yard
10 квадра́тных ме́тров	just under 12 square yards
два гекта́ра	nearly 5 acres (about the size of 3 football pitches)
250 гекта́ров	about 615 acres (roughly the area of Hyde Park)
20,000 квадра́тных киломе́тров	nearly 8,000 square miles (roughly the area of Wales)

5.1.3 Weight

Approximate metric equivalents of avoirdupois units of measure of weight:

1 ounce = 28.35 grams
1 pound = 0.45 kilograms
1 stone = 6.36 kilograms
1 hundredweight = 50.8 kilograms
1 ton = 1,016 kilograms

The Russian words for these avoirdupois units are **у́нция, фунт, сто́ун, ха́ндредвейт, то́нна** respectively.

The Russian words for the basic metric units of weight are:

миллигра́м	*milligram*
грамм	*gram*
килогра́мм	*kilogram*
це́нтнер	*100 kilograms*
то́нна	*(metric) tonne* (1,000 kg)

Some rough equivalents with avoirdupois weights:

200 грамм ма́сла	about 7 oz of butter
полкило́ мя́са	just over 1 lb of meat
мужчи́на ве́сом (в) 65 кило́	a man of just over 10 stone
мужчи́на ве́сом (в) 100 кило́/оди́н це́нтнер	a man of about 15 ½ stone
маши́на ве́сом (в) 1000 кило́/одну́ то́нну	a car weighing just under a ton

Note: the versions of the above phrases without the preposition **в** are more colloquial.

5.1.4 Volume

Approximate metric equivalents of imperial units of measure of volume:

1 cubic inch	= 16 cubic centimetres
1 cubic foot	= 0.03 cubic metres
1 cubic yard	= 0.8 cubic metres
1 pint	= 0.57 litres
1 gallon	= 4.55 litres

The Russian words for the last two imperial units are **пи́нта** and **галло́н** respectively.

The Russian adjective for *cubic* is **куби́ческий**; *litre* is **литр**.

Some rough equivalents:

полли́тра пи́ва	about a pint of beer
литр молока́	about $1^3/_4$ pints of milk
бензоба́к ёмкостью в 50 ли́тров	a petrol tank which holds about 11 gallons

Note: small quantities of drinks may be ordered by weight, eg **сто грамм во́дки**, *100 grams of vodka*; **двести́ грамм коньяка́**, *200 grams of brandy*.

5.1.5 Russian pre-revolutionary units of measure

Words relating to the earlier system of measurement will of course be found in pre-revolutionary literature and documents, and in some cases may persist in contexts in which they no longer have to do with precise measurement. The main units were:

length

вершо́к	= $1^3/_4''$ or 4.4 cm
арши́н	= 28″ or 71 cm

	са́же́нь (f)	= 7′ or 2.13 metres
	верста́	= $^{2}/_{3}$ mile or 1.07 km

Note: **ме́рить что́-н на свой арши́н**
to measure sth by one's own standards
ме́рить вёрсты
to travel a long way
хвата́ть вершки́ чего́-н
to get a smattering of sth

area	**десяти́на**	= 2.7 acres or 1.09 hectares
weight	**пуд**	= 36 lbs or 16.38 kg
dry measure	**га́рнец**	= 3.3 litres
	четвери́к	= 26.2 litres (8 x **га́рнец**)
	че́тверть (f)	= 210 litres (8 x **четвери́к**)
liquid measure	**штоф**	= 2 pints or 1.23 litres
	че́тверть (f)	= 5 pints or 3 litres
	ведро́	= 21 pints or 12.3 litres (10 x **штоф**, 4 x **че́тверть**)

5.1.6 Speed

Some rough equivalents:

60 киломе́тров в час	37 miles an hour
100 киломе́тров в час	62 miles an hour
160 киломе́тров в час	100 miles an hour
300 миллио́нов ме́тров в секу́нду	186,000 feet per second (the speed of light)

5.1.7 Temperature

The centigrade scale constructed by Celsius is used, and the Fahrenheit scale will not be generally understood. The formulae for conversion are:

$C = (F - 32) \times {}^{5}/_{9}$, eg 77°F = 25°C
$F = (C \times {}^{9}/_{5}) + 32$, eg 15°C = 59°F

Some equivalents:

по Це́льсию	**по Фаренге́йту**
сто гра́дусов (100°, **то́чка кипе́ния воды́,** ie *boiling point of water*)	212°
три́дцать гра́дусов (тепла́) (30° above zero)	86°
два́дцать гра́дусов (тепла́) (20° above zero)	68°
де́сять гра́дусов (тепла́) (10° above zero)	50°
четы́ре гра́дуса (тепла́) (4° above zero)	39°

нуль (m; 0°, **то́чка замерза́ния воды́,** ie *freezing point of water*)	32°
пять гра́дусов ни́же нуля́/моро́за (-5°)	23°
два́дцать гра́дусов ни́же нуля́/моро́за (-20°)	-4°
со́рок гра́дусов ни́же нуля́/моро́за (-40°)	-40°

The normal temperature of the human body (98.4°F) is just under 37°C, ie **три́дцать семь гра́дусов**, more precisely **три́дцать шесть и де́вять**.

5.2 Currency

The basic unit of currency is the rouble (**рубль**). The smaller unit, the kopeck (**копе́йка**), of which there are a hundred to the rouble, has with post-Soviet hyperinflation become valueless. The official rate of exchange (**курс**) was approximately £1 = 3,000 roubles in mid-1994, but the rate is so unstable that a list of equivalents would be of little use.

Salaries are described in monthly terms (eg **сто ты́сяч рубле́й в ме́сяц**, *100,000 roubles a month*).

Russian pre-revolutionary coins, the names of which may be encountered in classical literature and pre-revolutionary documents, included the **алты́н** (3 kopecks), **гри́вна** (10 kopecks) and **полти́нник** (50 kopecks).

5.3 Fractions and presentation of numerals

A decimal point is indicated in writing by a comma and is read as follows:

3,1 **три це́лых и одна́ деся́тая** [**часть**, *part*, is understood]
4,2 **четы́ре це́лых и две деся́тых**
5,5 **пять це́лых и пять деся́тых**
7,6 **семь це́лых и шесть деся́тых**
8,9 **во́семь це́лых и де́вять деся́тых**

Because the comma is used to indicate a decimal point it cannot be used to separate blocks in numbers involving thousands and millions, which may instead be spaced out in the following way:

23 987 **два́дцать три ты́сячи девятьсо́т во́семьдесят семь**
2 564 000 **два миллио́на пятьсо́т шестьдеся́т четы́ре ты́сячи**

5.4 Time

The 24-hour clock is widely used for all official purposes, eg

Конферéнция начинáется в 15.00 часóв.
The conference begins at 3.00 pm.
Пóезд отправля́ется в 21.00 час.
The train leaves at 9.00 pm.

If the 24-hour clock is not used, and one needs to specify which part of the day one is talking about, then one of the following forms (in the genitive case) should follow the stated time:

утрá *in the morning*
дня *in the afternoon*
вéчера *in the evening*
нóчи *in the night*

eg **в вóсемь часóв утрá**, *at 8 in the morning*; **в дéсять часóв вéчера**, *at 10 in the evening.*

Note: **вéчер** implies any time up until bedtime, whilst **ночь** indicates the period after midnight.

In R1/2 time is frequently presented in the simplified forms **три двáдцать**, *three twenty*; **вóсемь три́дцать пять**, *eight thirty-five*; rather than the more cumbersome **двáдцать мину́т четвёртого** and **без двадцати́ пяти́ дéвять** respectively. Forms such as **полседьмóго**, *half (past) six*, are also preferred in R1/2 to the fuller **полови́на седьмóго**.

Russia contains 11 time zones. Speakers may therefore need to specify which time zone they have in mind, eg **в дéсять часóв по москóвскому врéмени**, *at 10 o'clock Moscow time.*

5.5 Telephone numbers

In big cities these will normally consist of seven digits, which will be divided up and read in the following way:

243-71-59 **двéсти сóрок три/сéмьдесят оди́н/пятьдеся́т дéвять**
391-64-27 **три́ста девянóсто оди́н/шестьдеся́т четы́ре/двáдцать семь**

5.6 Postal addresses

These are presented in inverse order to that used in English, that is to say in the order country, code, town, street, building, addressee. The abbreviations **к. (кóрпус**, *block*), **д. (дом**, *house*), **кв. (кварти́ра**, *flat*), may be used. The name of the addressee is put in the dative case. Examples:

Росси́я 197343,
Москвá,

Украйна 253223,
г. Ки́ев,

ул. Ташке́нтская,	**ул. П. Вершиго́ры,**
д. 23, кв. 36,	**д. 3а, кв. 22,**
Елисе́евой, В.А.	**Па́влову, С.Г.**

5.7 Family relationships

The English-speaker is bewildered by the number of terms used in Russian to denote family relationships. Both the terms *father-in-law* and *mother-in-law*, for example, have to be rendered in different ways depending on whether the speaker has in mind the husband's or the wife's parents.

A man may have the following relations:

жена́	*wife*
тесть (m)	*father-in-law*
тёща	*mother-in-law*
шу́рин	*brother-in-law* (wife's brother)
своя́к	*brother-in-law* (husband of wife's sister)
своя́ченица	*sister-in-law* (wife's sister)

A woman on the other hand may have the following relations:

муж	*husband*
свёкор	*father-in-law*
свекро́вь (f)	*mother-in-law*
де́верь (m)	*brother-in-law* (husband's brother)
золо́вка	*sister-in-law* (husband's sister)

Note: the terms **шу́рин, своя́к, своя́ченица, де́верь, золо́вка** are more widespread in the provinces than in the city, not surprisingly in view of the fact that this complex terminology originally related to the extended family in the rural community. The foreign student need not be much troubled by them; some descriptive phrase, eg **брат жены́**, may be used instead.

Two further terms are particularly confusing, viz

зять (m)	*brother-in-law* (sister's husband or husband's sister's husband); also *son-in-law*
неве́стка	*sister-in-law* (brother's wife); also *daughter-in-law* (son's wife)

However, these relations are nowadays increasingly expressed by means of a description, eg **муж сестры́**, *sister's husband*; **жена́ бра́та**, *brother's wife*.

5.8 Public notices

A number of grammatical structures are characteristic of public notices, the language of which may be seen as a variety of R3b.

(a) Where an order or prohibition is expressed the imperative is often rendered by an infinitive form. In an instruction the infinitive is perfective, whilst in a prohibition it is imperfective, eg

Пристегну́ть ремни́.
Fasten seatbelts.
При ава́рии разби́ть стекло́ молотко́м.
In the event of an accident break the glass with the hammer. (in bus)
Убра́ть за собо́й посу́ду.
Clear away dishes after you. (in canteen)

Не кури́ть.
No smoking.
Не входи́ть в пальто́.
Do not enter in your coat. (in offices, etc)
Не бе́гать по эскала́торам.
Do not run up and down the escalators. (in underground)
Не прислоня́ться.
Do not lean. (on doors of underground train)
По газо́нам не ходи́ть.
Keep off the grass.
Приноси́ть и распива́ть спиртны́е напи́тки запрещено́.
It is forbidden to bring and consume alcoholic drinks.

(b) Instructions and prohibitions may also be couched in the imperative though, eg

Пройди́те да́льше в ваго́н.
Pass down the vehicle. (in tram)
Соблюда́й диста́нцию.
Keep your distance. (on back of vehicle)
Не отвлека́йте води́теля посторо́нними разгово́рами.
Do not distract the driver by talking to him.
Не стой под стрело́й.
Do not stand under the arm. (on crane)

(c) Prohibitions may also be expressed with a past passive participle, eg

Вход посторо́нним запрещён.
Unauthorised persons not admitted.
Кури́ть запрещено́.
Smoking prohibited.

(d) An exhortation may be couched in a third-person plural form, or with the word **про́сьба**, *request*, eg

У нас не ку́рят.
No smoking here.
Про́сьба закрыва́ть дверь.
Please close the door.

(e) Statements providing information, and also prohibitions, are often rendered by a reflexive verb, eg

Вы́емка пи́сем произво́дится в 8 часо́в.
Collection of letters takes place at 8.00. (on letter box)
Стол не обслу́живается.
No service at this table. (in restaurant)
Вход посторо́нним стро́го воспреща́ется.
Entry to people who have no business here strictly forbidden. (eg on building site)

(f) Some notices or instructions incorporate gerunds (see 8.7.1–2, 10.11.1), which are characteristic of R3, eg

Уходя́, гаси́те свет.
Turn out the light when you leave.
Опуска́я письмо́, прове́рьте нали́чие и́ндекса.
Check that you have put the postcode on when you post your letter.

(g) Miscellaneous notices:

закры́т на́ зиму	*closed for the winter* (on train windows)
закры́т на ремо́нт	*closed for repairs* (ubiquitous)
закры́т на учёт	*closed for stock-taking* (in shop)
иди́те	*go* (at road crossing)
к себе́	*pull* (on doors)
от себя́	*push* (on doors)
стоп!	*stop* (at road crossing, etc)
осторо́жно! высо́кое напряже́ние	*Warning. High voltage.*

5.9 Abbreviations of titles, weights, measures and common expressions

бул.	**бульва́р**	*boulevard, avenue*
в.	**век**	*century*
г	**грамм**	*gram*
г.	**год**	*year*
	гора́	*mountain*
	го́род	*town, city*
	господи́н	*Mr*
га	**гекта́р**	*hectare*
г-жа	**госпожа́**	*Mrs*
гл.	**гла́вный**	*main*
гос.	**госуда́рственный**	*state*
д.	**дом**	*house*
до н.э.	**до на́шей э́ры**	*BC*
ж.д.	**желе́зная доро́га**	*railway*

жит.	**жи́тели**	*inhabitants*
и т.д.	**и так да́лее**	*etc, and so on*
и т.п.	**и тому́ подо́бное**	*etc, and so on*
изд-во	**изда́тельство**	*publishing house*
им.	**и́мени**	*named after*
ин-т	**институ́т**	*institute*
кв.	**кварти́ра**	*flat, apartment*
кг	**килогра́мм**	*kilogram*
к-т	**комите́т**	*committee*
к/ч	**киломе́тры в час**	*kilometres per hour*
м	**метр**	*metre*
м.	**мину́та**	*minute*
мин-во	**министе́рство**	*ministry*
мор.	**морско́й**	*naval, marine*
напр.	**наприме́р**	*eg*
нар.	**наро́дный**	*people's*
нац.	**национа́льный**	*national*
н. ст.	**но́вый стиль**	*New Style* (post-revolutionary calendar)
н.э.	**на́шей э́ры**	*AD*
о.	**о́стров**	*island*
об.	**о́бласть**	*province*
оз.	**о́зеро**	*lake*
пл.	**пло́щадь**	*square*
пр.	**проспе́кт**	*avenue*
р.	**река́**	*river*
	рубль	*rouble*
р-н	**райо́н**	*region*
с.	**село́**	*village*
	страни́ца	*page*
с. г.	**сего́ го́да**	*of this year*
см.	**смотри́**	*see, vide*
ср.	**сравни́**	*compare, cf*
ст. ст.	**ста́рый стиль**	*Old Style* (pre-revolutionary calendar)
стр.	**страни́ца**	*page*
с.х.	**сельскохозя́йственный**	*agricultural*
т	**то́нна**	*tonne*

т.	**том**	*volume*
т.е.	**то есть**	*that is to say, ie*
т.к.	**так как**	*since*
ул.	**у́лица**	*street*
ун-т	**университе́т**	*university*
ф. ст.	**фунт стéрлингов**	*pound sterling*
ч.	**час**	*hour, o'clock*

5.10 Acronyms and alphabetisms

Acronyms and alphabetisms function as nouns. They have a gender of their own, and many (those which can be pronounced as a single word, as opposed to a succession of individual letters) also decline, eg **ЗАГС**, *register office*; **ООН**, *UNO*, which decline like masculine nouns ending in a hard consonant.

Acronyms and alphabetisms continue to abound in the Russian press. However, those denoting Soviet institutions and the names of institutions or countries in the communist world as a whole, which five years ago would have had to have been included in a list such as the following, for the most part now have only historical significance. (These are indicated below with an asterisk.)

Most of the acronyms and alphabetisms given below will be widely understood.

АН	**Акаде́мия нау́к**	*Academy of Sciences*
АН-	**Анто́нов-**	*Antonov* (Russian aircraft)
АСЕАН	**Ассоциа́ция госуда́рств Юго-Восто́чной А́зии**	*Association of Southeast Asian Nations (ASEAN)*
АЭС	**а́томная электроста́нция**	*atomic power-station*
БАМ	**Байка́ло-Аму́рская магистра́ль**	*Baikal-Amur Railway* (i.e. East Siberian railway)
БТР	**бронетранспортёр**	*armoured personnel carrier*
ВВП	**валово́й вну́тренний проду́кт**	*gross domestic product (GDP)*
ВВС	**Вое́нно-Возду́шные Си́лы**	*air force*
ВДНХ	**Вы́ставка достиже́ний наро́дного хозя́йства**	exhibition of Soviet economic achievement
ВМК	**вое́нно-промы́шленный ко́мплекс**	*military-industrial complex*
ВМФ	**Вое́нно-Морско́й Флот**	*(military) navy*
ВНП	**валово́й национа́льный проду́кт**	*gross national product (GNP)*
ВОЗ	**Всеми́рная организа́ция здравоохране́ния**	*World Health Organisation (WHO)*
ВС	**вооружённые си́лы**	*armed forces*

ГАИ	**Госуда́рственная автомоби́льная инспе́кция**	Soviet/Russian traffic police
ГАТТ	**Генера́льное соглаше́ние о тари́фах и торго́вле**	*General Agreement on Tariffs and Trade (GATT)*
ГДР*	**Герма́нская Демократи́ческая Респу́блика**	former East Germany
ГКЧП*	**Госуда́рственный Комите́т Чрезвыча́йного Положе́ния**	Committee responsible for putsch in USSR in August 1991
ГРУ*	**Гла́вное разве́дывательное управле́ние**	Soviet military intelligence
ГЭС	**гидроэлектроста́нция**	*hydroelectric power-station*
ЕС	**Европе́йское соо́бщество/ Европе́йский сою́з**	*European Community (EC)/European Union (EU)*
ЗАГС	**(отде́л) за́писи а́ктов гражда́нского состоя́ния**	register office
ИЛ-	**Илью́шин-**	*Iliushin* (Russian aircraft)
ИМЛИ	**Институ́т мирово́й литерату́ры**	*Institute of World Literature* (in Moscow)
КГБ*	**Комите́т госуда́рственной безопа́сности**	*Committee of State Security (KGB)*
КНДР	**Коре́йская Наро́дно-Демократи́ческая респу́блика**	*North Korea*
КПСС*	**Коммунисти́ческая па́ртия Сове́тского Сою́за**	*Communist Party of the Soviet Union (CPSU)*
МАГАТЭ	**Междунаро́дное аге́нтство по а́томной эне́ргии**	*International Atomic Energy Agency (IAEA)*
МБРР	**Междунаро́дный банк реконстру́кции и разви́тия**	*International Bank for Reconstruction and Development*
МНР	**Монго́льская Наро́дная респу́блика**	*Mongolian People's Republic*
МПС	**Министе́рство путе́й сообще́ния**	*Ministry of Communications*
МХАТ	**Моско́вский худо́жественный академи́ческий теа́тр**	*Moscow Arts Theatre*
НАТО	**Североатланти́ческий сою́з**	*North Atlantic Treaty Organisation (NATO)*
НКВД	**Наро́дный комиссариа́т вну́тренних дел**	*People's Commissariat of Internal Affairs* (Soviet police agency, 1934–43)
НЭП	**но́вая экономи́ческая поли́тика**	*New Economic Policy* (of 1920s)
ОАЭ	**Объединённые Ара́бские Эмира́ты**	*United Arab Emirates*
ОВД*	**Организа́ция Варша́вского Догово́ра**	*Warsaw Treaty Organisation*
ОВИР	**Отде́л виз и регистра́ции** (now also **УВИ́Р**, ie **Управле́ние** etc)	*visa and registration department*
ООН	**Организа́ция Объединённых На́ций**	*United Nations Organisation (UN)*

ООП	**Организа́ция Освобожде́ния Палести́ны**	*Palestine Liberation Organisation (PLO)*
ОПЕК	**Организа́ция стран-экспортёров не́фти**	*Organisation of Petroleum Exporting Countries (OPEC)*
ОЭСР	**Организа́ция экономи́ческого сотру́дничества и разви́тия**	*Organisation for Economic Co-operation and Development (OECD)*
ПВО	**противо-возду́шная оборо́на**	*anti-aircraft defence*
РСФСР*	**Росси́йская Сове́тская Федерати́вная Социалисти́ческая Респу́блика**	*Russian Soviet Federal Socialist Republic (RSFSR)*
СКВ	**свобо́дно-конверти́руемая валю́та**	*convertible currency*
СНГ	**Сою́з незави́симых госуда́рств**	*Union of Independent States (CIS)*
СП	**совме́стное предприя́тие**	*joint venture*
СССР*	**Сою́з Сове́тских Социалист-и́ческих Респу́блик**	*Union of Soviet Socialist Republics (USSR)*
США	**Соединённые Шта́ты Аме́рики**	*United States of America (USA)*
СЭВ*	**Сове́т Экономи́ческой взаимопо́мощи**	*Council for Mutual Economic Aid (COMECON)*
ТАСС	**Телегра́фное аге́нтство Сове́тского Сою́за**	*TASS*, ie the Soviet news agency
ТВ	**телеви́дение**	*TV*
ТНК	**транснациона́льные корпора́ции**	*multinational corporations*
ТУ-	**Ту́полев-**	*Tupolev* (Russian aircraft)
ФБР	**Федера́льное бюро́ рассле́дований**	*Federal Bureau of Investigation (FBI)*
ФРГ*	**Федерати́вная Респу́блика Герма́нии**	former West Germany
ФСК	**Федера́льная слу́жба контрразве́дки**	*Federal Counter-Intelligence Service* (former KGB)
ЦБР	**Центра́льный банк Росси́и**	*Central Bank of Russia*
ЦК*	**Центра́льный Комите́т**	*Central Committee* (of CPSU)
ЦРУ	**Центра́льное разве́дывательное управле́ние**	*Central Intelligence Agency (CIA)*
ЭВМ	**электро́нно-вычисли́тельная маши́на**	*electronic calculating machine* (ie *computer*, now replaced by **компью́тер**)
ЮНЕСКО	**Организа́ция ООН по вопро́сам образова́ния, нау́ки и культу́ры**	*United Nations Educational, Scientific and Cultural Organisation (UNESCO)*

5.11 Names of countries and nationalities

The following lists are not exhaustive, but give the names of most countries of the world, grouped according to continent or region, together with the adjectives formed from them and the nouns denoting male and female representatives of each nationality.

The suffixes most commonly used to denote nationality are **-ец** and **-нин**, for males, and **-ка** and **-нка** for females. However, in certain instances the expected feminine form cannot be used or at least seems unnatural to native-speakers (and is therefore omitted in the lists in the following sections). In other instances no noun at all is derived from the name of the country to denote nationality, or at least Russians might hesitate to use a form that does in theory exist. When in doubt as to whether a noun denoting nationality may be used one may have recourse to a phrase with **жи́тели**, *inhabitants*, eg **жи́тели Буру́нди**, *people who live in Burundi.*

In some foreign words the letter **е** is pronounced **э**; this pronunciation is indicated in brackets after the word in question.

* An asterisk after a place-name in this section indicates that the noun in question is indeclinable.

Note: nouns and adjectives denoting nationality do not begin with a capital letter in Russian (see also 10.16).

5.11.1 Russia and the other states of the former Soviet Union

Note: the name of the former Soviet republic is given in brackets where it differs from the name of the new state.

	country	adjective	man/woman
Russia	**Росси́я**	**ру́сский**	**ру́сский/ру́сская**
Russian Federation	**Росси́йская Федера́ция**	**росси́йский**	**россия́нин/россия́нка**

Note: **росси́йский** has come to be used to denote the nationality, which embraces people who are not ethnically Russian and things which are not culturally Russian.

	country	adjective	man/woman
Armenia	**Арме́ния**	**армя́нский**	**армяни́н/армя́нка**
Azerbaijan	**Азербайджа́н**	**азербайджа́нский**	**азербайджа́нец/ азербайджа́нка**
Belarus	**Белару́сь** (f) **(Белору́ссия)**	**белору́сский**	**белору́с/ белору́ска**
Estonia	**Эсто́ния**	**эсто́нский**	**эсто́нец/эсто́нка**
Georgia	**Гру́зия**	**грузи́нский**	**грузи́н/грузи́нка**
Kazakhstan	**Казахста́н**	**каза́хский**	**каза́х/каза́шка**
Kirgizia	**Кыргызста́н (Кирги́зия)**	**кирги́зский**	**кирги́з/кирги́зка**
Latvia	**Ла́твия**	**латви́йский**	**латы́ш/латы́шка**
Lithuania	**Литва́**	**лито́вский**	**лито́вец/лито́вка**
Moldova	**Молдо́ва (Молда́вия)**	**молда́вский** or **молдава́нский**	**молдава́нин/молдава́нка**

Tadjikistan	**Таджикиста́н**	**таджи́кский**	**таджи́к/таджи́чка**
Turkmenistan	**Туркмениста́н (Туркме́ния)**	**туркме́нский**	**туркме́н/туркме́нка**
Ukraine	**Украи́на**	**украи́нский**	**украи́нец/украи́нка**

Note: *in Ukraine*: **на Украи́не.**

Uzbekistan	**Узбекиста́н**	**узбе́кский**	**узбе́к/узбе́чка**

5.11.2 Other regions and national minorities of Russia and the former Soviet Union

	region	adjective	ethnic group
Abkhazia	**Абха́зия**	**абха́зский**	**абха́зец/абха́зка**
Baikal region	**Забайка́лье**	**забайка́льский**	**забайка́лец**
Baltic region	**Приба́лтика** (also **Ба́лтия**)	**прибалти́йский**	**приба́лт(и́ец)/ прибалти́йка**
Bashkiria	**Башки́рия**	**башки́рский**	**башки́р/башки́рка**
black earth region	**чернозём**	**чернозёмный**	
Buriat region	**Буря́тия**	**буря́тский**	**буря́т/буря́тка**
Caucasus	**Кавка́з**	**кавка́зский**	**кавка́зец/кавка́зка**
Chechnia	**Чечня́**	**чече́нский**	**чече́нец/чече́нка**
Chuvash region	**Чува́шия**	**чува́шский**	**чува́ш/чува́шка**
Crimea	**Крым**	**кры́мский**	**крымча́нин/крымча́нка**

Note: *in the Crimea*: **в Крыму́.**

Dagestan	**Дагеста́н**	**дагеста́нский**	**дагеста́нец/дагеста́нка**
Ingushetia	**Ингуше́тия**	**ингу́шский**	**ингу́ш/ингу́шка**
Kalmyk region	**Калмы́кия**	**калмы́цкий**	**калмы́к/калмы́чка**
Karelia	**Каре́лия**	**каре́льский**	**каре́л/каре́лка**
Kuban	**Куба́нь** (f)	**куба́нский**	**куба́нец/куба́нка**

Note: *in the Kuban*: **на Куба́ни.**

Mari Republic	**Мари́йская Респу́блика**	**мари́йский**	**мари́ец/мари́йка** or **ма́ри** (m and f, indecl)
Mordvin region	**Мордо́вия**	**мордо́вский**	**мордви́н/мордви́нка**; also **мордва́** (collect)
Moscow region	**Подмоско́вье**	**подмоско́вный**	
Ossetia	**Осе́тия**	**осети́нский**	**осети́н/осети́нка**
Siberia	**Сиби́рь** (f)	**сиби́рский**	**сибиря́к/сибиря́чка**
steppe	**степь** (f)	**степно́й**	
taiga	**тайга́**	**таёжный**	**таёжник**

Tatarstan	**Татарста́н**	**тата́рский**	**тата́рин/тата́рка**
Transcaucasia	**Закавка́зье**	**закавка́зский**	
tundra	**ту́ндра**	**ту́ндровый**	
Udmurt region	**Удму́ртия**	**удму́ртский**	**удму́рт/удму́ртка**
White Sea coast	**Се́верное помо́рье**	**помо́рский**	**помо́р/помо́рка**
Yakutia	**Яку́тия/Са́ха**	**яку́тский**	**яку́т/яку́тка**

5.11.3 Europe (Евро́па)

Albania	**Алба́ния**	**алба́нский**	**алба́нец/алба́нка**
Austria	**А́встрия**	**австри́йский**	**австри́ец/австри́йка**
Belgium	**Бе́льгия**	**бельги́йский**	**бельги́ец/бельги́йка**
Bosnia	**Бо́сния**	**босни́йский**	**босни́ец/босни́йка**
Bulgaria	**Болга́рия**	**болга́рский**	**болга́рин/болга́рка**
Croatia	**Аорва́тия**	**хорва́тский**	**хорва́т/хорва́тка**
Czech Republic	**Че́шская Респу́блика**	**че́шский**	**чех/че́шка**
Denmark	**Да́ния**	**да́тский**	**датча́нин/датча́нка**
England	**А́нглия**	**англи́йский**	**англича́нин/англича́нка**
Finland	**Финля́ндия**	**фи́нский**	**финн/фи́нка**
France	**Фра́нция**	**францу́зский**	**францу́з/францу́женка**
Germany	**Герма́ния**	**неме́цкий**	**не́мец/не́мка**
Great Britain	**Великобрита́ния**	**брита́нский/ англи́йский**	**брита́нец/брита́нка англича́нин/англича́нка**

Note: **англи́йский, англича́нин, англича́нка** tend to be used to encompass where necessary all things British or all British people unless it is intended to make specific reference to Scottish or Welsh things or people.

Greece	**Гре́ция**	**гре́ческий**	**грек/греча́нка**
Holland	**Голла́ндия/ Нидерла́нды**	**голла́ндский/ нидерла́ндский**	**голла́ндец/голла́ндка** or **нидерла́ндец/ нидерла́ндка**
Hungary	**Ве́нгрия**	**венге́рский**	**венгр/венге́рка**
Iceland	**Исла́ндия**	**исла́ндский**	**исла́ндец/исла́ндка**
Ireland	**Ирла́ндия**	**ирла́ндский**	**ирла́ндец/ирла́ндка**
Italy	**Ита́лия**	**италья́нский**	**италья́нец/италья́нка**
Luxembourg	**Люксембу́рг**	**люксембу́ргский**	**люксембу́ржец/ люксембу́ржка**
Norway	**Норве́гия**	**норве́жский**	**норве́жец/норве́жка**
Poland	**По́льша**	**по́льский**	**поля́к/по́лька**
Portugal	**Португа́лия**	**португа́льский**	**португа́лец/португа́лка**

Romania	**Румы́ния**	**румы́нский**	**румы́н/румы́нка**
Scotland	**Шотла́ндия**	**шотла́ндский**	**шотла́ндец/шотла́ндка**
Serbia	**Се́рбия**	**се́рбский**	**серб/се́рбка**
Slovakia	**Слова́кия**	**слова́цкий**	**слова́к/слова́чка**
Slovenia	**Слове́ния**	**слове́нский**	**слове́нец/слове́нка**
Spain	**Испа́ния**	**испа́нский**	**испа́нец/испа́нка**
Sweden	**Шве́ция**	**шве́дский**	**швед/шве́дка**
Switzerland	**Швейца́рия**	**швейца́рский**	**швейца́рец/швейца́рка**
Wales	**Уэ́льс**	**уэ́льский/валли́йский**	**уэ́льсец** or **валли́ец/валли́йка**

5.11.4 Africa (А́фрика)

Algeria	**Алжи́р**	**алжи́рский**	**алжи́рец/алжи́рка**
Angola	**Анго́ла**	**анго́льский**	**анго́лец/анго́лка**
Benin	**Бени́н**	**бени́нский**	**бени́ец/бени́йка**
Botswana	**Ботсва́на**	**ботсва́нский**	**жи́тели Ботсва́ны**
Burundi	**Буру́нди***	**бурунди́йский**	**жи́тели Буру́нди**
Cameroon	**Камеру́н**	**камеру́нский**	**камеру́нец/камеру́нка**
Chad	**Чад**	**ча́дский**	**жи́тели Ча́да**
Egypt	**Еги́пет**	**еги́петский**	**египтя́нин/египтя́нка**
Ethiopia	**Эфио́пия**	**эфио́пский**	**эфио́п/эфио́пка**
Ghana	**Га́на**	**га́нский**	**га́нец/га́нка**
Ivory Coast	**Бе́рег Слоно́вой Ко́сти**		**жи́тели Бе́рега Слоно́вой Ко́сти**
Kenya	**Ке́ния**	**кени́йский**	**кени́ец/кени́йка**
Libya	**Ли́вия**	**ливи́йский**	**ливи́ец/ливи́йка**
Mauritania	**Маврита́ния**	**маврита́нский**	**маврита́нец/маврита́нка**
Morocco	**Маро́кко***	**марокка́нский**	**марокка́нец/марокка́нка**
Mozambique	**Мозамби́к**	**мозамби́кский**	**жи́тели Мозамби́ка**
Namibia	**Нами́бия**	**намиби́йский**	**жи́тели Нами́бии**
Nigeria	**Ниге́рия**	**нигери́йский**	**нигери́ец/нигери́йка**
Rwanda	**Руа́нда**	**руанди́йский**	**руанди́ец/руанди́йка**
Senegal	**Сенега́л**	**сенега́льский**	**сенега́лец/сенега́лка**
Somalia	**Сомали́***	**сомали́йский**	**сомали́ец/сомали́йка**
South Africa	**Южно-Африка́нская Респу́блика (ЮАР)**	**южноафрика́нский**	**жи́тели ЮАР**
Sudan	**Суда́н**	**суда́нский**	**суда́нец/суда́нка**

Tanzania	**Танза́ния**	**танзани́йский**	**танзани́ец/танзани́йка**
Togo	**То́го**	**тоголе́зский**	**тоголе́зец/тоголе́зка**
Tunisia	**Туни́с**	**туни́сский**	**туни́сец/туни́ска**
Uganda	**Уга́нда**	**уга́ндский**	**уга́ндец/уга́ндка**
Zaire	**Заи́р**	**заи́рский**	**заи́рец/заи́рка**
Zambia	**За́мбия**	**замби́йский**	**замби́ец/замби́йка**
Zimbabwe	**Зимба́бве***	**зимбабви́йский**	**зимбабви́ец/зимбабви́йка**

5.11.5 America (Аме́рика)

Argentina	**Аргенти́на**	**аргенти́нский**	**аргенти́нец/аргенти́нка**
Bolivia	**Боли́вия**	**боливи́йский**	**боливи́ец/боливи́йка**
Brazil	**Брази́лия**	**брази́льский**	**брази́лец/бразилья́нка**
Canada	**Кана́да**	**кана́дский**	**кана́дец/кана́дка**
Chile	**Чи́ли***	**чили́йский**	**чили́ец/чили́йка**
Colombia	**Колу́мбия**	**колумби́йский**	**колумби́ец/колумби́йка**
Costa Rica	**Ко̀ста-Ри́ка**	**коста-рика́нский**	**костарика́нец/ костарика́нка**
Ecuador	**Эквадо́р**	**эквадо́рский**	**эквадо́рец/эквадо́рка**
El Salvador	**Сальвадо́р**	**сальвадо́рский**	**сальвадо́рец/ сальвадо́рка**
Guatemala	**Гватема́ла (тэ)**	**гватема́льский**	**гватема́лец/гватема́лка**
Guyana	**Гайа́на**	**гайа́нский**	**гайа́нец/гайа́нка**
Honduras	**Гондура́с**	**гондура́сский**	**гондура́сец/гондура́ска**
Mexico	**Ме́ксика**	**мексика́нский**	**мексика́нец/мексика́нка**
Nicaragua	**Никара́гуа**	**никарагуа́нский**	**никарагуа́нец/ никарагуа́нка**
Panama	**Пана́ма**	**пана́мский**	**жи́тели Пана́мы**
Paraguay	**Парагва́й**	**парагва́йский**	**парагва́ец/парагва́йка**
Peru	**Перу́* (Пэ)**	**перуа́нский**	**перуа́нец/перуа́нка**
United States of America	**Соединённые Шта́ты Аме́рики**	**америка́нский**	**америка́нец/америка́нка**
Uruguay	**Уругва́й**	**уругва́йский**	**уругва́ец/уругва́йка**
Venezuela	**Венесу́эла**	**венесу́эльский**	**венесу́элец/венесу́элка**

5.11.6 Asia (А́зия)

Afghanistan	**Афганиста́н**	**афга́нский**	**афга́нец/афга́нка**

Bangladesh	**Бангладе́ш**	**бангладе́шский**	**бангладе́шец/ бангладе́шка**
Burma	**Би́рма**	**бирма́нский**	**бирма́нец/бирма́нка**
Cambodia	**Камбо́джа/Кампучи́я**	**камбоджи́йский/ кампучи́йский**	**камбоджи́ец/ камбоджи́йка** or **кампучи́ец/кампучи́йка**
China	**Кита́й**	**кита́йский**	**кита́ец/китая́нка**

Note: **кита́йка** cannot be used for *Chinese woman*; it means *nankeen* (type of cloth).

India	**И́ндия**	**инди́йский**	**инди́ец/индиа́нка**

Note [1] The forms **инду́с/инду́ска**, originally *Hindu*, are often used instead of **инди́ец/индиа́нка**.

[2] The adjective **инде́йский** and the noun **инде́ец** refer to American Indians. The feminine form **индиа́нка** may refer to an Indian woman of either race. The noun **инде́йка** means *turkey*.

Indonesia	**Индоне́зия**	**индонези́йский**	**индонези́ец/индонези́йка**
Iran	**Ира́н**	**ира́нский**	**ира́нец/ира́нка**

Note: the forms **Пе́рсия, перси́дский**, and **перс/персия́нка** also occur, but like their English equivalents (*Persia, Persian, Persian man/woman*) they are not used with reference to the modern state of Iran.

Japan	**Япо́ния**	**япо́нский**	**япо́нец/япо́нка**
Korea	**Коре́я**	**коре́йский**	**коре́ец/корея́нка**

Note: **коре́йка** cannot be used for *Korean woman*; it means *brisket* (meat).

Laos	**Лао́с**	**лао́сский**	**лаотя́нин/лаотя́нка**
Malaya	**Мала́йя**	**мала́йский**	**мала́ец/мала́йка**
Malaysia	**Мала́йзия**	**малайзи́йский**	**малайзи́ец/малайзи́йка**
Mongolia	**Монго́лия**	**монго́льский**	**монго́л/монго́лка**
Nepal	**Непа́л**	**непа́льский**	**непа́лец/непа́лка**
Pakistan	**Пакиста́н**	**пакиста́нский**	**пакиста́нец/пакиста́нка**
Singapore	**Сингапу́р**	**сингапу́рский**	**сингапу́рец/сингапу́рка**
Sri Lanka	**Шри-Ла́нка**	**шри-ланки́йский**	**жи́тели Шри-Ла́нки**
Thailand	**Таила́нд**	**таила́ндский/та́йский**	**таила́ндец/таила́ндка** or (in pl) **та́йцы**
Tibet	**Тибе́т**	**тибе́тский**	**тибе́тец/тибе́тка**
Vietnam	**Вьетна́м**	**вьетна́мский**	**вьетна́мец/вьетна́мка**

5.11.7 The Middle East (Бли́жний Восто́к)

Iraq	**Ира́к**	**ира́кский**	**жи́тели Ира́ка**
Israel	**Изра́иль** (m)	**изра́ильский**	**израильтя́нин/ израильтя́нка**
Jordan	**Иорда́ния**	**иорда́нский**	**иорда́нец/иорда́нка**

Kuwait	**Куве́йт (вэ)**	**куве́йтский**	**жи́тели Куве́йта**
Lebanon	**Лива́н**	**лива́нский**	**лива́нец/лива́нка**
Palestine	**Палести́на**	**палести́нский**	**палести́нец/палести́нка**
Saudi Arabia	**Сау́довская Ара́вия**	**сау́довский**	**жи́тели Сау́довской Ара́вии**
Syria	**Си́рия**	**сири́йский**	**сири́ец/сири́йка**
Turkey	**Ту́рция**	**туре́цкий**	**ту́рок/турча́нка**
Note:	gen pl **ту́рок**, though **ту́рков** may be heard in R1.		
United Arab Emirates	**Объединённые Ара́бские Эмира́ты (ОАЭ)**		
Yemen	**Йе́мен (мэ)**	**йе́менский**	**йе́менец/йе́менка**

5.11.8 Australia and New Zealand

Australia	**Австра́лия**	**австрали́йский**	**австрали́ец/австрали́йка**
New Zealand	**Но́вая Зела́ндия**	**новозела́ндский**	**новозела́ндец/новозела́ндка**

5.12 Words denoting inhabitants of Russian towns

Nouns denoting natives or inhabitants of certain cities (eg *Bristolian, Glaswegian, Liverpudlian, Londoner, Mancunian, Parisian*) are rather more widely used in Russian than in English (at least in relation to natives or inhabitants of Russian cities). Moreover a wider range of suffixes (both masculine and feminine: **-ец/-ка, -анин/-анка, -янин/-янка, -ич/-ичка, -як/-ячка**) is in common use for this purpose than in English. However, it is not easy for the foreigner to predict which suffix should be applied to the name of a particular city. A list is therefore given below of the nouns denoting natives or inhabitants of the major Russian cities, and of some cities of other former republics of the USSR.

Note 1 In the case of some of the less important cities the nouns denoting their inhabitants may rarely be used or may have only local currency.

2 Where the name of a city has recently been changed (reverting to the pre-revolutionary name), the former Soviet name is given in brackets.

Арха́нгельск	**арха́нгельский**	**архàнгелогоро́дец/архàнгелогоро́дка**
А́страхань (f)	**астраха́нский**	**астраха́нец/астраха́нка**
Баку́	**баки́нский**	**баки́нец/баки́нка**
Ви́льнюс	**ви́льнюсский**	**ви́льнюсец/ви́льнюска**
Владивосто́к	**владивосто́кский**	**жи́тель(ница) Владивосто́ка**
Влади́мир	**влади́мирский**	**жи́тель(ница) Влади́мира** or **влади́мирец/влади́мирка**

Во́логда	**волого́дский**	**вологжа́нин/вологжа́нка** or **волого́дец/волого́дка**
Воро́неж	**воро́нежский**	**воро́нежец/воро́нежка**
Вя́тка (Ки́ров)	**вя́тский**	**вя́тич/вя́тичка**
Екатеринбу́рг (Свердло́вск)	**екатеринбу́ржский**	**екатеринобу́ржец/екатеринобу́рженка**
Екатериносла́в (Днепропетро́вск)	**екатеринosла́вский**	**екатериносла́вец/екатериносла́вка**
Ирку́тск	**ирку́тский**	**иркутя́нин/иркутя́нка**
Каза́нь (f)	**каза́нский**	**каза́нец/каза́нка**
Ки́ев	**ки́евский**	**киевля́нин/киевля́нка**
Кострома́	**костромско́й**	**костроми́ч/костроми́чка**
Краснода́р	**краснода́рский**	**краснода́рец/краснода́рка**
Красноя́рск	**красноя́рский**	**красноя́рец/красноя́рка**
Курск	**ку́рский**	**курча́нин/курча́нка**
Львов	**льво́вский**	**львовя́нин/львовя́нка**
Минск	**ми́нский**	**минча́нин/минча́нка**
Москва́	**моско́вский**	**москви́ч/москви́чка** (also **москвитя́нин/москвитя́нка**; obs)
Ни́жний Но́вгород (Го́рький)	**нижегоро́дский**	**нижегоро́дец/нижегоро́дка**
Но́вгород	**новгоро́дский**	**новгоро́дец/новгоро́дка**
Новоросси́йск	**новоросси́йский**	**новоросси́ец/новоросси́йка**
Новосиби́рск	**новосиби́рский**	**жи́тели Новосиби́рска** (also **новосиби́рец)**
Оде́сса	**оде́сский**	**одесси́т/одесси́тка (дэ** also possible)
Омск	**о́мский**	**оми́ч/омча́нка**
Псков	**пско́вский/псковско́й**	**псковитя́нин/псковитя́нка**
Пятиго́рск	**пятиго́рский**	**пятигорча́нин/пятигорча́нка**
Ри́га	**ри́жский**	**рижа́нин/рижа́нка**
Росто́в	**росто́вский**	**ростовча́нин/ростовча́нка**
Ряза́нь (f)	**ряза́нский**	**ряза́нец/ряза́нка**
Сама́ра (Ку́йбышев)	**сама́рский**	**самаровча́нин/самаровча́нка**
Санкт-Петербу́рг (Ленингра́д	**петербу́ргский ленингра́дский**	**петербу́ржец/петербу́ржка ленингра́дец/ленингра́дка)**
Сара́тов	**сара́товский**	**саратовча́нин/саратовча́нка** (also **сара́товец)**
Севасто́поль (m)	**севасто́польский**	**севасто́полец**
Смоле́нск	**смоле́нский**	**смоля́нин/смолянка**

Со́чи	**со́чинский**	**со́чинец/со́чинка**
Та́ллин	**та́ллинский**	**та́ллинец**
Тамбо́в	**тамбо́вский**	**тамбо́вец/тамбо́вка**
Та́рту	**та́ртуский**	**жи́тели Та́рту**
Тверь (Кали́нин)	**тверско́й**	**твер́як/твер́ячка**
Томск	**то́мский**	**томи́ч/томча́нка**
Ту́ла	**ту́льский**	**туля́к/туля́чка**
Хаба́ровск	**хаба́ровский**	**хабаровча́нин/хабаровча́нка**
Ха́рьков	**ха́рьковский**	**харьковча́нин/харьковча́нка**
Я́лта	**я́лтинский**	**я́лтинец/я́лтинка**
Я́рославль (m)	**яросла́вский**	**яросла́вец/яросла́вчанка**

Note: a noun of a similar sort to those denoting inhabitants of certain cities is derived from **земля́ (земля́к/земля́чка)**, with the meaning *person from the same region.*

6 Verbal etiquette

6.1 Introductory

Every language has conventional formulae to which its speakers resort in certain situations that constantly occur in everyday life: addressing others, attracting their attention, making acquaintance, greeting and parting, conveying congratulations, wishes, gratitude and apologies, making requests and invitations, giving advice, offering condolences and paying compliments. Telephone conversations take place and letters are written within established frameworks that vary according to the relationship between those communicating and the nature of the exchange.

Ignorance of the formulae in use for these purposes among speakers of a language may make dealings with them on any level difficult and unsuccessful or may even cause offence. Or to look at it from a more positive point of view, the speaker who has mastered a limited number of these formulae will make his or her intentions and attitudes clear, set a tone appropriate to the situation and thereby greatly facilitate communication and win social or professional acceptance.

One may say that there are particular advantages for the foreign student of Russian in deploying the correct formulae in a given situation. In the first place, Russians are aware of the difficulty of their language for the foreign student and have little expectation that a foreigner will speak it well, let alone that a foreigner should be sympathetic to their customs, of which they are inured to criticism. They therefore tend to be more impressed by and favourably disposed towards the foreigner who has mastered the intricacies of their language and is prepared to observe at least their linguistic customs than are perhaps the French towards foreign French-speakers. And in the second place, it would be true to say that Russian society has remained, at least until very recently, in many respects highly conservative and traditional and has adhered to conventional procedures, including linguistic usage, more rigidly than have the more highly industrialised societies of the West.

The following sections give some of the most common conventional formulae that are of use to the foreign student of Russian. Many of the formulae may occur in very numerous combinations of their parts, only a few of which can be given here. One may introduce many formulae, for example, with any one of the following phrases meaning *I want* or *I should like to*. (The phrases are arranged with the most direct first and the least direct last.)

Я хочу́
Я хоте́л бы
Мне хо́чется
Мне хоте́лось бы

Often the grammatical forms used in the formula (in particular choice of **ты** or **вы** forms) are determined by the context. A formula used exclusively in a formal situation, for example, is likely to contain only **вы** forms.

The formulae given in this chapter may be taken to be stylistically neutral and therefore of broad application unless an indication is given that they belong predominantly to R1 or R3. In general, formulae in the lower register are characterised by ellipsis (see 10.13) while those in the higher register are more periphrastic and often contain the imperative forms **позво́льте** or **разреши́те** (*allow [me]/permit [me]*).

Translations of the formulae given here are often inexact in a literal sense; an attempt has been made instead to render the spirit of the original by the most appropriate English formula.

6.2 Use of ты and вы

The English-speaking student, having only one second-person form of address (*you*), must take particular care with the second-person pronouns in Russian. To use them incorrectly is at best to strike a false note and at worst to cause offence.

If one is addressing more than one person, then only **вы** may be used. If on the other hand one is addressing only one person, then either **вы** or **ты** may be used. As a general rule one may say that **вы** is more respectful and formal than **ты**, but a fuller list of factors that determine choice of pronoun would include the following considerations.

	вы	**ты**
degree of intimacy	to adults on first meeting to adults not well known to the speaker	to people well known or close to the speaker to one's partner, parents, children children to other children

Note: one may switch from **вы** to **ты** as one comes to know the addressee better. This switch may take place almost immediately between people of the same age, especially young people, or it may be delayed until some closeness develops. Even when one knows a person well and feels close to them one may remain on **вы** terms; this is particularly the case among educated older people who wish to preserve the sense of mutual respect connoted by **вы**.

relative status	to seniors in age or rank	to juniors in age or rank

Note: one may address one's seniors as **ты** if one knows them well enough; conversely to address a junior as **ты** appears condescending unless there is some closeness and mutual trust between the speakers.

formality of situation	in formal or official contexts	in informal or unofficial contexts

Even if one normally addresses a person as **ты** one should switch to **вы** in a formal or official situation.

state of relations	cool, stiff, strained, excessively polite	disrespectful, over-familiar

The point here is that subversion of the normal rules indicates that the relationship is not as it should be, given the degree of intimacy, relative status and formality or informality of the situation. The speaker therefore chooses the pronoun which in normal circumstances would seem inappropriate.

6.3 Personal names

All Russians have three names: a first, or given name (**и́мя**), chosen by one's parents; a patronymic (**о́тчество**), derived from one's father's name; and a surname (**фами́лия**).

6.3.1 First names

Use of a person's first name only is an informal mode of address. The foreigner may use the first name, in its full form (**и́мя по́лное**) or in its shortened form (**и́мя сокращённое**), if one exists, in addressing children and students. However, it might seem impolite if one were to use the first name on its own on first acquaintance to an adult (particularly one's seniors in age or status) unless invited to do so (therefore see also 6.3.2).

The majority of Russian first names have shortened forms and diminutive forms. The foreigner must be aware of these forms, which may be confusing in their abundance and variety, because they will be frequently encountered in informal conversation and in imaginative literature. However, great care must be taken both to use them only in the right circumstances and to distinguish the nuances of the various forms. Three principal forms must be distinguished apart from the shortened forms that can be derived from most first names, viz:

- a truncated version of the shortened form which amounts to a form in the vocative case for use when a person is being called or addressed;
- a diminutive form which is a term of special endearment (hypocoristic). Such forms are usually derived from the shortened

form, if one exists, by using one or both of the suffixes **-енька** and **-очка/-ечка** for men and women alike, eg **Са́шенька**, **Па́шенька**, **Вале́рочка**, **Ле́ночка**, **Ната́шенька**, **Та́нечка**). These forms are used by parents or relations in talking to their children. Among older people they are used only when addressing those to whom one is very close;

- a further diminutive form derived from the shortened form by using the suffix **-ка** (eg **Ви́тька**, **Ко́лька**, **Пе́тька**, **Ле́нка**, **Ната́шка**, **Та́нька**). Such forms may be used by young children addressing one another. When used of adults about children or about other adults these forms may express disapproval or even verge on coarseness.

The following lists give the most common men's and women's first names in Russia today, and some, but by no means all of the shortened or diminutive forms that may be derived from them. Fashions vary over time and in different sections of the population, but the majority of the names given here have been widespread since pre-revolutionary times and now occur in most strata of the population.

men's first names

full form of name	shortened form	vocative of short form	hypocoristic diminutive	pejorative diminutive
Алекса́ндр	**Са́ша, Шу́ра**	**Саш, Шур**	**Са́шенька, Шу́рочка**	**Са́шка, Шу́рка**
Алексе́й	**Алёша, Лёша**	**Лёш, Алёш**	**Алёшенька, Лёшенька**	**Алёшка, Лёшка**
Анато́лий	**То́ля**	**Толь**	**То́ленька, То́лик**	**То́лька**
Андре́й	**Андрю́ша**	**Андрю́ш**	**Андрю́шенька**	**Андрю́шка**
Арка́дий	**Арка́ша**	**Арка́ш**	**Арка́шенька**	**Арка́шка**
Бори́с	**Бо́ря**	**Борь**	**Бо́ренька**	**Бо́рька**
Вади́м	**Ва́дя**	**Вадь**	**Ва́денька**	**Ва́дька**
Вален́тин	**Ва́ля**	**Валь**	**Ва́ленька**	**Ва́лька**
Вале́рий	**Вале́ра**	**Вале́р**	**Вале́рочка**	**Вале́рка**
Васи́лий	**Ва́ся**	**Вась**	**Ва́сенька**	**Ва́ська**
Ви́ктор	**Ви́тя, Витю́ша**	**Вить**	**Ви́тенька**	**Ви́тька**
Влади́мир	**Воло́дя**	**Воло́дь**	**Воло́денька**	**Во́вка**
Вячесла́в	**Сла́ва**	**Слав**	**Сла́вочка**	**Сла́вка**
Генна́дий	**Ге́на**	**Ген**	**Ге́ночка**	**Ге́нка**
Григо́рий	**Гри́ша**	**Гриш**	**Гри́шенька**	**Гри́шка**
Дми́трий	**Ди́ма, Ми́тя**	**Дим, Мить**	**Ди́мочка, Ми́тенька**	**Ди́мка, Ми́тька**

Евге́ний	**Же́ня**	**Жень**	**Же́нечка**	**Же́нька**
Ива́н	**Ва́ня**	**Вань**	**Ва́нечка**	**Ва́нька**
И́горь	**Го́ша**		**Игорёк**	
Константи́н	**Ко́стя**	**Кость**	**Ко́стенька, Ко́стик**	**Ко́стька**
Леони́д	**Лёня**	**Лёнь**	**Лёнечка**	**Лёнька**
Михаи́л	**Ми́ша**	**Миш**	**Ми́шенька**	**Ми́шка**
Никола́й	**Ко́ля**	**Коль**	**Ко́ленька**	**Ко́лька**
Оле́г			**Оле́жек, Оле́женька**	
Па́вел	**Па́ша**	**Паш**	**Па́шенька**	**Па́шка**
Пётр	**Пе́тя**	**Петь**	**Пе́тенька**	**Пе́тька**
Русла́н			**Ру́сик**	
Серге́й	**Серёжа**	**Серёж**	**Серёженька**	**Серёжка**
Станисла́в		**Слав, Стась**	**Ста́сенька, Ста́сечка**	**Ста́ська**
Степа́н	**Стёпа**	**Стёп**	**Стёпочка**	**Стёпка**
Ю́рий	**Ю́ра**	**Юр**	**Ю́рочка**	**Ю́рка**
Я́ков	**Я́ша**	**Яш**	**Я́шенька**	**Я́шка**

women's first names

full form of name	shortened form	vocative of short form	hypocoristic diminutive	pejorative diminutive
Алекса́ндра	**Са́ша, Шу́ра**	**Саш, Шур**	**Са́шенька, Шу́рочка**	**Са́шка, Шу́рка**
А́лла		**Ал**	**А́ллочка**	**А́лка**
А́нна	**А́ня, Ню́ра**	**Ань, Нюр**	**А́нечка, Ню́рочка**	**А́нька, Ню́рка**
Ве́ра		**Вер**	**Ве́рочка, Ве́руша**	**Ве́рка**
Викто́рия	**Ви́ка**	**Вик**	**Ви́кочка**	
Гали́на	**Га́ля**	**Галь**	**Га́лочка**	**Га́лька**
Евге́ния	**Же́ня**	**Жень**	**Же́нечка**	**Же́нька**
Екатери́на	**Ка́тя**	**Кать**	**Ка́тенька**	**Ка́тька**
Еле́на	**Ле́на, Алёна**	**Лен**	**Ле́ночка, Алёнушка**	**Ле́нка, Алёнка**
Зо́я		**Зой**	**Зо́ечка, Зо́енька**	**Зо́йка**
И́нна		**Инн**	**И́нночка, Ину́ся**	**И́нка**
Ири́на	**И́ра**	**Ир**	**И́рочка**	**И́рка**
Лари́са	**Ла́ра**	**Лар**	**Ла́рочка**	**Ла́рка**
Ли́лия	**Ли́ля**	**Лиль**	**Ли́лечка**	**Ли́лька**
Людми́ла	**Лю́да, Лю́ся, Ми́ла**		**Лю́дочка**	**Лю́дка, Лю́ська, Ми́лка**

Маргари́та	**Ри́та**	**Рит**	**Ри́точка**	**Ри́тка**
Мари́на		**Мари́н**	**Мари́ночка**	**Мари́нка**
Мари́я	**Ма́ша**	**Маш**	**Ма́шенька**	**Ма́шка**
Наде́жда	**На́дя**	**Надь**	**На́денька**	**На́дька**
Ната́лья	**Ната́ша**	**Ната́ш**	**На́точка, Ната́лочка, Ната́шенька**	**Ната́шка**
Ни́на		**Нин**	**Ни́ночка**	**Ни́нка**
О́льга	**О́ля**	**Оль**	**О́ленька**	**О́лька**
Раи́са	**Ра́я**	**Рай**	**Ра́ечка**	**Ра́йка**
Светла́на	**Све́та**	**Свет**	**Све́точка**	**Све́тка**
Софи́я/Со́фья	**Со́ня**	**Сонь**	**Со́нечка**	**Со́нька**
Тама́ра	**То́ма**	**Тама́р**	**Тама́рочка**	**Тама́рка, То́мка**
Татья́на	**Та́ня**	**Та́нь**	**Та́нечка, Таню́ша**	**Та́нька**
Эльви́ра	**Э́лла**	**Эл**	**Э́ллочка, Элю́ша**	**Э́лка**
Э́мма		**Эмм**	**Э́мочка**	**Э́мка**
Ю́лия	**Ю́ля**	**Юль**	**Ю́ленька, Ю́лечка**	**Ю́лька**

6.3.2 Patronymics

A patronymic is a name derived from the name of one's father. Russian patronymics are based on the full form of the first name and are obtained by the addition of one of the following suffixes:

	in men's names	in women's names
following hard consonants	**-ович**	**-овна**
following soft consonants or replacing **й**	**-евич**	**-евна**
replacing **а** or **я**	**-ич**	**-ична**

In colloquial speech the patronymics are shortened, and their normal pronunciation is given in the right-hand column of the table below. When the patronymic is combined with a first name, as it almost always is, then the two words in effect merge into one and only the ending of the patronymic is inflected.

first name	patronymic	pronunciation of patronymic
Алекса́ндр	**Алекса́ндрович**	**Алекса́ндрыч**
Алексе́й	**Алексе́евич**	**Алексе́ич**
Анато́лий	**Анато́льевич**	**Анато́льич**

Андре́й	**Андре́евич**	**Андре́ич**
Арка́дий	**Арка́дьевич**	**Арка́дьич**
Бори́с	**Бори́сович**	**Бори́сыч**
Вади́м	**Вади́мович**	**Вади́мыч**
Валенти́н	**Валенти́нович**	**Валенти́ныч**
Вале́рий	**Вале́р(и)евич**	**Вале́рьич**
Васи́лий	**Васи́льевич**	**Васи́льич**
Ви́ктор	**Ви́кторович**	**Ви́кторович**
Влади́мир	**Влади́мирович**	**Влади́мирыч**
Вячесла́в	**Вячесла́вович**	**Вячесла́вич**
Генна́дий	**Генна́дьевич**	**Генна́дич**
Григо́рий	**Григо́рьевич**	**Григо́рьич**
Дми́трий	**Дми́триевич**	**Дми́трич**
Евге́ний	**Евге́ньевич**	**Евге́ньич**
Ива́н	**Ива́нович**	**Ива́ныч**
И́горь	**И́горевич**	**И́горьевич**
Константи́н	**Константи́нович**	**Константи́ныч**
Леони́д	**Леони́дович**	**Леони́дыч**
Михаи́л	**Миха́йлович**	**Миха́йлыч**
Никола́й	**Никола́евич**	**Никола́ич**
Оле́г	**Оле́гович**	**Оле́гович**
Па́вел	**Па́влович**	**Па́(в)лыч**
Пётр	**Петро́вич**	**Петро́(в)ич**
Русла́н	**Русла́нович**	**Русла́ныч**
Серге́й	**Серге́евич**	**Серге́ич**
Станисла́в	**Станисла́вович**	**Станисла́вич**
Степа́н	**Степа́нович**	**Степа́ныч**
Ю́рий	**Ю́рьевич**	**Ю́рич**
Я́ков	**Я́ковлевич**	**Я́ковлич**

Note: the forms in the right-hand column above are not necessarily the only possible truncated forms, nor are all patronymics truncated in pronunciation.

Patronymics should as a rule be used in the following circumstances:

(a) when a person's full name is being given (eg in introductions or in answer to an official question);

(b) together with the first name, as a polite form of address to an adult with whom one is not on intimate terms. In this latter use it combines with the full form of the first name (eg **Ива́н Петро́вич**, **Еле́на Петро́вна**), not a shortened or diminutive form, and (as a rule) with the personal pronoun **вы**, not **ты**, and corresponds to an English form of address with title and surname (eg *Mr Smith, Mrs Johnson, Dr Collins*).

Note: the patronymic on its own may be encountered as a form of address among older people in the countryside, eg **Петро́вич! Ива́новна**!

6.4 Attracting attention (привлече́ние внима́ния)

The following formulae are commonly used to attract the attention of a stranger. With the exceptions indicated all are polite if not very polite. Some include part of the request that they generally introduce, eg for information of some sort.

seeking directions, help, or information

Извини́те (пожа́луйста)! Как пройти́ в метро́? **Прости́те (пожа́луйста)! Как пройти́ в метро́?** **Скажи́те, пожа́луйста, как пройти́ в метро́?**	*Excuse me, how do I get to the underground?*
Вы не мо́жете сказа́ть. . .? **Не мо́жете ли вы сказа́ть**. . .? **Вы не подска́жете. . .?** **Не могли́ бы вы сказа́ть. . .?** **Вас не затрудни́т сказа́ть. . .?** **Вам не тру́дно сказа́ть. . .?**	*Could you tell me. . .*
Бу́дьте добры́, скажи́те, кото́рый час? **Бу́дьте любе́зны, скажи́те, кото́рый час**?	*Could you tell me the time please?*

Note: because the above formulae are all polite and suitable for use to strangers it would not be appropriate to couch any of them in the **ты** form.

Мо́жно тебя́/вас на мину́тку?	*Could I speak to you for a moment?*

Note: this expression is more familiar, may be used to acquaintances, and is commonly couched in the **ты** form.

responses to requests for information

The initial response to an approach which does not itself include a request may be as follows:

Да.	*Yes.*
Да, пожа́луйста.	*Yes, please.*
Что?	*What?*
Слу́шаю.	*I'm listening.*
Слу́шаю вас.	*I'm listening to you.*

Чем могу́ быть поле́зен/поле́зна? (R3b)	*How can I be of help?*
Я к ва́шим услу́гам. (R3b or iron)	*At your service.*
Ну? (R1)	*Well?*
Что тебе́? (R1)	*What do you want?*
Чего́ тебе́? (R1)	*What do you want?*
Ну чего́ тебе́? (R1)	*Well what do you want?*

If the addressee is not sure that it is he or she who is being addressed, the response may be:

Вы меня́?
Вы ко мне? } *Are you talking to me?*

If the addressee has not heard or understood the request, the response may be:

Что-что? (R1)	*What was that?*
Повтори́те, пожа́луйста.	*Could you say that again?*
Прости́те, я не расслы́шал(а).	*I'm sorry, I didn't catch what you said.*
Что вы сказа́ли?	*What did you say?*

If the addressee cannot answer the question, the response may be as follows:

Не зна́ю.	*I don't know.*
Не могу́ сказа́ть.	*I can't say.*
Не скажу́. (R1)	*I can't say.*

calling for attention

The widespread forms of address for calling people unknown to the speaker, both of them stylistically neutral, are:

Молодо́й челове́к! (to males)	*Young man!*
Де́вушка! (to females)	*Young lady!*

Note: these forms of address are used, despite the literal meanings of the terms (*young man* and *girl* respectively) to call not just young people but also people up to middle age.

At a higher stylistic level an educated person might use:

Ю́ноша! — *Youth!*

At a lower stylistic level, one might use one of the following familiar forms of address, perhaps preceded by the coarse particle **Эй**!

Па́рень! (R1)	*Lad!*
Друг! (R1)	*Friend!*
Прия́тель! (R1)	*Friend!*

The pronoun **ты** would be appropriate, indeed expected, with these forms of address (which should, however, be avoided by the foreign student), eg

Эй, пáрень, у тебя́ есть закури́ть? (R1) — *Hey mate, have you got a light?*

At this level, one might – provocatively – use some attribute of the addressee as the form of address, eg

Эй, бородá! (D)	*Hey, you with the beard!*
Эй, в очкáх! (D)	*Hey, you in glasses!*

In familiar speech, older people, especially in the country, may be addressed as:

Дéдушка!	*Grandfather!*
Бáбушка!	*Grandmother!*

Young children might address older strangers as:

Дя́дя!	lit *Uncle!* (cf Eng *mister!*)
Дя́денька!	lit *Little uncle!*
Тётя!	*Auntie!* (cf Eng *missis!*)
Тётенька!	lit *Little auntie!*

Children speaking to their grandparents might use the words **дéдуля**, *grandad*, and **бабу́ля**, *granny*.

Foreigners may be addressed as **господи́н** (*Mr*) or **госпожá** (*Mrs*) + their surname, eg

Господи́н Смит!	*Mr Smith!*
Госпожá Брáун!	*Mrs Brown!*

other forms of address

Дóктор!	*Doctor!*
Сестрá!	*Nurse!*
Профéссор!	*Professor!*
Друзья́!	*Friends!*
Коллéги!	*Colleagues!*
Ребя́та!	*Lads!*
Мáльчики!	*Boys!*
Дéвушки!	*Girls!*
Дéвочки!	*(Young) girls!*
Ученики́!	*Pupils!*
Дáмы и господá!	*Ladies and gentlemen!*

Note: **Товáрищи!** *Comrades!* is also beginning to reappear.

6.5 Introductions (знакóмство)

introducing oneself

Я хочу́ с вáми познакóмиться.
Я хотéл бы с вáми познакóмиться
Мне хóчется с вáми познакóмиться.
Мне хотéлось бы с вáми познакóмиться.

lit *I want/should like to meet you/make your acquaintance.*

Дава́й(те) знако́миться! **Дава́й(те) познако́мимся!**	lit *Let's meet/get to know one another.*
Позво́льте (с ва́ми) познако́миться. (R3) **Разреши́те (с ва́ми) познако́миться.** (R3) **Позво́льте предста́виться.** (R3) **Разреши́те предста́виться.** (R3)	*Allow me to introduce myself to you.*

All the above formulae precede naming of oneself. The form of one's name which one gives depends on the degree of formality of the situation. Young people meeting in an informal situation would give only their first name, perhaps even in a diminutive form, eg

(Меня́ зову́т) Влади́мир.	*My name is Vladimir.*
(Меня́ зову́т) Воло́дя.	*My name is Volodia.*
(Меня́ зову́т) Татья́на.	*My name is Tat'iana.*
(Меня́ зову́т) Та́ня.	*My name is Tania.*

In a formal situation one would give one's first name and patronymic, eg

Меня́ зову́т Никола́й Петро́вич.	*My name is Nikolai Petrovich.*
Меня́ зову́т О́льга Серге́евна.	*My name is Ol'ga Sergeevna.*

or even all three names (first name, patronymic and surname), often with the surname first, eg

Евге́ний Бори́сович Попо́в	*Yevgenii Borisovich Popov*
Ири́на Па́вловна Тара́сова	*Irina Pavlovna Tarasova*
Гончаро́в, Серге́й Петро́вич	*Goncharov, Sergei Petrovich*

Note 1 The nominative case is preferred after the verb form **зову́т** when people are being named, although the instrumental is also grammatically possible after **звать** and is used when the name is not the person's real name, eg **И́мя моё—И́горь, а зову́т меня́ очка́риком** (R1), *My name is Igor, but people call me Specs.*

2 The formula **меня́ зову́т** tends to be omitted if the surname is included.

In a formal situation connected with one's work one might give one's position and surname, eg

Профе́ссор Моско́вского университе́та Кузнецо́в	*Moscow University Professor Kuznetsov*
Дире́ктор городско́го музе́я Гончаро́ва	*Director of the city museum Goncharova*

Having named oneself one may go on to ask for the same information from the other person in the following way:

А как вас зову́т?	*And what is your name?*
А как ва́ше и́мя?	*And what is your first name?*

	А как ва́ше и́мя и о́тчество?	*And what is your first name and patronymic?*
	А как ва́ша фами́лия?	*And what is your surname?*
responses to introductions	**О́чень прия́тно!**	*Very pleased to meet you.*
	Мне о́чень прия́тно с ва́ми познако́миться.	*I am very pleased to meet you.*
	О́чень ра́д(а)!	*Very glad (to meet you).*
	Я о вас слы́шал(а).	*I've heard about you.*
	Мне о вас говори́ли.	*I've been told about you.*

If the people have already met, one of the following formulae might be appropriate:

	Мы уже́ знако́мы.	*We're already acquainted.*
	Мы уже́ встреча́лись.	*We've already met.*
	Я вас зна́ю.	*I know you (already).*
	Я вас где́-то ви́дел(а).	*I've seen you somewhere.*
introducing other people	**Познако́мьтесь, пожа́луйста.**	lit *Meet each other.*
	Я хочу́ познако́мить вас с + instr **Я хоте́л(а) бы познако́мить вас с** + *instr* **Я хочу́ предста́вить вам** + acc	*I want to introduce you to*
	Позво́льте познако́мить вас с + instr (R3) **Разреши́те предста́вить вам** + acc (R3)	*Allow me to introduce you to*

6.6 Greetings (приве́тствие)

general greetings	**Здра́вствуй(те)!**	*Hello.*
	До́брый день!	*Good day.*
	До́брое у́тро!	*Good morning.*
	До́брый ве́чер!	*Good evening.*
	Приве́т! (R1)	*Hello.*
	Я ра́д(а) вас приве́тствовать. (formal; to audience)	*I am pleased to welcome you.*
	Добро́ пожа́ловать! (on sb's arrival for a stay)	*Welcome.*
	С прие́здом!	= добро́ пожа́ловать
	Хле́б-со́ль!	revived archaic welcome to guests at gathering, indicating hospitality
responses to greetings	**(Я) (о́чень) ра́д(а) тебя́/вас ви́деть**	*(I) am (very) glad to see you.*
	(Я) то́же ра́д(а) тебя́/вас ви́деть	*(I) am glad to see you too.*

enquiries about one's affairs and health	**Как живёшь/живёте?**	*How are you getting on?*
	Как пожива́ете?	*How are you getting on?*
	Как твоя́/ва́ша жизнь?	*How's life?*
	Как (иду́т) дела́?	*How are things going?*
	Что но́вого? (R1)	*What's new?*
	Как твой/ваш муж/сын/брат/оте́ц?	*How is your husband/son/brother/father?*
	Как твоя́/ва́ша жена́/до́чка/сестра́/мать?	*How is your wife/daughter/sister/mother?*
	Как вы себя́ чу́вствуете?	*How do you feel?*
	Ну, как ты? (solicitous, eg after illness)	*How are you then?*
responses to enquiries about one's affairs and health	**Замеча́тельно.**	*Marvellous.*
	Великоле́пно.	*Splendid.*
	Норма́льно.	*Fine.*
	Хорошо́.	*Fine.*
	Непло́хо.	*Fine.*
	Не жа́луюсь.	*I can't complain.*
	Ничего́.	*All right.*
	Ка́жется, ничего́ плохо́го.	*Not bad.*
	Ни ша́тко, ни ва́лко. (R1)	*Middling.*
	Так себе́. (R1)	*So-so.*
	Нева́жно.	*Not too good/well.*
	Пло́хо.	*Bad(ly).*
	Лу́чше не спра́шивай(те)! (R1)	*Better not to ask.*
	Ху́же не́куда! (R1)	*Couldn't be worse.*
	Из рук вон пло́хо! (R1)	*Dreadful(ly).*
unexpected meetings	**Кака́я (прия́тная) встре́ча!**	lit *What a (pleasant) meeting.*
	Кака́я (прия́тная) неожи́данность	*What a (pleasant) surprise.*
	Не ожида́л(а) тебя́/вас встре́тить (здесь).	*I didn't expect to meet you (here).*
	Каки́ми судьба́ми! (R1)	*Fancy meeting you here!*
	Как ты сюда́ попа́л(а)?	*How did you get here?*
meeting after long separation	**Кого́ я ви́жу?**	*Who's this?*
	Э́то ты?	*Is it you?*
	Ты ли э́то?	*Is it you?*
	Давно́ не ви́делись.	*We haven't seen each other for a long time.*
	Сто лет не ви́делись. **Це́лую ве́чность не ви́делись.** **Ско́лько лет, ско́лько зим!**	*We haven't seen each other for ages.*
meeting by arrangement	**Вот я и пришёл/пришла́.**	*Here I am.*
	Ты давно́ ждёшь/Вы давно́ ждёте?	*Have you been waiting long?*
	Я не опозда́л(а)?	*Am I late?*

	Я не заста́вил(а) вас ждать?	*I haven't kept you waiting, have I?*
responses at meeting by arrangement	**Я жду тебя́/вас.**	*I've been waiting for you.*
	Ты пришёл/пришла́ во́время/Вы пришли́ во́время.	*You're on time.*
	А, ну вот и ты. (R1)	*So here you are.*
	Лу́чше по́здно, чем никогда́.	*Better late than never.*

6.7 Farewells (проща́ние)

	До свида́ния.	*Goodbye.* (lit *until [the next] meeting*; cf Fr *au revoir*)
	До ско́рой встре́чи!	*Let's meet (again) soon.*
	До ве́чера!	*Till this evening.*
	До за́втра!	*Till tomorrow.*
	До понеде́льника!	*Till Monday.*
	Проща́й(те)!	= до свида́ния or may suggest parting for ever (cf Fr *adieu* as opposed to *au revoir*)
	Всего́ хоро́шего! **Всего́ до́брого!** **Всего́!** (R1)	*All the best.*
	Пока́! (R1)	*So long.*
	Счастли́во! (R1)	*Good luck.*
	Споко́йной но́чи!	*Good night.*
	Мы ещё уви́димся.	*We'll see each other again.*
phrases associated with parting	**Не забыва́й(те) нас.**	*Don't forget us.*
	Приходи́(те).	*Come again.*
	Заходи́(те).	*Drop in again.*
	Звони́(те).	*Give us a ring.*
	Приезжа́й(те).	*Come again.* (to sb travelling from afar)
	Пиши́(те).	*Write (to us).*
	Да́й(те) о себе́ знать.	lit *Let us hear from you.*
	Ми́лости про́сим, к нам ещё раз.	*You're always welcome to come again.*
	Переда́й(те) приве́т + dat	*Give my regards to*
	(По)целу́й(те) дете́й/дочь/сы́на.	*Give your children/daughter/son a kiss from me.*
	Не помина́йте ли́хом.	*Remember me kindly.* (to sb going away for good)

formulae preceding parting

It might be appropriate as one is preparing to part to use one of the following phrases:

Уже́ по́здно.	*It's late.*
Мне пора́ уходи́ть.	*It's time I was leaving.*

Мне было прия́тно с ва́ми поговори́ть.	*It's been nice talking to you.*

At the end of a business meeting it might be appropriate to use one of the following formulae:

Мы обо всём договори́лись.	*We've agreed about everything.*
Мы нашли́ о́бщий язы́к.	*We've found a common language.*
Извини́те, что я задержа́л(а) вас.	*I'm sorry I've kept you.*
Прости́те, что я о́тнял(а́) у вас сто́лько вре́мени.	*I'm sorry I've taken up so much of your time.*

6.8 Congratulation (поздравле́ние)

Congratulations are generally couched in a construction in which the verb **поздравля́ть/поздра́вить**, *to congratulate*, which is followed by **с** + instr, is used, or more often simply understood, eg

Серде́чно поздравля́ю вас с рожде́нием ребёнка!	*Congratulations on the birth of your child.*
С Рождество́м!	*Happy Christmas.*
С Но́вым го́дом!	*Happy New Year.*
С днём рожде́ния!	*Happy birthday.*
С годовщи́ной сва́дьбы!	*Happy wedding anniversary.*
С лёгким па́ром!	said to sb emerging from bath or shower

The phrase might end with **тебя́** or **вас** as a direct object of the verb, but the inclusion of this pronoun is not essential. Examples:

С сере́бряной сва́дьбой тебя́!	*Congratulations on your silver wedding anniversary.*
С оконча́нием университе́та вас!	*Congratulations on graduating.*

For more formal congratulations one of the following formulae may be used:

Позво́льте поздра́вить вас с + instr (R3)	*Allow me to congratulate you on*
Прими́те мои́ и́скренние/серде́чные/горя́чие/тёплые поздравле́ния с + instr (R3)	*(Please) accept my sincere/heartfelt/warmest/warm congratulations on*
От и́мени компа́нии/университе́та поздравля́ю вас с + instr (R3)	*On behalf of the company/university I congratulate you on*

giving presents

Congratulations might be accompanied by the giving of presents, in which case one of the following formulae might be used:

Вот тебе́ пода́рок. (R1)	*Here's a present for you.*
Э́то тебе́. (R1)	*This is for you.*

Я хочу́ подари́ть вам кни́гу.	*I want to give you a book.*
Прими́те наш пода́рок. (R3)	*(Please) accept our present.*

6.9 Wishing (пожела́ние)

Wishes are generally couched in a construction in which the imperfective verb **жела́ть**, *to wish*, is used or understood. In the full construction this verb is followed by an indirect object in the dative, indicating the recipient of the wish, and an object in the genitive indicating the thing wished for. The verb **жела́ть** may also be followed by an infinitive. Examples:

Жела́ю тебе́ сча́стья!	*I wish you happiness.*
Жела́ю вам больши́х успе́хов!	*I wish you every success.*
Всего́ наилу́чшего!	*All the best.*
Прия́тного аппети́та!	*Bon appétit.*
Счастли́вого пути́!	*Bon voyage.*
До́лгих лет жи́зни! (said to ageing person)	*Long life.*
Жела́ю поскоре́е вы́здороветь!	*Get better quickly.*

More formal wishes might be rendered thus:

Прими́те мои́ са́мые лу́чшие/и́скренние/серде́чные/тёплые пожела́ния.	*(Please) accept my best/most sincere/heartfelt/warmest wishes.*

Wishes, or an element of wishing, may also be expressed by means of the imperative or by **пусть**, *may*, eg

Выздора́вливай(те).	*Get better.*
Береги́(те) себя́.	*Look after yourself.*
Расти́ больши́м и у́мным. (said to child)	*Grow big and clever.*
Пусть тебе́ бу́дет хорошо́!	*May all be well for you.*
Пусть тебе́ повезёт!	*May you have good luck.*

Note: the expression **Ни пу́ха ни пера́**, *Good luck*, is said to a person about to take an examination. The response is **К чёрту!** *To the devil.*

toasts

Speeches and toasts are a very much more widespread feature of Russian life than of English life. Even at an informal gathering in the home speeches may well be delivered and toasts proposed to guests by the host and others, and the guests should themselves respond with speeches and toasts of their own. A toast might be proposed in one of the following ways:

(За) ва́ше здоро́вье!	*Your health.*
Я хочу́ вы́пить за + acc	*I want to drink to*
Я предлага́ю тост за + acc	*I propose a toast to*
Я поднима́ю бока́л за + acc	*I raise my glass to*

Позвóльте поднять бокáл за + acc (R3)	*Allow me to raise my glass to*
Разрешите провозгласить тост за + acc (R3)	*Allow me to propose a toast to*

6.10 Gratitude (благодáрность)

Спасибо.	*Thank you.*
Большóе спасибо.	*Thank you very much.*
Спасибо за внимáние. (said to audience after talk or lecture)	*Thank you for your attention.*
Спасибо, что вы́слушали меня́.	*Thank you for hearing me out.*
Благодарю́ вас за гостеприи́мство.	*Thank you for your hospitality.*
Я óчень благодáрен/благодáрна вам.	*I am very grateful to you.*
Я вам мнóгим обя́зан(а).	*I am much obliged to you.*
Я óчень признáтелен/признáтельна вам за цéнные совéты. (R3b)	*I am very grateful to you for your valuable advice.*
Я хотéл(а) бы вы́разить свою́ благодáрность за то, что (R3b)	*I should like to express my gratitude for the fact that*

Note: *for* is rendered by **за** + acc in such expressions.

responses to thanks

The recipient of thanks routinely dismisses gratitude as unnecessary:

Пожáлуйста.	*Don't mention it.* (cf Fr *de rien*; but note that **ничегó** is not used in this sense)
Нé за что. **Не стóит.**	*It's nothing.*
Ну да что ты, каки́е пустяки́! (R1)	*Don't be silly, it's nothing.*

Note: the expression **на здорóвье** is used as a response to some expression of thanks for hospitality such as **Спасибо за угощéние** (*Thanks for treating me/Thanks for the food and drink*). It should not be confused with **за вáше здорóвье** (see 6.9).

6.11 Apologising (извинéние)

Apologies are most often framed with one of the verbs **извиня́ть/извини́ть**, *to excuse*; **извиня́ться/извини́ться**, *to apologise*; or **прощáть/прости́ть**, *to forgive*.

Извини́(те), (пожáлуйста).	*I'm sorry.* (lit *Excuse me*)
Извини́(те) за беспокóйство.	*I'm sorry to trouble you.*
Извини́(те) меня́ за то, что забы́л(а) тебé/вам позвони́ть.	*I am sorry that I forgot to ring you.*

Прости́(те), (пожа́луйста).	= извини́(те)
Прости́(те) меня́.	*Forgive me.* (for more serious transgressions)
Я прошу́ проще́ния.	*Forgive me.*
Я до́лжен/должна́ извини́ться пе́ред ва́ми за то, что	*I must apologise to you for the fact that*
Я винова́т(а) пе́ред ва́ми.	*I owe you an apology.* (lit *I am guilty before you*)
Прими́те мои́ (глубо́кие) извине́ния. (R3)	*(Please) accept my (profound) apologies.*
Я бо́льше не бу́ду (так де́лать). (said by child)	*I shan't do it again.*

Note: *for* in apologies is rendered by **за** + acc.

responses to apologies

The recipient of an apology might respond in one of the following ways:

Ничего́!	*It's nothing.*
Не́ за что (извиня́ться).	*There's nothing to apologise for.*
Да что́ ты/вы! (R1)	*What are you (apologising for)?*
Ну, хорошо́. (R1) **Ну, ла́дно уж.** (R1)	*Well OK.*
Так и быть. (speaker not entirely happy to forgive)	*All right.*

6.12 Request (про́сьба)

Requests may of course be expressed by the imperative form of an appropriate verb (see 8.6.11 and 10.5.6). A request in the imperative may be introduced by the following very polite formulae:

Бу́дь любе́зен/любе́зна + imp **Бу́дьте любе́зны** + imp **Бу́дь добр/добра́** + imp **Бу́дьте добры́** + imp	*Would you be so good as to*
Е́сли вам не тру́дно + imp **Е́сли вас не затрудни́т** + imp	*If it's no trouble to you*

However, requests may also be framed in many other ways. Inclusion of **не** or **ли** in formulae of the sort which follow increases the politeness of the request. Examples:

О́чень прошу́ вас + infin	*I (do) ask you to*
Я хоте́л(а) бы попроси́ть у вас + acc	*I should like to ask you for*
Не могу́ ли я попроси́ть вас + infin	*Could I ask you to*

Я попроси́л(а) бы вас не кури́ть. (polite prohibition)	*I would ask you not to smoke.*
Мо́жет быть, вы сни́мете сапоги́?	*Would you take your boots off?*
Вы не пога́сите сигаре́ту? / **Не пога́сите ли вы сигаре́ту?**	*Would you put out your cigarette?*

In R1 a request might be couched as a question in the 2nd person singular of the perfective verb, eg

Зава́ришь мне чай?	*Will you make me a cup of tea?*

A request might also be introduced by one of the following formulae, all of which mean *Can you* or *Could you*, and all of which are followed by an infinitive:

Вы мо́жете
Вы не мо́жете
Вы не могли́ бы
Мо́жете ли вы
Не мо́жете ли вы
Не могли́ бы вы

Permission may be sought by means of one of the following phrases, all of which mean *May (I)*, and all of which are followed by an infinitive:

Мо́жно (мне)
Нельзя́ ли (мне)
Могу́ ли я
Не могу́ ли я
Позво́льте мне
Разреши́те мне

agreement

Accession to a request may be indicated by one of the following responses:

Пожа́луйста.	*By all means.*
Хорошо́.	*All right.*
Ла́дно. (R1)	*OK.*
Сейча́с.	*At once.*
Си́ю мину́ту.	*Straightaway.*
На́(те). (R1; said when sth is being handed over)	*Here you are.*
На́, возьми́. (R1)	*Here you are, take it.*

permission

The following responses indicate permission:

Да, коне́чно.	*Yes, of course.*
Да, пожа́луйста.	*Yes, by all means.*
Разуме́ется.	*Of course.*
Безусло́вно.	*It goes without saying.*

refusal

The following phrases might be used to indicate refusal:

Не хочу́.	*I don't want to.*
Не могу́.	*I can't.*
Жаль, но не могу́.	*I'm sorry, but I can't.*
Я не в си́лах + infin (R3b)	*I am not able to*

prohibition

Prohibition might be expressed by one of the following formulae:

Нельзя́.	*No, one/you can't.*
К сожале́нию, не могу́ разреши́ть вам + infin	*Unfortunately I can't allow you to*
Ни в ко́ем слу́чае.	*No way.*
Ни за что́.	*Not for anything.*
Ни при каки́х обстоя́тельствах.	*In no circumstances.*
Об э́том не мо́жет быть и ре́чи.	*There can be no question of it.*

6.13 Invitation (приглаше́ние)

Приглаша́ю тебя́/вас на ча́шку ко́фе.	*I invite you for a cup of coffee.*
Хочу́ пригласи́ть тебя́/вас к себе́.	*I want to invite you to my place.*
Приходи́(те) к нам.	*Come to our place.*
Придёшь/Придёте ко мне? (R1)	*Will you come and see me?*
Приезжа́й(те).	*Drive over to us.*
Заходи́(те) к нам.	*Call on us.*
Загля́дывай(те). (R1)	*Drop in.*
Входи́(те).	*Come in.*
Бу́дь(те) как до́ма.	*Make yourself at home.*

acceptance of invitation

Спаси́бо, с удово́льствием!	*Thank you, with pleasure.*
С ра́достью!	*Gladly.*
Охо́тно!	*Willingly.*
Я обяза́тельно приду́.	*I shall definitely come.*

6.14 Reassurance and condolence (утеше́ние, соболе́знование)

Успоко́йся/успоко́йтесь.	*Calm down.*
Не беспоко́йся/беспоко́йтесь.	*Don't worry.*
Не волну́йся/волну́йтесь.	*Don't get agitated.*
Не огорча́йся/огорча́йтесь.	*Cheer up.*
Не расстра́ивайся/расстра́ивайтесь.	*Don't be upset.*
Не па́дай(те) ду́хом.	*Don't lose heart.*
Не принима́й(те) э́того бли́зко к се́рдцу.	*Don't take this to heart.*

Не обраща́й(те) на э́то внима́ния.	*Don't pay any attention to this.*
Вы́брось(те) э́то из головы́.	*Put it out of your mind.*
Всё ко́нчится хорошо́.	*It'll all end up all right.*
Всё бу́дет в поря́дке!	*Everything will be all right.*
Всё э́то пройдёт!	*It'll all pass.*
Всё э́то обойдётся! (R1)	*Things will sort themselves out.*
Я тебе́/вам сочу́вствую.	*I sympathise with you.*
Мне жаль тебя́/вас.	*I'm sorry for you.*
Ничего́ не поде́лаешь.	*It can't be helped.*
Э́то не твоя́/ва́ша вина́.	*It's not your fault.*
Я тебе́/вам и́скренне соболе́зную.	*My sincere condolences.*
Приму́те мои́ глубо́кие соболе́знования. (R3)	*Please accept my deepest condolences.*
Разреши́те вы́разить вам мои́ глубо́кие соболе́знования. (R3)	*Permit me to express my deepest condolences.*
Я разделя́ю ва́ше го́ре.	*I share your grief.*

Note: the negative imperatives in these expressions are couched in imperfective forms.

6.15 Compliments (**комплиме́нты**)

Ты прекра́сно вы́глядишь!	*You look splendid.*
Вы так хорошо́ вы́глядите!	*You look so well.*
Како́й вы до́брый челове́к!	*What a kind person you are.*
Вы не измени́лись.	*You haven't changed.*
Вам не дашь ва́ших лет.	*You don't look your age.*
У тебя́ краси́вые во́лосы.	*You've got beautiful hair.*
Тебе́ идёт э́та причёска.	*This hair-style suits you.*
Тебя́ молоди́т коро́ткая стри́жка.	*Short hair makes you look younger.*
Вам к лицу́ я́ркие цвета́.	*Bright colours suit you.*

Note: compliments may of course be delivered with various degrees of expressiveness by the inclusion of such words as **о́чень**, **так**, **тако́й**, **како́й**.

responses to compliments

Спаси́бо за комплиме́нт.	*Thank you for (your) compliment.*
Вы льсти́те мне.	*You're flattering me.*
Вы преувели́чиваете.	*You're exaggerating.*
Прия́тно э́то слы́шать.	*It's nice to hear that.*
Я ра́д(а), что вам понра́вилось.	*I'm glad you liked it.*
То же мо́жно сказа́ть и о тебе́/вас.	*One could say the same about you.*

6.16 Telephone conversations (**телефо́нный разгово́р**)

The person picking up the telephone may use a formula of the following sort:

Алло́! (pronounced алё)	*Hello.*
Да.	*Yes.*
Слу́шаю.	lit *I'm listening.*
Петро́в слу́шает.	*Petrov speaking.*
Па́влова у телефо́на.	*Pavlova speaking.*

The person making the call might begin in one of the following ways:

Э́то Ива́н Серге́евич?	*Is that Ivan Sergeevich?*
Э́то ты, Ива́н?	*Is that you Ivan?*

If the caller has dialled the wrong number, one of the following responses might be used:

Вы ошибли́сь. **Вы непра́вильно набра́ли но́мер**. **Вы не туда́ попа́ли**.	*You've got the wrong number.*
Здесь таки́х нет.	*There's no one by that name here.*

If the caller wants to speak to someone other than the person who has answered the phone, he or she may use one of the following formulae:

Позови́(те), пожа́луйста, О́льгу Петро́вну.	*May I speak to Ol'ga Petrovna please?*
Попроси́(те) к телефо́ну Влади́мира Никола́евича.	*May I speak to Vladimir Nikolaevich?*
Мо́жно Ка́тю? (R1)	*Can I speak to Katia?*
Мне ну́жно Ива́на. (R1)	*I need Ivan.*
Мне Серге́я, пожа́луйста. (R1)	*I want Sergei.*
Та́ня до́ма? (R1)	*Is Tania in?*

The person who answers the telephone may call the person whom the caller is asking for in one of the following ways:

Ири́на Алексе́евна, вас про́сят к телефо́ну.	*Irina Alekseevna, you're wanted on the telephone.*
Ла́ру к телефо́ну!	*It's for you, Lara.*
Ната́ш, тебя́! (R1)	*Natasha, it's for you.*

In a place of work a person might be more formally called to the telephone in one of the following ways:

Ви́ктор Миха́йлович, вам звоня́т из министе́рства.	*Viktor Mikhailovich, there's a call for you from the ministry.*
Семён Степа́нович, с ва́ми хотя́т говори́ть из ба́нка.	*Semion Stepanovich, someone from the bank wants to talk to you.*
Ни́на Дми́триевна, вас спра́шивают из университе́та.	*Nina Dmitrievna, someone from the university wants to talk to you.*

The person who has answered the telephone and is summoning

the person whom the caller wants to speak to may say to the caller:

Сейча́с позову́.	*I'll get him/her.*
Сейча́с он(а́) подойдёт.	*He's/She's coming.*
Подожди́(те) мину́т(оч)ку.	*Just a moment.*
Не клади́(те) тру́бку.	*Don't put the receiver down.*
Жди́те.	*Wait (please).*
Одну́ мину́точку.	*Just a minute.*
Одну́ секу́нду.	*Just a second.*

If the person sought by the caller is not available, the person who answers the telephone may say:

Его́ сейча́с нет.	*He's not here at the moment.*
Позвони́(те) попо́зже.	*Ring a bit later.*
Вам не тру́дно позвони́ть ещё раз?	*Could you ring again?*

If the person sought is not available the caller may say:

Переда́й(те) ему́/ей, что звони́л Алекса́ндр.	*Tell him/her that Aleksandr rang.*
Попроси́(те) его́/её позвони́ть А́лле.	*Ask him/her to ring Alla.*
Я позвоню́/перезвоню́ че́рез час.	*I'll call again in an hour.*

In the event of problems with the telephone one might say:

Пло́хо слы́шно. Я перезвоню́.	*It's a bad line. I'll redial.*
Нас прерва́ли.	*We got cut off.*

The conversation may end thus:

Ну, всё.	lit *Well, that's all.*
Конча́ю.	*I must go.*
Пока́. (R1)	*So long.*
Созвони́мся. (R1)	*We'll talk again.*
Целу́ю. (among people close to one another, esp women)	lit *I kiss (you).*
Я вы́нужден(а) зако́нчить разгово́р. (R3)	*I must finish.*

6.17 Letter writing (перепи́ска)

Letters may be begun with the following formulae, which range from the intimate (R1) to the formal type of address used in official correspondence (R3b).

Ми́лая Та́ня!	*Darling Tania,*
Дорого́й Па́вел!	*Dear Pavel,*
Уважа́емый Михаи́л Петро́вич!	*Dear Mikhail Petrovich,*

Многоуважа́емый Ива́н Серге́евич!	*Dear Ivan Sergeevich,*
Глубокоуважа́емый Андре́й Па́влович!	*Dear Andrei Pavlovich,*

Note: the form of address may be affected by the form of first name (full form or diminutive) which the writer uses to the addressee and which, like the form of address itself, indicates the degree of intimacy, distance, respect between the writer and addressee.

The following formulae, again arranged in ascending order of formality, may be used at the end of a letter immediately before the signature:

Обнима́ю тебя́,	lit *I embrace you,*
Целу́ю тебя́,	lit *I kiss you,*
Пока́, (R1)	*So long,*
Всего́ хоро́шего, (R1)	*All the best,*
До свида́ния,	*Goodbye,*
Всего́ до́брого/хоро́шего,	*All the best,*
С любо́вью,	*With love,*
С серде́чным приве́том,	lit *With heartfelt greetings,*
С наилу́чшими пожела́ниями,	*With best wishes,*
С и́скренним уваже́нием,	*With sincere respect,*

Note: Russians tend to express themselves more effusively and in more emotional terms than the English, and such formulae reflect that fact.

In the formal official/business style of R3b formulae of the following sort may be employed:

В отве́т на Ва́ше письмо́ от 1-го ма́рта...
In reply to your letter of 1 March...
Подтвержда́ем получе́ние Ва́шего письма́ от 2-го апре́ля.
We confirm receipt of your letter of 2 April.
Конра́кт незамедли́тельно бу́дет Вам вы́слан.
A contract will be forwarded to you without delay.
Мы с интере́сом ожида́ем Ва́шего отве́та.
We look forward to receiving your reply.
Прилага́ем сле́дующие докуме́нты:
We append the following documents:

Note: it is conventional in letters in this style to begin the second-person plural forms of address with a capital letter (**Вы**, **Ваш**, etc).

7 Word-formation

7.1 Principles of word-formation

The stock of words in a language is increased over time by various procedures. In Russian the main procedures have been borrowing (see 4.1 on recent loanwords), affixation (with which this chapter is mainly concerned) and composition (see 7.12).

Knowledge of the main principles of Russian affixation helps a student to extend his or her vocabulary, because it enables the student in many cases to understand the precise sense of a word and to recognise the word's relationship with other words derived from the same root.

The student needs to be able to identify the basic components of a Russian verb, noun, or adjective, ie its prefix (if it contains one), root, and suffix (again, if it contains one), eg

	prefix	root	suffix
входи́ть, *to enter*, ie	**в**	**ход**	**и́ть**
развяза́ть, *to untie*, ie	**раз**	**вяз**	**а́ть**
стака́н, *a glass*, ie		**стака́н**	
подстака́нник, *glass-holder*, ie	**под**	**стака́н**	**ник**
описа́ние, *description*, ie	**о**	**пис**	**а́ние**
чита́тель, *reader*, ie		**чит**	**а́тель**
котёнок, *kitten*, ie		**кот**	**ёнок**
вку́сный, ie *tasty*		**вкус**	**ный**
бездо́мный, ie *homeless*	**без**	**до́м**	**ный**

Similar principles apply in English, but they are in evidence in words of Latin origin (eg *trans/late, in/scrip/tion*) rather than in the words of Germanic origin which constitute the bulk of the most common, everyday vocabulary of English. Some of the English prefixes and suffixes derived from Latin which are equivalent to Russian prefixes and suffixes are noted in the following sections.

It should be emphasised that while an understanding of Russian affixation and of the meanings of a word's components aids recognition of words and retention of vocabulary, the principles of word-formation cannot be applied in a wholly predictable way. The foreign student must therefore check that a word whose form may be inferred from the principles given here does actually exist.

The lists which follow are intended to illustrate the main principles of Russian affixation and in particular to give the student some knowledge of the main verbal prefixes and noun suffixes. However, the lists of affixes are not exhaustive, nor does the chapter describe all the functions which a given affix may have.

7.2 Types of consonant, spelling rules and consonant changes

It is helpful when studying Russian affixation (and grammatical inflection; see Chapter 8) to bear in mind the distinction which Russian makes between hard and soft consonants, certain spelling rules, and the transformation of certain consonants, in particular circumstances, into other consonants.

7.2.1 Hard and soft consonants

Russian has ten letters which represent vowel sounds: **а**, **е**, **ё**, **и**, **о**, **у**, **ы**, **э**, **ю**, **я**. These letters may be divided into two categories, viz

col 1	col 2
а	**я**
о	**ё**
у	**ю**
ы	**и**
э	**е**

The vowels represented by the letters in col 1 follow hard consonants, whereas those represented by the letters in col 2 follow soft consonants. Therefore letters in col 1, such as **а**, **у** and **ы**, which frequently occur in the standard endings of Russian nouns, are replaced by letters in col 2 (**я**, **ю** and **и** respectively) in endings which follow a soft consonant. Compare eg acc/gen/instr sg endings of **пила́**, which has a hard л, with those of **земля́**, which has a soft л:

пил**у́**	зе́мл**ю**
пил**ы́**	земл**и́**
пил**о́й**	земл**ёй**

7.2.2 Use of the hard sign

The sole function of this letter in the modern language is as a separative sign between the consonant with which a prefix ends and a root beginning with a vowel that would in other circumstances soften the preceding consonant (ie one of the vowels in col 2 in 7.2.1 above; in practice usually **е**, sometimes **ё** or **я**). Thus в**ъ**езжа́ть, *to drive in*; вз**ъ**еро́шенный, *dishevelled*; из**ъ**е́здить, *to travel all over*; от**ъ**е́хать, *to travel away*; раз**ъ**е́хаться, *to drive off in various directions*; с**ъ**е́зд, *congress*.

7.2.3 Devoicing of consonants

The consonants in col 1 below are voiced, whilst those in col 2 are their unvoiced equivalents. Col 2 also contains the unvoiced consonants which have no voiced equivalent.

col 1	col 2
б	**п**
в	**ф**
г	**к**
д	**т**
ж	**ш**
з	**с**
	х
	ц
	ч
	щ

If two consonants belonging to different categories fall adjacent then one of the consonants must change to its equivalent in the other category, and in prefixes ending in **з** (eg **без-**, **вз-**, **из-**, **раз-**) this change is reflected in the orthography: thus ра**с**ходи́ться, бе**с**полéзный.

In other circumstances, however, devoicing of consonants is not reflected in orthography. For example, the letters in col 1, which denote voiced consonants, are used in final position even though the consonants they represent are devoiced when they occur at the end of words (eg the words гроб, Ивано́в, друг, сад, нож, раз, are pronounced *gro**p***, *Ivano**f***, *dru**k***, *sa**t***, *no**sh***, *ra**s***, respectively).

7.2.4 Spelling rules

(a) After **г**, **к**, **х**, **ж**, **ч**, **ш** and **щ** the letter **ы** cannot occur (except in a very small number of words, especially names, of foreign origin). It must be replaced, in those endings where **ы** would be expected, by the letter **и**, eg ру́сск**ий**, ти́х**ий**, as opposed to кра́сн**ый**.

(b) The letters **я** and **ю** do not occur either after **г**, **к**, **х**, **ж**, **ц**, **ч**, **ш** and **щ**, except in a few words, especially proper nouns, of foreign origin (eg **Гю́**го, *Hugo*; **кю**расó, *Curaçao*; **жю**ри́, *jury*; **Цю́**рих, *Zurich*). They must be replaced, in those endings where they would be expected, by **а** and **у** respectively, eg леж**у́** and леж**а́т**, as opposed to говор**ю́** and говор**я́т**.

(c) Unstressed **о** is not found after **ж**, **ц**, **ч**, **ш** or **щ** and is replaced by **е** after these letters, eg in the neuter nominative singular adjectival ending хорóш**ее** (cf the normal ending for this form, as in кра́сн**ое**, ру́сск**ое**).

(d) The vowel **ё** is always stressed, eg in **полёт**, *flight*. It follows that **ё** cannot occur if the stress in a word is on any other syllable (contrast пойдёшь and вы́йдешь).

7.2.5 Consonant changes

A number of consonants (eg the velars **г**, **к**, **х**) are changed in certain circumstances into consonants of a different type (eg the hushing consonants **ж**, **ч**, **ш**). Thus it commonly happens that the consonant with which a root ends is transformed into a different consonant when certain suffixes are added to the root or when certain adjectival or verbal flexions are added to it (see 8.3.3, 8.6.8).

The main changes, which will be encountered frequently in the examples given in the following sections, are:

г → **ж**, as in дви**ж**е́ние, *movement*, from the root двиг
д → **ж**, as in бро**ж**е́ние, *ferment*, from the root брод
д → **жд**, as in освобо**жд**е́ние, *liberation*, from the root свобо́д
з → **ж**, as in выра**ж**е́ние, *expression*, from the root раз
к → **ч**, as in восто́**ч**ный, *eastern*, from восто́к
с → **ш**, as in отно**ш**е́ние, *attitude*, from the root нос
ст → **щ**, as in чи́**щ**е, *cleaner*, from the root чист
т → **ч**, as in я́р**ч**е, *brighter*, from я́ркий
т → **щ**, as in осве**щ**е́ние, *illumination*, from the root свет
х → **ш**, as in ти**ш**ина́, *tranquillity*, from the root тих

7.2.6 Epenthetic л

Before certain suffixes or flexions the consonant **л** is added to a root ending in **б**, **в**, **м**, **п**, **ф**, eg

у/глуб/**л**/е́ние, *deepening*
у/див/**л**/е́ние, *surprise*
из/ум/**л**/е́ние, *astonishment*
куп/**л**/ю́, *I shall buy*
по/тра́ф/**л**/ю, *I shall please*

7.3 Verbal prefixes

There are some two dozen prefixes which may be added to a simple verb in order to modify its meaning or to create a verb with a related but different meaning. A few of these prefixes are to be found in only a small number of verbs, but the majority occur in very many verbs.

Most of the widely used prefixes may themselves be used in various senses. They may indicate the direction of the movement denoted by the basic verb (eg **входи́ть**, *to go **into***), or they may in some other way define the precise nature of the action denoted by the verb (eg **за**пла́кать, ***to start*** *to cry*). In many instances the prefix, perhaps combined with some other affix, bears a subtle meaning which in English must be rendered by some adverbial modification of the verb (eg **за**стрели́ть, *to shoot* ***dead***; **на**бе́гать**ся**, ***to have had enough of*** *running about*; **по**сви́ст**ыв**ать, *to whistle* ***from time to time***; **при**откры́ть, *to open* ***slightly***).

Note [1] Prefix and aspect: normally the addition of a prefix to a simple imperfective verb makes the verb perfective, eg писа́ть (impf), **на**писа́ть (pf); вяза́ть (impf), связа́ть (pf). In some instances (eg in the verb **написа́ть**) the prefix has no function other than to make the verb perfective (ie it adds only the sense of completeness of the action to the sense already conveyed by the imperfective). However, in other instances (eg in the verb **связа́ть**) the prefix provides a further modification of the meaning (**вяза́ть** means *to tie*, but **связа́ть** means *to tie* ***together***, ie *to unite, to join, to link*). (See also 7.6 on infixes.)

[2] Prefixes consisting of a single consonant or ending in a consonant may have to add **о** for the sake of euphony, eg **во-**, **подо-**.

Most of the prefixes which verbs may bear are listed below. A few of the less common meanings which may be borne by some of the prefixes are omitted. The directional meaning of each prefix, if the prefix has such a meaning, is dealt with first in each instance.

в- (во-)

(a) movement *into*, or sometimes *upwards*, eg

ввози́ть/ввезти́	*to bring in (by transport), import*
вовлека́ть/вовле́чь	*to drag in, involve*
влеза́ть/влезть	*to climb into/up*

(b) + **-ся**: action carried out with care or absorption; not common in this sense:

вслу́шиваться/вслу́шаться в + acc	*to listen attentively to*
всма́триваться/всмотре́ться в + acc	*to peer at, scrutinise*

вз- (взо-)
вс- before unvoiced consonants

movement *up*, eg

взлета́ть/взлете́ть	*to fly up, to take off*
всходи́ть/взойти́	*to go up, mount, ascend,*
взва́ливать/взвали́ть	*to lift, load up on to*

воз- (вос- before unvoiced consonants)

of OCS origin; borne by verbs unlikely to occur in R1:

возде́рживаться/воздержа́ться	*to abstain, refrain from*
возобновля́ть/возобнови́ть	*to renew*
воскреша́ть/воскреси́ть	*to resurrect*

вы-

Note: this prefix is always stressed when it occurs in perfective verbs.

(a) movement *out of*, eg

вывози́ть/вы́везти	*to take out (by transport), export*
вынима́ть/вы́нуть	*to take out*

(b) action carried out to the fullest possible extent; uncommon in this meaning:

выва́ривать/вы́варить — *to boil thoroughly*

(c) action carried out to an extent sufficient to obtain the desired result; uncommon in this meaning:

выпра́шивать/вы́просить — *to obtain through asking*

Note: the imperfective here will carry a sense of *trying* to obtain through asking; see 10.5.3.

(d) + -**ся**: in a few perfective verbs indicating that an action has been carried out to a sufficient degree:

вы́плакаться — *to have a good cry*

вы́спаться — *to have a good sleep*

до-

(a) movement *as far as* or *up to* a certain point, eg

доходи́ть/дойти́ до + gen — *to reach (on foot)*

добира́ться/добра́ться до + gen — *to reach, get as far as*

(b) action supplementary to some action already carried out, eg

допла́чивать/доплати́ть — *to make an additional payment*

(c) + -**ся**: action carried through to its intended outcome; uncommon, eg

дозвони́ться — *to get through (on the telephone)*

за-

(a) movement *behind* or *beyond* or *a long way*, eg

заезжа́ть/зае́хать — *to drive beyond*

заходи́ть/зайти́ — *to go behind, set* (of sun)

закла́дывать/заложи́ть — *to put behind*

(b) in a number of verbs indicating that a call or visit is/was/will be made, eg

забега́ть/забежа́ть
загля́дывать/загляну́ть
заходи́ть/зайти́
} *to call in on/drop in on*

(c) used as a prefix to render simple verbs perfective, **за-** may indicate the beginning of an action; this usage is particularly common in verbs describing some sound, eg

зазвене́ть — *to start to ring*

засмея́ться — *to burst out laughing*

заходи́ть — *to start pacing around/up and down*

(d) may indicate that a space is filled or that sth is covered or closed by the action; fairly common:

зава́ливать/завали́ть — *to block up, obstruct, pile up with*

заполня́ть/запо́лнить — *to fill in* (form, questionnaire)

	(e)	used as a perfective prefix **за-** may indicate that an action, particularly a harmful one, has been carried to an extreme degree; uncommon in this meaning:	
		запоро́ть	*to flog to death*
		застрели́ть	*to shoot (and kill)*
	(f)	+ **-ся**: may indicate that action has gone on for longer than one might expect or that the agent has been more than normally engrossed in it; fairly common:	
		заба́лтываться/заболта́ться	*to be/get engrossed in conversation*
		зачи́тываться/зачита́ться	*to be/get engrossed in reading*
из- (**ис-** **before unvoiced consonants**)	(a)	in many verbs has original directional meaning *out of*, though now this meaning may not be obvious; cf Eng *ex-* (abridged form *e-*):	
		избира́ть/избра́ть	*to elect*
		извлека́ть/извле́чь	*to extract, derive*
		исключа́ть/исключи́ть	*to exclude, rule out*
	(b)	action affecting the entire surface of sth; not common in this meaning:	
		изгрыза́ть/изгры́зть	*to gnaw to shreds*
		изре́зывать/изре́зать	*to cut to pieces/cut in many places*
	(c)	exhaustion of a supply of sth; uncommon:	
		испи́сывать/исписа́ть	*to use up all of* (some writing material, eg paper, ink)
	(d)	action carried out to the fullest possible extent, eg	
		иссыха́ть/иссо́хнуть (intrans)	*to dry up altogether*
	(e)	+ **-ся**, and in perfective forms only: to do or suffer sth unpleasant to the extent that it becomes habitual, eg	
		изолга́ться	*to become an inveterate liar*
на-	(a)	movement *onto* or *into* (in the sense of collision), eg	
		налета́ть/налете́ть	*to swoop on, run into* (of vehicles)
		напада́ть/напа́сть	*to attack, fall upon*
	(b)	in some verbs, predominantly perfectives, to denote action affecting a certain quantity of an object; the direct object is generally in the genitive case, indicating partitive meaning, eg	
		навари́ть	*to boil a certain quantity of*
		накупи́ть	*to buy up a certain quantity of*
	(c)	+ **-ся**: in verbs (predominantly perfectives) denoting action carried out to satiety or even to excess, eg	
		нае́сться	*to eat one's fill*

Prefix		Meaning / Example	Translation
		напи́ться	*to drink as much as one wants; to get drunk*
недо-		insufficiency; attached to very few verbs, eg	
		недостава́ть/недоста́ть + gen	*to be insufficient*
		недооце́нивать/недооцени́ть	*to underestimate*
о- (об-, обо-)	(a)	movement *round* in various senses, viz comprehensive coverage, bypassing or overtaking, encircling or surrounding, eg	
		обходи́ть/обойти́	*to go all round, get round*
		обгоня́ть/обогна́ть	*to overtake*
		обрамля́ть/обра́мить	*to frame*
	(b)	thorough action covering the whole surface of sth, eg	
		окле́ивать/окле́ить	*to paste over*
		осма́тривать/осмотре́ть	*to look over, inspect*
	(c)	in verbs derived from a different part of speech, especially an adjective; very common in this function:	
		обогаща́ть/обогати́ть	*to enrich* (from бога́тый)
		освобожда́ть/освободи́ть	*to liberate, free* (from свобо́дный)
	(d)	+ **-ся**: in verbs indicating that an action is mistaken, eg	
		обсчи́тываться/обсчита́ться	*to make a mistake (in counting)*
		огова́риваться/оговори́ться	*to make a slip (in speaking)*
обез- (**обес-** before unvoiced consonants)		(= verbal prefix **о-** + adjectival prefix **без-/бес-**): loss or deprivation of the thing denoted by the root of the word; used with only a small number of verbs:	
		обезво́живать/обезво́дить	*to dehydrate* (ie *take away water*)
		обезвре́живать/обезвре́дить	*to render harmless, neutralise, defuse*
		обесси́ливать/обесси́лить	*to weaken* (ie *take away strength*)
от- (ото-)	(a)	movement *away from*, or *off* (cf **у-** below); very common in this meaning, eg	
		отлета́ть/отлете́ть	*to fly away, fly off, rebound*
		отходи́ть/отойти́	*to go away, go off, depart* (of transport), *come away from*
		отнима́ть/отня́ть	*to take away*
	(b)	in verbs with figurative meaning, may carry the sense of *back* (cf Eng *re-*); common in this meaning, eg	
		отбива́ть/отби́ть	*to beat back, repel*
		отража́ть/отрази́ть	*to reflect*

	(c)	in perfective verbs, to emphasise that action is at an end or has been carried out to its required limit; uncommon:	
		отдежу́рить	*to come off duty*
		отрабо́тать	*to finish one's work*
пере-	(a)	movement *across* or transference from one place to another (cf Eng *trans-*), eg	
		переходи́ть/перейти́	*to cross (on foot)*
		передава́ть/переда́ть	*to pass (across), transfer, transmit*
		переса́живаться/пересе́сть	*to change* (transport)
	(b)	to do sth again (cf Eng *re-*); common:	
		пересма́тривать/пересмотре́ть	*to look at again, review*
		перестра́ивать/перестро́ить	*to rebuild, reconstruct*
	(c)	to do sth too much (cf Eng *over-*), eg	
		перегрева́ть/перегре́ть	*to overheat*
		переоце́нивать/переоцени́ть	*to overestimate*
	(d)	+ **-ся**: reciprocal action, eg	
		перегля́дываться/перегляну́ться	*to exchange glances*
		перепи́сываться (impf only)	*to correspond* (ie *exchange letters*)
по-	(a)	in many perfective verbs, to indicate action of short duration or limited extent; it may be attached to indeterminate verbs of motion in this meaning; very common:	
		поговори́ть	*to have a talk, talk for a bit*
		погуля́ть	*to take a stroll*
		пое́сть	*to have a bite to eat*
		порабо́тать	*to do a bit of work*
		походи́ть	*to walk about for a bit*
	(b)	+ infix **-ыва-** or **-ива-**, to form imperfective verbs with iterative meaning (ie action repeated off and on for some time) or (it is argued by some, eg Bratus, pp 54–5; see Sources) with a nuance of reduced action and subjective expressive colouring, eg	
		погля́дывать	*to look at from time to time* or *to have a little look*
		погова́ривать	*to talk about every so often* or *to have a little talk*
		пока́шливать	*to cough from time to time*
		посви́стывать	*to whistle off and on*
под- (подо-)	(a)	action *from below*, eg	

		поддéрживать/поддержáть	*to support*
		подпи́сывать/подписáть	*to sign* (ie *write underneath*)
		подчёркивать/подчеркну́ть	*to stress, emphasise* (ie *underline*)
	(b)	movement *towards;* this is the commonest directional meaning of this prefix when it is used with verbs of motion:	
		подходи́ть/подойти́	*to approach, go towards/up to*
		подзывáть/подозвáть	*to call up, beckon*
	(c)	movement *upwards*, eg	
		подбрáсывать/подбрóсить	*to throw/toss up*
		поднимáть/поднять	*to lift, raise*
	(d)	action that is not far-reaching, eg	
		подкрáшивать/подкрáсить	*to tint, touch up*
		подрезáть/подрéзать	*to clip, trim*
	(e)	action that augments sth, eg	
		подрабáтывать/подрабóтать	*to earn some additional money*
	(f)	underhand action, eg	
		поджигáть/поджéчь	*to set fire to (criminally), commit arson*
		подкупáть/подкупи́ть	*to bribe, suborn*
		подслу́шивать (impf only)	*to eavesdrop*
пред- (**предо-**)		action that precedes or anticipates sth (cf Eng *fore-*); mainly in bookish words characteristic of R3, eg	
		предви́деть (impf; no pf)	*to foresee*
		предотвращáть/предотврати́ть	*to avert, prevent, stave off*
		предскáзывать/предсказáть	*to foretell, prophesy*
при-	(a)	movement *to* a destination, eg	
		приезжáть/приéхать	*to come, arrive (by transport)*
		приноси́ть/принести́	*to bring (by hand)*
		приходи́ть/прийти́	*to come, arrive (on foot)*
	(b)	attachment or fastening of an object to sth else, eg	
		привя́зывать/привязáть	*to tie/attach/fasten to*
		прикáлывать/приколóть	*to pin to*
	(c)	action that is not fully carried out, eg	
		приостанáвливать/приостанови́ть	*to halt*
		приоткрывáть/приоткры́ть	*to half-open*
		приспускáть/приспусти́ть	*to lower a little*

про-	(a)	movement *by* or *past*, eg	
		пробега́ть/пробежа́ть	*to run past*
		проходи́ть/пройти́	*to go past (on foot)*
	(b)	movement *through*, eg	
		проеда́ть/прое́сть	*to eat through, corrode*
		пропуска́ть/пропусти́ть	*to let through, admit, omit*
	(c)	as a perfective prefix, in many simple verbs when the duration of the action or the distance covered by it is defined, eg	
		просиде́ть два часа́	*to sit for two hours*
		пробежа́ть де́сять киломе́тров	*to run ten kilometres*
	(d)	thorough action, eg	
		проду́мывать/проду́мать	*to think over*
		прожа́ривать/прожа́рить	*to roast thoroughly*
	(e)	oversight (only a few verbs), eg	
		прогля́дывать/прогляде́ть	*to overlook*
	(f)	loss, eg	
		прои́грывать/проигра́ть	*to lose* (game, at cards)
	(g)	+ **-ся**: unintentional revelation, eg	
		прогова́риваться/проговори́ться	*to let the cat out of the bag*
раз- (разо-); рас- before unvoiced consonants	(a)	movement in various directions or distribution (cf Eng *dis-*); verbs of motion bearing this prefix become reflexive:	
		разбега́ться/разбежа́ться	*to run off (in various directions)*
		разлета́ться/разлете́ться	*to fly off, scatter, be shattered*
		размеща́ть/размести́ть	*to accommodate, place (in various places)*
	(b)	action that uncovers or undoes sth (cf Eng *un-*); common:	
		развя́зывать/развяза́ть	*to untie*
		разгружа́ть/разгрузи́ть	*to unload*
с- (со-)	(a)	movement *off* or *down from*, eg	
		сбега́ть/сбежа́ть	*to run down*
		слеза́ть/слезть	*to climb down/off*
		снима́ть/снять	*to take off*
		сходи́ть/сойти́	*to come down*
	(b)	convergence (cf Eng *con-*); verbs bearing the prefix in this sense may become reflexive:	
		сбега́ться/сбежа́ться	*to run and come together*

		сходи́ться/сойти́сь	*to come together, meet, gather, tally* (of figures)
		слива́ться/сли́ться	*to flow together, blend, mingle*
	(c)	joining, linking, eg	
		свя́зывать/связа́ть	*to tie together, connect, link, unite*
		соединя́ть/соедини́ть	*to unite, join*
	(d)	+ indeterminate verbs of motion to form perfective verbs which indicate that the subject moved in one direction and then back again; contrast homonyms or homographs which are imperfective verbs of motion indicating movement *down* or *off* (see (a) above), eg	
		сбе́гать	*to run somewhere and back again*
		сходи́ть	*to go somwehere and back again (on foot)*
у-	(a)	movement *away from*; this prefix differs from **от-** in that it suggests that the subject moves *right off*, whereas **от-** describes the progressive separation of the subject from the point of departure:	
		уезжа́ть/уе́хать	*to go away (by transport)*
		уходи́ть/уйти́	*to go away*
		убира́ть/убра́ть	*to remove, take away, clear away*
	(b)	in verbs with comparative meaning derived from an adjectival root, eg	
		улучша́ть(ся)/улу́чшить(ся)	*to improve* (from лу́чший)
		уменьша́ть(ся)/уме́ньшить(ся)	*to diminish* (from ме́ньший)
		ухудша́ть(ся)/уху́дшить(ся)	*to make worse* (non-refl)/*get worse* (refl; from худо́й)
		Note: the non-reflexive forms of the above verbs are transitive, the reflexive forms intransitive.	
	(c)	removal or diminution, eg	
		уре́зывать/уре́зать	*to cut, reduce*
		ушива́ть/уши́ть	*to take in (clothes)*
	(d)	achievement in spite of opposition; uncommon, eg	
		устоя́ть	*to stand one's ground*
	(e)	abundance, eg	
		усыпа́ть/усы́пать	*to strew with*

7.4 Noun prefixes

Although the main function of the prefixes listed in 7.3 above is to modify the meaning of verbs, they do also occur, with similar meaning, in many nouns. Some idea of their function and its extent in the formation of nouns may be gained from the following list of nouns which consist of prefix + the root **ход** (indicating *going, motion, movement on foot*) + (in some cases) a noun suffix.

восхóд (сóлнца)	*sunrise*
восхождéние	*ascent*
вход	*entrance, entry*
вы́ход	*exit, departure*
дохóд	*income*
захóд (сóлнца)	*sunset*
нахóдка	*a find*
обхóд	*round* (of doctor), *beat* (of policeman); *bypass*
отхóды	*waste-products*
перехóд	*crossing, transition*
подхóд	*approach*
прихóд	*arrival*
прохóд	*passage*
расхóд(ы)	*expense, outgoings*
расхóдование	*expenditure*
схóдни (pl; gen схóдней)	*gangplank*
схóдство	*similarity*
ухóд	*departure, withdrawal*

Note: adjectives may also be derived from some of these nouns, eg

выходнóй (день)	*rest-day*
дохóдный	*profitable, lucrative*
нахóдчивый	*resourceful*
обхóдный	*roundabout, circuitous*
перехóдный	*transitional*
схóдный	*similar*

7.5 Adjectival prefixes

A number of prefixes, some of them of foreign origin and international currency, may be attached to adjectives which also exist independently of them, eg

а/морáльный	*amoral*
анти/фаши́стский	*anti-Fascist*
все/си́льный	*all-powerful*
наи/лу́чший (bookish)	*best*
не/большóй	*small*
не/глу́пый	*not stupid*
не/без/основáтельный	*not without foundation*
пре/глу́пый (R1)	*really stupid*

про/америка́нский	*pro-American*
сверх/мо́щный (tech)	*extra-high-powered*
ультра/фиоле́товый	*ultraviolet*

Other prefixes, of Russian provenance, combine with the suffixes **-ный** and **-ский** to form adjectives, eg

без/вре́дный	*harmless*
бес/коне́чный	*infinite*
вне/бра́чный	*extramarital*
внутри/ве́нный	*intravenous*
до/вое́нный	*pre-war*
за/рубе́жный	*foreign* (lit *over the border*)
меж/плане́тный	*interplanetary*
между/наро́дный	*international*
на/сто́льный	*table* (eg те́ннис)
над/стро́чный	*superlinear*
по/дохо́дный	*(according to) income* (eg нало́г, *tax*)
по/сме́ртный	*posthumous*
под/во́дный	*underwater*
под/моско́вный	*near Moscow*
после/революцио́нный	*post-revolutionary*
пред/вы́борный	*pre-election* (ie *just before*)
при/балти́йский	*relating to the Baltic region*
сверх/есте́ственный	*supernatural*

7.6 The verbal infixes -ыва-/-ива-

These infixes have two functions:

(a) used in combination with the prefix **по-** they form iterative verbs (see 7.3, по- (b));

(b) they form secondary imperfectives (eg **подпи́сывать**, *to sign*), ie forms derived from a simple verb (eg **писа́ть**, *to write*) to which some prefix has been added, thus creating a perfective verb (eg **подписа́ть**) whose meaning needs to be preserved in an imperfective form. Further examples:

secondary impf	pf with prefix	simple verb
развя́зывать, *to untie*	**развяза́ть**	**вяза́ть**
переде́лывать, *to re-do*	**переде́лать**	**де́лать**
прои́грывать, *to lose*	**проигра́ть**	**игра́ть**
оты́скивать, *to find*	**отыска́ть**	**иска́ть**
прока́лывать, *to puncture*	**проколо́ть**	**коло́ть**
подка́пывать, *to undermine*	**подкопа́ть**	**копа́ть**
разма́тывать, *to unwind*	**размота́ть**	**мота́ть**
пересма́тривать, *to review*	**пересмотре́ть**	**смотре́ть**

всáсывать, *to suck in*	**всосáть**	**сосáть**
перестрáивать, *to rebuild*	**перестрóить**	**стрóить**

Note: 1 Unstressed **o** in the root of the simple verb, and sometimes stressed **ó**, change to **a** in secondary imperfective forms.

2 Secondary imperfectives belong to the conjugation 1A (see 8.6.2) and are characterised by stress on the syllable immediately before the infix.

7.7 Noun suffixes

The suffixes used in the formation of Russian nouns are very numerous. They may be used to indicate:

(a) people by reference to, eg, their qualities, characteristics, occupations or places of origin;
(b) types of animal;
(c) objects;
(d) abstract concepts;
(e) female representatives of a group;
(f) an attitude, ranging from affection to loathing, on the part of the speaker towards the object in question.

Note 1 Many suffixes are used within more than one of the above categories.

2 Properly speaking some of the 'suffixes' included in this section and almost all those in 7.9 might be treated as combinations of more than one suffix, eg **-н-ие**; **-ств-о**; **-ист-ый**; **-н-ый**.

7.7.1 The principal noun suffixes

The following list of noun suffixes is arranged in alphabetical order. The suffixes **-ация**, **-ение**, **-ец**, **-ин**, **-ость**, **-тель** are particularly common. The suffixes relating to categories (e) and (f) above are dealt with separately in 7.7.2 and 7.8 respectively.

-ак/-як

suffixes defining people by reference to their place of origin (see also 5.12), to some characteristic, or to the object with which their occupation is associated, eg

рыбáк	*fisherman*
бедня́к	*poor man*
моря́к	*seaman*
холостя́к	*bachelor*

-áла/-и́ла

very expressive suffixes used mainly in R1 to define people by reference to a particular action. The nouns formed with these suffixes are of common gender.

вороти́ла	*bigwig*
вышибáла	*bouncer*
громи́ла	*thug*
заправи́ла	*boss*

	кути́ла	*fast liver, hard drinker*
-анин/-янин	used to form nouns that indicate a person's status, ethnicity, or place of origin (see also 5.11–12), eg	
	горожа́нин	*town-dweller*
	граждани́н	*citizen*
	марсиа́нин	*Martian*
	мусульма́нин	*Moslem*
	христиани́н	*Christian*
	южа́нин	*southerner*
	дворяни́н	*nobleman*
	крестья́нин	*peasant*
	славяни́н	*Slav*
	Note: in some words the suffix used is **-ин**, eg **болга́рин**, *Bulgarian*; **боя́рин**, *boyar*; **грузи́н**, *Georgian*; **тата́рин**, *Tatar*.	
-ант/-ент	suffixes of foreign origin defining people in relation to some action or object, eg	
	демонстра́нт	*demonstrator*
	музыка́нт	*musician*
	эмигра́нт	*émigré*
	оппоне́нт	*opponent*
-ация/-яция	used in very numerous verbal nouns of international currency (cf Eng *-ation*; see also 4.1), eg	
	администра́ция	*administration*
	деклара́ция	*declaration*
	диссерта́ция	*dissertation*
	интона́ция	*intonation*
	консульта́ция	*consultation*
	милитариза́ция	*militarisation*
	модерниза́ция	*modernisation*
	организа́ция	*organisation*
	приватиза́ция	*privatisation*
	радиа́ция	*radiation*
	эвакуа́ция	*evacuation*
	эксплуата́ция	*exploitation*
	эскала́ция	*escalation*
Note 1	In words with a stem ending in a soft consonant the suffix used is **-я́ция**, eg **инфля́ция**, *inflation*; **корреля́ция**, *correlation*.	
2	The suffixes **-ция** and **-иция** also occur, eg **инстру́кция**, *instruction*; **экспеди́ция**, *expedition*.	
-ач	a relatively uncommon suffix defining people by reference to their occupational activity or salient characteristic, eg	
	бога́ч	*rich man*

	горба́ч	*hunchback*
	скрипа́ч	*violinist*
	ткач	*weaver*

-ёнок used to form nouns which denote the young of living creatures, eg

жеребёнок	*foal, colt*
котёнок	*kitten*
львёнок	*lion-cub*
поросёнок	*piglet*
ребёнок	*child*
цыплёнок	*chick*
ягнёнок	*lamb*

Note 1 After hushing consonants the suffix is **-о́нок**, eg **волчо́нок**, *wolf-cub*; **мышо́нок**, *baby mouse.*

2 The plural forms of nouns with this suffix are not formed in the usual way (see 8.1.9).

-ёр used in some words of international currency which define a person by reference to his field of activity (cf Eng *-er, -or*), eg

боксёр	*boxer*
дирижёр	*conductor* (of orchestra)
жонглёр	*juggler*
режиссёр	*producer* (of play, film)
суфлёр	*prompter* (in theatre)

-ец a very widespread suffix denoting a person by reference to (a) some action or occupation; (b) a certain quality; or (c) place of origin or residence (in which case the forms **-анец/-янец** (see also 5.11–12) are very common), eg

(a)	**бе́женец**	*refugee*
	гребе́ц	*rower, oarsman*
	живопи́сец	*painter*
	купе́ц	*merchant*
	очеви́дец	*witness*
	певе́ц	*singer*
	плове́ц	*swimmer*
	торго́вец	*trader*
(b)	**краса́вец**	*handsome man*
	скупе́ц	*miser, skinflint*
(c)	**америка́нец**	*American*
	африка́нец	*African*
	баки́нец	*person from Baku*
	перуа́нец	*Peruvian*
	япо́нец	*Japanese*

-ие/-ье with adjectival roots, in neuter abstract nouns which tend to be bookish and are therefore prevalent in R3, and which denote a quality, eg

вели́чие	*greatness*
изоби́лие	*abundance*
равноду́шие	*indifference*
уси́лие	*effort*
хладнокро́вие	*sang-froid*
здоро́вье	*health*

-изм of foreign origin, in nouns denoting a doctrine or system and also actions or tendencies (cf Eng *-ism*), eg

атеи́зм	*atheism*
капитали́зм	*capitalism*
коммуни́зм	*communism*
материали́зм	*materialism*
оптими́зм	*optimism*
романти́зм	*romanticism*
социали́зм	*socialism*
тури́зм	*tourism*
фанати́зм	*fanaticism*
эгои́зм	*egoism*

-ик used in words of international currency which define a person's field of activity, eg

акаде́мик	*academician*
исто́рик	*historian*
меха́ник	*mechanic*
те́хник	*technician*
хи́мик	*chemist* (not dispensing chemist: апте́карь (m))

-ика a suffix of foreign origin indicating a field of knowledge, a discipline (cf Eng *-ics*), eg

матема́тика	*mathematics*
поли́тика	*politics*
фи́зика	*physics*
фоне́тика	*phonetics*
эконо́мика	*economics*

-ина miscellaneous functions, including:

(a) with verbal roots, to indicate the result of actions, eg

впа́дина	*cavity*
морщи́на	*wrinkle*
цара́пина	*scratch*

(b) with noun roots, to denote an individual specimen of an object usually referred to collectively, eg

		жемчýжина	*a pearl*
		изю́мина	*a raisin*
		картóфелина	*a potato*
	(c)	to denote the meat of an animal or fish, eg	
		барáнина	*mutton*
		говя́дина	*beef*
		лососи́на	*salmon*
	(d)	to denote dimensions, and in some other abstract nouns:	
		глубинá	*depth*
		длинá	*length*
		тишинá	*silence*
		толщинá	*thickness*
		ширинá	*width*
-ионéр		used in words of international currency to define people by reference to their activity or outlook, eg	
		коллекционéр	*collector* (eg of stamps)
		реакционéр	*reactionary*
		революционéр	*revolutionary*
-ист		a suffix of foreign origin which defines people by reference to some doctrine they hold or art or skill they practise (cf Eng *-ist*; see also **-изм**), eg	
		атеи́ст	*atheist*
		велосипеди́ст	*cyclist*
		виолончели́ст	*cellist*
		журнали́ст	*journalist*
		очерки́ст	*essayist*
-ич		the suffix used to form male patronymics, and also to indicate place of origin (see also 5.12), eg	
		Ники́тич	*son of Nikita*
		Сергéич	*son of Sergei*
		оми́ч	*person from Omsk*
-ка	(a)	with verbal roots, in nouns denoting a process, an instrument, or the result of an action, eg	
		запи́ска	*note*
		заправка	*refuelling, seasoning*
		опи́ска	*slip of the pen*
		тёрка	*grater*
		чи́стка	*cleaning, purge*
	(b)	in R1 predominantly, with adjectival roots, to denote objects	

	which in R2 are described by the adjective in question + a noun, eg **пятиднéвка** = пятиднéвная недéля — *five-day week* **пятилéтка** = пятилéтний план — *five-year plan* **Третьякóвка** = Третьякóвская галерéя — *Tret'iakov Gallery*
-лка	often in R1, with verbal roots, to denote an instrument or place associated with an action, eg **вéшалка** — *clothes-hanger* **зажигáлка** — *cigarette-lighter* **качáлка** — *rocking-chair* **курúлка** (R1) — *smoking room* **раздевáлка** (R1) — *cloakroom*
-лог	a suffix of foreign origin denoting a specialist or person of learning in a particular field (cf Eng *-logist*; see also **-логия**), eg **биóлог** — *biologist* **геóлог** — *geologist* **метеорóлог** — *meteorologist*
-логия	a suffix of foreign origin denoting a science (cf Eng *-logy*; see also **-лог**), eg **биолóгия** — *biology* **гинеколóгия** — *gynaecology* **метеоролóгия** — *meteorology* **психолóгия** — *psychology* **социолóгия** — *sociology*
-ние	extremely common, in verbal nouns (cf Eng *-ing, -ment, -sion, -tion*), eg **восклицáние** — *exclamation* **выражéние** — *expression* **достижéние** — *achievement* **загрязнéние** — *pollution* **изобретéние** — *invention* **объявлéние** — *announcement, declaration* **объяснéние** — *explanation* **одобрéние** — *approval* **освобождéние** — *liberation* **осложнéние** — *complication* **отражéние** — *reflection* **пéние** — *singing* **повышéние** — *increase, elevation* **преувеличéние** — *exaggeration* **продолжéние** — *continuation* **произношéние** — *pronunciation*

	расшире́ние	*widening, expansion, extension*
	сочине́ние	*essay, composition*
	увеличе́ние	*increase*
	удивле́ние	*surprise*
	улучше́ние	*improvement*
	уменьше́ние	*lessening, decrease, reduction*
	упражне́ние	*exercise*
	ухудше́ние	*worsening, deterioration*
	чте́ние	*reading*

Note: consonant changes affecting the 1st person singular of second-conjugation verbs (8.6.8) are also in evidence in nouns of this type, eg **выраже́ние**.

-ник several uses, including:

(a) with noun roots, defining people by reference to their character, occupation or activity, eg

зави́стник	*envious person*
защи́тник	*defender*
помо́щник	*helper*

(b) with verbal roots, defining people by reference to their actions, eg

изме́нник	*traitor*
кочёвник	*nomad*
рабо́тник	*worker*

(c) denotation of objects which contain sth or accommodate some creature, eg

кофе́йник	*coffee-pot*
рудни́к	*mine*
коро́вник	*cowshed*

-ок with verbal roots, to indicate:

(a) a person who performs an action, eg

едо́к	*eater, mouth to feed*
знато́к	*expert, connoisseur*
игро́к	*player, gambler*

(b) the action itself or its result, eg

бросо́к	*a throw*; also *spurt*
зево́к	*a yawn*
обло́мок	*fragment*
объе́дки (pl; gen объе́дков)	*leftovers (of food)*
ога́рок	*candle-end* (after burning)
огры́зок	*core* (of fruit after eating)
оку́рок	*cigarette-end*
скачо́к	*a jump, leap*
спи́сок	*list*

толчóк	*a push, shove, jolt*

Note: the **o** in this suffix as used in (b) is a mobile vowel, hence gen sg **броскá**, etc.

-ор

a suffix of foreign origin denoting an agent (cf Eng *-or*; see also **-тор**), eg

профéссор	*professor*
сенáтор	*senator*
трáктор	*tractor*

-ость

this suffix, and related suffixes (eg **-ность**, **-нность**, **-мость**), are the most widespread suffixes used in the formation of abstract nouns. They are particularly prevalent in R3. With adjectival roots, **-ость** is used to form feminine nouns denoting a quality (cf Eng *-ness, -ery, -ity*, etc), eg

весёлость	*gaiety*
возмóжность	*possibility*
глýпость	*stupidity*
и́скренность	*sincerity*
мóлодость	*youth*
мýдрость	*wisdom*
скóрость	*speed*
спосóбность	*ability, capacity*
хрáбрость	*bravery, courage*
чéстность	*honesty*
я́сность	*clarity*

Note: after hushing consonants this unstressed suffix becomes **-есть**, eg **свéжесть**, *freshness* (see 7.2.4(c)).

Added to the roots of present active participles, or to the roots of adjectives derived from them, the suffixes **-ость** and **-мость** may be used to form nouns denoting a capacity or potentiality (cf Eng *-ity*), eg

ви́димость	*visibility*
заболевáемость	*sickness rate*
зави́симость	*dependence*
необходи́мость	*necessity, inevitability*
посещáемость	*attendance rate*

Added to the roots of past passive participles, the suffixes **-ость** and **-нность** may be used to form feminine nouns denoting a condition resulting from an action, eg

договорённость	*agreement, understanding*
изоли́рованность	*isolation*
срабóтанность	*wear and tear*

-ота́		with adjectival roots, to form abstract nouns denoting quality or condition (cf Eng *-ness*), eg	
		быстрота́	*speed*
		высота́	*height*
		глухота́	*deafness*
		густота́	*density*
		красота́	*beauty*
		острота́	*sharpness*
		пустота́	*emptiness*
		слепота́	*blindness*
		частота́	*frequency*
		чистота́	*cleanness, purity*
		широта́	*breadth, latitude* (geog)
-ство	(a)	with roots of nouns referring to people, in nouns denoting position, quality, branch of activity (cf Eng *-ship*), eg	
		а́вторство	*authorship*
		крестья́нство	*peasantry*
		чле́нство	*membership*
	(b)	with adjectival roots, in nouns denoting a quality or condition, eg	
		бога́тство	*richness, wealth*
		одино́чество	*solitude, loneliness*
		превосхо́дство	*superiority*
-тель (m)		a suffix added to the root of transitive verbs to form masculine nouns denoting an agent, usually a person, but also possibly a thing (cf Eng *-er, -or*), eg	
		води́тель	*driver*
		дви́гатель	*engine*
		зажига́тель	*ignition*
		зри́тель	*spectator, viewer*
		избира́тель	*elector, voter*
		изобрета́тель	*inventor*
		истреби́тель	*fighter* (aircraft)
		люби́тель	*amateur*
		огнетуши́тель	*fire-extinguisher*
		писа́тель	*writer*
		покупа́тель	*buyer, purchaser*
		потреби́тель	*consumer*
		преподава́тель	*teacher* (in higher education)
		роди́тель	*parent*
		руководи́тель	*leader*
		учи́тель	*teacher* (in school)
		чита́тель	*reader*

-тор	a suffix of foreign origin used to denote persons who do or things which carry out some activity denoted by a word with the suffix **-ация** or related suffixes (see **-ация**; cf Eng *-(a)tor*), eg	
	авиáтор	*aviator*
	дирéктор	*director*
	инкубáтор	*incubator*
	инстрýктор	*instructor*
	организáтор	*organiser*
-ун	mainly in R1, a suffix applied to verbal roots to form nouns which define persons by reference to some action which they perform or to which they are prone, eg	
	болтýн	*chatterbox*
	врун	*liar*
	говорýн	*talker*
	хвастýн	*braggart*
-щик/-чик	suffixes defining persons by reference to some object or institution associated with their occupation; also denoting some objects by reference to their function, eg	
	барабáнщик	*drummer*
	бомбардирóвщик	*bomber, bomber pilot*
	взлóмщик	*house-breaker*
	забастóвщик	*striker* (person on strike)
	кáменщик	*stone-mason, bricklayer*
	переп́исчик	*correspondent*
	подп́исчик	*subscriber*
	счётчик	*counter* (person, ie *teller*, or instrument, ie *meter*)
-щина	a suffix added mainly, but not exclusively, to proper nouns, to indicate a syndrome or set of circumstances associated with a person or place, eg	
	ежóвщина	*political terror associated with Yezhov* (chief of Stalin's secret police 1936–8)
	казёнщина	*red tape*
	облóмовщина	*behaviour associated with Oblomov* (eponymous hero of Goncharov's novel)
-ье	with noun roots and a spatial prefix, to form nouns denoting region, eg	
	заполя́рье	*polar region*
	поберéжье	*coast, littoral*
	предгóрье	*foothills*
	примóрье	*seaside*

Note: the prefix **-ие** may also have this function, eg **поднóжие**, *foot* (eg of mountain).

7.7.2 Noun suffixes denoting females

Several suffixes denote females of a type. These suffixes may correspond to suffixes denoting males of the same type (eg америкáн/**ка**, female equivalent of америкáнец), or they may be added to a masculine noun in order to transform it into a feminine one (eg тигр/**и́ца**, *tigress*). Sometimes the masculine noun to which the female suffix is added already bears a suffix itself (as in учи́тель/**ница**, *female teacher*, where the suffix **-ница** is added to учи́/тель).

Some of the commonest female suffixes are listed below, together with a note on their relation to masculine nouns denoting people of the same type and with a few examples.

-анка/-янка

feminine equivalents of **-анец/-янец** and **-анин/-янин** (see 7.7.1; also 5.11–12), eg

америкáнка	*American woman* (m америкáнец)
италья́нка	*Italian woman* (m италья́нец)
англичáнка	*English woman* (m англичáнин)
киевля́нка	*woman from Kiev* (m киевля́нин)

Note: the suffixes **-анка/-янка** may correspond simply to the masculine suffix **-ец**, eg **китая́нка**, *Chinese woman* (m китáец).

-иня/-ыня

бáрыня	*noble lady* (m бáрин)
герóиня	*heroine* (m герóй)
монáхиня	*nun* (m монáх)

-иса/-есса

suffixes of foreign origin, used in nouns of foreign origin, eg

актри́са	*actress* (m актёр)
поэтéсса	*poetess* (m поэ́т)

-иха

added to masculine nouns denoting persons and also to some nouns denoting animals, eg

повари́ха	*cook* (m пóвар)
труси́ха	*cowardess* (m трус)
слони́ха	*she-elephant* (m слон)

Note: the root of the masculine noun may undergo some change before the suffix is added, eg **зайчи́ха**, *doe-hare* (m зáяц).

-ица

added to some masculine nouns without a suffix; also feminine equivalent of **-ец** (see 7.7.1), eg

красáвица	*beautiful woman* (m красáвец)

	певи́ца	*singer* (m певе́ц)
	цари́ца	*tsarina* (m царь)
-ка	also a feminine equivalent of **-ец**; added to nouns in **-ист**, **-ич** (see 7.7.1), eg	
	арти́стка	*artiste* (m арти́ст)
	москви́чка	*Muscovite woman* (m москви́ч)
	япо́нка	*Japanese woman* (m япо́нец)
-ница	feminine equivalent of **-ник** and also added to nouns in **-тель** (see 7.7.1), eg	
	рабо́тница	*worker* (m рабо́тник)
	учи́тельница	*teacher* (m учи́тель)
-ша	added to masculine nouns to denote female of the type; also (in R1, but nowadays rare) to denote wife of the male, eg	
	секретáрша	*(woman) secretary* (m секретáрь)
	генерáльша	*general's wife* (m генерáл)
-ья	added to nouns in **-ун**, eg	
	болту́нья	*chatterbox* (m болту́н)

7.7.3 Miscellaneous noun suffixes

Although the commonest noun suffixes have been dealt with in the preceding sections, there are also many others, as briefly exemplified in the following list. (Suffixes, or groups of related suffixes, are arranged in alphabetical order.)

вольт/áж	*voltage*
сабот/áж	*sabotage*
пис/áка (R1, pej)	*hack*
брод/я́га	*tramp, vagrant*
покрыв/áло	*bedspread*
интриг/áн (R1, pej)	*intriguer*
груби/я́н (R1, pej)	*ruffian*
библиоте́к/арь m)	*librarian*
слов/áрь (m)	*dictionary*
старик/áшка (R1, pej)	*old man*
борь/бá	*struggle*
дру́ж/ба	*friendship*
жáл/оба	*complaint*
уч/ёба	*tuition*
клáд/бище	*cemetery*
убе́ж/ище	*refuge*
учи́л/ище	*college*

сердц/еви́на	*heart(land)*
пут/ёвка	*travel permit, pass* (to sanatorium)
плат/ёж	*payment*
сласт/ёна	*person with a sweet tooth*
пе́рв/енство	*first place, championship*
боле́/знь(f)	*illness*
боя́/знь(f)	*fear*
жи/знь(f)	*life*
то́пл/иво	*fuel*
дорогов/и́зна	*expensiveness*
нов/изна́	*novelty*
бронх/и́т	*bronchitis*
безрабо́т/ица	*unemployment*
больн/и́ца	*hospital*
пе́пель/ница	*ashtray*
владе́/лец	*owner*
буди́/льник	*alarm clock*
холоди́/льник	*refrigerator*
боле́/льщик	*fan, supporter*
колоко́ль/ня	*belfry*
па́ш/ня	*ploughed land*
то́п/от	*stamping*
шёп/от	*whisper*
бег/отня́	*scurrying*
прави́/тельство	*government*
закры́/тие	*closure*
бри/тьё	*shaving*
пас/ту́х	*shepherd*
лен/тя́й (R1)	*idler*
аспирант/у́ра	*postgraduate study, postgraduate student body*
литерат/у́ра	*literature*
де́д/ушка	*grandad*
весель/ча́к (R1)	*cheerful person*
мал/ы́ш (R1)	*kid*
обо́рв/ыш (R1)	*ragamuffin*
гнёзд/ышко (R1)	*little nest*
тел/я́тина	*veal*

7.8 Diminutive, augmentative and expressive suffixes

Russian is rich in suffixes which either indicate the size, especially smallness, of an object or are indicative of the speaker's attitude (which may be affectionate, tender, attentive or scornful, ironic, disparaging) towards it. Many suffixes may serve both a diminutive and an affectionate (hypocoristic) purpose. Note though that in certain nouns, or in some nouns when they are used in certain meanings, the suffix has lost its original diminutive or hypocoristic function (eg when the noun **ру́чка** means the *handle* of a door).

As a rule diminutives and augmentatives are of the same gender as the noun to which the suffix is attached, even when the suffix ends with a vowel normally associated with another gender. The noun **городи́шко**, *god-forsaken town*, for example, is masculine like го́род even though nouns in -o are generally neuter.

Because they are highly expressive colloquial forms diminutives belong primarily to R1, although they are also widely used in the literary variety of the written language and in folk poetry. They are less likely to be encountered in the neutral R2 and are generally altogether absent in the more formal varieties of R3, especially R3a and R3b.

The following lists of diminutive, augmentative and expressive suffixes are not exhaustive; they contain only some of the more productive suffixes.

7.8.1 Diminutive and hypocoristic suffixes

-енька

a diminutive of heightened expressiveness, used mainly with nouns denoting people and with proper names already in a diminutive form, eg Са́ша:

ду́шенька	*darling*
Са́шенька	*Sasha dear*

-ик

added to masculine nouns; may also convey scorn:

гво́здик	*little nail, tack*
до́ждик	*shower*
до́мик	*little house, cottage*
но́сик	*spout* (of jug, teapot)
сто́лик	*little table*
студе́нтик	*so-called student*
ча́сик	*hour*

-инка

diminutive form of suffix **-ина** when it denotes single specimens of an object, eg

песчи́нка	*grain of sand*
пыли́нка	*speck of dust*
снежи́нка	*snowflake*
соло́минка	*piece of straw*
чаи́нка	*tea leaf*

-ка

the most widespread diminutive suffix; added to feminine nouns; may also convey scorn: eg

	голо́вка	*little head* (eg of pin)
	до́чка	*daughter*
	ёлка	*little fir-tree*
	иде́йка	*a silly idea*
	кры́шка	*lid*
	но́жка	*little leg, leg* (eg of chair)
	пе́сенка	*a (nice) song*
	ру́чка	*little hand, handle* (eg of door), *arm* (eg of chair)
	стре́лка	*little arrow, hand* (eg of clock)
	ча́шка	*cup*
-ок/-ёк	added to masculine nouns, which may have to undergo a final consonant change (see 7.2.5); may also convey scorn:	
	ветеро́к	*breeze*
	городо́к	*small town*
	дурачо́к	*idiot, clot*
	листо́к	*little leaf, leaflet*
	конёк	*hobby-horse*
-це (-ице)/-цо́ (-ецо́)	added to neuter nouns, eg	
	зе́ркальце	*little mirror* (eg in car)
	пла́тьице	*little dress*
	деревцо́	*small tree*
	письмецо́	*little letter*
-чик	added to masculine nouns ending in **в, л, м, н, р, й**, eg	
	бараба́нчик	*little drum*
	бли́нчик	*pancake*
	колоко́льчик	*little bell*
	рома́нчик	*novel* (pej)

7.8.2 Double diminutive suffixes

Some suffixes are really double diminutives which may help to form nouns denoting particularly small objects or may serve as terms of special endearment:

-о́чек	added to masculine nouns, eg	
	листо́чек	*tiny little leaf*
	цвето́чек	*little flower*
-е́чко	added to neuter nouns, eg	
	месте́чко	*little place*
	слове́чко	*little word*

-очка/-ечка/-ичка added to feminine suffixes, eg

де́вочка	*little girl*
звёздочка	*tiny little star, asterisk*
стре́лочка	*tiny little arrow, little hand* (eg on watch)
води́чка	*nice little (bottle/drink of) water*
сестри́чка	*dear little sister*

7.8.3 The augmentative suffix -**ище**/-**ища**

-**ище** is added to masculine and neuter nouns, -**ища** to feminine nouns, eg

городи́ще	*a very large town*
бороди́ща	*a massive beard*

7.8.4 Pejorative suffixes

Pejorative suffixes indicate scorn or contempt on the part of the speaker or writer towards the object in question. The main pejorative suffixes are:

-ишка/-ишко The suffix -**ишка** may be added to masculine animate and feminine nouns; -**ишко** may be added to masculine inanimate and neuter nouns, eg

лгуни́шка (m)	*a wretched liar*
кварти́ришка (f)	*a horrible flat*
пого́дишка (f)	*horrible weather*
городи́шко (m)	*an awful town*
доми́шко (m)	*a beastly house*
письми́шко (n)	*letter* (pej)

Note: the form **брати́шка**, *brother*, is affectionate.

-ёнка/-онка This suffix is applied mainly to feminine nouns. The form -**онка** follows hushing consonants, which may result from a consonant change in the root of the noun when the suffix is added.

Examples:

бабёнка	*foul old hag*
лошадёнка	*wretched nag*
книжо́нка	*dreadful book*
собачо́нка	*cur*

7.9 Adjectival suffixes

7.9.1 The principal adjectival suffixes

In this section some of the commoner adjectival suffixes are given. Closely related suffixes are treated together.

Note: **-о́й** is used when the ending is stressed.

-анный/-янный
-аный/-ано́й
-яный/-яно́й

variations on the same suffix, used in many adjectives indicating the material or thing from which sth is made eg

деревя́нный	*wooden*
стекля́нный	*glass*
ко́жаный	*leather*
ржано́й	*rye*
шерстяно́й	*woollen*

Note: there are also many adjectives denoting material which do not have one of these suffixes, eg **желе́зный, шёлковый**.

-атый

a suffix indicating that the thing denoted by the noun from which the adjective is derived is characteristic of or conspicuous in the subject, eg

борода́тый	*bearded*
крыла́тый	*winged*
полоса́тый	*striped*
рога́тый	*horned*

Note: **жена́тый**, *married* (of man to woman, ie *having a wife*), belongs in this category.

-енький/-онький

diminutive suffixes which carry a nuance of smallness, tenderness or sometimes disparagement; **-онький** is used after the velars **г, к, х**:

бе́ленький	*little white*
ми́ленький	*dear, sweet*
хоро́шенький	*pretty*
ти́хонький	*quiet little*

-ивый -ливый
-чивый

suffixes which may be applied to noun or verbal roots and which indicate that the subject is inclined or prone to some conduct, eg

красноречи́вый	*eloquent*
лени́вый	*lazy*
брезгли́вый	*squeamish*
молчали́вый	*taciturn*
терпели́вый	*patient, tolerant*
трусли́вый	*cowardly*
дове́рчивый	*trustful, credulous*
заду́мчивый	*pensive*

-ин in R1, indicating possession; applied to roots of nouns in **-а/-я** denoting people, including diminutive forms of first names, eg

ма́мин	*mum's*
па́пин	*dad's*
Пе́тин	*Pete's*
Та́нин	*Tania's*
тётин	*auntie's*

Note: these adjectives are similar in meaning to adjectives from the same roots in **-инский** and adjectives in **-овский/-евский**, eg **матери́нский**, **никола́евский** (see section (c) under the suffix **-ский** below). However, whereas adjectives in **-ин** tend to indicate possession by a particular individual, the forms in **-инский**, etc denote general association with a person or type of person.

-ний used in a number of common adjectives indicating place or time, sometimes with the help of a further letter or morpheme between root and ending. These adjectives are important because their flexions cannot be explained by the spelling rules which normally dictate variations from the standard type of adjectival ending (see 8.3.1).

по́здний	*late*
ра́нний	*early*
весе́нний	*spring*
ле́тний	*summer*
осе́нний	*autumn(al)*
зи́мний	*winter*
у́тренний	*morning*
вече́рний	*evening*
вчера́шний	*yesterday's*
сего́дняшний	*today's*
за́втрашний	*tomorrow's*
ны́нешний	*present-day*
да́вний	*of long standing*
дре́вний	*ancient*
пре́жний	*former, previous*
после́дний	*last*
бли́жний	*near, neighbouring*
да́льний	*far, distant*
ве́рхний	*upper*
ни́жний	*lower*
пере́дний	*front*
за́дний	*back*
вне́шний	*outer, external*
вну́тренний	*inner, internal*
сре́дний	*middle, medium, average*
кра́йний	*extreme*
посторо́нний	*extraneous*
дома́шний	*domestic*

	ли́шний	*superfluous*
-ный/-но́й	the most common suffix applied to inanimate nouns, including nouns of foreign origin, with the meanings *relating to* or *consisting of*, or denoting possession of the quality to which the noun refers, eg	
	вку́сный	*tasty*
	во́дный	*(relating to) water*
	вре́дный	*harmful*
	голо́дный	*hungry*
	перехо́дный	*transitional*
	спо́рный	*debatable*
	транзи́тный	*transit*
	ую́тный	*comfortable*
	шу́мный	*noisy*
	глазно́й	*eye*
	головно́й	*head*
	зубно́й	*tooth, dental*
	лесно́й	*forest*
	As with adjectives in **-ский**, there are also many further suffixes that are developed on the basis of this suffix, including suffixes of foreign origin which are applied to foreign roots, eg	
	суд/е́бный	*judicial*
	госуда́рств/енный	*state*
	иску́сств/енный	*artificial*
	худо́жеств/енный	*artistic*
	боле́зн/енный	*sickly, unhealthy*
	неб/е́сный	*heavenly*
	чуд/е́сный	*marvellous*
	втор/и́чный	*secondary*
	купа́/льный	*bathing*
	верх/о́вный	*supreme*
	душ/е́вный	*spiritual*
	избира́/тельный	*electoral*
	убеди́/тельный	*convincing*
	раздраж/и́тельный	*irritating*
	театр/а́льный	*theatrical*
	элемент/а́рный	*elementary*
	прогресс/и́вный	*progressive*
	конструк/ти́вный	*constructive*
-ова́тый/-ева́тый	used to indicate that a quality is possessed in some degree (cf Eng *-ish*). Especially common with adjectives of colour, eg	
	белова́тый	*whitish*
	кислова́тый	*a bit sour*
	синева́тый	*bluish*

-овый/-ово́й
-евый/-ево́й

used with inanimate nouns. (English may make no distinction between the equivalent adjective and the noun which possesses the quality denoted by the adjective.) Examples:

бамбу́ковый	*bamboo*
берёзовый	*birch*
кла́ссовый	*class*
боково́й	*side*
мирово́й	*world*
боево́й	*combat*

-ский/-ско́й

(a) An extremely widespread suffix that is applied to the roots of nouns, mainly masculine, to form adjectives indicating relationship to the thing denoted by the root. Many adjectives denoting nationality or describing place of origin (see 5.11–12) or a person's designation contain this suffix.

а́вторский	*author's, authorial*
бра́тский	*brotherly, fraternal*
де́тский	*child's, infantile*
же́нский	*wife's, female*
ма́йский	*May*
городско́й	*town, urban*
донско́й	*(relating to the River) Don*

(b) There is a very large number of adjectives, formed from roots of international currency, in **-и́ческий** (cf Eng *-ic/-ical*), eg

географи́ческий	*geographical*
климати́ческий	*climatic*
коми́ческий	*comic*
реалисти́ческий	*realistic*

There are also many other adjectives in **-и́ческий**, formed from nouns of international currency in **-ика** (see 7.7.1). (Strictly speaking the suffix in these adjectives is **-еский**.)

математи́ческий	*mathematical*
полити́ческий	*political*
экономи́ческий	*economic*

(c) numerous other adjectival suffixes are developed on the basis of **-ский**, eg

африк/а́нский	*African*
венец/иа́нский	*Venetian*
итал/ья́нский	*Italian*
рожд/е́ственский	*Christmas*
альп/и́йский	*Alpine*
олимп/и́йский	*Olympian, Olympic*
матер/и́нский	*maternal*
отц/о́вский	*paternal*

ма́рт/овский	*March*
корол/е́вский	*royal*
никола́/евский	*(relating to Tsar) Nicholas*

7.9.2 Miscellaneous adjectival suffixes

The following list, arranged in alphabetical order according to the basic suffix, gives some idea of the range of further suffixes available.

кров/а́вый	*bloody*
кудр/я́вый	*curly*
зуб/а́стый (R1)	*large-toothed, toothy*
бугр/и́стый	*hilly*
напо́р/истый	*pushy*
плодов/и́тый	*fruitful, fertile*
ядов/и́тый	*poisonous*
гро́м/кий	*loud*
ли́п/кий	*sticky*
ско́льз/кий	*slippery*

7.10 Suffixes of participial origin

Many words of participial origin which bear one of the following suffixes have become established in the language as adjectives.

-аный/-еный/-ёный suffixes indicating that some process has been carried out. Many of the adjectives with this suffix are culinary terms.

рва́ный	*torn, lacerated*
жа́реный	*roast(ed)*
ра́неный	*wounded, injured*
сушёный	*dried*
тушёный	*stewed, braised*

-ачий/-ячий
-учий/-ючий adjectives derived from Old Russian participial forms which stand alongside active participles in -щий from the same verbal roots. (In cases where the use of a form of this type is restricted the adjective is given in a phrase in which it commonly occurs.)

лежа́чий	*lying, recumbent*
горя́чий	*hot* (cf горя́щий, *burning*)
сидя́чий	*sedentary*
стоя́чая вода́	*stagnant* (ie *standing*) *water*
лету́чая мышь	*bat* (ie *flying mouse*)
колю́чий	*prickly*

-лый adjectives derived from the roots of some intransitive verbs and describing a condition that is the result of some action, eg

быва́лый	*worldly-wise*
вя́лый	*limp*
зре́лый	*mature*
отста́лый	*backward*
уста́лый	*tired*

-мый/-емый used in the formation of present passive participles (see 8.7.5; cf Eng *-able, -ible*), many of which have become established as adjectives and which occur most commonly in R3. Participles of this type have also given rise to many adjectives with the prefix **не-** (cf Eng *-in/un-*), eg

осяза́емый	*tangible*
допусти́мый	*admissible*
несгора́емый	*fireproof*
непобеди́мый	*invincible*
неуязви́мый	*invulnerable*

-нный/-енный/-ённый suffixes used to form the past passive participles of many verbs (see 8.7.6; cf Eng *-ed*), eg

взволно́ванный	*agitated*
уме́ренный	*moderate*
влюблённый	*in love*
истощённый	*exhausted*

-тый used to form the past passive participle of verbs of certain types (see 8.7.6; cf Eng *-ed*), some of which have become established as adjectives, eg

за́нятый	*occupied*
изби́тый	*hackneyed*
смя́тый	*crumpled*

-ший used to form past active participles (see 8.7.4), a few of which have become established as adjectives, eg

бы́вший	*former*
проше́дший	*past*
сумасше́дший	*mad*

-щий used to form present active participles (see 8.7.3), many of which have become established as adjectives, eg

блестя́щий	*brilliant*
подходя́щий	*suitable*
сле́дующий	*following*

7.11 The verbal suffixes **-ничать** and **-ануть**

There are many suffixes which are used in the formation of the infinitive and stems of verbs. As a rule verbal suffixes do not bear specific meaning, but it is worth noting here two suffixes which do indicate certain types of action and which are characteristic of R1 and D respectively.

(a) **-ничать**: used in R1 to form imperfectives, often with a jocular tone, which describe a certain pattern of behaviour, eg

бродя́жничать	*to be a tramp* (from бродя́га)
во́льничать	*to take liberties*
ехи́дничать	*to be malicious, go in for innuendo*
жема́нничать	*to behave in an affected way*
секре́тничать	*to be secretive*
скро́мничать	*to be over-modest*
скря́жничать	*to behave like a miser*

(b) **-ануть**: used freely in D, to form highly expressive semelfactive perfectives indicating that an action was carried out suddenly on one occasion, eg

махану́ть	*to wave*
резану́ть	*to cut*
сказану́ть	*to blurt out*
тряхану́ть	*to shake*
чесану́ть	*to scratch*
шагану́ть	*to step*

7.12 Composition

7.12.1 Compound nouns

Russian has many nouns which have been formed by the various types of composition or abbreviation illustrated below.

compound hyphenated nouns

га́лстук-ба́бочка (m)	*bow tie*
шко́ла-интерна́т (f)	*boarding-school*
штаб-кварти́ра (f)	*headquarters*

Note: the gender of such nouns is that of the key noun of the pair, which is generally the first noun (as in the first two examples above), but may also be the second noun (as in the third example).

stump compounds This type of word-formation was rarely used in pre-revolutionary times but became common in the 1920s, particularly in relation to political and administrative innovations in the early Soviet period.

	авиа/ба́за	*air base*
	авто/тра́нспорт	*road transport*
	зав/ка́федрой (R1/2; заве́дующий ка́федрой)	*head of department*
	зар/пла́та	*wages, pay, salary*
	кол/хо́з (коллекти́вное хозя́йство)	*collective farm*
	лин/ко́р (лине́йный кора́бль)	*battleship*
	нарко/би́знес	*(illegal) drugs business*
	проф/сою́з	*trade union*
	са́мбо (n, indecl; само/оборо́на без ору́жия)	*unarmed combat*
	сек/со́т (секре́тный сотру́дник)	*secret agent*
	стен/газе́та (стенна́я газе́та)	*wall newspaper*
	физ/культу́ра (физи́ческая культу́ра)	*physical training*
	хоз/расчёт (хозя́йственный расчёт)	see 4.1.2
	эс/ми́нец (эска́дренный миноно́сец)	*destroyer* (naval)
	Note: nouns of this type fall within the normal declensional pattern (see 8.1.2) and their gender is determined by their ending in the usual way.	
abbreviated nouns	**метро́** (метрополите́н)	*underground (railway system)*
	Пи́тер (R1; Петербу́рг)	*St Petersburg*
acronyms	**вуз** (вы́сшее учёбное заведе́ние)	*higher educational institution*
	ЗИЛ (заво́д и́мени Лихачёва)	type of car (esp *limousine*) produced in Likhachev factory
	СПИД (синдро́м приобретённого имму́нного дефици́та)	*AIDS*
	See also eg **бич**, **бомж** (4.1.2), **ЗАГС** (5.10).	
	Note: nouns of this type fall within the normal declensional pattern (see 8.1.2) and their gender is determined as a rule in the usual way.	

7.12.2 Compound adjectives

The following list gives examples of the process of adjectival formation through various types of composition.

земледе́ль/ческий	root of compound noun + adj suffix	*agricultural*
железно/доро́жный	adj + adj derived from noun	*railway*
много/чи́сленный	adv + adj derived from noun	*numerous*
дико/расту́щий	adv + pres act part	*(growing) wild*
светло-/зелёный	two adj roots	*light green*
англо-/ру́сский	two adj denoting equivalent concepts	*Anglo-Russian*

двух/ле́тний	numeral + adj derived from noun	*two-year, biennial*
все/сторо́нний	pron + adj	*thorough*
еже/го́дный	pron + adj	*annual*
огне/упо́рный	adj derived from two noun roots	*fireproof*

8 Inflection

Russian is a highly inflected language. Meaning is much more dependent on the ending of words and less dependent on word order than is the case in English. Without a thorough knowledge of the many flexions used on Russian nouns, pronouns, adjectives, numerals and verbs it is impossible not only to speak and write Russian correctly but even to arrive at an accurate understanding of what one hears or reads.

However, the difficulty of learning the numerous flexions is not so great as seems at first to be the case if the learner keeps in mind the distinction between hard and soft consonants and the spelling rules listed in 7.2.1 and 7.2.4 and takes the trouble to study the basic declensional and conjugational patterns set out in this chapter.

8.1 Declension of the noun

The Russian declensional system has six cases and distinguishes between singular and plural. The six cases are nominative, accusative, genitive, dative, instrumental, prepositional. There is a very small number of relics of the vocative case and dual number (see Glossary). Some nouns exist only in a plural form (eg **су́тки**), at least in certain meanings (eg **часы́**, *clock*; 2.6.1). Some nouns borrowed from other languages are indeclinable (8.1.12).

8.1.1 Gender

The gender of most nouns is easily determined:

masculine

(a) all nouns ending in a hard consonant, eg стол;
(b) all nouns ending in **-й**, eg музе́й;
(c) a minority of nouns ending in **-ь**, especially:
 i. all those denoting males, eg зять, *son-in-law* or *brother-in-law*;
 ii. nouns ending in the suffix **-тель** (see 7.7.1), eg покупа́тель, *shopper*;
(d) some nouns in **-а** and **-я** which denote males or people who may be of either sex, eg мужчи́на, *man*; дя́дя, *uncle*; слуга́, *servant*.

neuter

(a) most nouns in **-о**, eg окно́, *window*;
(b) most nouns in **-е**, eg мо́ре, *sea*; упражне́ние, *exercise*; except подмасте́рье, *apprentice* (m);
(c) all nouns in **-ё**, eg ружьё, *gun*.

Note: nouns derived from masculine nouns with the pejorative suffix **-ишко** (7.8.4) are masculine.

feminine

(a) most nouns ending in **-а**, eg де́вушка, *girl*; кни́га, *book*;
(b) most nouns ending in **-я**, eg тётя, *aunt*; ба́шня, *tower*;
(c) the majority of nouns ending in **-ь**, especially:
i. nouns denoting females, eg мать, *mother*;
ii. nouns in which the soft sign is preceded by one of the hushing consonants **ж**, **ч**, **ш**, or **щ**, eg рожь, *rye*; ночь, *night*; мышь, *mouse*; вещь, *thing*;
iii. abstract nouns ending in **-ость** or **-есть**, eg мо́лодость, *youth*; све́жесть, *freshness*.

Note: nouns derived from animate masculine nouns with the pejorative suffix **-ишка** (see 7.8.4) are masculine.

A few nouns, eg **сирота́**, *orphan*, are of common gender, ie they may be either masculine or feminine depending on whether they denote a male or female.

On the gender of indeclinable nouns see 8.1.12.

8.1.2 Basic declensional patterns of the noun

The main declensional types may be classified according to gender.
For the purposes of this book Russian nouns are treated as divisible into ten basic declensional patterns (three masculine, three neuter and four feminine). Groups of nouns, individual nouns, and particular case endings which do not conform to these patterns are dealt with in sections 8.1.3 to 8.1.12 inclusive.

Note: many of the nouns which have been chosen to illustrate the various declensional types and whose paradigms are given below have fixed stress. However, the stress patterns of Russian nouns are extremely complex, and in several of the declensional categories nouns of various stress patterns are to be found.

		HARD ENDINGS		SOFT ENDINGS	
		sg	pl	sg	pl
MASCULINE[1]	nom	**авто́бус**	**авто́бусы**[3]	**трамва́й**	**трамва́и**
	acc	**авто́бус**	**авто́бусы**	**трамва́й**	**трамва́и**
	gen	**авто́буса**	**авто́бусов**[4]	**трамва́я**	**трамва́ев**
	dat	**авто́бусу**	**авто́бусам**	**трамва́ю**	**трамва́ям**
	instr	**авто́бусом**[2]	**авто́бусами**	**трамва́ем**	**трамва́ями**
	prep	**авто́бусе**	**авто́бусах**	**трамва́е**	**трамва́ях**
				сти́ль	**сти́ли**
				сти́ль	**сти́ли**
				сти́ля	**сти́лей**
				сти́лю	**сти́лям**
				сти́лем	**сти́лями**
				сти́ле	**сти́лях**

NEUTER	nom	**сло́во**	**слова́**[5]	**по́ле**[6]	**поля́**[7]
	acc	**сло́во**	**слова́**	**по́ле**	**поля́**
	gen	**сло́ва**[5]	**слов**	**по́ля**[7]	**поле́й**
	dat	**сло́ву**	**слова́м**	**по́лю**	**поля́м**
	instr	**сло́вом**	**слова́ми**	**по́лем**	**поля́ми**
	prep	**сло́ве**	**слова́х**	**по́ле**	**поля́х**
				зда́ние	**зда́ния**
				зда́ние	**зда́ния**
				зда́ния	**зда́ний**
				зда́нию	**зда́ниям**
				зда́нием	**зда́ниями**
				зда́нии	**зда́ниях**
FEMININE	nom	**газе́та**	**газе́ты**[9]	**неде́ля**	**неде́ли**
	acc	**газе́ту**[8]	**газе́ты**[9]	**неде́лю**	**неде́ли**
	gen	**газе́ты**[9]	**газе́т**	**неде́ли**	**неде́ль**[12]
	dat	**газе́те**	**газе́там**	**неде́ле**	**неде́лям**
	instr	**газе́той**[10]	**газе́тами**	**неде́лей**[11]	**неде́лями**
	prep	**газе́те**	**газе́тах**	**неде́ле**	**неде́лях**
				фами́лия	**фами́лии**
				фами́лию	**фами́лии**
				фами́лии	**фами́лий**
				фами́лии	**фами́лиям**
				фами́лией	**фами́лиями**
				фами́лии	**фами́лиях**
				кость	**ко́сти**
				кость	**ко́сти**
				ко́сти	**косте́й**
				ко́сти	**костя́м**[13]
				ко́стью	**костя́ми**
				ко́сти	**костя́х**

1 All the examples of masculine nouns given here denote inanimate objects. In nouns of the animate category the accusative form coincides in both singular and plural with the genitive (see 10.1.3).

2 The instrumental singular form in unstressed endings after a hushing consonant is **-ем**, eg му́жем, from муж, *husband*. However, the ending **-ом** is retained after hushing consonants if stress is on the ending, eg ножо́м, from нож, *knife*.

3 Nouns with stems in **г**, **к**, **х**, **ж**, **ч**, **ш**, **щ** have nominative/accusative plural in **-и**, eg враги́, *enemies*; со́ки, *juices*; ножи́, *knives*; карандаши́, *pencils*.

4 Nouns in **ж**, **ч**, **ш**, **щ** have genitive plural in **-ей**, eg ноже́й, карандаше́й.

5 Many nouns in **-о** distinguish genitive singular from nominative/accusative plural by means of stress, though the stress shift in the plural forms may be forward (eg gen sg **окна́** but nom/acc pl **о́кна**) rather than back as is the case in сло́во.

6 Nouns with stem in **ж**, **ц**, **ч**, **ш**, **щ** have endings with **а** for **я** and **у** for **ю**; thus кла́дбище, *cemetery*, has gen sg кла́дбища, dat sg кла́дбищу, nom/acc pl кла́дбища, dat/instr/prep pl кла́дбищам, кла́дбищами, кла́дбищах respectively.

7 The same considerations of stress apply here as to сло́во (see note 5 above).

8 Feminine nouns of the animate category have accusative forms that coincide with the genitive in the plural only, eg acc pl же́нщин, but acc sg же́нщину.

9 (a) Nouns with stems in **г**, **к**, **х**, **ж**, **ч**, **ш**, **щ** have **и** for ы, eg нога́, *leg*, has gen sg ноги́, nom/acc pl но́ги. (b) Some nouns in **-а** distinguish genitive singular from nominative/accusative plural by means of stress shift, eg **ноги́**, **но́ги** (see notes 5 and 7 above).

10 (a) The instrumental singular form in unstressed endings after a hushing consonant is **-ей**, eg больни́цей, from больни́ца, *hospital*. However, the ending **-ой** is retained after hushing consonants if stress is on the ending, eg душо́й from душа́, *soul*. (b) An instrumental singular form in **-ою** is also found (eg газе́тою), but in the modern language this form is used mainly in literary contexts or in poetry where the metre requires an additional syllable.

11 An instrumental singular ending in **-ею** may also be found, in the same circumstances as -ою (see note 10 (b) above).

12 The zero ending which occurs in the genitive plural forms of nouns in **-а** is in effect retained, the soft sign merely serving to indicate that the consonant remains soft in this case just as it is when followed by any of the vowels used in the other endings of this declension.

13 Nouns ending in **-жь**, **-чь**, **-шь**, **-щь** have **а** for я, eg dat/instr/prep pl forms ноча́м, ноча́ми, ноча́х from ночь, *night*; веща́м, веща́ми, веща́х, from вещь, *thing*.

8.1.3 Mobile vowels

Many masculine nouns have a mobile vowel, ie **о** or **е** or **ё** which is found in the last syllable of the nominative/accusative singular form but which disappears in all other cases, eg

nom/acc sg	gen sg
кусо́к *piece*	**куска́**
ого́нь *fire*	**огня́**
ве́тер *wind*	**ве́тра**
день *day*	**дня**
козёл *goat*	**козла́**
шатёр *tent*	**шатра́**

Note 1 When a mobile **е** follows the letter **л** it must be replaced by **ь** in order to indicate that the **л** remains soft, eg лев, *lion*, has gen sg **льва**.

2 The feminine nouns **вошь**, *louse*; **ложь**, *lie*; **любо́вь**, *love*, and **рожь**, *rye*, lose their **о** in all oblique cases except the instrumental singular. Thus любо́вь has gen/dat/prep sg **любви́**, but instr sg **любо́вью**.

8.1.4 Genitive singular forms in -у/-ю

- A small number of masculine nouns, including a few abstract nouns, may have genitive singular forms in **-у** (or **-ю** if they have a soft stem) which may be used when the genitive has partitive meaning (ie when it denotes a quantity of sth), eg

купи́ть горо́ху, лу́ку, ри́су	*to buy some peas, onions, rice*
буты́лка коньяку́, лимона́ду	*a bottle of brandy, lemonade*
ба́нка мёду	*a jar of honey*
доста́ть кероси́ну, клею́,	*to get some paraffin, glue,*
ме́лу, миндалю́, пе́рцу,	*chalk, almonds, pepper,*
скипида́ру, тёсу	*turpentine, planks*
мно́го наро́ду, шу́му	*a lot of people, noise*
па́чка са́хару	*a packet of sugar*

кило́ сы́ру, чесноку́	*a kilo of cheese, garlic*
стака́н ча́ю	*a glass of tea*

Note [1] The normal genitive forms for such nouns must be used whenever a genitive is used with any meaning other than partitive meaning (eg цвет **мёда**, *the colour of honey*), or when the noun is qualified by an adjective, eg стака́н **кре́пкого ча́я**, *a glass of strong tea.*

[2] Even when the meaning is partitive the forms in -у and -ю are now infrequently used in R2/R3, except in the established phrases **мно́го наро́ду** and **стака́н ча́ю**. They are perhaps more widespread in R1 and among older speakers.

- Genitive endings in **-у** or **-ю** also occur in some set phrases including a preposition which governs the genitive case. In this use they persist in all registers, though many of the phrases tend to be colloquial. The examples below are arranged in order according to the preposition which governs the noun in question.

Note: the stress tends to be capricious in such phrases.

бе́з году неде́ля (R1)	*only a few days*
без ро́ду, без пле́мени	*without kith or kin*
говори́ть без у́молку	*to talk incessantly*
ну́жно до заре́зу	*needed urgently*
не до сме́ху	*in no mood for laughter*
упусти́ть что́-н и́з виду	*to overlook sth*
ей пять лет о́т роду	*she is five years old*
с гла́зу на́ глаз	*eyeball-to-eyeball*
умере́ть с го́лоду	*to starve to death*
кри́кнуть с испу́гу	*to cry out from fright*
с кру́гу спи́ться	*to go to seed from drink*
сбива́ть/сбить кого́-н с то́лку	*to confuse sb*

8.1.5 Locative singular forms in -у́/-ю́/

Quite a large number of masculine nouns which denote inanimate objects have a special prepositional singular ending (**-у́** after hard consonants, **-ю́** when the nominative ends in -й) when they are used after **в** or **на** in a locative sense (ie when they indicate the place where sth is situated or happening). In a few cases usage wavers between this form and the normal ending for such nouns (-**е**), in which case the irregular ending may seem more colloquial.

в аэропорту́ (R1)	*at the airport*
на балу́	*at a ball* (dance)
на берегу́	*on the bank, shore*
на боку́	*on (one's) side*
на борту́	*on board* (ship, plane)
в бою́	*in battle*
в бреду́	*in a fever, delirium*
в глазу́	*in the eye*
в году́	*in a year*

на Дону́	*on the (River) Don*
в жару́	*in the heat*
на краю́	*on the edge*
в кругу́	*in a circle*
в Крыму́	*in the Crimea*
на лбу́	*on (one's) forehead*
в лесу́	*in the forest*
на лугу́	*in the meadow*
на льду́	*on ice*
в меду́	*in honey*
в мозгу́	*in the brain*
на мосту́	*on the bridge*
на носу́	*on (one's) nose*
в отпуску́ (R1)	*on leave*
в полку́	*in a regiment*
на полу́	*on the floor*
в порту́	*in port*
весь в поту́	*bathed in sweat*
в пруду́	*in the pool*
в раю́	*in paradise*
во рту́	*in (one's) mouth*
в ряду́	*in a row* (tier)
в саду́	*in a garden/orchard*
в снегу́	*in the snow*
в строю́	*in service*
в углу́	*in the corner*
в цвету́	*in bloom*
в часу́	*in an hour*
в шкафу́	*in the cupboard*

Note 1 The locative ending in **-у́** is also embodied in various set expressions, eg **име́ть в виду́**, *to have in mind*; **в про́шлом году́**, *last year*; **В кото́ром часу́**? *At what time?*

2 Not all the nouns in the list above invariably have locative singular in **-у́/-ю́**; in certain meanings or phraseological combinations they may have the regular ending in -е, eg **в Краснода́рском кра́е**, *in the Krasnodar region*; **в по́те лица́**, *by the sweat of one's brow*; **в це́лом ря́де слу́чаев**, *in a whole series of instances.*

3 The endings **-у́/-ю́** are used only after в and на, not after the other prepositions, о, по and при, which may govern the prepositional case (thus в лесу́/краю́ but **о ле́се/кра́е**).

4 Even after в and на the special locative endings are only used when the meaning is literally locative, and not in such phrases as **знать толк в ле́се**, *to be knowledgeable about timber*; **в «Вишнёвом са́де»**, *in 'The Cherry Orchard'* (ie Chekhov's play); **в «Ти́хом До́не»**, *in 'Quiet flows the Don'* (ie Sholokhov's novel).

8.1.6 Masculine nouns with nominative plural in -á/-я́

Over the last two hundred years the endings **-á** (after hard consonants) and **-я́** (after soft consonants) have been steadily extended to more and more masculine nouns (both nouns of Russian origin and nouns of foreign origin). Some such nouns denote objects which, when referred to in the plural, usually occur in pairs and some are nouns of foreign origin ending in **-ор** or **-ер**. Many of the indigenous nouns have stress on the first syllable in the singular.

In many instances the plural in **-а́/-я́** is now firmly established as the only possible plural for the noun in question. In other instances both the form in **-а́/-я́** and a regular form in **-ы** (**-и** after soft consonants, velars and hushing consonants) are possible, in which case the form in **-а́/-я́** may have a colloquial or popular flavour or may belong to the professional jargon of a particular group.

Note: most of the nouns in the following lists (which are not exhaustive) are inanimate and their accusative plural form is therefore the same as the nominative plural form given here; animate nouns, on the other hand, have accusative plural forms which coincide with the genitive plural form.

- Nouns with firmly established plural in **-а́/-я́**:

а́дрес *address*	**адреса́**
бег *race*	**бега́**
бе́рег *shore, bank* (of river)	**берега́**
бок *side* (see 3.1)	**бока́**
борт *side* (of ship)	**борта́**
бу́фер *buffer*	**буфера́**
ве́ер *fan*	**веера́**
век *century, age*	**века́**

Note: the obsolete form ве́ки persists in certain set expressions, eg **в ко́и-то ве́ки**, *once in a blue moon*; **во ве́ки веко́в**, *for all time.*

ве́ксель *bill of exchange*	**векселя́**
ве́чер *evening*	**вечера́**
глаз *eye*	**глаза́**
го́лос *voice, vote*	**голоса́**
го́род *town*	**города́**
дире́ктор *manager, headmaster*	**директора́**
до́ктор *doctor*	**доктора́**
дом *house*	**дома́**
жёлоб *gutter, trough*	**желоба́**
же́мчуг *pearl*	**жемчуга́**
за́кром *cornbin; granary* (rhet)	**закрома́**
инспе́ктор *inspector*	**инспектора́**
ка́тер *small boat*	**катера́**
ко́локол *bell*	**колокола́**
край *edge, region*	**края́**
ку́пол *cupola, dome*	**купола́**
ле́мех *ploughshare*	**лемеха́**
лес *forest*	**леса́**
луг *meadow*	**луга́**
ма́стер *craftsman*	**мастера́**
но́мер *number, hotel room*	**номера́**

обшла́г *cuff*	**обшлага́**
о́круг *district*	**округа́**
о́рдер *order, warrant, writ*	**ордера́**
о́стров *island*	**острова́**
о́тпуск *(period of) leave*	**отпуска́**
па́рус *sail*	**паруса́**
па́спорт *passport*	**паспорта́**
пе́репел *quail*	**перепела́**
по́вар *cook*	**повара́**
по́греб *cellar*	**погреба́**
по́езд *train*	**поезда́**
профе́ссор *professor*	**профессора́**
рог *horn*	**рога́**
рука́в *sleeve*	**рукава́**
сви́тер *sweater*	**свитера́**
снег *snow*	**снега́**
сорт *sort*	**сорта́**
стог *stack, rick*	**стога́**
сто́рож *watchman*	**сторожа́**
те́нор *tenor* (mus)	**тенора́**
те́терев *black grouse*	**тетерева́**
том *volume*	**тома́**
фли́гель *wing* (of building)	**флигеля́**
флю́гер *weather-vane*	**флюгера́**
хлев *cattle-shed, pigsty*	**хлева́**
хо́лод *cold spell*	**холода́**
ху́тор *farmstead*	**хутора́**
че́реп *skull*	**черепа́**
ша́фер *best man* (at wedding)	**шафера́**
шёлк *silk*	**шелка́**
шу́лер *card-sharp, cheat*	**шулера́**
я́корь *anchor*	**якоря́**

- Nouns whose standard nominative plural form may be felt to be **-ы/-и** but which may have **-а́/-я́** in R1, D, or professional jargon. Forms marked † may be particularly frowned upon in the standard language.

бу́нкер *bunker*	**бункера́/бу́нкеры**
бухга́лтер *book-keeper, accountant*	**†бухгалтера́/бухга́лтеры**
год *year*	**года́/го́ды**
до́гово́р *treaty, pact*	**договора́/догово́ры**
инжене́р *engineer*	**†инженера́/инжене́ры**
констру́ктор *designer, constructor*	**†конструктора́/ констру́кторы**
кре́йсер *cruiser* (naval)	**крейсера́/кре́йсеры**
ку́зов *body* (of carriage)	**кузова́/ку́зовы**
офице́р *officer*	**†офицера́/офице́ры**

пéкарь *baker*	**пекаря́/пéкари**
прожéктор *searchlight*	**прожектора́/прожéкторы**
редáктор *editor*	**†редактора́/редáкторы**
рéктор *rector* (head of university)	**ректора́/рéкторы**
сéктор *sector*	**сектора́/сéкторы**
слéсарь *metal-worker, locksmith*	**слесаря́/слéсари**
тóполь *poplar tree*	**тополя́/тóполи**
трáктор *tractor*	**†трактора́/трáкторы**
цех *workshop*	**цеха́/цéхи**
шофёр *chauffeur*	**†шофера́/шофёры**

8.1.7 Irregularities in the genitive plural of nouns

There are more irregularities that affect this case than any other, viz

insertion of о or е

(a) affects many feminine and neuter nouns in which loss of final **а** or **о** of the nominative singular forms leaves a zero ending, eg

бéлка *squirrel*	**бéлок**
ви́лка *fork*	**ви́лок**
окнó *window*	**óкон**
дéвочка *small girl*	**дéвочек**
дерéвня *village*	**деревéнь**
метла́ *broom*	**мётел**

(b) **е** also occurs in the genitive plural forms of most neuter nouns in **-це** and **-цó**, eg

полотéнце *towel*	**полотéнец**
сéрдце *heart*	**сердéц**
кольцó *ring*	**колéц**
крыльцó *porch*	**крылéц**

Note: яйцó, *egg*, has **яи́ц**.

change of ь to е

affects feminine and neuter nouns in which the first of two consonants preceding the final **а** or **о** is soft, eg

письмó *letter*	**пи́сем**
свáдьба *wedding*	**свáдеб**
тюрьма́ *prison*	**тю́рем**

Note: прóсьба, *request*, has **прóсьб**.

change of й to е

affects feminine nouns ending in **-йка**, eg

балала́йка *balalaika*	**балала́ек**
гáйка *nut*	**гáек**
кóйка *bunk, berth*	**кóек**
копéйка *kopeck*	**копéек**
чáйка *seagull*	**чáек**
шáйка *gang*	**шáек**

zero ending some masculine nouns ending in a hard consonant have a genitive plural form that is the same as the nominative singular form, eg **раз**, *time, occasion*. Other nouns with this so-called zero ending include:

(a) some nouns which, when used in the plural, refer to pairs of things, eg

боти́нок	*(ankle-high) boot*
ва́ленок	*felt boot*
глаз	*eye*
пого́н	*(military) shoulder strap*
сапо́г	*boot*
чуло́к	*stocking*

- But **носко́в** (from носо́к, *sock*).

(b) the names of certain nationalities, including those formed with the suffix **-нин** (see 5.11–12), eg

англича́н (← англича́нин)	*Englishman*
армя́н (← армяни́н)	*Armenian*
башки́р	*Bashkir*
болга́р (← болга́рин)	*Bulgarian*
буря́т	*Buriat*
грузи́н	*Georgian*
румы́н	*Romanian*
ту́рок (or ту́рков in R1)	*Turk*

- But:

бедуи́нов (← бедуи́н)	*Bedouin*
кирги́зов (← кирги́з)	*Kirgiz*
монго́лов (← монго́л)	*Mongol*
таджи́ков (← таджи́к)	*Tadjik*
узбе́ков (← узбе́к)	*Uzbek*
хорва́тов (← хорва́т)	*Croat*

(c) certain nouns denoting military personnel, eg

партиза́н	*guerrilla*
солда́т	*soldier*

(d) some units of measure, eg

ампе́р	*ampere*
арши́н	*arshin* (see 5.1.5)
ватт	*watt*
вольт	*volt*
герц	*hertz*
ом	*ohm*

Several other nouns have a variant with a zero ending in R1, but the full ending in **-ов** is considered the norm, eg

апельси́н	*orange*
баклажа́н	*aubergine*
гекта́р	*hectare*
грамм	*gram*
кара́т	*carat*
килогра́мм	*kilogram*
мандари́н	*mandarin*
помидо́р	*tomato*

Note 1 челове́к, *person*, also has gen pl **челове́к**, which is used after certain numerals (10.4.8), though in most contexts the genitive plural of лю́ди, **люде́й**, is used instead.

2 во́лос, *hair*, has gen pl **воло́с**. This noun is always used in the plural form (nom/acc **во́лосы**) in the sense of *hair on one's head*.

nouns in -ье, -ьё

most have genitive plural forms in **-ий**, eg

захолу́стье *out-of-the-way place*	**захолу́стий**
побере́жье *seaboard*	**побере́жий**
уще́лье *gorge*	**уще́лий**
копьё *spear*	**ко́пий**

- But:

пла́тье *dress*	**пла́тьев**
подмасте́рье (m) *apprentice*	**подмасте́рьев**
у́стье *mouth of river*	**у́стьев**
ружьё *gun*	**ру́жей**

nouns in -жа, -ча, -ша, -ща

some have genitive plural forms in **-ей**, eg

ханжа́ *sanctimonious person*	**ханже́й**
ю́ноша *youth*	**ю́ношей**

nouns in -я

although most nouns in -я have genitive plural in a soft consonant (see 8.1.2), some have genitive plural forms in **-ей**, eg

дя́дя *uncle*	**дя́дей**
ноздря́ *nostril*	**ноздре́й**
тётя *aunt*	**тётей**

Note: ту́фля, *shoe* (see 3.1), has gen pl **ту́фель** in R2 but the form **ту́флей** may be encountered in R1.

nouns in -ня

many nouns in -ня preceded by another consonant have a zero ending with a hard consonant rather than the soft ending that is normal for nouns in -я, eg

ба́шня *tower*	**ба́шен**
ви́шня *cherry-tree*	**ви́шен**
пе́сня *song*	**пе́сен**
спа́льня *bedroom*	**спа́лен**
тамо́жня *customs* (at frontier post)	**тамо́жен**

- But:

дере́вня *village*	**дереве́нь**

	ку́хня *kitchen*	**ку́хонь**
nouns in -ая, -ея, -уя	have genitive plural forms in **-ай**, **-ей**, **-уй** respectively, eg	
	ста́я *flock, shoal*	**стай**
	иде́я *idea*	**иде́й**
	ста́туя *statue*	**ста́туй**
nouns in -ья́	have genitive plural forms in **-е́й**, eg	
	семья́ *family*	**семе́й**
	статья́ *article*	**стате́й**
	судья́ *judge, referee*	**суде́й**

о́блако (***cloud***) has gen pl **облако́в**, although in all other cases it conforms to the same pattern as standard neuter nouns in -о (see 8.1.2).

8.1.8 Irregularities in dative/instrumental/prepositional plural forms

це́рковь (***church***) in R3 generally has dat/instr/prep pl **церква́м**, **церква́ми**, **церква́х**, even though it is a noun ending in a soft sign. However, in R1 and R2 soft endings are now more usual in these cases too (**церквя́м**, **церквя́ми**, **церквя́х**).

instr pl in -ьми́ A very small number of nouns have (or may have) instrumental plural in **-ьми́**, although with some of the nouns in question such usage is restricted to certain registers or expressions:

де́ти *children*	**детьми́** (all registers)
ло́шадь *horse*	**лошадьми́** (all registers)
лю́ди *people*	**людьми́** (all registers)
дверь *door*	**дверьми́** (R1) **дверя́ми** (R2–3)
дочь *daughter*	**дочерьми́** (R1) **дочеря́ми** (R2–3)
кость *bone*, in the expression	**лечь костьми́** (R3, arch/rhet), *to lay down one's life (in battle)*

8.1.9 Nouns which are irregular throughout the plural

стул (***chair***)
де́рево (***tree***)

A few masculine nouns which end in a hard consonant and a few neuter nouns in **-о** have regular endings in the singular but have plural forms of the following type:

nom/acc pl	**сту́лья**	**дере́вья**
gen pl	**сту́льев**	**дере́вьев**
dat pl	**сту́льям**	**дере́вьям**
instr pl	**сту́льями**	**дере́вьями**
prep pl	**сту́льях**	**дере́вьях**

Like стул and де́рево are:

кол *stake*	**ко́лья, ко́льев**, etc
ком *lump*	**ко́мья, ко́мьев**, etc
прут *twig*	**пру́тья, пру́тьев**, etc
звено́ *link* (in chain)	**зве́нья, зве́ньев**, etc

крыло́ *wing*	**кры́лья, кры́льев**, etc
перо́ *feather*	**пе́рья, пе́рьев**, etc
поле́но *log*	**поле́нья, поле́ньев,** etc

Note 1 **брат**, *brother*, declines in exactly the same way, except that, being animate, it has acc pl **бра́тьев**.

2 **лист** declines like стул when it means *leaf* (ie *foliage*), but it declines like a regular masculine noun of the same type as авто́бус when it means *sheet of paper* (**листы́**, etc).

3 **сук**, *branch, bough*, declines like стул, but undergoes a consonant change in its stem: thus **су́чья, су́чьев, су́чьям**, etc.

друг (***friend***)
сын (***son***)

These nouns are similar to стул and де́рево, but the stem for their plural forms is not the same as that for their singular forms, and they have accusative/genitive plural in **-ей**:

nom pl	**друзья́**	**сыновья́**
acc/gen pl	**друзе́й**	**сынове́й**
dat pl	**друзья́м**	**сыновья́м**
instr pl	**друзья́ми**	**сыновья́ми**
prep pl	**друзья́х**	**сыновья́х**

Note 1 **сын** also has regular plural forms (**сыны́, сыно́в, сына́м, сына́ми, сына́х**) when it has a figurative sense, as in **сыны́ оте́чества**, *sons of the fatherland*.

2 **князь**, *prince*, and **муж**, *husband*, have similar plural endings but no consonant change in the stem:

nom pl	**князья́**	**мужья́**
acc/gen pl	**князе́й**	**муже́й**
dat pl	**князья́м**	**мужья́м**
instr pl	**князья́ми**	**мужья́ми**
prep pl	**князья́х**	**мужья́х**

коле́но (***knee***)
у́хо (***ear***)

nom/acc pl	**коле́ни**	**у́ши**
gen pl	**коле́ней**	**уше́й**
dat pl	**коле́ням**	**уша́м**
instr pl	**коле́нями**	**уша́ми**
prep pl	**коле́нях**	**уша́х**

Note: **плечо́**, *shoulder*, has nom/acc pl **пле́чи**, but regular forms in the oblique cases (**плеч, плеча́м, плеча́ми, плеча́х**).

не́бо (***sky***, ***heaven***)
чу́до (***miracle, wonder***)

These nouns have plural forms with a stem in **с**:

nom/acc pl	**небеса́**	**чудеса́**
gen pl	**небе́с**	**чуде́с**
dat pl	**небеса́м**	**чудеса́м**
instr pl	**небеса́ми**	**чудеса́ми**
prep pl	**небеса́х**	**чудеса́х**

сосе́д (***neighbour***)
чёрт (***devil***)

These nouns have soft endings in the plural:

nom pl	**сосе́ди**	**че́рти**
acc/gen pl	**сосе́дей**	**черте́й**
dat pl	**сосе́дям**	**чертя́м**

instr pl	**сосе́дями**	**чертя́ми**
prep pl	**сосе́дях**	**чертя́х**

nouns in -нин

Nouns of this type (see also 5.11–12) are regular in the singular but in the plural the last two letters (-ин) are removed to form the stem:

nom pl	**англича́не**
acc/gen pl	**англича́н**
dat pl	**англича́нам**
instr pl	**англича́нами**
prep pl	**англича́нах**

Note
1. All these nouns are animate, hence the coincidence of accusative/genitive forms.
2. **болга́рин**, *Bulgarian*, and **тата́рин**, *Tartar*, also follow this pattern, except that they have nom pl **болга́ры** and **тата́ры** respectively.
3. **цыга́н**, *gipsy*, has plural forms **цыга́не, цыга́н, цыга́нам**, etc in the modern language, but nom pl **цыга́ны** in the nineteenth century (eg in the title of Pushkin's narrative poem).
4. **хозя́ин**, *landlord, host*, has plural forms **хозя́ева, хозя́ев, хозе́явам, хозя́евами, хозя́евах**.
5. **господи́н**, *master, gentleman, Mr*, has plural forms **господа́, госпо́д, господа́м, господа́ми, господа́х**.

nouns in -ёнок

Nouns of this type (see also 7.7.1) are regular in the singular (except that they have a mobile **о**), but in the plural have the following pattern:

nom pl	**теля́та**
acc/gen pl	**теля́т**
dat pl	**теля́там**
instr pl	**теля́тами**
prep pl	**теля́тах**

Note
1. All these nouns are animate, hence the coincidence of accusative/genitive forms.
2. **ребёнок**, *child*, does have a plural of this type (**ребя́та**, etc), but this is a more colloquial word for *children* than **де́ти**, and it is also used in the sense of *lads*.

8.1.10 Nouns with irregular declension throughout

neuters in -мя

There is a small group of nouns ending in **-мя** which are neuter and which have a stem in **н** in all except nominative/accusative singular forms, eg **и́мя**, *name*:

	sg	pl
nom	**и́мя**	**имена́**
acc	**и́мя**	**имена́**
gen	**и́мени**	**имён**
dat	**и́мени**	**имена́м**
instr	**и́менем**	**имена́ми**
prep	**и́мени**	**имена́х**

Like и́мя (but with some exceptions listed below) are:

бре́мя[1]	*burden*
вре́мя	*time*
вы́мя[1]	*udder*
зна́мя[2]	*flag*
пла́мя[3]	*flame*
пле́мя	*tribe*
се́мя[4]	*seed*
стре́мя[5]	*stirrup*
те́мя[1]	*crown of the head*

Note
1 No plural forms.
2 nom/acc pl **знамёна**, gen pl **знамён**, dat pl **знамёнам**, etc.
3 For a plural form the expression **языки́ пла́мени**, *tongues of flame*, is used; язы́к is put in the case appropriate in the context.
4 gen pl **семя́н**.
5 gen pl **стремя́н**.

мать (***mother***)
дочь (***daughter***)

These two nouns have a stem in **р** in all oblique cases in the singular and throughout the plural:

	sg	pl	sg	pl
nom	**мать**	**ма́тери**	**дочь**	**до́чери**
acc	**мать**	**матере́й**	**дочь**	**дочере́й**
gen	**ма́тери**	**матере́й**	**до́чери**	**дочере́й**
dat	**ма́тери**	**матеря́м**	**до́чери**	**дочеря́м**
instr	**ма́терью**	**матеря́ми**	**до́черью**	**дочеря́ми***
prep	**ма́тери**	**матеря́х**	**до́чери**	**дочеря́х**

* in R1, instr pl **дочерьми́**.

муравей (***ant***)

	sg	pl
nom	**мураве́й**	**муравьи́**
acc/gen	**муравья́**	**муравьёв**
dat	**муравью́**	**муравья́м**
instr	**муравьём**	**муравья́ми**
prep	**муравье́**	**муравья́х**

Like мураве́й are **воробе́й**, *sparrow*; **солове́й**, *nightingale*; **руче́й**, *stream* (but руче́й, being inanimate, has acc sg **руче́й**).

путь (***way***, ***path***)

This is a masculine noun, but its genitive/dative/prepositional singular forms are those of a feminine noun:

	sg	pl
nom/acc	**путь**	**пути́**
gen	**пути́**	**путе́й**
dat	**пути́**	**путя́м**
instr	**путём**	**путя́ми**
prep	**пути́**	**путя́х**

8.1.11 Declension of surnames

men's names in -ов, -ёв, -ев, -ин, -ын

These surnames decline like nouns ending in a hard consonant in the accusative/genitive, dative and prepositional singular forms and in the nominative plural, but in the remaining cases they have adjectival endings:

	sg	pl	sg	pl
nom	**Че́хов**	**Че́ховы**	**Пу́шкин**	**Пу́шкины**
acc/gen	**Че́хова**	**Че́ховых**	**Пу́шкина**	**Пу́шкиных**
dat	**Че́хову**	**Че́ховым**	**Пу́шкину**	**Пу́шкиным**
instr	**Че́ховым**	**Че́ховыми**	**Пу́шкиным**	**Пу́шкиными**
prep	**Че́хове**	**Че́ховых**	**Пу́шкине**	**Пу́шкины**

Note: foreign surnames ending in -ин, however, follow the normal declension pattern for nouns of this type, eg instr sg **Да́рвином**.

women's names in -ова, -ёва, -ева, -ина, -ына

These surnames have accusative singular in **-у** (eg **Ивано́ву**, **Ники́тину**) and the ending **-ой** in all the oblique cases in the singular (eg **Ивано́вой**, **Ники́тиной**).

Note: surnames which end in a hard consonant, whether they are Russian or foreign, do not decline when a woman is denoted, eg the forms **Ку́чер**, **Тэ́тчер** (*Mrs Thatcher*) are used for all cases.

names in -ский, -ская

Surnames with these endings decline in exactly the same way as adjectives of this type (8.3.1).

indeclinable surnames

Surnames ending in **-их**, **-ых**, **-ово**, **-аго** (eg Долги́х, Бессме́ртных, Черны́х, Дурново́, Хитрово́, Жива́го) are indeclinable.

Surnames in **-ко** and **-енко** (eg Котько́, Решетко́, Евтуше́нко, Черне́нко), which are of Ukrainian origin, are not normally declined, especially in R3b in which it is essential to avoid the confusion that may arise from the difficulty of inferring the nominative form of a name from an oblique case. However, some speakers may still decline these names like feminine nouns in -а.

Also indeclinable are Georgian surnames in **-адзе**, **-идзе**, **-вили** (eg Чавчава́дзе, Орджоники́дзе, Джугашви́ли), and foreign surnames ending in a vowel other than unstressed -а or -я, eg Дюма́, Да́нте, Гюго́, Шо́у, Золя́ (*Dumas, Dante, Hugo, Shaw, Zola*).

Note 1 Most foreign surnames ending in unstressed -а or -я do decline (eg соне́ты **Петра́рки**, *Petrarch's sonnets*), but those in **-иа** do not, eg Гарси́а, *Garcia*.

2 Georgian names in **-ава** (eg Окуджа́ва) may decline like nouns in -а, but are sometimes also treated as indeclinable.

8.1.12 Indeclinable nouns

Russian has quite a large number of common nouns that are indeclinable, most of them fairly recent borrowings from other languages that do not easily fit into the Russian declensional pattern. The gender of indeclinable nouns is governed by such factors as whether they denote male or female persons or creatures or by the gender of the generic noun that describes the class of thing to which the object in question belongs (generic nouns are given in brackets in the lists below). Indeclinable nouns may be allocated to the following types.

(a) Nouns of foreign origin denoting inanimate objects: generally neuter, eg

бюро́	*office*
ви́ски	*whisky*
ге́тто	*ghetto*
депо́	*depot*
жюри́	*judges* (of competition)
интервью́	*interview*
кака́о	*cocoa*
кафе́	*café*
кино́	*cinema*
коммюнике́	*communiqué*
купе́	*compartment*
меню́	*menu*
метро́	*underground*
пальто́	*overcoat*
пари́	*bet*
пиани́но	*upright piano*
плато́	*plateau*
резюме́	*résumé*
такси́	*taxi*
шоссе́	*highway*

- But:

ко́фе (m)	*coffee* (influenced by the older form ко́фей)
сиро́кко (m)	*sirocco* (ве́тер)
хи́нди (m)	*Hindi* (язы́к)
бе́ри-бе́ри (f)	*beri-beri* (боле́знь)
кольра́би (f)	*kohlrabi* (капу́ста)
саля́ми (f)	*salami* (колбаса́)

(b) Nouns of foreign origin denoting people, including proper nouns: masculine or feminine depending on whether the person is male or female, eg

атташе́	*attaché*
Ве́рди	*Verdi*
ку́ли	*coolie*

(c) Nouns of foreign origin denoting animate beings other than people: generally masculine, eg

кенгуру́	*kangaroo*

ки́ви	*kiwi*
коли́бри	*humming-bird*
по́ни	*pony*
шимпанзе́	*chimpanzee*

Note: if the noun specifically denotes the female of the species then it may be treated as feminine, eg Кенгуру́ корми́ла кенгурёнка, *The kangaroo was feeding its cub.*

- But:

иваси́ (f)	*iwashi* (small far-eastern fish; ры́ба)
цеце́ (f)	*tsetse* (му́ха)

(d) Indeclinable Russian words which are not nouns but are used as such: neuter, eg

ве́жливое «здра́вствуйте»	*a polite 'hello'*
мона́ршее «мы»	*the royal 'we'*
све́тлое за́втра	*a bright tomorrow*

8.2 Declension of pronouns

я/ты/мы/вы

nom	**я**	**ты**	**мы**	**вы**
acc/gen	**меня́**	**тебя́**	**нас**	**вас**
dat	**мне**	**тебе́**	**нам**	**вам**
instr	**мно́й (мно́ю)**	**тобо́й (тобо́ю)**	**на́ми**	**ва́ми**
prep	**мне**	**тебе́**	**нас**	**вас**

он/она́/оно́/они́

nom.	**он**	**оно́**	**она́**	**они́**
acc/gen	**его́**		**её**	**их**
dat	**ему́**		**ей**	**им**
instr	**им**		**ей (е́ю)**	**и́ми**
prep	**нём**		**ней**	**них**

Note: 1 The letter **н-** must be added to the third-person pronouns when they occur after the great majority of prepositions, eg **от него́**, **к нему́**, **с ним**, **без неё**, **по ней**, **пе́ред ней**, **из них**, **к ним**, **ме́жду ни́ми**, and all prepositions governing the prepositional case. Prosthetic **н-** is not required after **вне**, **внутри́**, **благодаря́**, **вопреки́**, **подо́бно**, **согла́сно** (see 9.1.3–4) or after short comparative adjectives. Nor may it be used when **его́**, **её**, **их** are possessive pronouns, ie when they mean *his/its, (belonging to) her, their* respectively as opposed to *him, her, them.*

2 The instrumental forms **мно́ю**, **тобо́ю**, **е́ю** are alternatives to мной, тобо́й, ей respectively. They may be used in the written language for stylistic or rhythmic reasons, especially with past passive participles, eg подпи́санный **мно́ю** докуме́нт, *the document signed by me*, and are particularly associated with the absence of a preposition.

сам

	m	n	f	pl
nom	**сам**	**само́**	**сама́**	**са́ми**
acc	**сам/самого́**	**само́**	**саму́**	**са́ми/сами́х**
gen	**самого́**		**само́й**	**сами́х**

		m/n	f	pl
	dat	**самому́**	**само́й**	**сами́м**
	instr	**сами́м**	**само́й (само́ю)**	**сами́ми**
	prep	**само́м**	**само́й**	**сами́х**

себя́	acc/gen	**себя́**
	dat	**себе́**
	instr	**собо́й**
	prep	**себе́**

друг дру́га	acc/gen	**друг дру́га**
	dat	**друг дру́гу**
	instr	**друг дру́гом**
	prep	**друг (о) дру́ге**

мой (твой, свой)		m	n	f	pl
	nom	**мой**	**моё**	**моя́**	**мои́**
	acc	**мой/моего́**	**моё**	**мою́**	**мои́/мои́х**
	gen	**моего́**		**мое́й**	**мои́х**
	dat	**моему́**		**мое́й**	**мои́м**
	instr	**мои́м**		**мое́й**	**мои́ми**
	prep	**моём**		**мое́й**	**мои́х**

наш (ваш)		m	n	f	pl
	nom	**наш**	**на́ше**	**на́ша**	**на́ши**
	acc	**наш/на́шего**	**на́ше**	**на́шу**	**на́ши/на́ших**
	gen	**на́шего**		**на́шей**	**на́ших**
	dat	**на́шему**		**на́шей**	**на́шим**
	instr	**на́шим**		**на́шей**	**на́шими**
	prep	**на́шем**		**на́шей**	**на́ших**

его́, её, их These forms are invariable when they are used as possessive pronouns (*his, her, their* respectively). In D the adjectival form **и́хний** may be found instead of их.

э́тот		m	n	f	pl
	nom	**э́тот**	**э́то**	**э́та**	**э́ти**
	acc	**э́тот/э́того**	**э́то**	**э́ту**	**э́ти/э́тих**
	gen	**э́того**		**э́той**	**э́тих**
	dat	**э́тому**		**э́той**	**э́тим**
	instr	**э́тим**		**э́той**	**э́тими**
	prep	**э́том**		**э́той**	**э́тих**

тот		m	n	f	pl
	nom	**тот**	**то**	**та**	**те**
	acc	**тот/того́**	**то**	**та**	**те/тех**
	gen	**того́**		**той**	**тех**
	dat	**тому́**		**той**	**тем**
	instr	**тем**		**той**	**те́ми**
	prep	**том**		**той**	**тех**

весь

	m	n	f	pl
nom	**весь**	**всё**	**вся**	**все**
acc	**весь/всегó**	**всё**	**всю**	**все/всех**
gen	**всегó**		**всей**	**всех**
dat	**всемý**		**всей**	**всем**
instr	**всем**		**всей**	**всéми**
prep	**всём**		**всей**	**всех**

что, ничтó, нéчто

nom	**что**	**ничтó**	**нéчто**
acc/gen	**чегó**	**ничегó**	**нéчего**
dat	**чемý**	**ничемý**	**нéчему**
instr	**чем**	**ничéм**	**нéчем**
prep	**чём**	**ни (о) чем**	**нé (о) чём**

кто, никтó, нéкто

nom	**кто**	**никтó**	**нéкто**
acc/gen	**когó**	**никогó**	**нéкого**
dat	**комý**	**никомý**	**нéкому**
instr	**кем**	**никéм**	**нéкем**
prep	**ком**	**ни (о) ком)**	**нé (о) ком**

Note: the elements of ничтó, нéчто, никтó, нéкто are usually split when combined with a preposition, whatever the case governed by the preposition, eg **ни с кéм**, *not with anybody*.

чей

	m	n	f	pl
nom	**чей**	**чьё**	**чья**	**чьи**
acc	**чей**	**чьё**	**чью**	**чьи**
gen	**чьегó**		**чьей**	**чьих**
dat	**чьемý**		**чьей**	**чьим**
instr	**чьим**		**чьей (чьéю)**	**чьíми**
prep	**чьём**		**чьей**	**чьих**

8.3 Adjectival forms

8.3.1 Declension of adjectives

Accurate declension of adjectives should be taken for granted in the advanced student. Although there are various types of adjectival declension, the main differences are for the most part explained entirely by the spelling rules given in 7.2.4.

standard type

	m	n	f	pl
nom	**нóвый**	**нóвое**	**нóвая**	**нóвые**
acc	**нóвый/ нóвого**	**нóвое**	**нóвую**	**нóвые/ нóвых**
gen	**нóвого**		**нóвой**	**нóвых**
dat	**нóвому**		**нóвой**	**нóвым**
instr	**нóвым**		**нóвой**	**нóвыми**
prep	**нóвом**		**нóвой**	**нóвых**

Note: adjectives with stressed endings have masculine nominative/accusative singular forms in **-ой**, eg **молодо́й**.

stem in г, к, х

	m	n	f	pl
nom	**ру́сский**	**ру́сское**	**ру́сская**	**ру́сские**
acc	**ру́сский/ ру́сского**	**ру́сское**	**ру́сскую**	**ру́сские/ ру́сских**
gen	**ру́сского**		**ру́сской**	**ру́сских**
dat	**ру́сскому**		**ру́сской**	**ру́сским**
instr	**ру́сским**		**ру́сской**	**ру́сскими**
prep	**ру́сском**		**ру́сской**	**ру́сских**

Note: adjectives with stem in **г**, **к**, **х** and stressed endings have forms in **-о́й** in the masculine nominative/accusative singular, eg **дорого́й**.

stem in ж, ч, ш, щ

	m	n	f	pl
nom	**хоро́ший**	**хоро́шее**	**хоро́шая**	**хоро́шие**
acc	**хоро́ший/ хоро́шего**	**хоро́шее**	**хоро́шую**	**хоро́шие/ хоро́ших**
gen	**хоро́шего**		**хоро́шей**	**хоро́ших**
dat	**хоро́шему**		**хоро́шей**	**хоро́шим**
instr	**хоро́шим**		**хоро́шей**	**хоро́шими**
prep	**хоро́шем**		**хоро́шей**	**хоро́ших**

Note: adjectives with stressed endings have masculine nominative/accusative singular forms in **-ой**, and **о́** in all endings that in хоро́ший have е, eg

	m	n	f	pl
nom	**большо́й**	**большо́е**	**больша́я**	**больши́е**
acc	**большо́й/ большо́го**	**большо́е**	**большу́ю**	**больши́е/ больши́х**
gen	**большо́го**		**большо́й**	**больши́х**
dat	**большо́му**		**большо́й**	**больши́м**
instr	**больши́м**		**большо́й**	**больши́ми**
prep	**большо́м**		**большо́й**	**больши́х**

adjectives in -ний

	m	n	f	pl
nom	**си́ний**	**си́нее**	**си́няя**	**си́ние**
acc	**си́ний/ си́него**	**си́нее**	**си́нюю**	**си́ние/си́них**
gen	**си́него**		**си́ней**	**си́них**
dat	**си́нему**		**си́ней**	**си́ним**
instr	**си́ним**		**си́ней**	**си́ними**
prep	**си́нем**		**си́ней**	**си́них**

For a list of adjectives like си́ний see 7.9.1.

adjectives like тре́тий

	m	n	f	pl
nom	**тре́тий**	**тре́тье**	**тре́тья**	**тре́тьи**
acc	**тре́тий/ тре́тьего**	**тре́тье**	**тре́тью**	**тре́тьи/ тре́тьих**
gen	**тре́тьего**		**тре́тьей**	**тре́тьих**
dat	**тре́тьему**		**тре́тьей**	**тре́тьим**

instr	**трéтьим**	**трéтьей**	**трéтьими**
prep	**трéтьем**	**трéтьей**	**трéтьих**

Like трéтий are a number of adjectives derived from the names of living creatures, eg **вóлчий**, *wolf's*; **корóвий**, *cow's, bovine*; **кошáчий**, *cat's, feline*; **птúчий**, *bird's*; **собáчий**, *dog's, canine*.

8.3.2 Formation of short adjectives

- Short adjectives have four indeclinable forms which distinguish gender and number. The masculine form is found by removing the masculine nominative singular ending (-ый, -ий, or -ой); the feminine, neuter and plural forms are found by adding **-а**, **-о** (**-е** in unstressed endings after hushing consonants) and **-ы** (**-и** after velars and hushing consonants) respectively to the masculine form, eg

нóвый, *new*: **нов, новá, нóво, нóвы**
свéжий, *fresh*: **свеж, свежá, свежó, свéжи**
блестя́щий, *brilliant*: **блестя́щ, блестя́ща, блестя́ще, блестя́щи**
стрóгий, *strict*: **строг, строгá, стрóго, стрóги**
молодóй, *young*: **мóлод, молодá, мóлодо, мóлоды**

Note 1 Some adjectives have short forms which may not be used in the whole range of meanings of which the long form is capable, eg **жив, живá, жúво, жúвы** (← живóй) may mean *alive* but not *lively*; **стар, старá, стáро, стáры** (← стáрый) may mean *old* in the sense *not young* and *not new*, but not in the sense *of long-standing*.

2 **большóй**, *big*, has short forms **велúк, великá, великó, великú**; мáленький, *small*, has **мал, малá, малó, малы́**.

3 **рад, рáда, рáдо, рáды**, *glad*, has short forms only.

- In many adjectives a vowel must be inserted between the last two consonants of the masculine short form, eg

(a) common adjectives with **о** inserted, eg **блúзок** (← блúзкий): **гúбкий, глáдкий, дéрзкий, дóлгий, крéпкий, лёгкий, лóвкий, мя́гкий, нúзкий, рéдкий, рéзкий, слáдкий, тóнкий, ýзкий**;
(b) common adjectives with **е** inserted, eg **бéден** (← бéдный): **блéдный, врéдный, грýстный, интерéсный, крáсный, прия́тный, свéтлый, скýчный, тóчный, трýдный, чéстный, я́сный**;
(c) common adjectives with **ё** (**о** after hushing consonants) inserted: **умён** (← ýмный), **смешóн** (← смешнóй).

Note: **сúльный**, *strong*, has **сúлен**.

- Many adjectives have no short form. These include all or most adjectives of the following types:

(a) denoting material, many of which end in **-áн(н)ый** or **-я́н(н)ый/-янóй**, eg **кóжаный**, *leather*; **серéбряный**, *silver*; **деревя́нный**, *wooden*; **шерстянóй**, *woollen* (see 7.9.1);
(b) of participial origin ending in **-лый** (see 7.10) eg **устáлый**, *tired*;

(c) ending in **-ний**, **-шний**, eg **весéнний**, *spring*; **послéдний**, *last*; **домáшний**, *domestic* (see 7.9.1);

(d) ending in **-óвый/-овóй**, eg **фиолéтовый**, *violet*;

(e) ending in **-ский/-скóй**, eg **англи́йский**, *English*.

Note 1 **вéский**, *weighty*, does have short forms (**вéсок, вéска, вéско, вéски**) because its suffix is not -ский but **-кий**, the -**с**- being part of the stem.

2 Many adjectives in **-и́ческий** have synonyms in **-и́чный** which do have short forms, eg **траги́чный** (= траги́ческий), *tragic*: short forms **траги́чен, траги́чна, траги́чно, траги́чны**.

8.3.3 Formation of short comparatives

- Most adjectives have a short comparative form, which is indeclinable and which is derived from the long form of the adjective in one of the following ways:

(a) in most adjectives, by addition of -**ее** to the stem, eg

нóвый *new*	**новéе**
интерéсный *interesting*	**интерéснее**
полéзный *useful*	**полéзнее**

(b) in adjectives whose stem ends in **г**, **д**, **т**, **х**, or the combination **ст**, by a consonant change (to **ж**, **ж**, **ч**, **ш** or **щ** respectively) and the addition of -**е**, eg

стрóгий *strict*	**стрóже**
твёрдый *firm*	**твёрже**
богáтый *rich*	**богáче**
сухóй *dry*	**сýше**
чи́стый *clean*	**чи́ще**

Note: жёлтый has **желтée**.

(c) in many adjectives ending in **-кий**, by the consonant change к → **ч**, and the addition of -**е**, eg

грóмкий *loud*	**грóмче**
крéпкий *strong*	**крéпче**
мя́гкий *soft*	**мя́гче**
я́ркий *bright*	**я́рче**

Note: лёгкий → **лéгче**.

(d) in many other common adjectives, including many which end in **-кий**, by some other means, eg

бли́зкий *near*	**бли́же**
глáдкий *smooth*	**глáже**
глубóкий *deep*	**глýбже**
далёкий *distant*	**дáльше**
дешёвый *cheap*	**дешéвле**
дóлгий *long* (of time)	**дóльше**

коро́ткий *short*	**коро́че**
ме́лкий *shallow*	**ме́льче**
по́здний *late*	**по́зже** (or **поздне́е**)
ра́нний *early*	**ра́ньше** (or **ра́нее**)
ре́дкий *rare*	**ре́же**
сла́дкий *sweet*	**сла́ще**
то́нкий *thin*	**то́ньше**
у́зкий *narrow*	**у́же**
широ́кий *wide*	**ши́ре**

Note: го́рький, *bitter*, has **го́рче** in its literal meaning, but when used figuratively has **го́рше**.

- The short comparative forms of eight adjectives which are themselves already comparatives give particular difficulty:

бо́льший *bigger*	**бо́льше**
ме́ньший *smaller*	**ме́ньше**
лу́чший *better*	**лу́чше**
ху́дший *worse*	**ху́же**
ста́рший *older* (of people), *senior*	**ста́рше**
мла́дший *junior*	**мла́дше**
высо́кий *high*	**вы́ше**
ни́зкий *low*	**ни́же**

Note: the form **моло́же** must be used as a comparative of мла́дший when it means *younger.*

- Outside R2 the suffix **-ей** may be encountered, as an alternative to -ee, eg **нове́й**. This suffix may have an archaic or colloquial flavour, or it may be used in verse for metrical reasons.
- The prefix **по-** is frequently attached to the short comparative, especially in R1, to modify the meaning, eg **побо́льше**, *a little bigger*; **полу́чше**, *a bit better.*
- There are many adjectives from which short comparative forms cannot be derived, especially:

(a) those in **-ский** or **-ско́й**, eg **ру́сский, мастерско́й**;
(b) those in **-овый/-ово́й** or **-евый/-ево́й**, eg **ма́ссовый, передово́й**;
(c) those of verbal origin in **-лый**, eg **уста́лый**;
(d) some in **-кий**, eg **де́рзкий, ли́пкий, ро́бкий, ско́льзкий**;
(e) miscellaneous adjectives, eg **больно́й, ве́тхий, го́рдый, ли́шний**.

8.4 Formation of adverbs

Adverbs are formed in the following ways:

(a) from adjectives with a stem in a hard consonant and from present and past passive participles (or adjectives derived from them), by addition of **-о** to the stem, eg

бы́стрый *quick*	**бы́стро**
необходи́мый *inevitable*	**необходи́мо**
взволно́ванный *agitated*	**взволно́ванно**

(b) from adjectives with a stem in a soft consonant and from adjectives derived from present active participles, by addition of **-е** to the stem, eg

кра́йний *extreme*	**кра́йне**
блестя́щий *brilliant*	**блестя́ще**

Note: some adjectives in -ний have adverbs in **-о**, eg **давно́** (← да́вний); **по́здно** (← по́здний); **ра́но** (← ра́нний); и́скренний has either **и́скренно** or **и́скренне**.

(c) from adjectives in **-ский**, **-ско́й**, **-цкий**, by addition of **-и** to the stem, eg

дру́жеский *amicable*	**дру́жески**
мастерско́й *masterly*	**мастерски́**
молоде́цкий *spirited*	**молоде́цки**

(d) by prefixing **по-** to a masculine/neuter dative form of the adjective or an adverb of the type in (c) above, to form adverbs of manner, eg

по-друго́му	*in a different way*
по-пре́жнему	*as before*
по-мо́ему	*in my opinion*
по-ру́сски	*(in) Russian*
по-челове́чьи	*like a human being*

(e) by a combination of preposition + short adjective or long adjective or noun, eg

напра́во	*to the right*
слегка́	*slightly*
вполне́	*fully*
вкруту́ю	*hard-boiled* (of egg)
наконе́ц	*finally*
подря́д	*in succession*
снача́ла	*at first*
за́мужем	*married* (of woman)
накану́не	*on the eve*

(f) in miscellaneous other ways, such as by use of the instrumental form of a noun or on the basis of a numeral, eg

шёпотом	*in a whisper*
весно́й	*in spring*
пешко́м	*on foot*
вдвоём	*as a pair*

8.5 Declension of numerals

оди́н

	m	n	f	pl
nom	**оди́н**	**одно́**	**одна́**	**одни́**
acc	**оди́н/одного́**	**одно́**	**одну́**	**одни́/одни́х**
gen	**одного́**		**одно́й**	**одни́х**
dat	**одному́**		**одно́й**	**одни́м**
instr	**одни́м**		**одно́й**	**одни́ми**
prep	**одно́м**		**одно́й**	**одни́х**

два/две, три, четы́ре

	m/n	f	all genders	all genders
nom	**два**	**две**	**три**	**четы́ре**
acc	**два/двух**	**две/двух**	**три/трёх**	**четы́ре/ четырёх**
gen	**двух**		**трёх**	**четырёх**
dat	**двум**		**трём**	**четырём**
instr	**двумя́**		**тремя́**	**четырьмя́**
prep	**двух**		**трёх**	**четырёх**

о́ба/о́бе

	m/n	f
nom	**о́ба**	**о́бе**
acc	**о́ба/обо́их**	**о́бе/обе́их**
gen	**обо́их**	**обе́их**
dat	**обо́им**	**обе́им**
instr	**обо́ими**	**обе́ими**
prep	**обо́их**	**обе́их**

Note: in R1 the distinctive feminine form may be lost in the oblique cases, eg в **обо́их** ко́мнатах, *in both rooms*.

пять

nom/acc	**пять**
gen/dat/prep	**пяти́**
instr	**пятью́**

Like пять are all cardinal numerals up to **два́дцать** and **три́дцать**.

Note: the normal instrumental singular form of во́семь is **восьмью́**; the form восемью́ is obsolescent.

со́рок, девяно́сто, сто

nom/acc	**со́рок**	**девяно́сто**	**сто**
gen/dat/instr/prep	**сорока́**	**девяно́ста**	**ста**

пятьдеся́т

nom/acc	**пятьдеся́т**
gen/dat/prep	**пяти́десяти**
instr	**пятью́десятью**

Like пятьдеся́т are **шестьдеся́т**, **се́мьдесят** and **во́семьдесят**.

Note: the genitive/dative/prepositional form of во́семьдесят is **восьми́десяти** and the instrumental form is **восьмью́десятью**.

две́сти, три́ста, четы́реста

nom/acc	**две́сти**	**три́ста**	**четы́реста**
gen	**двухсо́т**	**трёхсо́т**	**четырёхсо́т**
dat	**двумста́м**	**тремста́м**	**четырёмста́м**

instr	**двумястáми**	**тремястáми**	**четырьмястáми**
prep	**двухстáх**	**трёхстáх**	**четырёхстáх**

пятьсóт

nom/acc	**пятьсóт**	**восемьсóт**
gen	**пятисóт**	**восьмисóт**
dat	**пятистáм**	**восьмистáм**
instr	**пятьюстáми**	**восьмьюстáми**
prep	**пятистáх**	**восьмистáх**

Like пятьсóт are **шестьсóт**, **семьсóт**, **девятьсóт**.

двóе, трóе, чéтверо

nom	**двóе**	**трóе**	**чéтверо**
acc	**двóе/двои́х**	**трóе/трои́х**	**чéтверо/четверы́х**
gen	**двои́х**	**трои́х**	**четверы́х**
dat	**двои́м**	**трои́м**	**четверы́м**
instr	**двои́ми**	**трои́ми**	**четверы́ми**
prep	**двои́х**	**трои́х**	**четверы́х**

мнóго, немнóго

nom/acc	**мнóго**	**немнóго**
acc/gen	**мнóгих**	**немнóгих**
dat	**мнóгим**	**немнóгим**
instr	**мнóгими**	**немнóгими**
prep	**мнóгих**	**немнóгих**

скóлько, нéсколько, стóлько

nom/acc	**нéсколько**	**скóлько**	**стóлько**
acc/gen	**нéскольких**	**скóльких**	**стóльких**
dat	**нéскольким**	**скóльким**	**стóльким**
instr	**нéсколькими**	**скóлькими**	**стóлькими**
prep	**нéскольких**	**скóльких**	**стóльких**

other words denoting number

The collective noun **сóтня**, *hundred*, declines like a noun in -ня (gen pl сóтен).

The word **ты́сяча**, *thousand*, declines like a noun in -а (instr sg **ты́сячей**), but may also be used as a numeral in which case it has instr sg **ты́сячью**.

The words **миллиóн**, *million*, and **миллиáрд**, *billion*, are nouns and decline like other nouns ending in a hard consonant.

Ordinal numbers **пéрвый**, **вторóй**, **трéтий**, etc decline like adjectives of the type in question (see 8.3.1 above).

8.6 Verb forms

8.6.1 The system of conjugation

Russian verbs may be divided into two broad conjugations.

conjugation 1

Endings characterised by the vowel **е** (or **ё** under stress) in the 2nd and 3rd persons singular and the 1st and 2nd persons plural (ie ты, он/онá/онó, мы, вы forms).

This conjugation may be subdivided into a further two types and sub-types:

1A stem of present/future tense is derived by removing final -ть of the infinitive, eg рабо́та/ть;

1B stem of present/future tense is derived in some other way (in many instances because the infinitive ends in some combination other than vowel + ть, eg **везти́, лезть, вести́, класть, жечь, идти́**). 1B may be further subdivided into the following sub-types:

i. vowel stem + unstressed ending, eg мыть (**мо́-ю**);
ii. vowel stem + stressed ending, eg дава́ть (**да-ю́**);
iii. consonant stem + unstressed ending, eg ре́зать (**ре́ж-у**);
iv. consonant stem + stressed ending, eg жить (**жив-у́**).

conjugation 2 Endings characterised by the vowel **и** in the 2nd and 3rd persons singular and the 1st and 2nd persons plural (ie ты, он/она́/оно́, мы, вы forms).

In this conjugation the 1st person singular and the 3rd person plural (ie я and они́ forms) are modified in certain verbs in accordance with basic spelling rules (see 7.2.4(b) above). Moreover, in the 1st person singular certain consonants at the end of the stem have to be changed (7.2.5) or require the insertion after them of the letter -л- (7.2.6).

The endings of verbs in the two conjugations therefore are:

	conjugation 1	**conjugation 2**
(я)	**-ю** (**-у** after consonant*)	**-ю** (**-у** after hushing consonant)
(ты)	**-ешь** (**-ёшь** under stress)	**-ишь**
(он/она́)	**-ет** (**-ёт** under stress)	**-ит**
(мы)	**-ем** (**-ём** under stress)	**-им**
(вы)	**-ете** (**-ёте** under stress)	**-ите**
(они́)	**-ют** (**-ут** after consonant*)	**-ят** (**-ат** after hushing consonant)

* except **л** and sometimes **р**

Note: the vast majority of Russian verbs have two aspects, imperfective and perfective. The use of these aspects is dealt with below (see 10.5).

In the following tabulations of conjugation patterns there are many simple verbs from which a vast number of perfective forms (eg **зарабо́тать, откры́ть, наре́зать, подписа́ть, собра́ть, привести́, пойти́, заже́чь, рассмотре́ть**) are derived by the addition of prefixes (see 7.3). All such perfective derivatives conjugate in the same way as the simple verb itself.

8.6.2 1A verbs

Stem of present/future tense formed by removing final -ть of the infinitive; unstressed endings **-ю**, **-ешь**, **-ет**, **-ем**, **-ете**, **-ют**, eg

рабо́тать	**теря́ть**	**красне́ть**	**дуть**
to work	*to lose*	*to blush*	*to blow*
рабо́таю	**теря́ю**	**красне́ю**	**ду́ю**
рабо́таешь	**теря́ешь**	**красне́ешь**	**ду́ешь**
рабо́тает	**теря́ет**	**красне́ет**	**ду́ет**
рабо́таем	**теря́ем**	**красне́ем**	**ду́ем**
рабо́таете	**теря́ете**	**красне́ете**	**ду́ете**
рабо́тают	**теря́ют**	**красне́ют**	**ду́ют**

In 1A are a very large number of verbs in **-ать** or **-ять** and many in **-еть** (but not all such verbs); also **обу́ть**.

8.6.3 1B verbs with vowel stems and unstressed endings

мыть	**организова́ть**	**воева́ть**	**ла́ять**	**брить**
to wash	*to organise*	*to make war*	*to bark*	*to shave*
мо́ю	**организу́ю**	**вою́ю**	**ла́ю**	**бре́ю**
мо́ешь	**организу́ешь**	**вою́ешь**	**ла́ешь**	**бре́ешь**
мо́ет	**организу́ет**	**вою́ет**	**ла́ет**	**бре́ет**
мо́ем	**организу́ем**	**вою́ем**	**ла́ем**	**бре́ем**
мо́ете	**организу́ете**	**вою́ете**	**ла́ете**	**бре́ете**
мо́ют	**организу́ют**	**вою́ют**	**ла́ют**	**бре́ют**

Like мыть: **выть**, **крыть**, **ныть**, **рыть**.
Like организова́ть: the great majority of verbs in **-овать**, including many verbs of foreign origin, eg **атакова́ть**, as well as verbs from Slavonic roots, eg **волнова́ть**. Similarly **танцева́ть** (**танцу́ю**, **танцу́ешь**, etc).
Like воева́ть: most other verbs in **-евать**.
Like ла́ять: **та́ять**, **се́ять**, **ве́ять**, **наде́яться**.

8.6.4 1B verbs with stems in л and р and unstressed endings

коло́ть	**боро́ться**	**колеба́ться**	**сы́пать**
to prick	*to struggle*	*to hesitate*	*to pour*
колю́	**борю́сь**	**коле́блюсь**	**сы́плю**
ко́лешь	**бо́решься**	**коле́блешься**	**сы́плешь**
ко́лет	**бо́рется**	**коле́блется**	**сы́плет**
ко́лем	**бо́ремся**	**коле́блемся**	**сы́плем**
ко́лете	**бо́ретесь**	**коле́блетесь**	**сы́плете**
ко́лют	**бо́рются**	**коле́блются**	**сы́плют**

Like коло́ть: **поло́ть**; also **моло́ть** but with **е** in the stem (**мелю́**, **ме́лешь**, etc).

Like боро́ться: **поро́ть**.
Like сы́пать: **трепа́ть, щипа́ть, дрема́ть**.

8.6.5 1B verbs with vowel stems and stressed endings

дава́ть	**узнава́ть**	**встава́ть**	**плева́ть**
to give	*to find out*	*to get up*	*to spit*
даю́	**узнаю́**	**встаю́**	**плюю́**
даёшь	**узнаёшь**	**встаёшь**	**плюёшь**
даёт	**узнаёт**	**встаёт**	**плюёт**
даём	**узнаём**	**встаём**	**плюём**
даёте	**узнаёте**	**встаёте**	**плюёте**
даю́т	**узнаю́т**	**встаю́т**	**плюю́т**

петь	**смея́ться**	**пить**
to sing	*to laugh*	*to drink*
пою́	**смею́сь**	**пью́**
поёшь	**смеёшься**	**пьёшь**
поёт	**смеётся**	**пьёт**
поём	**смеёмся**	**пьём**
поёте	**смеётесь**	**пьёте**
пою́т	**смею́тся**	**пью́т**

Like узнава́ть: cognate verbs in **-знава́ть**, eg **признава́ть**.
Like встава́ть: cognate verbs in **-става́ть**, eg **остава́ться**.
Like плева́ть: **клева́ть**; also **кова́ть (кую́, куёшь**, etc).
Like пить (which has a stem in a soft consonant rather than a vowel, but conjugates in the same way): **бить, вить, лить, шить**.

Note: **слать**, which has a consonant stem (**шл-**), conjugates in the same way (**шлю, шлёшь**, etc).

8.6.6 1B verbs with consonant stems and unstressed endings

Note: the stress is often on the ending in the infinitive and the 1st person singular of verbs of this type, but is always on the stem throughout the remaining persons of the present/future tense.

(a) Verbs with a stem in a hushing consonant:

ре́зать	**пла́кать**	**писа́ть**	**иска́ть**
to cut	*to cry*	*to write*	*to look for*
ре́жу	**пла́чу**	**пишу́**	**ищу́**
ре́жешь	**пла́чешь**	**пи́шешь**	**и́щешь**
ре́жет	**пла́чет**	**пи́шет**	**и́щет**
ре́жем	**пла́чем**	**пи́шем**	**и́щем**
ре́жете	**пла́чете**	**пи́шете**	**и́щете**
ре́жут	**пла́чут**	**пи́шут**	**и́щут**

Like ре́зать: **вяза́ть, каза́ться, сказа́ть, ма́зать**.

Like пла́кать: **скака́ть**; also **шепта́ть (шепчу́, ше́пчешь**, etc), **бормота́ть, пря́тать, топта́ть, хохота́ть, щекота́ть**.
Like писа́ть: **теса́ть, чеса́ть**; also ***маха́ть (машу́, ма́шешь**, etc), ***колыха́ть, паха́ть**.
Like иска́ть: ***плеска́ть, *полоска́ть**; also **трепета́ть (трепещу́, трепе́щешь**, etc), **ропта́ть**; also **свиста́ть (свищу́, сви́щешь**, etc), **хлеста́ть**.

* These verbs may also be 1A in R1/D, eg **маха́ю**.

(b) Verbs with a stem in **м** or **н**:

приня́ть	**стать**	**наде́ть**
to receive	*to become*	*to put on*
приму́	**ста́ну**	**наде́ну**
при́мешь	**ста́нешь**	**наде́нешь**
при́мет	**ста́нет**	**наде́нет**
при́мем	**ста́нем**	**наде́нем**
при́мете	**ста́нете**	**наде́нете**
при́мут	**ста́нут**	**наде́нут**

Like приня́ть: **отня́ть, подня́ть, снять**.

Note: a few other verbs from the same root, and which also have **м** stems in the present/future tense, have stressed endings throughout (see 8.6.7(b) below).

Like наде́ть: the simple verb **деть** and its perfective derivatives, eg **оде́ть(ся), переоде́ть(ся), разде́ть(ся)**.

(c) Verbs in -**нуть**:

гло́хнуть
to go deaf
гло́хну
гло́хнешь
гло́хнет
гло́хнем
гло́хнете
гло́хнут

Like гло́хнуть:

i. many other verbs which denote change of state, eg **блёкнуть, ки́снуть, мёрзнуть, мо́кнуть, сле́пнуть, со́хнуть**;
ii. many verbs derived from the following roots -**бег**-, -**верг**-, -**вык**-, -**ник**-, -**стиг**-, -**тих**-, -**чез**-, eg **прибе́гнуть, опрове́ргнуть, све́ргнуть, привы́кнуть, возни́кнуть, прони́кнуть, дости́гнуть, зати́хнуть, исче́знуть**;
iii. many semelfactive verbs, eg **кри́кнуть, пры́гнуть**;
iv. miscellaneous, eg **вспы́хнуть, дви́нуть, тону́ть, тро́нуть, тяну́ть**.

Note: there are also many verbs in -нуть that have stressed endings (see 8.6.7(c) below).

(d) Miscellaneous verbs:

быть	**е́хать**	**сесть**
to be	*to go*	*to sit down*
бу́ду	**е́ду**	**ся́ду**
бу́дешь	**е́дешь**	**ся́дешь**
бу́дет	**е́дет**	**ся́дет**
бу́дем	**е́дем**	**ся́дем**
бу́дете	**е́дете**	**ся́дете**
бу́дут	**е́дут**	**ся́дут**

Note: **бу́ду**, etc, is the future tense of быть, there being no present tense of this verb in modern Russian (except the form **есть** in certain circumstances; see 3.2).

лезть	**лечь**	**мочь**
to climb	*to lie down*	*to be able*
ле́зу	**ля́гу**	**могу́**
ле́зешь	**ля́жешь**	**мо́жешь**
ле́зет	**ля́жет**	**мо́жет**
ле́зем	**ля́жем**	**мо́жем**
ле́зете	**ля́жете**	**мо́жете**
ле́зут	**ля́гут**	**мо́гут**

8.6.7 1B verbs with consonant stems and stressed endings

(a) Various verbs with stems in **в**:

жить	**плыть**	**звать**	**рвать**
to live	*to swim*	*to call*	*to tear*
живу́	**плыву́**	**зову́**	**рву**
живёшь	**плывёшь**	**зовёшь**	**рвёшь**
живёт	**плывёт**	**зовёт**	**рвёт**
живём	**плывём**	**зовём**	**рвём**
живёте	**плывёте**	**зовёте**	**рвёте**
живу́т	**плыву́т**	**зову́т**	**рвут**

Like плыть: **слыть**.

(b) Verbs with stem in **м** or **н**:

поня́ть	**взять**	**жать**
to understand	*to take*	*to press*
пойму́	**возьму́**	**жму**
поймёшь	**возьмёшь**	**жмёшь**
поймёт	**возьмёт**	**жмёт**
поймём	**возьмём**	**жмём**
поймёте	**возьмёте**	**жмёте**
пойму́т	**возьму́т**	**жмут**

Like поня́ть: **заня́ть, наня́ть**. (But see 8.6.6(b) above for verbs in **-нять** which have a stem in **м** and unstressed endings.)

нача́ть	**мять**	**жать**	**клясть**
to begin	*to crumple*	*to reap*	*to swear*

начну́	**мну**	**жну**	**кляну́**
начнёшь	**мнёшь**	**жнёшь**	**клянёшь**
начнёт	**мнёт**	**жнёт**	**клянёт**
начнём	**мнём**	**жнём**	**клянём**
начнёте	**мнёте**	**жнёте**	**клянёте**
начну́т	**мнут**	**жнут**	**кляну́т**

(c) Verbs in **-нуть**:

гнуть
to bend
гну
гнёшь
гнёт
гнём
гнёте
гнут

Like гнуть: **косну́ться**, **махну́ть**, **улыбну́ться**.

(d) Various verbs with stem in **р**:

брать	**врать**	**умере́ть**
to take	*to lie*	*to die*
беру́	**вру**	**умру́**
берёшь	**врёшь**	**умрёшь**
берёт	**врёт**	**умрёт**
берём	**врём**	**умрём**
берёте	**врёте**	**умрёте**
беру́т	**врут**	**умру́т**

Like брать: **дра́ть(ся)**.
Like умере́ть: **пере́ть**, **тере́ть** (**тру́**, **трёшь**, etc).

(e) Verbs in **-сти́** (with stem in **б**, **д**, **с**, or **т**) and in **-сть** (with stem in **д** or **т**):

грести́	**вести́**	**нести́**	**мести́**
to row	*to lead*	*to carry*	*to sweep*
гребу́	**веду́**	**несу́**	**мету́**
гребёшь	**ведёшь**	**несёшь**	**метёшь**
гребёт	**ведёт**	**несёт**	**метёт**
гребём	**ведём**	**несём**	**метём**
гребёте	**ведёте**	**несёте**	**метёте**
гребу́т	**веду́т**	**несу́т**	**мету́т**

Like грести́: **скрести́**.
Like вести́: **блюсти́**.
Like нести́: **спасти́**, **трясти́**.
Like мести́: **плести́**, **цвести́**.

класть	**прочёсть**
to put	*to read*

кладу́	**прочту́**
кладёшь	**прочтёшь**
кладёт	**прочтёт**
кладём	**прочтём**
кладёте	**прочтёте**
кладу́т	**прочту́т**

Like класть: **красть, пасть, прясть**.
Like проче́сть: **счесть** (**сочту́, сочтёшь**, etc).

(f) **идти́**
to go
иду́
идёшь
идёт
идём
идёте
иду́т

(g) Verbs in **-зти́** and **-зть** with stem in **з**:

везти́	**грызть**
to take	*to gnaw*
везу́	**грызу́**
везёшь	**грызёшь**
везёт	**грызёт**
везём	**грызём**
везёте	**грызёте**
везу́т	**грызу́т**

Like везти́: **ползти́**.

(h) Verbs in **-чь** with stem in **г/ж**:

бере́чь	**жечь**	**стричь**	**запря́чь**
to guard	*to burn*	*to cut*	*to harness*
берегу́	**жгу**	**стригу́**	**запрягу́**
бережёшь	**жжёшь**	**стрижёшь**	**запряжёшь**
бережёт	**жжёт**	**стрижёт**	**запряжёт**
бережём	**жжём**	**стрижём**	**запряжём**
бержёте	**жжёте**	**стрижёте**	**запряжёте**
берегу́т	**жгут**	**стригу́т**	**запрягу́т**

Note: **жечь** loses the **е** of the infinitive in its present/future tense stem, whereas other verbs of this type preserve the vowel of the infinitive in those tenses.

Like бере́чь: **пренебре́чь, стере́чь**.

(i) Verbs in **-чь** with stem in **к/ч**:

печь	**воло́чь**
to bake	*to drag*

пеку́	**волоку́**
печёшь	**волочёшь**
печёт	**волочёт**
печём	**волочём**
печёте	**волочёте**
пеку́т	**волоку́т**

Like печь: **влечь, сечь, течь**.

(j) Miscellaneous verbs:

ждать	**лгать**	**ошиби́ться**	**расти́**	**соса́ть**	**ткать**
to wait	*to lie*	*to be mistaken*	*to grow*	*to suck*	*to weave*
жду	**лгу**	**ошибу́сь**	**расту́**	**сосу́**	**тку**
ждёшь	**лжёшь**	**ошибёшься**	**растёшь**	**сосёшь**	**ткёшь**
ждёт	**лжёт**	**ошибётся**	**растёт**	**сосёт**	**ткёт**
ждём	**лжём**	**ошибёмся**	**растём**	**сосём**	**ткём**
ждёте	**лжёте**	**ошибётесь**	**растёте**	**сосёте**	**ткёте**
ждут	**лгут**	**ошибу́тся**	**расту́т**	**сосу́т**	**ткут**

Like ошиби́ться: **ушиби́ть(ся)**.

8.6.8 Second-conjugation verbs

The stem of the present/future tense is found by removing vowel + ть (-ить/-ать/-еть/-ять) from the end of the infinitive.

(a) Verbs with infinitives in **-ить, -еть, -ять, -ать**:

говори́ть	**смотре́ть**	**стоя́ть**	**гнать**	**спать**
to speak	*to look at*	*to stand*	*to chase*	*to sleep*
говорю́	**смотрю́**	**стою́**	**гоню́**	**сплю*****
говори́шь	**смо́тришь**	**стои́шь**	**го́нишь**	**спишь**
говори́т	**смо́трит**	**стои́т**	**го́нит**	**спит**
говори́м	**смо́трим**	**стои́м**	**го́ним**	**спим**
говори́те	**смо́трите**	**стои́те**	**го́ните**	**спи́те**
говоря́т	**смо́трят**	**стоя́т**	**го́нят**	**спят**

* See (d) below for explanation of this form.

Like говори́ть: the vast majority of verbs that have an infinitive ending in **-ить**.
Like смотре́ть: **боле́ть, верте́ть, ви́деть, висе́ть, горе́ть, зави́сеть, лете́ть, ненави́деть, оби́деть, перде́ть** (R1, vulg), **свисте́ть, сиде́ть, смотре́ть, терпе́ть**; also **блесте́ть**, though this verb may also be conjugated as a 1B verb with a stem in **щ (блещу́, бле́щешь**, etc).

Note: most of these verbs undergo a consonant change in the 1st person singular form (see (c) below).

Like стоя́ть: **боя́ться**.

(b) Verbs with a stem in a hushing consonant:

лежа́ть	**молча́ть**	**слы́шать**
to lie	*to be silent*	*to hear*

лежу́	**молчу́**	**слы́шу**
лежи́шь	**молчи́шь**	**слы́шишь**
лежи́т	**молчи́т**	**слы́шит**
лежи́м	**молчи́м**	**слы́шим**
лежи́те	**молчи́те**	**слы́шите**
лежа́т	**молча́т**	**слы́шат**

Like лежа́ть: **держа́ть, дрожа́ть, принадлежа́ть.**
Like молча́ть: **звуча́ть, крича́ть, стуча́ть.**
Like слы́шать: **дыша́ть.**

Note: not all verbs ending in -жать, -чать, or -шать belong to the second conjugation. For example, **дорожа́ть, получа́ть, слу́шать** all belong to type 1A, while **жать**, in both its meanings (*to press; to reap*), belongs to type 1B (see 8.6.7(b) above).

(c) Verbs with one of the following consonant changes in the 1st person singular:

д → **ж**
з → **ж**
с → **ш**
т → **ч**
т → **щ**
ст → **щ**

ходи́ть	*to go*	хожу́, хо́дишь
вози́ть	*to transport*	вожу́, во́зишь
носи́ть	*to carry*	ношу́, но́сишь
лете́ть	*to fly*	лечу́, лети́шь
посети́ть	*to visit*	посещу́, посети́шь
чи́стить	*to clean*	чи́щу, чи́стишь

Like посети́ть: all verbs in -**ти́ть** which have imperfectives in -**ща́ть**, eg **возмути́ть** (impf возмуща́ть), **запрети́ть, защити́ть, обогати́ть, обрати́ть, освети́ть, ощути́ть, укроти́ть.**

Note
1. The following 'defective' verbs have no first-person singular form: **победи́ть, убеди́ть, очути́ться, ощути́ть, чуди́ть.**
2. **чтить**, *to honour*, is a second-conjugation verb but has 3rd pers pl **чтут** as well as **чтят**.
3. **зи́ждиться** (на + prep; R3), *to be founded on*, has 3rd pers sg/pl **зи́ждется, зи́ждутся**.

(d) Verbs with epenthetic **л** in the 1st person singular.

The consonant **л** is inserted between the present/future tense stem and the ending in verbs whose stem ends in one of the consonants **б, в, м, п, ф**.

люби́ть	*to love*	люблю́, лю́бишь
ста́вить	*to put*	ста́влю, ста́вишь
корми́ть	*to feed*	кормлю́, ко́рмишь
купи́ть	*to buy*	куплю́, ку́пишь
графи́ть	*to rule (line)*	графлю́, гра́фишь

Like люби́ть: many verbs, eg **долби́ть, истреби́ть, осла́бить, руби́ть**.
Like ста́вить: many verbs, eg **объяви́ть, пра́вить, предста́вить, соста́вить**.
Like корми́ть: many verbs, eg **вы́прямить, обра́мить, ошеломи́ть, стреми́ться**.
Like купи́ть: many verbs, eg **копи́ть, ослепи́ть, ступи́ть, топи́ть**.

There are no common second-conjugation verbs in the modern language with present/future tense stem in **ф**.

8.6.9 Irregular verbs

бежа́ть	**дать**	**есть**	**хоте́ть**
to run	*to give*	*to eat*	*to want*
бегу́	**дам**	**ем**	**хочу́**
бежи́шь	**дашь**	**ешь**	**хо́чешь**
бежи́т	**даст**	**ест**	**хо́чет**
бежи́м	**дади́м**	**еди́м**	**хоти́м**
бежи́те	**дади́те**	**еди́те**	**хоти́те**
бегу́т	**даду́т**	**едя́т**	**хотя́т**

8.6.10 Formation of the past tense

The past tense has only four forms, which are differentiated according to gender and number rather than person. Masculine forms end in **-л** or some other hard consonant. Feminine, neuter and plural forms end in **-ла**, **-ло**, **-ли** respectively; these endings are added to the masculine form in verbs in which the masculine form ends in some consonant other than л.

Note: in many 1B verbs in **-зти́**, **-сти́** and **-ечь** the vowel е is replaced by **ё** in the masculine form of the past tense.

The following types of past tense can be distinguished:

(a) verbs with infinitive ending in vowel + **ть**: the final -ть is replaced by **-л**, **-ла**, **-ло**, **-ли**, eg

чита́ть *to read*	**чита́л, чита́ла, чита́ло, чита́ли**
теря́ть *to lose*	**теря́л, теря́ла, теря́ло, теря́ли**
пе́ть *to sing*	**пе́л, пе́ла, пе́ло, пе́ли**
дуть *to blow*	**дул, ду́ла, ду́ло, ду́ли**
откры́ть *to open*	**откры́л, откры́ла, откры́ло, откры́ли**
коло́ть *to prick*	**коло́л, коло́ла, коло́ло, коло́ли**
пить *to drink*	**пил, пила́, пи́ло, пи́ли**
лечи́ть *to cure*	**лечи́л, лечи́ла, лечи́ло, лечи́ли**

(b) verbs in **-зти́**, **-зть**: the final -ти́ or -ть is lost and the remaining stem serves as the masculine form, eg

везти́ *to take*	**вёз, везла́, везло́, везли́**
лезть *to climb*	**лез, ле́зла, ле́зло, ле́зли**

(c) verbs in **-сти́** with stems in **б** or **с**: the masculine form ends in the consonant with which the present/future tense stem ends, eg

грести́ *to row* (гре**б**/у́)	**грёб, гребла́, гребло́, гребли́**
нести́ *to carry* (не**с**/у́)	**нёс, несла́, несло́, несли́**

(d) verbs in **-сть** or **-сти́** with stems in **д** or **т**: the consonant with which the present/future tense stem ends is replaced with **-л** in the masculine form, eg

вести́ *to lead* (ве**д**/у́)	**вёл, вела́, вело́, вели́**
мести́ *to sweep* (ме**т**/у́)	**мёл, мела́, мело́, мели́**
класть *to put* (кла**д**/у́)	**клал, кла́ла, кла́ло, кла́ли**
красть *to steal* (кра**д**/у́)	**крал, кра́ла, кра́ло, кра́ли**

(e) verbs in **-чь**: the final **-чь** of the infinitive is replaced with the velar with which the stem of the 1st person singular form of the present/future tense ends, eg

бере́чь *to be careful* (бере**г**/у́)	**берёг, берегла́, берегло́, берегли́**
лечь *to lie down* (ля́**г**/у)	**лёг, легла́, легло́, легли́**
стричь *to cut* (hair; стри**г**/у́)	**стриг, стри́гла, стри́гло, стри́гли**
мочь *to be able* (мо**г**/у́)	**мог, могла́, могло́, могли́**
печь *to bake* (пе**к**/у́)	**пёк, пекла́, пекло́, пекли́**

Note: **жечь**, *to burn* (жг/у), has **жёг, жгла, жгло, жгли**.

(f) **идти́**: **шёл, шла, шло, шли**

Note: stress in **вы́шел** is on the prefix.

(g) verbs in **-ере́ть** lose the final **-е́ть** in their masculine form, eg

умере́ть *to die*	**у́мер, умерла́, у́мерло, у́мерли**
запере́ть *to lock*	**за́пер, заперла́, за́перло, за́перли**
стере́ть *to rub off*	**стёр, стёрла, стёрло, стёрли**

(h) some verbs in **-нуть** with stress on stem, including verbs denoting change of state (see 8.6.6(c)) lose this suffix in the masculine form, eg

возни́кнуть *to arise*	**возни́к, возни́кла, возни́кло, возни́кли**
дости́гнуть *to attain*	**дости́г, дости́гла, дости́гло, дости́гли**
замёрзнуть *to freeze*	**замёрз, замёрзла, замёрзло, замёрзли**
исче́знуть *to disappear*	**исче́з, исче́зла, исче́зло, исче́зли**
поги́бнуть *to perish*	**поги́б, поги́бла, поги́бло, поги́бли**

Note: the tendency is for verbs of this type to lose their suffix in the past tense, and forms which preserve it have an archaic flavour.

(i)

ошиби́ться *to be mistaken*	**оши́бся, оши́блась, оши́блось, оши́блись**
ушиби́ться *to hurt oneself*	**уши́бся, уши́блась, уши́блось, уши́блись**

8.6.11 Formation of the imperative

The second-person imperative may be formed from either aspect of the Russian verb (on usage see 10.5.6).

The basic forms are used if the form of address used by the speaker is ты. The suffix **-те** is added to this basic form if the form of address used by the speaker is вы.

The imperative of most Russian verbs is formed by removing the last two letters of the 3rd person plural of the present/future tense and adding one of the following endings:

(a) **й**, if the stem ends in a vowel, eg

конча́ть *to finish* (конча́/ют)	**конча́й(те)**
объясня́ть *to explain* (объясня́/ют)	**объясня́й(те)**
организова́ть *to organise* (организу́/ют)	**организу́й(те)**
закры́ть *to close* (закро́/ют)	**закро́й(те)**
петь *to sing* (по/ю́т)	**пой(те)**

Note: a few second-conjugation verbs with stressed endings in -ить in the infinitive have the ending -й in R2/3, eg **кройть**, *to cut out* (кро/я́т) → **крой(те)**. In R1/D, though, the form **кро́й(те)** is also possible.

(b) **и**, if the stem ends in a single consonant and the stress in the 1st person singular is on the ending or if the stem ends in two or more consonants and irrespective of the position of the stress, eg

писа́ть *to write* (пи́ш/ут, пишу́)	**пиши́(те)**
вести́ *to lead* (вед/у́т, веду́)	**веди́(те)**
нести́ *to carry* (нес/у́т, несу́)	**неси́(те)**
говори́ть *to speak* (говор/я́т, говорю́)	**говори́(те)**
купи́ть *to buy* (ку́п/ят, куплю́)	**купи́(те)**
ждать *to wait* (жд/ут, жду́)	**жди(те)**
объясни́ть *to explain* (объясн/я́т, объясню́)	**объясни́(те)**

Note: verbs with stems ending in the consonants **ст** or **р** + another consonant have parallel forms in **-ь** in the singular form of the imperative, eg **почи́сть**, **не порть**.

(c) **ь**, if the stem ends in a single consonant and the stress in the 1st person singular is on the stem, eg

ре́зать *to cut* (ре́ж/ут, ре́жу)	**ре́жь(те)**
отве́тить *to reply* (отве́т/ят, отве́чу)	**отве́ть(те)**

Note: some imperative forms derived from simple verbs which have end stress but which have the stressed prefix **вы́-** retain the ending **-и**, eg вы́бежать, *to run out* (вы́бег/ут, вы́бегу) → **вы́беги(те)**; вы́йти, *to go out* (вы́йд/ут, вы́йду) → **вы́йди(те)**.

- The following verbs or types of verb have imperatives that depart from the above patterns:

(a) monosyllabic verbs in **-ить**: бить, *to beat* → **бей(те)**;

(b) 1B verbs in **-ва́ть**: дава́ть, *to give* → **дава́й(те)**;
(c) **е́хать** and **пое́хать**, *to go*, both have **поезжа́й(те)**;
(d) **дать**, *to give* → **да́й(те)**;
(e) **есть**, *to eat* → **е́шь(те)**;
(f) **лечь**, *to lie down* → **ля́г(те)**.

- A few common verbs may have forms in R1/D which differ from the standard forms of R2/3, eg

		R2/3	R1/D
взгляну́ть	*to glance*	взгляни́	**взгля́нь**
вы́йти	*to go out*	вы́йди	**вы́дь**
е́хать	*to go (by transport)*	поезжа́й	**езжа́й**
красть	*to steal*	кради́	**кра́дь**
обня́ть	*to embrace*	обними́	**обойми́**
пойти́	*to go*	пойди́	**поди́**
положи́ть	*to put*	положи́	**поло́жь***

* As in the expression **вынь да поло́жь**, *here and now, on the spot.*

- The reflexive particle **-ся** is reduced to **-сь** after the vowel ending **и** and after the particle **-те**, eg **береги́сь**, **береги́тесь**, *be careful.*

8.7 Formation of gerunds and participles

8.7.1 Formation of imperfective gerunds

Imperfective gerunds are formed by replacing the last two letters of the third-person plural form of the present tense with **-я** or (after hushing consonants) **-а**. These forms are invariable.

начина́ть (начина́/ют)	**начина́я** *beginning*
кома́ндовать (кома́нду/ют)	**кома́ндуя** *commanding*
жить (жив/у́т)	**живя́** *living*
приходи́ть (прихо́д/ят)	**приходя́** *arriving*
держа́ть (де́рж/ат)	**де́ржа** *holding*

Note
1. 1B verbs in **-ва́ть** have imperfective gerunds in **-ва́я**, eg дава́ть → **дава́я**, *giving.*
2. быть → **бу́дучи**, *being.*
3. In reflexive verbs **-ся** is contracted to **-сь** after the vowel ending, eg улыба́ться → **улыба́ясь**, *smiling.*
4. Many verbs, the vast majority of them 1B, are not capable of forming imperfective gerunds, viz 1B verbs in **-зать** or **-сать** (eg **вяза́ть, писа́ть**); verbs with no vowel in their present tense stem (eg monosyllables in **-ить** such as **лить**; **ждать, мять, рвать, слать, тере́ть**); verbs in **-чь** such as **печь**; verbs in **-нуть** (eg **ги́бнуть**); miscellaneous common verbs (eg **бежа́ть, гнить, драть, е́хать, звать, лезть, петь**). It is often possible, though, to form an imperfective gerund from a related 1A verb from the same root, eg **налива́ть** (← лить), **ожида́ть** (← ждать), **посыла́ть** (← слать), **вытира́ть** (← тере́ть), **погиба́ть** (← ги́бнуть) in the normal way.

8.7.2 Formation of perfective gerunds

Like imperfective gerunds, perfective gerunds are invariable. They are formed in the following ways:

(a) in most verbs the final -л of the masculine form of the past tense is replaced by **-в**, eg

прочита́ть (прочита́л)	**прочита́в** *having read*
откры́ть (откры́л)	**откры́в** *having opened*
потяну́ть (потяну́л)	**потяну́в** *having pulled*
почи́стить (почи́стил)	**почи́стив** *having cleaned*

Note: forms in **-вши** (eg **прочита́вши**, etc) have an archaic flavour but may also occur in R1 or D.

(b) most perfective verbs which do not form their past tense by adding **-л** to the final vowel of the infinitive are capable in theory of forming gerunds by adding **-ши** to the masculine form of the past tense, eg дости́гнуть (дости́г) → **дости́гши**, *having attained*.

Note: in practice such gerunds are nowadays rarely used, and may be replaced, in some types of verb, by forms in **-в**, eg привы́кнуть (привы́к) → **привы́кнув**, *having become accustomed*; запере́ть (за́пер) → **запере́в**, *having locked*.

(c) in perfective verbs of motion of the determinate category which have infinitive in **-ти́** (see 10.7) the gerund is formed by attaching **-я** to the stem of the future tense, eg

войти́ (войд/у́)	**войдя́** *having entered*
привести́ (привед/у́)	**приведя́** *having brought*
ввезти́ (ввез/у́)	**ввезя́** *having imported*
унести́ (унес/у́)	**унеся́** *having carried away*

Note: alternative gerunds in **-ши** for such verbs, eg **воше́дши**, are archaic.

(d) in reflexive verbs the perfective gerund is formed by replacing the final -л of the masculine form of the past tense by **-вшись**, eg верну́ться (верну́лся) → **верну́вшись**, *having returned*.

8.7.3 Formation of present active participles

Present active participles may be formed only from imperfective verbs. They are formed by replacing the final -т of the 3rd person plural of the present tense by **-щий**, eg

покупа́ть (покупа́ю/т)	**покупа́ющий** *who is buying*
пить (пью/т)	**пью́щий** *who is drinking*
идти́ (иду́/т)	**иду́щий** *who is going*
говори́ть (говоря́/т)	**говоря́щий** *who is speaking*
лежа́ть (лежа́/т)	**лежа́щий** *who is lying*
интересова́ться (интересу́ю/тся)	**интересу́ющийся** *who is interested in*

Note 1 Present active participles decline like adjectives of the type хоро́ший (8.3.1).
2 The reflexive particle -**ся**, when it occurs in such participles, is not contracted to -сь after vowels (eg m/n gen sg интересу́ющего**ся**).

8.7.4 Formation of past active participles

Past active participles may be formed from verbs of either aspect. They are formed in the following ways:

(a) in most verbs the final -л of the masculine form of the past tense is replaced with -**вший**, eg

покупа́ть (покупа́/л) **покупа́вший** *who was buying*
петь (пе/л) **пе́вший** *who was singing*
купи́ть (купи́/л) **купи́вший** *who bought*
закры́ть (закры́/л) **закры́вший** *who closed*
объясня́ть (объясня́/л) **объясня́вший** *who was explaining*

(b) verbs whose masculine past tense form ends in a consonant other than л form their past active participle by adding -**ший** to that consonant, eg

нести́ (нёс) **нёсший** *who was carrying*
мочь (мог) **мо́гший** *who was able*
умере́ть (у́мер) **у́мерший** *who died*
дости́гнуть (дости́г) **дости́гший** *who attained*

(c) verbs in -**сти́** which have a present/future tense stem in **д** or **т** retain this consonant and add -**ший**, eg

вести́ → **ве́дший**, *who was leading*
изобрести́ → **изобре́тший**, *who invented*

Note 1 Similarly идти́ (шёл) → **ше́дший**, *who was going*.
2 Many participles of this type, whilst theoretically possible, are rarely encountered in modern Russian.

- Past active participles decline like adjectives of the type хоро́ший (8.3.1). The reflexive particle -**ся**, when it occurs in such participles, is not contracted to -сь after vowels (eg m/n gen sg интересова́вшего**ся**).

8.7.5 Formation of present passive participles

Present passive participles may as a rule be formed only from verbs which are imperfective and transitive (eg **открыва́ть**). They may not therefore be formed from verbs which are perfective (eg откры́ть) or intransitive (eg стоя́ть); nor can they be formed from reflexive verbs (eg смея́ться), since these verbs are intransitive.

Present passive participles are formed by adding -**ый** to the 1st person plural of imperfective verbs. They decline like adjectives of the type но́вый (see 8.3.1), eg

рассма́тривать → **рассма́триваемый**, *being examined*
организова́ть → **организу́емый**, *being organised*

Note [1] 1B verbs in **-ава́ть** do not form their present passive participles in the normal way, eg дава́ть → **дава́емый**, *being given*.
[2] A few verbs with 1st person plural in **-ём** have participle in **-о́мый**, eg вести́ → **ведо́мый**, *being led*; such forms are rarely used.
[3] Many imperfective transitive verbs have no present passive participle, eg **брать, класть, петь, писа́ть**, monosyllables in **-ить** (see 8.6.5).

8.7.6 Formation of past passive participles

Past passive participles may as a rule be formed only from verbs which are perfective and transitive (eg **откры́ть**). They may not therefore be formed from verbs which are imperfective (eg открыва́ть) or intransitive (eg стоя́ть); nor can they be formed from reflexive verbs (eg смея́ться), since these verbs are intransitive.

Past passive participles have one of the following types of ending.

-тый

The suffix **-ый** is added to the final т of the infinitive in verbs of the following types (note stress changes):

(a) basically monosyllabic in **-ыть** (8.6.3): закры́ть → **закры́тый**, *shut*;
(b) basically monosyllabic in **-ить** (8.6.5): разби́ть → **разби́тый**, *broken*;
(c) basically monosyllabic in **-еть** (8.6.6(b)): оде́ть → **оде́тый**, *dressed*;
(d) in **-оть** (8.6.4): проколо́ть → **проко́лотый**, *punctured*;
(e) in **-уть**: упомяну́ть → **упомя́нутый**, *mentioned*;
(f) in **-ере́ть** (8.6.7(d)): запере́ть → **за́пертый**, *locked*; стере́ть → **стёртый**, *rubbed off*.

Note: the final **е** of the infinitive form of derivatives of тере́ть is lost, and the remaining **е** changes to **ё**.

(g) 1B in **-ать** or **-ять** which have a stem in **-м** or **-н** (8.6.6(b) and 8.6.7(b)): нача́ть (начн-у́) → **на́чатый**, *begun*; снять (сним-у́) → **сня́тый**, *taken off*.

-нный

In verbs with infinitive ending in -ать or -ять, including 1B verbs (except those in (g) above) and second-conjugation verbs, the final -ть of the infinitive is replaced by **-нный** (note stress changes):

прочита́ть → **прочи́танный**, *read*
взволнова́ть → **взволно́ванный**, *agitated*
написа́ть → **напи́санный**, *written*
потеря́ть → **поте́рянный**, *lost*

-енный
-ённый

The ending **-енный** is used when stress is on the stem, **-ённый** when stress is on the ending. These endings are used in verbs of the following types:

(a) 1B verbs with consonant stems which do not fall into any of the above categories, eg

ввести́ → **введённый**, *introduced*
принести́ → **принесённый**, *brought*
смести́ → **сметённый**, *swept off*
ввезти́ → **ввезённый**, *imported*
зажéчь → **зажжённый**, *set light to*
испéчь → **испечённый**, *baked*

Note: of the two stems which verbs in **-чь** have in their present/future tense (**г/ж** or **к/ч**) it is the stem in a hushing consonant (ж or ч) that is used in this participle.

(b) Second-conjugation verbs other than those in -ать. Any irregularities affecting the 1st person singular of second-conjugation verbs (consonant changes or insertion of epenthetic **-л-** (see 8.6.8(c) and (d)) also occur in these participles, eg

заморо́зить → **заморо́женный**, *frozen*
реши́ть → **решённый**, *decided*
встрéтить → **встрéченный**, *met*
просвети́ть → **просвещённый**, *enlightened*
поста́вить → **поста́вленный**, *put*
купи́ть → **ку́пленный**, *bought*

Note 1 Verbs in **-дить** which have imperfective form in **-ждать** have the combination **-жд-** in their participle, even though this combination does not occur in their 1st person singular, eg **освобождённый** from освободи́ть (impf освобожда́ть).

2 Position of stress in past passive participles in **-енный** and **-ённый** is determined by position of stress in the 2nd person singular of the present/future tense (заморо́зишь, реши́шь, встрéтишь, просвети́шь, поста́вишь, ку́пишь, освободи́шь in the verbs given above).

(c) Some verbs which do not quite conform to the above rules:

укра́сть → **укра́денный**, *stolen*
derivatives of есть: съесть → **съéденный**, *eaten up*
найти́ → **на́йденный**, *found*
уви́деть → **уви́денный**, *seen*

- The long forms of past passive participles of all types decline like adjectives. Past passive participles also have short forms which, like the short forms of adjectives, distinguish gender and number, eg

откры́тый	**откры́т**	**откры́та**	**откры́то**	**откры́ты**
прочи́танный	**прочи́тан**	**прочи́тана**	**прочи́тано**	**прочи́таны**
потéрянный	**потéрян**	**потéряна**	**потéряно**	**потéряны**
решённый	**решён**	**решена́**	**решено́**	**решены́**
поста́вленный	**поста́влен**	**поста́влена**	**поста́влено**	**поста́влены**

Note 1 In all past passive participles ending in **-нный** only one **н** survives in the short form.

2 The short forms of participles in **-ённый** are always stressed on the last syllable, with the result that **ё** changes to **е** in the feminine, neuter and plural forms.

9 Prepositions

It is worth devoting a separate chapter to Russian prepositions, and the rendering of English prepositions into Russian. For one thing knowledge of prepositions in a foreign language tends to be a good indicator of command of that language in general. More importantly, the meanings of Russian prepositions coincide with the meanings of their most common English equivalents only to a limited degree. Russian prepositions are also extremely precise in their meanings. The English-speaker must therefore think particularly carefully about the meaning of the English preposition in a given context before rendering it into Russian. Moreover, some of the most widespread English prepositions (*for*, *of*, *to*, *with*) may not be rendered in Russian by any preposition at all, since their meaning is often implicit in the use of a certain Russian case. Attention must also be paid to the differences in meaning that many prepositions have when they are used with different cases.

This chapter examines the most important meanings of Russian and English prepositions respectively, and also deals with common verbs which govern an object indirectly through a particular preposition. The last section (9.4), which deals with the rendering of each English preposition in Russian, draws attention to expressions where usage in the two languages is quite different.

9.1 Valency of prepositions

9.1.1 Prepositions governing the nominative

В

in a few expressions denoting change of status, promotion:

произвести́ **в полко́вники**	*to promote to the rank of colonel*
пойти́ **в лётчики**	*to become a pilot*

ЗА

governs the nominative case in the interrogative expression **Что э́то за...?** *What sort of... is...?* (cf Ger *Was für ein Buch ist das?*) and the interjectional expression **Что за ...!** *What a...!*

Что э́то за **маши́на?**	*What sort of car is it?*
Что за **день!**	*What a (wonderful) day!*

9.1.2 Prepositions governing the accusative

В

(a) *into*, *to*, *in*, when movement is involved (cf в + prep):

Она́ вошла́ **в ко́мнату**.	*She went into the room.*

	Он положи́л ве́щи **в чемода́н**.	*He put his things in a case.*
(b)	*at* a time on the hour or past the hour, *at* an age:	
	в час	*at one o'clock*
	в че́тверть пя́того	*at a quarter past four*
	в два́дцать мину́т шесто́го	*at twenty past five*
	в де́вять лет	*at nine years of age*
	Also **в по́лдень**, *at midday*, and **в по́лночь**, *at midnight*.	
(c)	*on* a day of the week:	
	в понеде́льник	*on Monday*
	в сре́ду	*on Wednesday*
(d)	to express dimension and measurement:	
	стол ширино́й **в оди́н метр**	*a table a metre wide*
	дом **в два** этажа́	*a two-storey house*
	моро́з **в де́сять** гра́дусов	*a 10-degree frost*
(e)	to denote pattern:	
	ю́бка **в кле́точку**	*a check shirt*
	пла́тье **в кра́пинку**	*a spotted dress* (tiny spots)
	ю́бка **в горо́шек**	*a spotted skirt* (larger spots)
	руба́шка **в поло́ску**	*a striped shirt*

ЗА

(a)	*behind* or *beyond*, when movement into a position is involved:	
	Со́лнце зашло́ **за горизо́нт**.	*The sun went behind the horizon* [ie *set*].
	Мы пое́хали **за́ город**.	*We went out of town* [ie *into the country*].
	This is the sense in which **за** is used in certain phrases, eg	
	сади́ться/сесть **за стол**	*to sit down at table*
	е́хать/пое́хать **за грани́цу**	*to go abroad*
(b)	*for*, when some sort of exchange or reciprocity is involved:	
	благодари́ть/поблагодари́ть кого́-н **за гостеприи́мство**	*to thank sb for their hospitality*
	плати́ть/заплати́ть **за кни́гу**	*to pay for a book*
(c)	*during*, *in the space of*, *over* a period of time:	
	за́ ночь	*during the night*
	За три дня вы́пало две ме́сячные но́рмы оса́дков.	*In the space of three days there was twice the usual monthly rainfall.*
(d)	*after a period of time*, or *over/beyond* a certain age:	
	далеко́ **за́ полночь**	*long after midnight*
	Ему́ уже́ **за со́рок**.	*He is already over 40.*

	(e)	*at a distance* in space or time (especially in combination with **от** and **до** respectively):
		Э́то произошло́ **за сто** киломе́тров **отсю́да**. — *This happened 100 kilometres from here.*
		за оди́н день до его́ сме́рти — *a day before his death*
НА	(a)	*on to, on*, when movement is involved:
		класть/положи́ть что́-н **на пол** — *to put sth on the floor*
		сади́ться/сесть **на стул** — *to sit down on the chair*
	(b)	*to, into* with those nouns listed in 9.1.6 (на (b)) which require **на** + prepositional case for the translation of *in* or *at*, eg
		на вы́ставку — *to the exhibition*
		на ры́нок — *to the market*
	(c)	*for* a period of time, when one is defining what period an action is intended or expected to cover (cf use of accusative without a preposition; see 9.4 (*for*) and 10.1.2):
		Он е́дет в Москву́ **на неде́лю**. — *He is going to Moscow for a week.*
		Она́ прие́хала к нам **на́ год**. — *She came to us for a year.*
	(d)	*for* a certain purpose:
		тало́ны **на мя́со** — *(rationing) coupons for meat*
		обе́д **на пять** челове́к — *dinner for five people*
	(e)	*by* a certain margin:
		Он **на два го́да** ста́рше бра́та. — *He is two years older than his brother.*
		Э́ти проду́кты подорожа́ли **на ты́сячу** проце́нтов. — *These products have become a thousand per cent more expensive.*
О		*against* in the sense of *in contact with*:
		спотыка́ться/споткну́ться **о ка́мень** — *to stumble against a stone*
		как бара́н **о но́вые воро́та** (R1) — *like a ram against a new gate* (of sth having no effect)
		бок **о́ бок** — *side by side*
ПО		*up to* a certain point in space or time:
		стоя́ть **по ше́ю** в воде́ — *to stand up to one's neck in water*
		Ви́за действи́тельна **по двадца́тое** ма́я. — *The visa is valid up to 20 May inclusive.*
ПОД	(a)	*under*, when movement into a position is involved:
		Ко́шка зале́зла **под крова́ть**. — *The cat went under the bed.*
		Я положи́л(а) кни́ги **под стол**. — *I put the books under the table.*

(b) *towards*, in a temporal sense, or *just before*:

под ве́чер	*towards evening*
Ему́ **под со́рок** лет.	*He is getting on for 40.*

(c) *to* the accompaniment of a sound:

танцева́ть **под му́зыку**	*to dance to music*
писа́ть **под дикто́вку**	*to write to dictation*

(d) *in imitation of*:

кольцо́ **под зо́лото**	*an imitation gold ring*
писа́ть **под Го́голя**	*to write in the style of Gogol*

ПРО

(a) *about* or *concerning*; more or less synonymous with о + prep, but characteristic of R1; used only with the accusative:

говори́ть **про Ма́шу**	*to speak about Masha*
петь **про любо́вь**	*to sing about love*

(b) + **себя́**, *to* in certain phrases:

ду́мать **про себя́**	*to think to oneself*
чита́ть **про себя́**	*to read to oneself*

С

with nouns denoting measurement, distance, time, etc, in the sense of *approximately*, *about*:

ве́сить **с килогра́мм**	*to weigh about a kilogram*
Мы прошли́ **с ми́лю**.	*We walked about a mile.*
Я про́был(а́) там **с неде́лю**.	*I was there about a week.*

СКВОЗЬ

through, esp when passage through sth is difficult; used only with the accusative:

смех **сквозь слёзы**	*laughter through tears*
пробира́ться/пробра́ться **сквозь толпу́**	*to force one's way through a crowd*

ЧЕ́РЕЗ

(a) *across*, *through*, or *over* when this preposition means *across*; used only with the accusative:

переходи́ть **че́рез доро́гу**	*to cross (over) the road*
перелеза́ть/переле́зть **че́рез забо́р**	*to climb over the fence*

(b) *in* (a certain amount of time from the time of speaking):

Че́рез неде́лю он верну́лся.	*In a week he returned.*

Note: there is a similar spatial use in phrases such as **че́рез две остано́вки**, *in two stops* (ie of getting out of bus or train).

(c) *via* a place:

Он пое́хал туда́ **че́рез Москву́**.	*He went there via Moscow.*

(d) *through* an intermediary:

говори́ть с ке́м-н **че́рез перево́дчика**	*to speak to sb through an interpreter*

(e) when an action affects alternate objects in a series:

рабо́тать **че́рез день**	*to work every other day*
печа́тать/напеча́тать **че́рез строку́**	*to print on every other line* (ie *to double-space*)

9.1.3 Prepositions governing the genitive

A very large number of prepositions may govern the genitive case. The most common ones are **из**, **от**, **с**, and **у**. All of the prepositions listed in this section, with the exception of **ме́жду** and **с**, invariably govern the genitive case.

БЕЗ *without*:

(a)

без значе́ния	*without significance*
без оши́бок	*without mistakes*

(b) in expressions of time, to indicate minutes before the hour, eg

без пяти́ (мину́т) де́сять	*(at) five to ten*
без че́тверти два (часа́)	*(at) a quarter to two*

ВВИДУ́ *in view of*; rather formal:

Ввиду́ вну́треннего кри́зиса президе́нт реши́л не выезжа́ть за грани́цу.	*In view of the internal crisis the president decided not to go abroad.*

ВДОЛЬ *along* (ie adhering to a line; see also 9.4):

Нефтяно́е пятно́ растекло́сь **вдоль побере́жья**.	*The oil slick flowed out along the coast.*

ВМЕ́СТО *instead of, in place of*:

Он пошёл на собра́ние **вме́сто своего́ бра́та**.	*He went to the meeting instead of his brother.*

Note: **вме́сто** should not be confused with **вме́сте**, *together*.

ВНЕ *outside* (as opposed to *inside*):

вне го́рода	*outside the town*
вне зако́на	*outside the law*

Note: **вне** is narrower in meaning than Eng *outside*, which may have to be translated into Russian with other prepositions such as **о́коло** or **пе́ред** (see 9.4).

ВНУТРИ́

inside, to indicate the position in which sth is located; (**внутри́** is itself a form in the prepositional case):

Внутри́ корабля́—торпе́ды с я́дерными боеголо́вками. — *Inside the ship are torpedoes with nuclear warheads.*

ВНУТРЬ

inside, to indicate movement inwards (**внутрь** is itself a form in the accusative case):

Войска́ бы́стро продви́нулись **внутрь страны́**. — *The troops quickly moved inland.*

ВО́ЗЛЕ

by, near:

Воздви́гли па́мятник **во́зле собо́ра**. — *They erected a monument near the cathedral.*

ВОКРУ́Г

round:

путеше́ствие **вокру́г све́та** — *a journey round the world*

ВПЕРЕДИ́

in front of, ahead of:

Впереди́ по́езда стоя́л сугро́б. — *In front of the train was a snowdrift.*

ВСЛЕ́ДСТВИЕ

because of, owing to:

Вследствие тума́на ма́тч не состоя́лся. — *Owing to the fog the match did not take place.*

ДЛЯ

for in the sense of *for the benefit of* or *for the purpose of*:

пода́рок **для дру́га** — *a present for (one's) friend*
ору́дие **для** — *a tool for*

Note: **для** is much narrower in meaning than English *for*, which may have to be translated by other prepositions such as **за** + acc or **на** + acc (see 9.4), or indeed by no preposition at all.

ДО

(a) *before* and *until* in a temporal sense:

Э́то произошло́ **до войны́**. — *This happened before the war.*
Он рабо́тает **до шести́ часо́в**. — *He works until six o'clock.*

(b) *up to* or *as far as* in a spatial sense:

Он дое́хал **до Владивосто́ка**. — *He went as far as Vladivostok.*

ИЗ

(a) *out of*, when movement is involved:

выходи́ть/вы́йти **из ко́мнаты** — *to go out of/leave the room*
вынима́ть/вы́нуть **из карма́на** — *to take out of one's pocket*

(b) to indicate that sb or sth is of a particular origin, or that an object is made of or consists of sth, or is one out of a larger number:

		из крестья́нской семьи́	*from a peasant family*
		пла́тье **из шёлка**	*a silk dress*
		обе́д **из пяти́ блюд**	*a five-course dinner*
		одна́ **из са́мых лу́чших книг**	*one of the best books*
	(c)	to indicate that some action results from a certain experience or feeling:	
		Из до́лгого о́пыта зна́ю, что...	*From long experience I know that...*
		Она́ э́то сде́лала **из любви́** к де́тям.	*She did this out of love for the children.*
ИЗ-ЗА	(a)	*out from behind*:	
		из-за угла́	*from round the corner*
		встава́ть/встать **из-за стола́**	*to get up from the table*
	(b)	*because of* when the cause of sth is regarded unfavourably:	
		Она́ не могла́ рабо́тать **из-за головно́й бо́ли**.	*She could not work because of a headache.*
ИЗ-ПОД	(a)	*out from under*:	
		из-под посте́ли	*out from under the bed*
		торго́вля **из-под прила́вка**	*under-the-counter trade*
	(b)	to indicate the purpose for which an object is designed:	
		ба́нка **из-под варе́нья**	*a jam-jar*
		бо́чка **из-под пи́ва**	*a beer-barrel*
КРО́МЕ		*except, apart from*:	
		Она́ ничего́ не е́ла **кро́ме бу́лочки**.	*She didn't eat anything apart from a bun.*
МЕ́ЖДУ		*between*; used with the genitive only in a few phrases:	
		чита́ть **ме́жду строк**	*to read between the lines*
		ме́жду двух огне́й	*between the devil and the deep blue sea* (lit *between two fires*)
МИ́МО		*past*:	
		проходи́ть/пройти́ **ми́мо до́ма**	*to go past the house*
НАПРО́ТИВ		*opposite*:	
		Мы договори́лись встре́титься **напро́тив це́ркви**.	*We agreed to meet opposite the church.*
НАСЧЁТ		*about, as regards*:	
		Как **насчёт ва́шего докла́да**?	*What about your report?*

О́КОЛО	(a)	*near* or *by*:	
		Он сиде́л **о́коло своего́ друга́**.	*He was sitting by his friend.*
	(b)	*around*, *about* or *approximately*:	
		о́коло полу́ночи	*around midnight*
		о́коло миллио́на	*about a million*
ОТ (ОТО)	(a)	*away from*:	
		По́езд отхо́дит **от платфо́рмы**.	*The train is moving away from the platform.*
	(b)	to indicate distance from:	
		в двух киломе́трах **от це́нтра**	*two kilometres from the centre*
		в пяти́ мину́тах ходьбы́ **от вокза́ла**	*five minutes' walk from the station*
	(c)	to indicate the source of sth:	
		узнава́ть/узна́ть **от кого́-н**	*to find out from sb*
		Я получи́л(а) **от неё** письмо́.	*I received a letter from her.*
	(d)	to indicate the date of a letter:	
		его́ письмо́ **от пе́рвого ма́рта**	*his letter of 1 March*
	(e)	to indicate the purpose for which sth is intended:	
		ключ **от две́ри**	*the door key*
		пу́говица **от руба́шки**	*a shirt button*
	(f)	to indicate that sth may be used to counter sth else:	
		страхова́ние **от огня́**	*fire insurance*
		табле́тки **от головно́й бо́ли**	*headache tablets*
	(g)	to indicate that sth is prompted by a certain cause:	
		Стол ломи́лся **от еды́**.	*The table was groaning with food.*
	(h)	to describe the emotional state a person is in, when the feelings that prompted an action are being defined:	
		кипе́ть **от негодова́ния**	*to seethe with indignation*
		дрожа́ть **от стра́ха**	*to tremble with fear*
	(i)	in miscellaneous common phrases:	
		не/далеко́ от	*not/far from*
		вре́мя от вре́мени	*from time to time*
		от всей души́	*with all one's heart*
		от и́мени кого́-н	*on behalf of sb*
ОТНОСИ́ТЕЛЬНО		*concerning*; formal, used mainly in R3:	

		вопро́сы **относи́тельно процеду́ры**	*questions concerning procedure*
ПОМИ́МО		*besides, apart from*:	
		поми́мо всего́ про́чего	*apart from everything else*
ПО́СЛЕ		*after*:	
		по́сле у́жина	*after supper*
ПОСРЕДИ́		*in the middle of*:	
		Он стоя́л **посреди́ пло́щади**.	*He was standing in the middle of the square.*
ПОСРЕ́ДСТВОМ		*by means of, by dint of*:	
		посре́дством усе́рдной рабо́ты	*by means of hard work*
ПРО́ТИВ		*against*:	
		про́тив тече́ния выступа́ть **про́тив си́льного оппоне́нта**	*against the current* *to take on* [lit *come out against*] *a strong opponent*
ПУТЁМ		*by means of, by dint of*:	
		путём хи́трости	*by means of cunning*
РА́ДИ		*for the sake of*:	
		ра́ди семьи́	*for the sake of the family*
С (СО)	(a)	*off* the surface of sth, *down from*:	
		снима́ть/снять **со стола́** приходи́ть/прийти́ **с рабо́ты**	*to take off the table* *to come home from work*
	Note:	**с** translates *away from* or *out of* when the following noun is one of those nouns that require **на** rather than **в** to translate *in(to)* or *at/on to* (see 9.1.6, на (b–e)).	
	(b)	*since* in a temporal sense:	
		с нача́ла января́	*since the beginning of January*
	(c)	*from* in the sense of *as a result of:*	
		умира́ть/умере́ть **с го́лода** **со стыда́**	*to die of hunger/starve to death* *from shame*
	(d)	*with* in the sense of *on the basis of*:	
		с ва́шего разреше́ния	*with your permission*
	(e)	*from*:	
		Ма́льчик запры́гал **с ра́дости**.	*The boy began jumping for joy.*

Note: in this sense **с** is synonymous with (though a little more colloquial than) **от** as a preposition describing the emotional state that causes some action.

(f) in miscellaneous common expressions:

с одно́й стороны́	*on the one hand*
с друго́й стороны́	*on the other hand*
с како́й ста́ти?	*to what purpose?*
с пе́рвого взгля́да	*at first sight*
с тех пор, как	*since* (conj)
с то́чки зре́ния кого́-н	*from the point of view of sb*

СВЕРХ *on top of, over and above*:

сверх зарпла́ты	*on top of wages*
сверх вся́кого ожида́ния	*beyond expectations*

СВЫ́ШЕ *over, more than*; used mainly in numerical contexts:

свы́ше миллио́на люде́й	*more than a million people*

СРЕДИ́ *among, amid*:

среди́ молодёжи	*among the young*
Среди́ бе́женцев—старики́, же́нщины и де́ти.	*Among the refugees are old men, women and children.*

У (a) *by* in the sense of *near*:

Она́ стоя́ла **у окна́**.	*She was standing by the window.*
дом **у мо́ря**	*a house by the sea*

(b) *at* in the sense of Fr *chez* and related meanings:

Мы поу́жинаем **у вас**.	*We shall have supper at your place.*
Он ещё живёт **у роди́телей**.	*He still lives with his parents.*

(c) + nouns and personal pronouns to indicate possession; in this sense corresponds to the English verb *to have* (3.1):

У нас есть но́вая маши́на.	*We've got a new car.*
У меня́ к вам одна́ про́сьба.	*I've got a request to make of you.*

(d) + personal pronouns, in R1, in lieu of possessive pronoun:

Са́ша **у меня́** до́брый челове́к.	*My Sasha's a good man.*

(e) + nouns and personal pronouns in expressions indicating pain or discomfort:

У меня́ боли́т зуб.	*I've got toothache.*
У неё боли́т го́рло.	*She's got a sore throat.*

(f) to denote dispossession or taking away:

занима́ть/заня́ть де́ньги **у кого́-н**	*to borrow money from sb*

		У нас о́тняли всё.	*They've taken everything away from us.*

9.1.4 Prepositions governing the dative

The commonest preposition governing the dative case is **по**, which is used much more widely with the dative than with the accusative or the prepositional, and which has many meanings. **К** is also very common, but the remaining prepositions which may govern the dative are very restricted in their use.

БЛАГОДАРЯ́ *thanks to*:

благодаря́ её **хладнокро́вию**	*thanks to her presence of mind*

ВОПРЕКИ́ *despite, contrary to*:

вопреки́ мои́м распоряже́ниям	*contrary to my instructions*

К (КО)

(a) *towards, up to* in a spatial sense:

Он подхо́дит **к мосту́**.	*He is going towards the bridge.*
Она́ подошла́ **ко мне**.	*She came up to me.*

(b) *by* or *towards* in a temporal sense:

Он придёт **к ве́черу**.	*He will arrive by evening.*

(c) in combination with many nouns to indicate attitude:

жа́лость к	*pity for*
интере́с к	*interest in*
любо́вь к	*love for*
не́нависть к	*hatred of*
отноше́ние к	*attitude towards, relation to*
презре́ние к	*contempt for*
равноду́шие к	*indifference towards*
скло́нность к	*inclination towards, penchant for*
страсть к	*passion for*
стремле́ние к	*striving for*
уваже́ние к	*respect for*

(d) in miscellaneous common phrases:

к сожале́нию	*unfortunately*
к сча́стью	*fortunately*
к тому́ же	*moreover, besides*
к моему́ удивле́нию	*to my surprise*
к на́шему изумле́нию	*to our astonishment*
к ва́шим услу́гам	*at your service*
лицо́м к лицу́	*face to face*

ПО	(a)	*along, down*:	
		Она́ идёт **по у́лице**.	*She is walking along the street.*
		Он спуска́ется вниз **по ле́стнице**.	*He is coming down the stairs.*
	(b)	*round* in the sense of *in various directions*:	
		Он хо́дит **по ко́мнате**.	*He is pacing round the room.*
		броди́ть **по го́роду**	*to wander round the town*
	(c)	*according to, in accordance with*:	
		по расписа́нию	*according to the timetable*
		по подсчётам экспе́ртов	*according to the calculations of experts*
		по официа́льному ку́рсу	*according to the official rate of exchange*
	(d)	*by* a means of communication:	
		по телефо́ну	*by telephone*
		по по́чте	*by post*
		по желе́зной доро́ге	*by rail*
	(e)	*at*, *on* or *in* in the sense of *in the field of* or *on the subject of*:	
		чемпио́ны **по футбо́лу**	*champions at football*
		специали́ст **по полити́ческим вопро́сам**	*a specialist on political matters*
		мини́стр **по дела́м** Шотла́ндии	*Minister for Scottish affairs*
		уро́к **по матема́тике**	*a mathematics lesson*
	(f)	*on* days of the week and in other expressions of time to indicate regular occurrence:	
		по понеде́льникам	*on Mondays*
		по пра́здникам	*on holidays*
		по утра́м	*in the mornings*
	(g)	+ the numeral **оди́н**, *one*, and also the nouns **ты́сяча**, *thousand*, and **миллио́н**, *million*, to indicate distribution; cf **по** + acc in this sense with other numerals (see 10.4.9):	
		Мы получи́ли **по одному́ фу́нту**.	*We received a pound each.*
	(h)	+ the negative particle **не** in phrases in which inconsistency is indicated; in this sense **по** may sometimes be translated by the English *for*:	
		Он **не по во́зрасту** высо́к.	*He is tall for his age.*
		Э́та маши́на мне **не по карма́ну**.	*I can't afford this car.*

Note: **по** has also made some progress in the language at the expense of more precise forms, eg **програ́мма по литерату́ре** (= програ́мма литерату́ры), *programme of literature*; **приз по стрельбе́** (= приз за стрельбу́), *prize for shooting*.

ПОДО́БНО *like, similar to*:

кричáть **подóбно сумасшéдшему**	*to shout like a madman*

СОГЛА́СНО *in accordance with*; official in tone, characteristic of R3b:

соглáсно глáвной статьé договóра	*in accordance with the main article of the treaty*

9.1.5 Prepositions governing the instrumental

ЗА *behind, beyond, on the far side of*, and *at* in the sense of *behind*; when location is being defined; cf **за** + acc when movement into a position is indicated:

за дóмом	*behind the house*
за границéй	*abroad (beyond the border)*
за бóртом	*overboard*
за столóм	*at the table*
за роя́лем	*at the piano*
за пи́вом	*over a beer*

МЕ́ЖДУ *between*; followed only by the instrumental case except in a few fixed expressions in which it governs the genitive (see 9.1.3)

мéжду параллéльными ли́ниями	*between parallel lines*
мéжду нáми	*between ourselves*

НАД (НА́ДО) *over, above, on top of*; used only with the instrumental:

Над столóм виси́т лю́стра.	*A chandelier hangs over the table.*
нáдо мной	*over me*

ПЕ́РЕД (ПЕ́РЕДО) used only with the instrumental:

(a) *in front of* or *before* in a spatial sense:

сидéть **пéред телеви́зором**	*to sit in front of the television*
пéредо мной	*in front of me*

(b) *before* in a temporal sense, especially *shortly before*; cf **до** (see 9.1.3) which may indicate any time before:

пéред смéртью	*before death*

ПОД (ПО́ДО) (a) *under, below, beneath*, when actual or figurative location is defined; cf **под** + acc when movement into a position is indicated:

под мостóм	*under the bridge*
под арéстом	*under arrest*
под влия́нием	*under the influence*

(b) *with* a certain dressing, in culinary expressions, in which the literal meaning of *under* is retained:

рыба **под томатным соусом** — *fish in tomato sauce*
яйцо **под майонезом** — *egg mayonnaise*

(c) *in the region of*:

под Москвой — *in the region of Moscow*

(d) *of* in the names of battles:

битва под Полтавой — *the Battle of Poltava*

С (СО)

(a) *with*, when *with* means *together with* or *in the company of*, or when it refers to some connection or attendant characteristic; cf omission of **с** when *with* denotes agency (see 9.4):

Он пошёл в кино **с сестрой**. — *He went to the cinema with his sister.*
в связи **с этим** — *in connection with this*
человек **с голубыми глазами** — *a person with (light) blue eyes*
с радостью — *gladly (with gladness)*

(b) together with personal pronouns in an inclusive sense, eg:

он с сестрой — *he and his sister*
мы с братом — *my brother and I*
мы с матерью — *my mother and I*

(c) in the expression **Что с вами/с тобой**? *What is the matter with you?*

(d) *with* the passage of time, eg **с каждым днём**, *with each (passing) day*.

9.1.6 Prepositions governing the prepositional or locative

The prepositional case, as its name suggests, may only be used with certain prepositions (**в, на, о, по, при**). It is also sometimes called the locative case, since when used with the prepositions **в** and **на** it may define location.

В (ВО)

(a) *in* or *at* to define location, the place where sth is situated or happening; cf use of accusative when movement is involved:

Он живёт **в Москве**. — *He lives in Moscow.*
Мы сидели **в спальне**. — *We were sitting in the bedroom.*

(b) to express the distance at which sth is located:

в одном километре от центра города — *a kilometre from the centre of town*
в трёх минутах ходьбы от школы — *three minutes' walk from the school*
в пяти часах езды от Парижа — *five hours' journey/travel from Paris*

(c) *in* in certain expressions of time (to indicate the month, year, decade, century, or period of one's life, or stage in a period in which an event took place):

в январé	*in January*
в прóшлом годý	*last year*
в двадцáтых годáх	*in the 1920s*
в двадцáтом вéке	*in the twentieth century*
в дéтстве	*in childhood*
в начáле гóда	*at the beginning of the year*
в концé войны́	*at the end of the war*

(d) *at* half past an hour:

в половúне пéрвого	*at half past twelve*

(e) to describe what sb is wearing:

Онá **в крáсной блýзке**.	*She's got a red blouse on.*
Он был **в чёрном костю́ме**.	*He was wearing a black suit.*

НА

(a) *on, in* or *at* to define location, the place where sth is situated; cf use of accusative when movement is involved:

Кни́га лежи́т **на столé**.	*The book is on the table.*

(b) *on, in* or *at* before many common nouns, where English-speakers might expect **в** to be used; many of these nouns denote some sort of occasion, or refer to both the place and the event or activity associated with it:

вéчер *party* (reception)	**на вéчере**
войнá *war*	**на войнé**
вокзáл *station*	**на вокзáле**
вы́ставка *exhibition*	**на вы́ставке**
завóд *factory*	**на завóде**
заседáние *meeting, session*	**на заседáнии**
кáфедра *department* (in higher educational institution)	**на кáфедре**
конферéнция *conference*	**на конферéнции**
концéрт *concert*	**на концéрте**
курóрт *resort*	**на курóрте**
курс *year* (of course in higher educational institution)	**на кýрсе**
лéкция *lecture*	**на лéкции**
óпера *opera*	**на óпере**
плóщадь (f) *square*	**на плóщади**
пóчта *post-office*	**на пóчте**
рабóта *work*	**на рабóте**
ры́нок *market*	**на ры́нке**
свáдьба *wedding*	**на свáдьбе**
собрáние *meeting, gathering*	**на собрáнии**

ста́нция *station*	**на ста́нции**
съезд *congress*	**на съе́зде**
у́лица *street*	**на у́лице**
уро́к *lesson*	**на уро́ке**
фа́брика *factory*	**на фа́брике**
факульте́т *faculty* (of higher educational institution)	**на факульте́те**
фронт *front* (mil)	**на фро́нте**
ша́хта *mine*	**на ша́хте**
экза́мен *examination*	**на экза́мене**

(c) *in* with points of the compass, islands, peninsulas, mountainous regions of the former USSR, the word *Ukraine*, and names of streets and squares, eg

на за́паде	*in the west*
на ю́ге	*in the south*
на се́веро-восто́ке	*in the north-east*
на о́строве	*on the island*
на Ки́пре	*in Cyprus*
на Ку́бе	*in Cuba*
на Сахали́не	*in Sakhalin*
на Аля́ске	*in Alaska*
на Камча́тке	*in Kamchatka*
на Кавка́зе	*in the Caucasus*
на Ура́ле	*in the Urals*
на Украи́не	*in the Ukraine*
на Арба́те	*in the Arbat*
на Не́вском проспе́кте	*in Nevsky Prospect*
на Кра́сной пло́щади	*in Red Square*

Note: with names of mountain ranges outside the former Soviet Union, though, **в** + prep is more usual, eg

в А́льпах	*in the Alps*
в А́ндах	*in the Andes*
в Гимала́ях	*in the Himalayas*

(d) *in* with certain nouns (especially nouns denoting means of transport, eg **авто́бус**, **автомоби́ль**, **маши́на**, **по́езд**) when presence in the place in question is associated with the activity for which the place is designed:

е́хать **на авто́бусе**	*to go by bus*
гото́вить **на ку́хне**	*to cook in the kitchen*

cf чита́ть газе́ту **в авто́бусе**, *to read a newspaper on the bus*

(e) in miscellaneous expressions of place or time, eg

на моро́зе	*in the frost*
на сквозняке́	*in a draught*
на со́лнце	*in the sun*

		на рассве́те	*at dawn*
		на пе́нсии	*retired* (on a pension)
		на откры́том во́здухе	*in the open air*
		на све́жем во́здухе	*in the fresh air*
		на бу́дущей неде́ле	*next week*
		на про́шлой неде́ле	*last week*
		на сле́дующей неде́ле	*the following week*
		на э́той неде́ле	*this week*

О (ОБ, ОБО) when the following noun or adjective begins with one of the vowels **а, о, у, э** (ie a vowel without an initial *j* sound), then the letter **б** is generally added to **о** for the sake of euphony; **о́бо** occurs only in the expressions given below.

(a) *about, concerning*:

Он ду́мает **о бра́те**.	*He is thinking about his brother.*
Поговори́м **об э́том**.	*Let's speak about this.*
обо всём/всех	*about everything/everybody*
обо мне	*about me*

(b) *with* when the properties of sth are being described; this use is uncommon:

па́лка **о двух конца́х**	*a two-ended stick* (ie *a double-edged weapon*)

ПО *after, following*, or *on completion of*; most commonly found with verbal nouns; this usage is rather literary or official and confined to R3, especially R3b:

по истече́нии ви́зы	*on expiry of the visa*
по оконча́нии университе́та	*on completing university* (ie *on graduation*)
по получе́нии письма́	*on receipt of the letter*

ПРИ used only with the prepositional:

(a) *at the time of*:

Он жил **при Ле́нине**.	*He lived at the time of Lenin.*
Достое́вский на́чал писа́ть **при Никола́е Пе́рвом**.	*Dostoevsky started writing in the reign of Nicholas I.*

(b) *adjacent/attached to*:

я́сли **при фа́брике**	*a nursery attached to the factory*
буфе́т **при вокза́ле**	*a station buffet*

(c) *in the presence of*:

ссо́риться **при гостя́х**	*to quarrel in front of the guests*

(d) *given the availability of*:

Я э́то сде́лаю **при трёх усло́виях**.	*I'll do this on three conditions.*

(e) *while* sth is being done (R3); in this sense the phrase with **при** is synonymous with an imperfective gerund:

Мы теря́ем много проду́ктов **при транспортиро́вке**.	*We lose a lot of foodstuffs while they are being transported.*

9.2 Prepositional phrases based on nouns

Prepositional phrases based on nouns, such as the following, are a feature of the official register (see 1.3.4(b)):

в де́ле + gen	*in the matter of*
в отли́чие от + gen	*unlike, in contradistinction to*
в отноше́нии + gen	*in respect of*
в связи́ с + instr	*in connection with*
в си́лу + gen	*by virtue of*
в соотве́тсвии с + instr	*in accordance with*
в тече́ние + gen	*in the course of*
в це́лях + gen	*with the object of*
за счёт + gen	*at the expense of*
на основа́нии + gen	*on the basis of*
по ли́нии + gen	*through the channel of*
по направле́нию к + dat	*in the direction of*
по отноше́нию к + dat	*with respect to*
по причи́не + gen	*by reason of*
по слу́чаю + gen	*by reason of*

9.3 Verbs followed by prepositions

Many verbs may be followed by certain prepositions. In the following sections some common combinations of verb + preposition are given.

9.3.1 Verbs followed by prepositions governing the accusative

В + acc

ве́рить/пове́рить в	*to believe in*
вме́шиваться/вмеша́ться в	*to interfere, intervene in*
вторга́ться/вто́ргнуться в	*to invade*
игра́ть в	*to play* (a game, sport)
одева́ть(ся)/оде́ть(ся) в	*to dress (oneself in)*
поступа́ть/поступи́ть в	*to enter* (institution)
превраща́ть(ся)/преврати́ть(ся) в	*to turn/be turned into*
стреля́ть в	*to shoot at* (fixed target)

ЗА + acc	(a)	after verbs with the sense of *taking hold of*:	
		брать/взять кого́-н **за́ руку**	*to take sb by the hand*
		вести́ кого́-н **за́ руку**	*to lead sb by the hand*
		держа́ть кого́-н **за́ руку**	*to hold sb by the hand*
		держа́ться за (eg **пери́ла**)	*to hold on to* (eg *the handrail*)
		хвата́ть/схвати́ть кого́-н **за ши́ворот**	*to seize sb by the scruff of the neck*
	(b)	*for the sake of*:	
		боро́ться за что́-н	*to fight/struggle for sth*
		заступа́ться/заступи́ться за кого́-н	*to stand up/plead/intercede for sb*
		пить/вы́пить за (eg **чьё-н здоро́вье**)	*to drink to* (eg *sb's health)*
		сража́ться/срази́ться за (eg **ро́дину**)	*to fight for* (eg *one's country*)
НА + acc		**гляде́ть/погляде́ть на**	*to look at*
		дели́ть/раздели́ть на	*to divide into*
		жа́ловаться/пожа́ловаться на	*to complain of*
		наде́яться на	*to hope for, count on, rely on*
		напада́ть/напа́сть на	*to attack, fall upon*
		отвеча́ть/отве́тить на	*to reply to* (letter, question)
		полага́ться/положи́ться на	*to count on, rely on*
		серди́ться/рассерди́ться на	*to be angry at, cross with*
		смотре́ть/посмотре́ть на	*to look at*
		соглаша́ться/согласи́ться на	*to agree to* (but not *to agree with*)

9.3.2 Verbs followed by prepositions governing the genitive

ИЗ + gen	**состоя́ть из**	*to consist of*
	стреля́ть из	*to shoot, fire* (a weapon)
ОТ + gen	**отка́зываться/отказа́ться от**	*to refuse, decline, turn down*
	отлича́ться/отличи́ться от	*to differ from*
	страда́ть от	*to suffer from*

Note: **страда́ть от** means to suffer from some temporary or slight problem as opposed to a chronic problem (in the latter meaning страда́ть is followed by the instrumental).

С + gen	**начина́ть(ся)/нача́ть(ся) с чего́-н**	*to begin with sth*
	сбива́ть/сбить спесь с кого́-н	*to take sb down a peg*

9.3.3 Verbs followed by prepositions governing the dative

К + dat especially verbs indicating approach or attachment:

	относи́ться/отнести́сь к	*to relate to, have an attitude to*
	подходи́ть/подойти́ к	*to approach, match, suit*
	приближа́ться/прибли́зиться к	*to approach, draw near to*
	привлека́ть/привле́чь к	*to attract to*
	привыка́ть/привы́кнуть к	*to get used/grow accustomed to*
	прилипа́ть/прили́пнуть к	*to stick/adhere to*
	прислоня́ться/прислони́ться к	*to lean against*
	присоединя́ться/присоедини́ться к	*to join*
	стреми́ться к	*to strive towards, aspire to*

Note: the verb **принадлежа́ть** is followed by **к** when it denotes membership (cf ownership; see 10.1.8) eg

	принадлежа́ть к полити́ческой па́ртии	*to belong to a political party*
ПО + dat	**стреля́ть по чему́-н**	*to shoot at*

Note: used if the target is a moving or mobile one, or if random shots are fired at a target; cf **стреля́ть в** + acc, 9.3.1)

	ударя́ть/уда́рить кого́-н/что́-н **по чему-н** (eg **по щеке́**)	*to hit sb/sth on sth* (eg *on the cheek*)
	скуча́ть по кому́-н/чему́-н	*to miss sb/sth*
	суди́ть по чему́-н	*to judge by sth*
	тоскова́ть по кому́-н/чему́-н	*to long for sb/sth*

9.3.4 Verbs followed by prepositions governing the instrumental

ЗА + instr verbs indicating pursuit of sth, supervision or caring for sth:

	идти́/пойти́ за	*to go for, fetch*
	наблюда́ть за	*to supervise*
	надзира́ть за	*to supervise*
	присма́тривать/присмотре́ть за	*to look after, keep an eye on*
	следи́ть за	*to track, shadow, follow, keep an eye on*
	сле́довать/после́довать за	*to go after, follow*
	уха́живать за	*to court, look after, tend to*
НАД + instr	**возвыша́ться/возвы́ситься над**	*to tower over*
	госпо́дствовать над	*to dominate, tower above*
	издева́ться над	*to mock*
	рабо́тать над	*to work at/on*
	смея́ться над	*to laugh at*
ПЕ́РЕД + instr	**извиня́ться/извини́ться пе́ред**	*to apologise to*
	преклоня́ться/преклони́ться пе́ред	*to admire, worship*
С + instr	**встреча́ться/встре́титься с**	*to meet* (by arrangement)

здоро́ваться/поздоро́ваться с	*to greet, say hello to*
знако́миться/познако́миться с	*to meet, get acquainted with*
проща́ться/попроща́ться с	*to say goodbye to*
расстава́ться/расста́ться с	*to part with*
сове́товаться/посове́товаться с	*to consult*
соглаша́ться/согласи́ться с	*to agree with*
ссо́риться/поссо́риться с	*to quarrel with*
ста́лкиваться/столкну́ться с	*to collide with, run into*

9.3.5 Verbs followed by prepositions governing the prepositional

В + prep

нужда́ться в	*to need, be in need of*
обвиня́ть/обвини́ть в	*to accuse of*
признава́ться/призна́ться в	*to confess, own up to*
сомнева́ться в	*to doubt, question*
убежда́ть(ся)/убеди́ть(ся) в	*to convince/be convinced of*
уверя́ть/уве́рить в	*to assure of*
уча́ствовать в	*to participate in, take part in*

НА + prep

говори́ть на како́м-н языке́	*to speak in a language*

Note: used when one is specifying in which language communication takes place, eg на э́той се́ссии конфере́нции **говоря́т на ру́сском**, *at this session of the conference they are speaking in Russian.*

жени́ться на	*to get married to* (of man marrying woman)
игра́ть на	*to play* (a musical instrument)
остана́вливаться/останови́ться на	*to dwell on* (eg of conversation, lecture)
ска́зываться/сказа́ться на	*to tell on, have an effect on*

О + prep

жале́ть о	*to regret, be sorry about*
забо́титься/позабо́титься о	*to worry about*
знать о	*to know about*
мечта́ть о	*to dream about*
расска́зывать/рассказа́ть о	*to recount, relate, tell*
слы́шать о	*to hear about*
сообща́ть/сообщи́ть о	*to inform about*
узнава́ть/узна́ть о	*to find out about, discover*

9.4 Rendering of English prepositions in Russian

In this section the most common Russian rendering of the principal meanings of English prepositions is given. Some examples of equivalents of the English prepositions in certain idiomatic contexts are also given.

ABOUT

(a) meaning *concerning*: **о** + prep; **про** + acc (R1); **насчёт** + gen; **относи́тельно** + gen (*with regard to*; R3, esp R3b):

a book about football	кни́га **о футбо́ле**
a film about the war	фильм **про войну́** (R1)
What about your essay?	Как **насчёт ва́шего сочине́ния**?
concerning your letter of 1 June	**относи́тельно Ва́шего письма́** от 1-го ию́ня (R3b)

(b) meaning *around* a place: **по** + dat:

She was pacing about the room.	Она́ расха́живала **по ко́мнате**.

(c) expressing approximation, rendered in one of the following ways: **о́коло** + gen; **с** + acc (R1); **приблизи́тельно**; **приме́рно**; by inversion of numeral and noun:

about two hours	**о́коло двух часо́в**
about a week	**с неде́лю** (R1)
about forty pounds	**приблизи́тельно** со́рок фу́нтов **приме́рно** со́рок фу́нтов **фу́нтов со́рок**

ABOVE

(a) meaning *over, higher than*: **над** + instr; **вы́ше** + gen:

above the clouds	**над облака́ми**
above zero	**вы́ше нуля́**

(b) in various expressions:

above all	**пре́жде всего́**
above-board	**че́стный, откры́тый**
above suspicion	**вне подозре́ния**
to get above oneself	**зазнава́ться/зазна́ться** (R1)

ACCORDING TO **по** + dat; **согла́сно** + dat (R3):

according to Tolstoy	**по Толсто́му**
according to the timetable	**по расписа́нию**
according to the treaty	**согла́сно догово́ру** (R3)

Note: *the Gospel according to Mark*, **ева́нгелие от Ма́рка**.

ACROSS

(a) indicating movement to the other side: **че́рез** + acc:

a bridge across the river	мост **че́рез реку́**
We went across the desert.	Мы перее́хали **че́рез пусты́ню**.

Note: with transitive verbs bearing the prefix **пере-** **че́рез** may be omitted, eg **переходи́ть доро́гу**, *to cross the road*.

(b) indicating position on the other side of: **на той стороне́** or **по ту сто́рону** + gen; **за** + instr (= *beyond*); **напро́тив** (= *opposite*):

There's a park across the road.	**По ту сто́рону доро́ги** располо́жен парк.

		They live across the ocean.	Они́ живу́т **за океа́ном**.
		They live across the road.	Они́ живу́т **напро́тив**.
	(c)	indicating movement over the surface of sth: **по** + dat:	
		Clouds were scudding across the sky.	Облака́ несли́сь **по не́бу**.
	(d)	crosswise, obstructing: **поперёк** + gen:	
		A lorry stood across the road.	Грузови́к стоя́л **поперёк доро́ги**.

AFTER

(a) in temporal sense: **по́сле** + gen:

after work	**по́сле рабо́ты**

(b) indicating that a period of time has elapsed: **че́рез** + acc; **спустя́** + acc; and also **по́сле** + gen:

after a while	**че́рез не́которое вре́мя**
after a week	**спустя́ неде́лю**
after a long absence	**по́сле до́лгого отсу́тствия**

(c) indicating succession: **за** + instr:

day after day	**день за днём**
page after page	**страни́ца за страни́цей**

(d) meaning *following* or *in pursuit of*: **за** + instr; **вслед за** + instr; **вслед** + dat:

to run after a tram	бежа́ть **за трамва́ем**
He got in after the driver.	Он влез **вслед за води́телем**.
She shouted after him.	Она́ крича́ла **ему́ вслед**.

(e) in certain expressions:

after all	**в конце́ концо́в**
after you	**прошу́ вас**
named after	**на́званный по** + dat; **на́званный в честь** + gen (= *named in honour of*)
to take after	**быть похо́жим/похо́жей на** + acc
the day after tomorrow	**послеза́втра**

AGAINST

(a) meaning *in opposition to*: **про́тив** + gen:

I voted against the plan.	Я проголосова́л(а) **про́тив пла́на.**

Note: with verbs indicating contest *against* may be translated by **с** + instr, eg **боро́ться с ке́м-н**, *to fight against sb.*

(b) meaning *in collision with*: **о** + acc; **на** + acc:

to bang one's head against a wall	сту́кнуться голово́й **о сте́ну**
We ran up against a problem.	Мы натолкну́лись **на пробле́му**.

(c) meaning *in contact with*: **к** + dat:

He was leaning against the door.	Он прислоня́лся **к две́ри**.

(d) indicating protection against: **от** + gen; **на слу́чай** + gen:

to protect against disease	предохраня́ть/предохрани́ть **от заболева́ния**
precautions against infection	предосторо́жности **на слу́чай инфе́кции**

ALONG

по + dat; also **вдоль** + gen (= *down the side of*):

She was walking along the path.	Она́ шла **по тропи́нке**.
We were driving along the border.	Мы е́хали **вдоль грани́цы**.

AMONG

(a) meaning *in the midst of*: **среди́** + gen:

There was a Spanish girl among the students.	**Среди́ студе́нтов** была́ испа́нка.
Among the little houses was a church.	**Среди́ до́миков** была́ це́рковь.

(b) meaning *between*: **ме́жду** + instr:

They quarrelled among themselves.	Они́ поссо́рились **ме́жду собо́й**.

(c) indicating one of a number, usually with superlative adjective: **из** + gen:

The Don is among the longest rivers in Russia.	Дон—**одна́ из са́мых дли́нных рек** Росси́и.

AT

(a) indicating location: **в** + prep; **на** + prep:

at school	**в шко́ле**
at work	**на рабо́те**

Note: **на** is used to express *at* with many Russian nouns which an English-speaker might expect would combine with **в** (see 9.1.6 for a list).

(b) indicating location *in the vicinity of* or *at* sb's house: **у** + gen:

I left my car at the station.	Я оста́вил(а) маши́ну **у вокза́ла**.
I'm having dinner at a friend's place.	Я обе́даю **у дру́га**.

(c) indicating location *behind* certain objects: **за** + instr:

at the table	**за столо́м**
at the piano	**за роя́лем**
at the wheel (of car, boat)	**за рулём**

(d) in certain expressions defining point in time: **в** + prep:

at half past one	**в полови́не** второ́го
at the beginning of April	**в нача́ле** апре́ля
at an early age	**в ра́ннем во́зрасте**
At what time?	**В кото́ром часу́**?

(e) in other expressions defining point in time, including minutes past the hour: **в** + acc:

at one o'clock	**в час**
at midday	**в пóлдень**
at five past two	**в пять** минýт трéтьего
at that time	**в то врéмя**
at a given moment	**в дáнный момéнт**
at dusk	**в сýмерки**

Note: in expressions indicating time before the hour *at* is not translated, eg *at five to ten*, **без пяти́ дéсять**.

(f) in yet other expressions defining point in time: **на** + prep:

at dawn	**на зарé**
	на рассвéте
at sunset	**на закáте**

(g) in the following expressions of time: **на** + acc:

at Christmas	**на Рождествó**
at Easter	**на Пáсху**

(h) indicating direction of an action: **в** + acc; **на** + acc:

to shoot at sth	**стреля́ть во чтó-н**
to throw sth at sb	**бросáть/брóсить** чтó-н **в когó-н**
to look at sth	**смотрéть/посмотрéть** на чтó-н
to point at sth	**укáзывать/указáть на** чтó-н

(i) in miscellaneous other expressions:

at 100°	**при ста грáдусах**
at 100 kilometres per hour	**со скóростью сто** киломéтров в час
at any price	**любóй ценóй**
at one's own expense	**за свой счёт**
at first sight	**на пéрвый взгляд**
at home	**дóма**
at last	**наконéц**
at least	**по крáйней мéре**
at leisure	**на досýге**
at night	**нóчью**
at once	**срáзу**
at the request of	**по прóсьбе**

BECAUSE OF **из-за** + gen (esp for negative reason); **благодаря́** + dat (= *thanks to*); **вслéдствие** + gen (= *owing to*; more formal, R2/3)

because of an earthquake	**из-за землетрясéния**
thanks to your foresight	**благодаря́ вáшей предусмотри́тельности**

		Owing to the rain the fair did not take place.	**Вслéдствие дождя́** я́рмарка не состоя́лась.
BEFORE	(a)	in a temporal sense: **до** + gen (= *previous to, earlier than*); **пéред** + instr (= *[just] before*):	
		before the revolution	**до револю́ции**
		long before	**задóлго до**
		We changed before dinner.	Мы переодéлись **пéред обéдом**.
	(b)	when *before* is followed by an English gerund it may be translated by **пéред** + a verbal noun or by **прéжде чем** + infin, eg	
		before leaving	**пéред отъéздом**
		before replying	**прéжде чем отвéтить**
	(c)	indicating location: **пéред** + instr:	
		You see before you a list.	Вы ви́дите **пéред собóй** спи́сок.
		before the court	**пéред судóм**
	(d)	in other expressions:	
		before long	**скóро**
		before now	**рáньше**
		before the other pupils	**впереди́ други́х ученикóв**
		before witnesses	**при свидéтелях**
		the day before yesterday	**позавчерá**
BEHIND	(a)	indicating motion behind: **за** + acc:	
		The sun went behind a cloud.	Сóлнце зашлó **за óблако**.
		He put his hands behind his back.	Он заложи́л рýки **зá спину**.
	(b)	indicating location: **за** + instr:	
		She was walking behind me.	Онá шла **за мной**.
		He was hiding behind a tree.	Он пря́тался **за дéревом**.
	(c)	in other senses and expressions:	
		She is behind the other girls in her class.	Онá **отстаёт от други́х дéвушек** в клáссе.
		The team is behind the captain.	Комáнда **поддéрживает** капитáна.
		What's behind this?	**Что за э́тим крóется**?
BELOW/ BENEATH	(a)	indicating motion below: **под** + acc:	
		The swimmer dived below the water.	Пловéц нырнýл **под вóду**.
	(b)	indicating location: **под** + instr:	
		below ground	**под землёй**
		below the surface	**под повéрхностью**

(c) meaning *lower than, inferior to*: **ни́же** + gen:

below average	**ни́же сре́днего**
below a captain in rank	**ни́же капита́на** по ра́нгу
beneath criticism	**ни́же вся́кой кри́тики**
beneath my dignity	**ни́же моего́ досто́инства**

BEYOND

= *behind* in the senses described in (a) and (b) above; also in certain expressions, eg

beyond belief	**невероя́тно**
beyond one's means	**не по сре́дствам**
beyond reach	**вне досяга́емости**
beyond one's understanding	**вы́ше понима́ния**

BY

(a) indicating agent or instrument or means of transport: instrumental case with no preposition:

The play was written by Chekhov.	Пье́са была́ напи́сана **Че́ховым**.
The building was destroyed by a fire.	Зда́ние бы́ло уничто́жено **пожа́ром**.
by train	**по́ездом**

Note: in phrases of the following sort, which lack a verb, the genitive may be used:

a play by Chekhov	пье́са **Че́хова**
a speech by the president	речь **президе́нта**

(b) meaning *in accordance with*, and also indicating means of communication: **по** + dat:

by nature	**по приро́де**
by origin	**по происхожде́нию**
by this clock	**по э́тим часа́м**
by television	**по телеви́дению**

(c) meaning *in the vicinity of*: **у** + gen; **о́коло** + gen; **во́зле** + gen; **ря́дом с** + instr (= *next to*); **вдоль** + gen (= *alongside*):

to sit by the window	сиде́ть **у/о́коло окна́**
She was standing by the bus-stop.	Она́ стоя́ла **у/о́коло авто́бусной остано́вки**.
She was sitting by me.	Она́ сиде́ла **во́зле меня́**.
The shop is by the theatre.	Магази́н нахо́дится **ря́дом с теа́тром.**
a track by the river	доро́жка **вдоль реки́**

(d) meaning *past*: **ми́мо** + gen:

She went by the bank.	Она́ прошла́ **ми́мо ба́нка**.

(e) meaning *by way of*: **че́рез** + acc:

She came in by the side entrance.	Она́ вошла́ **че́рез боково́й вход**.

(f) meaning *not after*: **к** + dat:

by Saturday	**к суббо́те**
It always snows by Christmas.	Всегда́ идёт снег **к Рождеству́**.

(g) indicating a margin of difference, and also expressing multiplication, division or combination of dimensions: **на** + acc:

older by one week	ста́рше **на одну́ неде́лю**
They increased my salary by a thousand pounds.	Увели́чили мою́ зарпла́ту **на ты́сячу** фу́нтов.
ten by five	де́сять **на пять**

(h) after verbs meaning *to take hold of*: **за** + acc:

He took her by the hand.	Он взял её **за́ руку**.
I seized him by the neck.	Я схвати́л(а) его́ **за ше́ю**.

(i) in miscellaneous other expressions:

by chance	**случа́йно**
by means of	**посре́дством** + gen; **путём** + gen
by no means	**во́все не**; **отню́дь не** (R3)
by mistake	**по оши́бке**
by the way	**ме́жду про́чим/кста́ти**
to know sb by sight	**знать кого́-н в лицо́**
to learn sth by heart	**вы́учить что́-н наизу́сть**
to pay by the month	**плати́ть/заплати́ть поме́сячно**
one by one	**оди́н за одни́м**
step by step	**шаг за ша́гом**

DOWN

(a) meaning *along*: **по** + dat:

down the corridor	**по коридо́ру**
He is going down the road.	Он идёт **по доро́ге**.

(b) meaning *descending along*: **вниз по** + dat; **с** + gen:

I am going downstairs.	Иду́ **вниз (по ле́стнице)**.
downstream	**вниз по тече́нию**
They came down the hill.	Они́ спусти́лись **с горы́**.

DURING

(a) meaning *at some point in*: **во вре́мя** + gen:

He died during the war.	Он у́мер **во вре́мя войны́**.
I left during the interval.	Я ушёл/ушла́ **во вре́мя антра́кта**.

(b) meaning *throughout, in the course of*: **в тече́ние** + gen; **на протяже́нии** + gen; these expressions are used mainly with nouns which have temporal meaning:

During the 80s the USSR was collapsing.	**В тече́ние восьмидеся́тых годо́в** СССР распада́лся.

		During the last century Russian literature flourished.	**На протяже́нии про́шлого ве́ка** процвета́ла ру́сская литерату́ра.
	(c)	meaning *in the reign/rule/time of*: **при** + prep:	
		censorship during the reign of Nicholas	цензу́ра **при Никола́е**
		the terror during Stalin's rule	терро́р **при Ста́лине**

EXCEPT FOR

кро́ме + gen; **за исключе́нием** + gen (= *with the exception of*); **исключа́я** + acc (= *excepting*; R3):

Everybody left except me.	Все ушли́ **кро́ме меня́**.
All the students passed the exam except for one.	Все студе́нты **за исключе́нием одного́** сда́ли экза́мен.
All the conditions were agreed except for one.	Все усло́вия бы́ли согласо́ваны **исключа́я одно́**.

FOR

(a) indicating benefit, purpose, suitability or unsuitability: **для** + gen:

a present for you	пода́рок **для тебя́**
clothes for big people	оде́жда **для люде́й** больши́х разме́ров
The book is useful for foreigners.	Уче́бник поле́зен **для иностра́нцев**.
Polluted air is bad for one's health.	Загрязнённый во́здух вре́ден **для здоро́вья**.

Note: with verbs, or when a verb is understood, the person benefiting may be in the dative, eg

She bought a tie for me.	Она́ купи́ла **мне** га́лстук.
There's a letter for you.	**Вам** письмо́. (R1)

(b) expressing duration, time spent doing sth or distance covered: accusative case with no preposition; **в тече́ние** + gen:

He lay for a week in hospital.	Он пролежа́л **неде́лю** в больни́це.
I have been living here for a year.	Я здесь живу́ **оди́н год**.
I ran (for) a mile.	Я пробежа́л(а) **ми́лю**.
for a month	**в тече́ние ме́сяца**

(c) indicating the amount of time action is expected to last, or that sth is arranged for a certain time or intended for a certain purpose: **на** + acc:

He has gone to Moscow for a week.	Он пое́хал в Москву́ **на неде́лю**.
closed for the winter	закры́то **на́ зиму**
for a long time	**надо́лго**
forever	**навсегда́**
a meeting arranged for two o'clock	встре́ча, назна́ченная **на два** часа́
dinner for two	обе́д **на двои́х**

a house for sale	дом **на продáжу**
for example	**напримéр**

(d) meaning *in recompense of*, and also indicating support for sb or sth: **за** + acc:

I paid the cashier for the book	Я заплати́л(а) касси́рше **за кни́гу**.
We thanked them for their hospitality.	Мы поблагодари́ли их **за гостеприи́мство**.
an eye for an eye	**óко за óко**
He is voting for me.	Он голосýет **за меня́**.

(e) meaning *in quest of*: **за** + instr:

I sent for a doctor.	Я послáл(а) **за дóктором**.

(f) after many nouns indicating attitude: **к** + dat:

love for one's country	**любóвь к рóдине**
a passion for music	**страсть к мýзыке**
respect for foreigners	**уважéние к инострáнцам**

(g) in miscellaneous other expressions, eg

for and against	**за и прóтив**
for certain	**наверня́кá**
for the first time	**в пéрвый раз** **впервы́е**
for hours on end	**цéлыми часáми**
for this reason	**по э́той причи́не**
for God's sake	**рáди Бóга**
as for me	**что касáется меня́**
known for	**извéстный** + instr
once for all	**раз навсегдá**
There were no houses for miles around.	**На мнóгие ми́ли вокрýг** нé было домóв.
to cry for joy	**плáкать от рáдости**
to get married for love	**жени́ться по любви́**
He is tall for his age.	**Он высóк не по летáм**.
to ask for	**проси́ть/попроси́ть** + acc or gen or **о** + prep
to long for	**тосковáть по** + dat
to look for	**искáть** + acc or gen
to be sorry for sb	**жалéть когó-н**
to wait for	**ждать/подождáть** + acc or gen

FROM

(a) meaning *out of* (ie the opposite of **в** + acc); *originating from, made of*: **из** + gen:

We went from Moscow to Minsk.	Мы поéхали **из Москвы́** в Минск.
from afar	**издалекá**

fruit from Spain	фру́кты **из Испа́нии**
sausages made from pork	соси́ски, **сде́ланные из свини́ны**

(b) meaning *away from* (ie the opposite of **до** or **к**); expressing distance *from*; indicating person *from* whom sth originates; indicating protection, freedom, concealment, separation, difference *from*; meaning *by reason of*: **от** + gen:

The train is drawing away from the platform.	По́езд отхо́дит от **платфо́рмы**.
from here/there	**отсю́да/отту́да**
two minutes from the centre	в двух мину́тах **от це́нтра**
a present from my mother	пода́рок **от мое́й ма́тери**
protection from the gale	защи́та **от урага́на**
exemption from taxation	освобожде́ние **от нало́гов**
cut off from civilisation	отре́занный **от цивилиза́ции**
Russian architecture differs from ours.	Ру́сская архитекту́ра **отлича́ется от на́шей**.
He collapsed from exhaustion.	Он свали́лся **от изнеможе́ния**.

(c) meaning *off, down from* (ie the opposite of **на** + acc; therefore used to mean *from* before nouns in 9.1.6, на (b–e)); meaning *by reason of* in R1; and also *since*: **с** + gen:

The book fell from the shelf.	Кни́га упа́ла **с по́лки**.
from east to west	**с восто́ка на за́пад**
from the Urals	**с Ура́ла**
from above/below	**све́рху/сни́зу**
from boredom	**со ску́ки**
from 1 April	**с пе́рвого** апре́ля
from childhood	**с де́тства**

(d) indicating removal of sth that belongs to sb else: **у** + gen:

She took the toy away from the child.	Она́ отняла́ **у ребёнка** игру́шку.
He borrowed a mower from his neighbour.	Он за́нял газо̀нокоси́лку **у сосе́да**

(e) preceding a gerund: infinitive form of verb:

You are preventing me from working.	Ты меша́ешь **мне рабо́тать**.

(f) in many other expressions:

from bad to worse	**всё ху́же и ху́же**
from behind	**из-за** + gen
from generation to generation	**из поколе́ния в поколе́ние**
from time to time	**вре́мя от вре́мени**
from under	**из-под** + gen
change from a pound	**сда́ча с фу́нта**
The town dates from the tenth century.	**Го́род отно́сится к деся́тому ве́ку**.

	a year from now	**чéрез год**

IN

(a) indicating location; indicating a point in a month, decade, year, century, time of life, or in the past, present or future; also describing attire: **в** + prep:

in the garden	**в садý**
I read it in a newspaper.	Я читáл(а) э́то **в газéте**.
in March	**в мáрте**
in 1994	**в** ты́сяча девятьсóт девянóсто **четвёртом годý**
in the last decade of the century	**в послéднем десятилéтии** вéка
in the twentieth century	**в двадцáтом вéке**
in old age	**в стáрости**
in the future	**в бýдущем**
in a blue shirt	**в си́ней рубáшке**

(b) indicating motion *into* or duration of an action or period: **в** + acc:

She went in the canteen.	Онá вошлá **в столóвую**.
In the Golden Age Russian writers created a rich literature.	**В золотýю эпóху** рýсские писáтели сóздали богáтую литератýру.

(c) expressing *in* with periods of the day and seasons of the year; expressing *in* in some adverbial phrases of manner; indicating material used in some action; also indicating method of arranging people or things: instrumental case with no preposition:

in the morning	**ýтром**
in winter	**зимóй**
in a loud voice	**грóмким гóлосом**
to write in ink	писáть **черни́лами**
in small groups	**небольши́ми грýппами**
in rows	**рядáми**

(d) meaning *in* with certain nouns listed in 9.1.6, на (b–e); defining time in relation to the beginning of a certain period; also in certain set phrases: **на** + prep:

in the street	**на ýлице**
in Cuba	**на Кýбе**
in the north	**на сéвере**
in the war	**на войнé**
in the kitchen (in order to cook)	**на кýхне**
in the first minute of the second half	**на пéрвой минýте** вторóго тáйма
in my lifetime	**на моём векý**
in old age	**на стáрости лет** (R1)

(e) indicating time taken to complete an action or meaning *over* a period: **за** + acc:

Five centimetres of rain fell in one day.	**За оди́н день** вы́пало пять сантиме́тров дождя́.

(f) indicating time after a certain interval: **че́рез** + acc:

I'll come back in a week.	Я верну́сь **че́рез неде́лю**.

(g) meaning *on the subject of*: **по** + dat:

an exam in geography	**экза́мен по геогра́фии**
research in electronics	**иссле́дования по электро́нике**

(h) meaning *in the reign/time of*, and in phrases indicating attendant circumstances: **при** + prep:

in Pushkin's time	**при Пу́шкине**
in the Brezhnev era	**при Бре́жневе**
in complete silence	**при по́лном молча́нии**

(i) in other expressions:

in advance	**зара́нее**
in all respects	**во всех отноше́ниях**
in answer to	**в отве́т на** + acc
in any case	**во вся́ком слу́чае**
in the circumstances	**при э́тих усло́виях**
in custody	**под аре́стом**
in the end	**в конце́ концо́в**
in the evenings	**по вечера́м**
in general	**вообще́**
in good time	**заблаговре́менно** (R3)
in honour of	**в честь** + gen
in memory of	**в па́мять** + gen
in a minute	**сейча́с**
in the name of	**от и́мени** + gen
in my opinion	**по моему́ мне́нию** **по-мо́ему** (R1/2)
in respect of	**по отноше́нию к** + dat (R3)
in spite of	**несмотря́ на** + acc
in succession	**подря́д**
in turn	**по о́череди**
to believe in God	**ве́рить в Бо́га**
blind in one eye	**слепо́й/слепа́я на оди́н глаз**
deaf in one ear	**глухо́й/глуха́я на одно́ у́хо**
I'm in my twenties.	**Мне за два́дцать.**
an interest in politics	**интере́с к поли́тике**
just in case	**на вся́кий слу́чай**
to be in power	**быть у вла́сти**
The word ends in a soft sign.	**Сло́во конча́ется на мя́гкий знак.**

INSIDE (a) indicating location: **в** + prep; **внутри́** + gen:

inside the house	**в до́ме**
We do not know what is happening inside the country.	Мы не зна́ем, что̀ происхо́дит **внутри́ страны́**.

(b) indicating motion: generally **в** + acc:

to go inside the house	**входи́ть/войти́ в дом**

INSTEAD OF **вме́сто** + gen:

Have some juice instead of water.	Вы́пейте со́ка **вме́сто воды́**.

Note: this preposition should not be confused with **вме́сте**, *together*.

INTO (a) generally **в** + acc:

They went into the hall.	Они́ вошли́ **в зал**.
to fall into a trap	попада́ть/попа́сть **в лову́шку**
The water turned into ice.	Вода́ преврати́лась **в лёд**.

(b) with some nouns denoting open spaces (see 9.1.6, на (b–c)); after certain verbs with the prefix **на-**; indicating division: **на** + acc:

She came out into the street.	Она́ вы́шла **на у́лицу**.
I cut the loaf into pieces.	Я разре́зал(а) хлеб **на куски́**.

OF (a) expressing possession or quantity and in other functions: genitive case with no preposition:

the roof of the house	**кры́ша до́ма**
the end of the lecture	**коне́ц ле́кции**
a slice of bread	**ломо́ть хле́ба**
a litre of beer	**литр пи́ва**
a bunch of keys	**свя́зка ключе́й**
the rector of the institute	**ре́ктор институ́та**

(b) expressing identity or definition: noun in apposition, or use of adjective:

the city of London	**го́род Ло́ндон**
the Isle of Wight	**о́стров Уайт**
the month of May	**ме́сяц май**
the University of Oxford	**О́ксфордский университе́т**
the Battle of Borodino	**Бороди́нское сраже́ние**
the Sea of Azov	**Азо́вское мо́ре**
Lawrence of Arabia	**Ло́уренс арави́йский**

(c) meaning *out of* or *consisting of*; also indicating material of which sth is made: **из** + gen:

one of the students	**оди́н/одна́ из студе́нтов**
some of them	**не́которые из них**
a family of four	семья́ **из четырёх челове́к**
a table made of wood	стол **из де́рева**

(d) indicating amount, capacity, dimension: **в** + acc:

an article of twenty pages	статья́ **в два́дцать** страни́ц
an army of 100,000 men	а́рмия **в сто** ты́сяч солда́т
a building of ten stories	зда́ние **в де́сять** этаже́й
a field of three hectares	по́ле пло́щадью **в три** гекта́ра

(e) in other functions and expressions:

of course	**коне́чно**
your letter of 2 May	**Ва́ше письмо́ от второ́го ма́я**
the Battle of Stalingrad	**би́тва под Сталингра́дом**
capable of anything	**спосо́бный на всё**
characteristic of	**характе́рный для** + gen
typical of	**типи́чный для** + gen
a charge of murder	**обвине́ние в уби́йстве**
east of Moscow	**к восто́ку от Москвы́**
envy of one's neighbour	**за́висть к сосе́ду**
news of the accident	**весть об ава́рии**
a view of the forest	**вид на лес**
a copy of a document	**ко́пия с докуме́нта**
The room smells of smoke.	**В ко́мнате па́хнет табако́м.**

OFF

(a) meaning *off* the surface of sth, *down from*: **с** + gen:

I took the saucepan off the stove.	Я снял(а́) кастрю́лю **с плиты́.**
He fell off the ladder.	Он упа́л **с ле́стницы.**

(b) meaning *at a distance from*: **от** + gen:

2 kilometres off the coast	на расстоя́нии двух киломе́тров **от бе́рега**
not far off	**недалеко́ от** **неподалёку от**

(c) indicating dispossession or removal: **у** + gen:

I borrowed a book off him.	Я взял(а́) **у него́** кни́гу почита́ть. (R1)
He broke the handle off the door	Он отби́л ру́чку **у две́ри.**

(d) in certain expressions:

off the beaten track	**по непроторённой доро́ге**
off colour (unwell)	**нездоро́вый/нездоро́вая**
(not in form)	**не в фо́рме**
off work	**не на рабо́те**
goods at 10% off	**това́ры на де́сять проце́нтов** ни́же обы́чной цены́
Keep off the grass.	**Не ходи́ть по траве́.**
She's off her food.	**У неё нет аппети́та.**
He's off his rocker.	**Он спя́тил с ума́.** (R1)

ON

(a) indicating location: **на** + prep:

He's sitting on a stool.	Он сиди́т **на табуре́тке**.
on board	**на борту́**

(b) indicating movement *on to*: **на** + acc:

He climbed on the roof.	Он влез **на кры́шу**.
They got on the train.	Они́ се́ли **на по́езд**.

(c) *on* a day of the week: **в** + acc:

on Wednesday	**в сре́ду**
on that day	**в тот день**

(d) repeatedly *on* a certain day: **по** + dat pl:

on Saturdays	**по суббо́там**
on free days	**по свобо́дным дням**

(e) expressing a date: genitive case with no preposition:

on 1 March	**пе́рвого** ма́рта
on 22 June	два́дцать **второ́го** ию́ня

(f) in certain other expressions of time: **на** + acc:

on the following day	**на сле́дующий день**
on the fourth day	**на четвёртый день**
on this occasion	**на э́тот раз**

(g) meaning *immediately after, on the expiry of*: **по́сле** + gen; **по** + prep (R3):

on arrival	**по́сле прие́зда**
on expiry of the visa	**по истече́нии** ви́зы
On graduating she went abroad.	**По оконча́нии** университе́та, она́ пое́хала за грани́цу.

(h) indicating means of transport; also in certain expressions of time: instrumental case with no preposition:

on a bus	**авто́бусом**
on horseback	**верхо́м**
on a spring evening	**весе́нним ве́чером**

(i) meaning *on the subject of*: **по** + dat; **о** + prep:

a lecture on geology	ле́кция **по геоло́гии**
an article on Blok	статья́ **о Бло́ке**

(j) indicating a means of communication: **по** + dat:

I heard about it on the radio.	Я слы́шал(а) об э́том **по ра́дио**.

(k) in other meanings and expressions:

on average	**в сре́днем**
on no account	**ни в ко́ем слу́чае**
on behalf of	**от и́мени** + gen

on the contrary	**наоборо́т**
on leave	**в о́тпуске**
on the left	**сле́ва**
on the right	**спра́ва**
on the occasion of	**по слу́чаю** + gen
on the one hand	**с одно́й стороны́**
on the other hand	**с друго́й стороны́**
on one condition	**при одно́м усло́вии**
on purpose	**наро́чно**
on the quiet	**потихо́ньку** (R1)
on time	**во́время**
on time (according to timetable)	**по расписа́нию**
on the way home	**по доро́ге домо́й**
cash on delivery	**с упла́той при доста́вке**
The house is on fire.	**Дом гори́т.**
I had no money on me.	**У меня́ не́ было де́нег с собо́й.**
The workers are on strike.	**Рабо́чие басту́ют.**
to work on sth	**рабо́тать над че́м-н**

OPPOSITE

про́тив + gen; **напро́тив** + gen:

They were sitting opposite each other.	Они́ сиде́ли друг **про́тив дру́га.**
He is standing opposite the Kremlin.	Он стои́т **напро́тив Кремля́.**

Note: in the meaning of *opposite* **про́тив** and **напро́тив** are interchangeable, but only **про́тив** may mean *against.*

OUT OF

(a) in most meanings: **из** + gen:

She came out of the shop.	Она́ вы́шла **из магази́на.**
He took a coin out of his pocket.	Он вы́нул моне́ту **из карма́на.**
a chapter out of a novel	глава́ **из рома́на**
four out of five students	че́тверо **из пяти́ студе́нтов**
It's made out of iron.	Сде́лано **из желе́за.**

(b) meaning *outside*: **вне** + gen; **за** + instr (= *beyond*):

out of control	**вне контро́ля**
out of danger	**вне опа́сности**
out of earshot	**вне преде́лов слы́шимости**
out of reach/range	**вне преде́лов досяга́емости**
out of sight	**вне по́ля зре́ния**
out of turn	**вне о́череди**
out of town	**за́ городом**
out of the country	**за грани́цей**

(c) indicating cause or motive: **из** + gen; **от** + gen; **с** + gen (R1):

out of respect for you	**из уваже́ния** к вам
out of pity	**из/от жа́лости**
out of spite	**от зло́сти** (R2)
	со зло́сти (R1)

(d) in certain other expressions:

out of breath	**запыха́вшийся**
out of doors	**на у́лице/на дворе́**
(in the open air)	**на откры́том во́здухе**
out of fashion	**не в мо́де**
out of order	**не в поря́дке**
(not working)	**неиспра́вный/не рабо́тает**
Out of my sight!	**Убира́йся!**
out of work	**без рабо́ты**
to get out of bed	**встава́ть/встать с посте́ли**
We're out of bread.	**У нас ко́нчился хлеб.**
It's out of the question.	**Об э́том не мо́жет** быть и ре́чи.

OUTSIDE

(a) meaning *in the vicinity of*: **о́коло** + gen; **у** + gen; **пе́ред** + instr (= *in front of*):

I met her outside the park.	Я встре́тился с ней **о́коло/у па́рка**.
The car's outside the house.	Маши́на стои́т **пе́ред до́мом**.

(b) meaning *on the outside of, beyond*: **вне** + gen; **за** + instr; **за преде́лами** + gen (= *beyond the bounds of*):

It's outside my competence.	Э́то **вне моей компете́нции**.
There was a policeman outside the window.	**За окно́м** стоя́л полице́йский.
He is not known outside Russia.	Он неизве́стен **за преде́лами Росси́и**.

OVER

(a) meaning *across*: **че́рез** + acc; **за** + acc:

a bridge over the river	мост **че́рез ре́ку́**
He crossed over the threshold.	Он перешёл **за поро́г**.
to throw overboard	выки́дывать/вы́кинуть **за́ борт**

Note: **че́рез** may be omitted when the verb bears the prefix **пере-**, which may carry the same meaning (see the second example above; see also 9.1.2).

(b) indicating location *beyond, on the other side of*: **за** + instr; **по ту сто́рону** + gen:

I heard a voice over the fence.	Я услы́шал(а) го́лос **за и́згородью**.
They live overseas.	Они́ живу́т **за́ морем**.
the forest over the border	лес **по ту сто́рону грани́цы**

(c) meaning *above*: **над** + instr:

A chandelier hangs over the table.	**Над столо́м** виси́т лю́стра.
A threat hangs over us.	**Над на́ми** виси́т угро́за.

(d) meaning *over the top of*: **пове́рх** + gen:

to look over one's spectacles	смотре́ть **пове́рх очко́в**

(e) meaning *on to*: **на** + acc:

She drew a blanket over the child. — Она́ натяну́ла одея́ло **на ребёнка**.

(f) meaning *across the surface* of sth; also *by* a means of communication: **по** + dat:

A boat sped over the water. — Ка́тер помча́лся **по воде́**.
all over the world — **по всему́ све́ту**
over the radio — **по ра́дио**

(g) meaning in the course of a certain period: **в тече́ние** + gen; **за** + acc:

The situation deteriorated over many years. — Ситуа́ция ухудша́лась **в тече́ние мно́гих лет**.
They have all fallen ill over the last week. — Они́ все заболе́ли **за после́днюю неде́лю**.

Note: **в тече́ние** emphasises duration and therefore occurs with an imperfective verb, whilst **за** emphasises the completed nature of the event and therefore tends to dictate the use of a perfective.

(h) meaning *more than*: **бо́льше** + gen; **свы́ше** + gen (used with numerals); **сверх** + gen (= *over and above, in excess of*):

He drank over a litre of wine. — Он вы́пил **бо́льше ли́тра** вина́.
over a million voters — **свы́ше миллио́на** избира́телей
over (and above) the norm — **сверх но́рмы**

(i) in other expressions:

over a cup of tea — **за ча́шкой ча́я**
It's over my head. — **Э́то вы́ше моего́ понима́ния.**
to go head over heels — **полете́ть кувырко́м**
to stumble over sth — **спотыка́ться/споткну́ться** о что́-н

PAST

(a) indicating motion alongside and beyond sth: **ми́мо** + gen:

He ran past me. — Он пробежа́л **ми́мо меня́**.

(b) indicating location *beyond*: **за** + instr:

The theatre is past the church. — Теа́тр нахо́дится **за це́рковью**.

(c) meaning *after*: **по́сле** + gen; **за** + acc; **по́зже** + gen:

past midnight — **по́сле полу́ночи**; **за́ полночь**
She's past fifty. — Ей **за пятьдеся́т**.
It's past ten o'clock. — **По́зже десяти́.**

(d) in expressions of time: no preposition:

ten past one — **де́сять мину́т второ́го**
at half past six — **в полови́не седьмо́го**

ROUND

(a) indicating rotation and encirclement: **вокру́г** + gen; **круго́м** (+ gen; encirclement only):

All the guests were sitting round the table.	Все го́сти сиде́ли **вокру́г стола́**.
The earth revolves round the sun.	Земля́ враща́ется **вокру́г со́лнца**.

(b) expressing approximation: **о́коло** + gen:

round(about) midnight	**о́коло полу́ночи**
round a thousand dollars	**о́коло ты́сячи до́лларов**

Note: the adverbs **приблизи́тельно**, *approximately*, and **приме́рно**, *roughly*, may also be used, with no preposition, to express approximation with numbers, eg **приме́рно сто фу́нтов**, *round a hundred pounds*.

(c) expressing motion in various directions (often with indeterminate verbs of motion): **по** + dat:

She's walking round the garden.	Она́ хо́дит **по са́ду**.
His things are scattered round the room.	Его́ ве́щи разбро́саны **по ко́мнате**.

(d) after verbs bearing the prefix **об-** *round* may have no prepositional equivalent:

He walked round the puddle.	**Он обошёл лу́жу.**
The nurse put pillows round him.	**Медсестра́ обложи́ла его́ поду́шками.**

THROUGH

(a) indicating passage through: **че́рез** + acc (also meaning *via*); **сквозь** + acc (often implying difficulty); **в** + acc:

I went through France.	Я прое́хал(а) **че́рез** Фра́нцию.
We went to Moscow through Minsk.	Мы прое́хали в Москву́ **че́рез Минск**.
He squeezed through the crowd.	Он проти́снулся **сквозь толпу́**.
through a thick fog	**сквозь густо́й тума́н**
He was looking through the window.	Он смотре́л **че́рез/в окно́**.

(b) meaning *around, over, through* an element: **по** + dat:

He was walking through the streets.	Он шёл **по у́лицам**.
The ball was flying through the air.	Мяч лете́л **по во́здуху**.

(c) meaning *for the duration of, throughout*: accusative case with no preposition:

It rained all through/throughout the day.	**Весь день** шёл дождь.
Work will continue through the winter.	Рабо́та бу́дет продолжа́ться **всю зи́му**.

(d) meaning *as a result of*: **благодаря́** + dat (= *thanks to* a favourable cause); **из-за** + gen (= *because of* some unfavourable cause); **по** + dat (= *for* some abstract reason):

through far-sightedness	**благодаря́ предусмотри́тельности**
He had to leave work through illness.	Ему́ пришло́сь уйти́ с рабо́ты **из-за боле́зни**.
to know through experience	знать **по о́пыту**

(e) in other expressions:

to get through an exam	**сдать экза́мен**
to go through a fortune	**прома́тывать/промота́ть состоя́ние**
to see through sb	**ви́деть кого́-н насквозь**

TO

(a) expressing indirect object: dative case without any preposition:

He gave his brother a book.	Он дал **бра́ту** кни́гу.
Tell us what to do.	Скажи́те **нам**, что̀ де́лать.
Greetings to you.	Приве́т **тебе́/вам**!

(b) indicating direction of movement: **в** + acc; **на** + acc (with certain nouns; see 9.1.6, на (b–e)); **к** + dat (with persons and with sth approached but not entered):

We are going to Russia.	Мы е́дем **в Росси́ю**.
She is going to a concert.	Она́ идёт **на конце́рт**.
to the left/right	**нале́во/напра́во**
I am going to the rector.	Я иду́ **к ре́ктору**.
Come to the table.	Подойди́(те) **к столу́**.
to the south of Voronezh	**к ю́гу** от Воро́нежа

(c) indicating distance, limit or extent: **до** + gen; **по** + acc (= *up to and including*):

the distance from London to Moscow	расстоя́ние от Ло́ндона **до Москвы́**
to the end	**до конца́**
to a certain extent	**до не́которой сте́пени**
He got soaked to the skin.	Он промо́к **до мо́зга** косте́й.
to 1 May	**по пе́рвое** ма́я
He was standing (up) to his knees in water.	Он стоя́л **по коле́ни** в воде́.

(d) indicating attachment, membership, proximity: **к** + dat:

to add five to ten	прибавля́ть/приба́вить пять **к десяти́**
to belong [expressing membership] *to a club*	принадлежа́ть **к клу́бу**
a preface to a book	предисло́вие **к кни́ге**
shoulder to shoulder	плечо́м **к плечу́**

(e) expressing time *to* the hour: a construction with **без** + gen:

five to ten	**без пяти́ де́сять**

(f) meaning *to the accompaniment of* a sound: **под** + acc:

to dance to a record	танцева́ть **под пласти́нку**

(g) in miscellaneous expressions:

to my surprise	**к моему́ удивле́нию**
an answer to sth	**отве́т на что́-н**
a tendency to	**скло́нность к** + dat
a claim to sth	**прете́нзия на что́-н**
a right to sth	**пра́во на что́-н**
an exception to a rule	**исключе́ние из пра́вила**
the key to a door	**ключ от две́ри**
compared to	**по сравне́нию с** + instr
harmful to	**вре́дный для** + gen
near to	**бли́зкий от** + gen
similar to	**похо́жий на** + acc
a visit to the Ukraine	**посеще́ние Украи́ны**
I have been to Moscow.	**Я был(а́) в Москве́.**

TOWARDS

(a) in most meanings: **к** + dat:

They were travelling towards the lake.	Они́ е́хали **к о́зеру**.
He was standing with his back towards me.	Он стоя́л **ко мне** спино́й.
attitude towards	**отноше́ние к**

(b) in other expressions:

towards evening	**под ве́чер**
responsibility towards	**отве́тственность пе́ред** + instr

UNDER

(a) indicating location: **под** + instr:

to sit under the trees	сиде́ть **под дере́вьями**
to be under suspicion	быть **под подозре́нием**

(b) indicating motion: **под** + acc:

She shoved a note under the door.	Она́ подсу́нула запи́ску **под дверь**.

(c) meaning *according to*: **по** + dat:

under Roman law	**по ри́мскому пра́ву**

(d) in other expressions:

under five dollars	**ме́ньше пяти́ до́лларов**
children under five	**де́ти до пяти́ лет**
under those circumstances	**при тех обстоя́тельствах**

		under Lenin	**при Ле́нине**
		under one's arm	**под мы́шкой**
		under repair	**в ремо́нте**
		The matter is under consideration.	**Де́ло рассма́тривается**. (R3b)

UNTIL

(a) in most contexts: **до** + gen:

until Wednesday	**до среды́**
until three o'clock	**до трёх часо́в**

(b) meaning *up to and including*: **по** + acc:

The visa is valid until 1 March.	Ви́за действи́тельна **по пе́рвое** ма́рта.

(c) with negated verb: **то́лько**:

I shall not do it until tomorrow.	**Я то́лько за́втра сде́лаю** э́то.

UP

(a) indicating location: **на** + prep:

The cat is up the tree.	Ко́шка сиди́т **на де́реве**.

(b) indicating motion: **на** + acc; **(вверх) по** + dat:

He went up the hill.	Он пошёл **на́ гору**.
The smoke goes up the chimney.	Дым поднима́ется **по трубе́**.
They sailed up the Volga.	Они́ поплы́ли **вверх по Во́лге**.

WITH

(a) in the majority of meanings, especially *in the company of, together with*: **с** + instr:

I work with him.	Я рабо́таю **с ним**.
She went there with a friend.	Она́ пошла́ туда́ **с дру́гом**.
a man with a red face	мужчи́на **с румя́ным лицо́м**
with pleasure	**с удово́льствием**
I agree with you.	**Я соглаша́юсь с ва́ми.**

(b) indicating instrument; also indicating what sth is covered or surrounded by: instrumental case without a preposition:

She is eating with a spoon.	Она́ ест **ло́жкой**.
I saw it with my own eyes.	Я ви́дел(а) э́то **свои́ми глаза́ми**.
The lake is covered with ice.	О́зеро **покры́то льдом**.
a house surrounded with flowers	дом **окружённый цвета́ми**

(c) indicating presence at sb's home, or entrustment of sth to sb: **у** + gen:

I lodge with them.	Я снима́ю ко́мнату **у них**.
I left my things with the concierge.	Я оста́вил(а) свои́ ве́щи **у вахтёра**.

(d) indicating source or cause: **от** + gen:

He is trembling with cold.	Он дрожит **от холода**.
She is blushing with shame.	Она краснеет **от стыда**.

(e) in miscellaneous other functions:

with all one's heart	**от всей души**
with the exception of	**за исключением** + gen
with regard to	**в связи с** + instr
	по отношению к + dat (R3)
	что касается + gen
with your consent	**с вашего согласия**
with your permission	**с вашего разрешения**
to go with/match	**подходить к** + dat
satisfied with	**доволен/довольна** + instr
to speak with a stutter	**говорить заикаясь**
Down with the government!	**Долой правительство!**
What's it to do with me?	**При чём тут я?**

10 Syntax

10.1 Use of the cases

A sound understanding of the functions of the cases in Russian is crucial to an ability to master the language, for grammatical relationships in the sentence, and therefore meaning, depend on inflection. The sections which follow examine the basic function or functions of each of the six cases of modern Russian and also the use of those cases with verbs. The use of the case after prepositions, some of which may invariably govern it and others of which govern it when they have certain meanings, is examined thoroughly in 9.1–3.

10.1.1 Use of the nominative

(a) The nominative is the case used to indicate the subject of a clause:

Кни́га лежа́ла на столе́.	*The book lay on the table.*
В саду́ сиде́ла **ко́шка**.	*A cat was sitting in the garden.*
Ива́н зовёт бра́та.	*Ivan is calling his brother.*

Note: in Russian the subject may follow the verb; it is inflection, not word order (on which see 10.14), that makes clear the grammatical relationships in the sentence.

(b) The complement of the verb *to be* may also stand in the nominative when the verb *to be* is not actually stated, ie in the present tense, eg

Моя́ мать—**врач**.	*My mother is a doctor.*
Он—**грузи́н**.	*He is a Georgian.*

A nominative complement is also used when the verb form **есть** is used, in the sense of *is*, and the complement is the same as the subject (see 3.2), eg

Пра́вда есть **пра́вда**.	*The truth is the truth.*

When the verb *to be* occurs in the past tense a nominative complement may be used (although the instrumental is now preferred; see 10.1.10(e)), eg

Он был **выдаю́щийся писа́тель**.	*He was an outstanding writer.*

10.1.2 Use of the accusative

(a) The principal use of the accusative case is to express the direct object of a transitive verb, eg

Я чита́ю **кни́гу**.	*I am reading a book.*
Он пи́шет **письмо́**.	*He is writing a letter.*
Она́ лю́бит **отца́**.	*She loves her father.*

Note 1 See 10.1.3 on the animate category of nouns.

2 No reflexive verb, with the partial exception of **слу́шаться/послу́шаться** (see 10.1.5(b)), may govern the accusative.

(b) The accusative is also used, without any preposition, to express the duration of an action, the distance covered, price, and weight. In the first two meanings it often follows a verb with the prefix **про-** (see 7.3, про- (c)).

Рабо́та продолжа́лась **всю зи́му**.	*Work continued all winter.*
Они́ прое́хали **ты́сячу** киломе́тров.	*They travelled a thousand kilometres.*
Дом сто́ит **миллио́н** до́лларов.	*The house costs a million dollars.*
Маши́на ве́сит **то́нну**.	*The car weighs a tonne.*

10.1.3 Use of case to denote animate direct object

Many animate nouns must be put in the genitive case when they are used as direct objects. This usage arises from the fact that in most types of noun the nominative and accusative forms have come to coincide. Given the flexibility of Russian word order clauses in which both subject and object are animate could be ambiguous were the grammatical forms of subject and object to remain undifferentiated. (Take, eg, the hypothetical statement Ива́н уби́л брат.) By marking the object by use of the genitive form, which in all categories of noun is distinct from the accusative, no confusion can arise as to which noun is subject and which is object. (Cf the similar function of the preposition **a** to mark an animate direct object in Spanish, eg Él mató a un toro, *He killed a bull.*)

Animate nouns include those denoting people, animals, birds, reptiles, fish and insects, and embrace all three genders. The following table shows which types of Russian animate noun have to be marked in this way when they function as the direct object of a transitive verb.

accusative form preserved	genitive form required	
	masculine singular	
	бра́та	*brother*
	ти́гра	*tiger*
	орла́	*eagle*
	пито́на	*python*
	ка́рпа	*carp*
	паука́	*spider*

		masculine plural	
		сыновéй	*sons*
		слонóв	*elephants*
		сóколов	*falcons*
		крокоди́лов	*crocodiles*
		осетрóв	*sturgeons*
		муравьёв	*ants*
feminine singular and masculine singular in -а/-я		feminine plural	
жéнщину	*woman*	**дéвушек**	*girls*
лóшадь	*horse*	**собáк**	*dogs*
лáсточку	*swallow*	**сорóк**	*magpies*
змею́	*snake*	**кобр**	*cobras*
акýлу	*shark*	**щук**	*pikes*
бáбочку	*butterfly*	**пчёл**	*bees*
Сáшу	*Sasha*		
дя́дю	*uncle*		
neuter singular		neuter plural	
		должностны́х лиц	*officials*
млекопитáющее	*mammal*	**млекопитáющих**	*mammals*
пресмыкáющееся	*reptile*	**пресмыкáющихся**	*reptiles*
насекóмое	*insect*	**насекóмых**	*insects*
miscellaneous		miscellaneous	
толпý	*crowd*		
нарóд	*a people*		
войскá (n pl)	*troops*		
труп	*dead body, corpse*	**мертвецá**	*dead man*
		покóйника	*the deceased*
дáму	*queen* (cards)	**ферзя́**	*queen* (chess)
		короля́	*king* (cards, chess)
		тузá	*ace*
		валéта	*jack*
		(пусти́ть) **бумáжного змéя**	*to fly a kite*

Note 1 The words **Марс**, **Меркýрий**, **Нептýн**, **Плутóн**, **Урáн**, **[Ю]пи́тер** are treated as inanimate when they denote planets in the solar system but as animate when they denote the classical gods after whom the planets are named, eg наблюдáть **Юпи́тер**, *to observe Jupiter*; прогнéвать **Юпи́тера**, *to anger Jupiter*.

2 Usage is less clear-cut when the direct object denotes a low or as yet unborn form of life, eg **бактéрия**, *bacterium*; **баци́лла**, *bacillus*; **зарóдыш**, *foetus*; **личи́нка**, *larva, grub*; **микрóб**, *microbe*; **эмбриóн**, *embryo*. In everyday speech such objects tend to be treated as inanimate, eg изучáть **бактéрии**, *to study bacteria*, but in scientific parlance they may be treated as animate (**бактéрий**).

10.1.4 Basic uses of the genitive

(a) To express possession, origin, relationship of part to whole, the nature, quality, measurement, or quantity *of* sth, eg

кни́га **моего́ бра́та**	*my brother's book*
стихи́ **Пу́шкина**	*Pushkin's poetry*
пе́рвый ваго́н **по́езда**	*the first coach of the train*
мужчи́на **большо́го ро́ста**	*a man of large stature*
за́пах **цвето́в**	*the scent of flowers*
метр **тка́ни**	*a metre of fabric*
литр **вина́**	*a litre of wine*

Note: the genitive case is not used in a number of contexts where English has *of* (see 9.4, *of* (b)).

(b) After words indicating quantity, eg

ма́ло **вре́мени**	*little/not much time*
мно́го **цвето́в**	*many/a lot of flowers*
немно́го **студе́нтов**	*not many/a few students*
не́сколько **пе́сен**	*a few/some/several songs*
Ско́лько **вина́**?	*How much wine?*
Сто́лько **впечатле́ний**!	*How/So many impressions!*

(c) To denote a certain quantity, some of a given object (cf Fr *du pain, de l'eau*, etc), eg

нали́ть **молока́**	*to pour some milk*
Она́ ничего́ не е́ла, то́лько вы́пила **ча́я**.	*She didn't eat anything, she just drank some tea.*

Note 1 The accusative case in such contexts would denote not *some* of the object but *the* object, eg нали́ть **молоко́**, *to pour the* (ie some specific) *milk*, perhaps the milk left in the bottle, the milk on the table.

2 A genitive form with partitive meaning is often found after verbs bearing the prefix **на-** in its meaning of *a certain quantity of* (see 7.3, **на-** (b)), eg накупи́ть **книг**, *to buy up a number of books*.

(d) To express lack or absence of sth or sb in constructions with **нет**, *there is/are not*; **не́ было**, *there was/were not*; and **не бу́дет**, *there will not be*. These three Russian expressions, when they have the meanings given above, are invariable.

Хле́ба нет.	*There is no bread.*
Его́ здесь нет сего́дня.	*He is not here today.*
Сне́га не́ было.	*There was no snow.*
Дождя́ не бу́дет.	*There will not be any rain.*

Note: in the past or future tense absence may also be expressed by using a nominative form of the noun or personal pronoun: **Она́** не была́ до́ма, *She wasn't at home*; **Они́** там не бу́дут, *They won't be there.*

(e) To express sufficiency or insufficiency after the impersonal verbs **хвата́ть/хвати́ть**, *to suffice* (+ **у** + gen of person who has enough/

not enough of sth) and **недоставáть/ недостáть**, *to be insufficient/ not to have enough* (+ dat of person who is short of sth):

У нас **врéмени** не хватáет.	*We don't have enough time.*
Емý недостаёт **óпыта**.	*He doesn't have enough experience.*

Note: the genitive has a similar meaning of sufficiency after certain reflexive verbs bearing the prefix **на-** which mean to do sth to satiety or to excess (see 7.3, **на-** (c)), eg Онá наéлась **икры́**, *She ate a great deal of caviare*; Они́ напи́лись **воды́**, *They drank a lot of water (as much as they wanted)*.

(f) After short comparative adjectives, eg

бóльше **гóда**	*more than a year*
ни́же **нуля́**	*below zero*

(g) After cardinal numerals (provided that the numeral itself is in the nominative or accusative case), except *one* and compound numbers in which *one* is the last component (see 10.4.2).

(h) The genitive case of an ordinal numeral is used without a preposition to express *on* a certain date, eg

трéтьего áвгуста	*on 3 August*
двáдцать **шестóго** октября́	*on 26 October*

10.1.5 Verbs governing the genitive

(a) Many verbs which express fear, avoidance or apprehension, eg

боя́ться (no pf as a rule)	*to fear, be afraid of*
избегáть/избежáть	*to avoid*
опасáться (no pf)	*to fear, shun, avoid*
пугáться/испугáться	*to be afraid of*
стесня́ться/постесня́ться	*to be shy of*
стыди́ться/постыди́ться	*to be ashamed of*

Note: in R1 these verbs may now be found with the accusative of animate nouns (ie of those animate nouns that have a distinct accusative form), eg Он бои́тся **тётю**, *He's afraid of his aunt.*

(b) Miscellaneous other verbs, eg

алкáть (impf only; R3)	*to hunger for, crave*
держáться (no pf in this sense)	*to keep to, hold on to*
добивáться[1] (impf)	*to strive for*
доби́ться[1] (pf)	*to get, procure*
достигáть/дости́гнуть	*to attain, achieve*
заслýживать (impf)	*to deserve*
касáться/коснýться	*to touch, concern*
лишáть/лиши́ть	*to deprive* (sb of sth)
лишáться/лиши́ться	*to lose, be deprived of*
слýшаться/послýшаться[2]	*to obey*
стóить[3] (no pf)	*to be worth*

Note [1] The different aspects of this verb have different meanings when the verb refers to a single instance.

[2] In R1 this verb may now govern the accusative of an animate object, eg Ребёнок слу́шается **Веру**, *The child obeys Vera.*

[3] But this verb governs the accusative when it means *to cost* (see 10.1.2).

(c) A number of verbs may govern either the genitive or the accusative, eg

дожида́ться/дожда́ться	*to wait until*
ждать/подожда́ть	*to wait for, expect*
иска́ть (various pf)	*to look for, seek*
ожида́ть (no pf)	*to expect*
проси́ть/попроси́ть	*to ask for*
тре́бовать/потре́бовать	*to require, need*
хоте́ть/захоте́ть	*to want*

The reasons for choosing one case in preference to the other after these verbs are not very clear-cut, and educated Russians may be unable to explain them or even to agree on which case should be used in certain contexts. One may say that the genitive tends to be used if the object of the verb is general and abstract, whilst the accusative tends to prevail if the object is particular and concrete, ie is a specific thing or person. Thus:

- genitive object

Он ждал **отве́та**.	*He was waiting for an answer.*
Он и́щет **рабо́ты**.	*He is looking for work.*
Прошу́ **проще́ния**.	*I beg (your) pardon.*
Тре́буют **аре́ста** президе́нта.	*They are demanding the arrest of the president.*

- accusative object

Он ждёт **дя́дю**.	*He is waiting for his uncle.*
Он и́щет **тётю**.	*He is looking for his aunt.*
Про́сим **ви́зу** на въезд в Росси́ю.	*We are asking for a Russian entry visa.*

Note: the genitive is understood in set phrases expressing wishes (see 6.9), eg

Всего́ до́брого!	*All the best!*
Споко́йной но́чи!	*Good night!*

10.1.6 Case of direct object after a negated verb

The genitive may be used instead of the accusative to express the direct object of a negated verb. The foreign student needs to know when one case or the other is obligatory or strongly preferred, but should also be aware that there are many instances where the question is finely balanced and either case might be acceptable to a native-speaker.

Note: there is no question of a genitive object being used if the negated verb is one which, when it is used affirmatively, governs the dative or instrumental case. Thus in the statement *I am not interested in music* the noun *music* would be rendered by an instrumental form (я не интересу́юсь **му́зыкой**) just as it would if the verb интересова́ться were not negated. Only verbs which, when affirmative, govern the accusative case may govern a direct object in the genitive when they are negated.

(a) The genitive is preferred in the following circumstances:

- when the negation is intensive, ie if the negated verb is strengthened by some form of **никако́й**, or **ни одного́/одно́й**, or **ни. . .ни**, eg

Никаки́х реше́ний приня́ть не смогли́.	*They could not take any decisions at all.*

- when the absence of sth or any part of sth is indicated. (The English translation in such contexts may well contain the word *any*.) A genitive object is therefore naturally to be expected after the verb **име́ть** when it is negated.

Мото́рных ло́док здесь ещё не приобрели́.	*They have not yet acquired motor boats here.*
Мы не име́ем **доста́точного запа́са** то́плива.	*We don't have a sufficient supply of fuel.*

- when the negated verb and its object combine to form a common expression, a set phraseological combination, eg

Э́то не игра́ет **ро́ли**.	*This plays no role.*
Я не обраща́ю **внима́ния** на э́то.	*I pay no attention to this.*
Мы не пожале́ем **сил**.	*We shall spare no efforts.*
Они́ не сложи́ли **ору́жия**.	*They did not lay down (their) arms.*
Она́ не несёт **отве́тственности** за э́то.	*She does not bear responsibility for this.*

- when the negated verb is a verb of perception, especially **ви́деть**, *to see*, or **слы́шать**, *to hear*, eg

Он не ви́дел **трамва́я**, кото́рый ме́дленно шёл по у́лице.	*He did not see the tram which was slowly going down the street.*
Я не слы́шал(а) **звонка́**.	*I didn't hear the bell.*

- when the form of the verb which is negated is a gerund or active participle, eg

не читая **газе́ты**	*not reading the paper*
не написа́в **письма́**	*without having written the letter*
пробле́ма, не наше́дшая **отраже́ния** в кни́ге	*a problem which did not find reflection in the book*

- when the object of the negated verb is **э́то**, *this/that/it*, eg

Я **э́того** не забу́ду.	*I shan't forget this.*
Мно́гие не хоте́ли бы **э́того**.	*Many people would not want this.*

Note: it may happen that more than one of the above considerations applies and that it is therefore difficult to define the overriding criterion for using the genitive in the given context.

(b) The accusative is preferred in the following circumstances:

- when there is a double negative or when the negative occurs in a combination such as **чуть не**, *almost*, or **едва́ не**, *barely*, ie when the basic idea is not negative but affirmative, eg

Он не мог не заме́тить **пятно́**.	*He could not help noticing the stain.*
Она́ чуть не разби́ла **ва́зу**.	*She almost broke the vase.*
Как тут не вспо́мнить **э́то**?	*How can one not recall this?*

- when the object of the negated verb is qualified by an instrumental predicate, eg

Я не нахожу́ **францу́зский язы́к** тру́дным.	*I do not find French difficult.*
Он не счита́ет **э́тот отве́т** удовлетвори́тельным.	*He does not consider this answer satisfactory.*

- when it is not the verb but some part of speech other than the verb that is being negated, eg

Не он **э́то** сде́лал.	*It was not he who did this.*
Она́ купи́ла не **газе́ту**, а **журна́л**.	*It was a magazine, not a newspaper, that she bought.*
Они́ не то́лько сообщи́ли **ма́ссу** све́дений. . .	*They not only communicated a mass of information. . .*

- when the object of the negated verb is a place or specific concrete object, eg

Э́ти де́ньги **Нью-Йо́рк** не спасу́т.	*This money will not save New York.*
Радиослу́шатели не выключа́ли **радиоприёмники** в тече́ние двух неде́ль.	*Radio listeners did not turn off their sets for a fortnight.*

- when the object is a feminine noun referring to a person (or a masculine noun of the type Са́ша), eg

Я не зна́ю **Ири́ну** в лицо́.	*I don't know Irina by sight.*

(c) The accusative is more common than the genitive (but is not obligatory) when the negated verb is an auxiliary verb while the verb which governs the direct object is an infinitive, eg

Он не мог поня́ть **план**.	*He could not understand the plan.*
Не ста́ну приводи́ть **конкре́тные аргуме́нты**.	*I shall not put forward any concrete arguments.*

10.1.7 Basic uses of the dative

(a) To express the indirect object of a verb, ie the person or thing to which sth is given or done, or which is indirectly affected by an action, eg

Почтальо́н даёт **ему́** письмо́.	*The postman is giving him a letter.*
Он заплати́л **официа́нту**.	*He paid the waiter.*
Портно́й сшил **мне** костю́м.	*The tailor made me a suit.*
Я пожа́л(а) **ему́** ру́ку.	*I shook his hand.*

Note: the dative form of the reflexive pronoun **себе́** is commonly used in phrases describing injury to oneself or action on part of oneself, eg

лома́ть/слома́ть **себе́** ру́ку	*to break one's arm*
потира́ть/потере́ть **себе́** лоб	*to wipe one's brow*

(b) To indicate the subject in common impersonal expressions, such as:

мо́жно	*it is possible to/one can*
на́до/ну́жно	*it is necessary to/one must*
нельзя́	*it is impossible to/one cannot/ one must not*
жаль	*to be sorry for, to be sorry to*
пора́	*to be time to*

If past meaning is intended these expressions are followed by the neuter form **бы́ло**, and if future meaning is intended they are followed by the third-person singular form **бу́дет**.

Ему́ на́до бы́ло вы́йти.	*He had to go out.*
Нам ну́жно сде́лать пра́вильный вы́бор.	*We must make the right choice.*
Мне жаль э́тих люде́й.	*I am sorry for these people.*

Note: these impersonal expressions are also often used without any subject, eg

Здесь **мо́жно** кури́ть.	*One can smoke here.*
Нельзя́ входи́ть в пальто́.	*One mustn't go in with one's coat on.*

(c) In impersonal expressions with the neuter short form of many adjectives, eg

Мне пло́хо.	*I don't feel well.*
Тебе́ хо́лодно?	*Are you cold?*
Вам не ду́шно?	*It's not too stuffy for you?*
Вам бу́дет жа́рко.	*You'll be (too) hot.*

(d) In impersonal expressions with many verbs, eg

каза́ться/показа́ться	*to seem to*
надоеда́ть/надое́сть	*to make tired, sicken, bore* (used in translation of *to be fed up with*)
недостава́ть/недоста́ть	*to be insufficient*
нра́виться/понра́виться	*to be pleasing to* (used in translation of *to like*)
приходи́ться/прийти́сь	*to have to*

слéдовать (no pf in this sense)	*ought, should*
удавáться/удáться	*to succeed*

Examples:

мне кáжется, что...	*I think* (lit *it seems to me*) *that...*
Нам понрáвилась э́та пьéса.	*We liked this play.*
Вам слéдовало бы сказáть мне э́то вчерá.	*You ought to have told me that yesterday.*

(e) With negative pronouns which mean *to have nothing to* or *there is nothing to*, etc (see 10.2.4).

(f) To express a subject's age. The invariable forms **бы́ло** and **бýдет** are used to convey past and future meaning respectively.

Андрéю пятнáдцать лет.	*Andrei is 15.*
Сáше бы́ло пять лет.	*Sasha was 5.*
В áвгусте **мне** бýдет три́дцать лет.	*I'll be 30 in August.*

10.1.8 Verbs governing the dative

(a) Many verbs which indicate either advantage, assistance, permission or disadvantage, hindrance, prohibition to the object of the verb, eg

вреди́ть/повреди́ть[1]	*to injure, harm, hurt*
грози́ть (impf)	*to threaten*
запрещáть/запрети́ть[2]	*to forbid, prohibit*
изменя́ть/измени́ть[3]	*to betray*
мешáть/помешáть	*to prevent, hinder, bother, disturb*
позволя́ть/позвóлить	*to allow, permit*
помогáть/помóчь	*to help*
препя́тствовать/воспрепя́тствовать	*to obstruct*
противорéчить (impf only)	*to contradict*
разрешáть/разреши́ть[2]	*to allow, permit*
служи́ть/послужи́ть	*to serve*
совéтовать/посовéтовать	*to advise*
сопротивля́ться (impf only)	*to resist*
спосóбствовать/поспосóбствовать	*to assist, promote, contribute to*

Note [1] The pair **повреждáть/повреди́ть**, which also means *to damage, to injure*, or *to hurt*, takes the accusative case, eg Он повреди́л себé **нóгу**, *He hurt his leg.*

[2] When it is a thing that is prohibited or allowed **запрещáть/запрети́ть** and **разрешáть/разреши́ть** govern a direct object in the accusative, eg Прави́тельство запрети́ло/разреши́ло **нóвую газéту**, *The government prohibited/permitted the new newspaper.*

[3] When **изменя́ть/измени́ть** means *to change* or *to alter* it governs the accusative

case, eg Диpéктор шкóлы решúл изменúть **учéбную прогрáмму**, *The headmaster decided to change the curriculum.*

(b) Some verbs indicating attitude towards an object, eg

вéрить/повéрить[1]	*to believe, give credence to*
завúдовать/позавúдовать[2]	*to envy*
изумля́ться/изумúться	*to be astonished at*
рáдоваться/обрáдоваться	*to rejoice at, be gladdened by*
сочýвствовать (impf)	*to sympathise with*
удивля́ться/удивúться	*to be surprised at*

Note 1 **Вéрить/повéрить** takes **в** + acc if it means *to believe in* sth, eg Он вéрит **в бóга**, *He believes in God.* Contrast the use of the two cases with this verb in the sentence Не знáют, **во что и комý** вéрить, *They don't know what to believe in and whom to believe.*

2 **Завúдовать/позавúдовать** cannot govern a direct object as can the English verb *to envy* in phrases such as *I envy you your health.*

(c) Miscellaneous other verbs, eg

велéть (impf and pf)	*to order, command*
звонúть/позвонúть	*to ring, telephone*
льстить/польстúть[1]	*to flatter*
повиновáться (impf, and in past tense also pf)	*to obey*
подражáть (impf only)	*to imitate*
прикáзывать/приказáть	*to order*
принадлежáть[2] (impf only)	*to belong to*
слéдовать/послéдовать[3]	*to follow*
соответствовать (impf only)	*to correspond to*
учúть/научúть[4]	*to teach*
учúться/научúться[4]	*to learn* (a subject)

Note 1 Although **льстить/польстúть** normally governs the dative case, the accusative form of the reflexive pronoun is used in the expression **льстить/польстúть себя́ надéждой**, *to flatter oneself with the hope.*

2 When **принадлежáть** denotes ownership it is followed by the dative case without any preposition, eg Э́та кнúга принадлежúт **моемý брáту**, *This book belongs to my brother.* When on the other hand it denotes membership it must be followed by **к** and the dative, eg Он принадлежúт **к лейборúстской пáртии**, *He belongs to the Labour Party.*

3 **Слéдовать/послéдовать** is followed by the dative case only when it means *to follow* in the sense of *to emulate.* When it means *to go after* it takes **за** + instr (see 9.3.4).

4 After **учúть/научúть**, *to teach* and **учúться/научúться**, *to learn*, it is the subject taught or the thing learnt that is denoted by a noun in the dative case, eg Он ýчит сестрý **францýзскому языкý**, *He is teaching his sister French*; Онá ýчится **францýзскому языкý**, *She is learning French.* However, after the verb **изучáть/изучúть**, which means *to study*, the thing learnt is denoted by a noun in the accusative case, eg Он изучáет **математúку**, *He is studying mathematics.*

(d) The adjective **рад**, **рáда**, **рáды**, *glad*, which may only be used predicatively and which exists only in a short form, is also followed by a noun or pronoun in the dative, eg Онá былá рáда **моемý счáстью**, *She was glad at my good fortune.*

10.1.9 Basic uses of the instrumental

(a) To indicate the agent by whom or the instrument with which or by means of which an action is carried out, eg

Он был убит **солда́том**.	*He was killed by a soldier.*
Она́ ест **ви́лкой**.	*She is eating with a fork.*

(b) To denote the thing with which sth is supplied or endowed, eg

Госуда́рство обеспе́чивает всех гра́ждан **образова́нием**.
The state provides all citizens with an education.
А́томная электроста́нция снабжа́ет го́род **электри́чеством**.
The atomic power station supplies the town with electricity.

(c) In many adverbial phrases of manner, including indication of means of transport, eg

автомоби́лем	*by car*
самолётом	*by plane*
шёпотом	*in a whisper*
идти́ **бы́стрыми шага́ми**	*to walk with quick steps*

(d) In certain expressions of time which define the point at which sth happens; cf use of the accusative to indicate duration (see 10.1.2(b)), eg

ве́чером	*in the evening*
о́сенью	*in autumn*

(e) In the literary variety of R3, to define route taken and to indicate likeness, eg

е́хать **бе́регом** (ie по бе́регу)	*to travel along the bank*
зе́ркалом (ie как зе́ркало)	*like a mirror*

(f) In certain impersonal constructions indicating the agency of some force of nature, eg

Доро́гу занесло́ **сне́гом**.
The road was covered in snow.
Луга́ за́лило **водо́й**.
The meadows were flooded with water.
Кры́шу сду́ло **ве́тром**.
The roof was blown off by the wind.

10.1.10 Verbs governing the instrumental

(a) Many verbs indicating control, command, government, direction or use. Some of these verbs are by their nature not capable of having perfective forms.

владе́ть	*to command, master, own*
дирижи́ровать	*to conduct* (orchestra)

заве́довать	*to be in charge of, manage, run*
кома́ндовать	*to command* (armed forces)
облада́ть	*to possess*
по́льзоваться/воспо́льзоваться	*to use, make use of, enjoy* (in sense *dispose of*)

Note: the verb **испо́льзовать** (no pf), *to utilise*, on the other hand, governs the accusative case.

пра́вить	*to govern, rule, drive* (vehicle)
располага́ть	*to have at one's disposal*
распоряжа́ться/распоряди́ться	*to manage, deal with*
руководи́ть	*to manage, direct*
управля́ть	*to govern, rule, drive* (vehicle)

(b) A number of verbs indicating attitude towards sth. Some of these too exist only in an imperfective form.

восхища́ться/восхити́ться	*to admire* (ie *to be very impressed by*)
горди́ться (no pf)	*to be proud of*
дорожи́ть (no pf)	*to value, prize*
интересова́ться/ заинтересова́ться	*to be interested in*
любова́ться/полюбова́ться	*to admire* (ie *to enjoy looking at*)
наслажда́ться/наслади́ться	*to enjoy*
пренебрега́ть/пренебре́чь	*to ignore, neglect*
увлека́ться/увле́чься	*to be fond of, be carried away by, be obsessed with*
хва́статься/похва́статься	*to boast of*

(c) A number of verbs which indicate movement of sth, especially of part of the subject's body, or making a sound with sth, eg

бряца́ть це́пью (no pf)	*to rattle, clank a chain*
виля́ть/вильну́ть хвосто́м	*to wag (its) tail*
дви́гать/дви́нуть ного́й	*to move (one's) foot*
звене́ть деньга́ми (no pf)	*to jingle money*
кача́ть/покача́ть голово́й	*to shake (one's) head*
кива́ть/кивну́ть голово́й	*to nod (one's) head*
маха́ть/махну́ть руко́й	*to wave (one's) hand*
мига́ть/мигну́ть гла́зом **морга́ть/моргну́ть гла́зом**	*to wink, blink (one's) eye*
пожима́ть/пожа́ть плеча́ми	*to shrug (one's) shoulders*
разма́хивать мечо́м (no pf)	*to brandish a sword*
то́пать/то́пнуть ного́й	*to stamp (one's) foot*
хло́пать/хло́пнуть две́рью	*to slam a door*
ша́ркать/ша́ркнуть ного́й	*to shuffle (one's) foot*

Note: when the part of the body belongs to someone other than the subject the accusative is used, eg пожима́ть/пожа́ть кому́-н **ру́ку**, *to shake sb's* [ie *sb else's*] *hand*.

(d) Miscellaneous other verbs, eg

дыша́ть (no pf)	*to breathe*
же́ртвовать/поже́ртвовать	*to sacrifice*
занима́ться/заня́ться	*to be engaged in, be occupied with, study*
злоупотребля́ть/злоупотреби́ть	*to abuse*
па́хнуть (impf only)	*to smell of* (used impersonally)
рискова́ть (no pf)	*to risk, hazard*
страда́ть (no pf)	*to suffer from*

Note: used with the instrumental case **страда́ть** implies chronic or permanent predicament, eg страда́ть **диабе́том**, *to suffer from diabetes*; **страда́ть от** implies more temporary suffering, eg страда́ть **от зубно́й бо́ли**, *to suffer from toothache.*

(e) The instrumental is also used in nouns which function as the complement of **быть**, *to be*. Modern usage is as follows.

- The instrumental is used when the verb occurs in the infinitive (**быть**), future (**бу́ду**, etc), conditional (**был/была́/бы́ло/бы́ли бы**), imperative (**будь** or **бу́дьте**) or as a gerund (**бу́дучи**), eg

Он хо́чет быть **инжене́ром**.	*He wants to be an engineer.*
Он бу́дет **диплома́том**.	*He will be a diplomat.*
Бу́дьте **врачо́м**.	*Be a doctor.*
Бу́дучи **дурако́м**, он не по́нял.	*Being a fool, he didn't understand.*

- The instrumental is also normally used nowadays with the past tense (**был**, etc), eg

В мо́лодости он был **выдаю́щимся спортсме́ном**.
In his youth he was an outstanding sportsman.
Толсто́й был **вели́ким писа́телем**.
Tolstoy was a great writer.

Note: grammarians make a distinction between temporary state (in which case the instrumental is obligatory) and permanent state (as in the second example above, in which case the nominative may be used, giving **вели́кий писа́тель**). However, the choice is not one the student needs to agonise over, and one is now on safe ground if one always uses an instrumental complement with **быть**. (On identification of subject and complement see 3.2, явля́ться, note 2.)

- When on the other hand the verb *to be* is in the present tense, and is therefore understood but not actually stated in the Russian, a nominative complement must be used, eg

Он **профе́ссор**.	*He is a professor.*
Мой брат—**инжене́р**.	*My brother is an engineer.*

Departures from this rule are rare, unless the complement is **вина́**, *fault, blame*, or **причи́на**, *cause*, eg Тут, коне́чно, не одно́ телеви́дение **вино́й**, *Here, of course, television alone is not to blame.*

Note: the noun which in English functions as the complement is not in the instrumental in the following type of Russian construction:

Э́то был Ива́н.	*It was Ivan.*
Э́то была́ Татья́на.	*It was Tat'iana.*
Э́то бы́ло францу́зское сло́во.	*It was a French word.*
Э́то бы́ли дере́вья.	*They were trees.*

(f) A number of other verbs, apart from **быть**, require an instrumental complement, at least in some contexts, eg

вы́глядеть (impf)	*to look (like)*
де́латься/сде́латься	*to become*
каза́ться/показа́ться	*to seem*
называ́ть/назва́ть	*to call, name*
ока́зываться/оказа́ться	*to turn out to be, prove to be*
остава́ться/оста́ться	*to remain*
притворя́ться/притвори́ться	*to pretend to be*
рабо́тать (no pf)	*to work as*
служи́ть/послужи́ть	*to serve as*
слыть/прослы́ть	*to be reputed to be*
станови́ться/стать	*to become*
счита́ться (no pf)	*to be considered*
явля́ться/яви́ться	*to be*

(g) Some verbs take a direct object in the accusative and a complement in the instrumental, eg **Я нахожу́** э́ту о́перу **ску́чной**, *I find this opera boring*. Similarly:

выбира́ть/вы́брать	*to elect*
назнача́ть/назна́чить	*to appoint*
счита́ть/счесть	*to consider*

10.1.11 Use of the prepositional

This case, as its name suggests, is used only after certain prepositions (on which see 9.1.6) and can only be governed by verbs through those prepositions (see 9.3.5).

10.2 Use of pronouns

10.2.1 Use of кото́рый as a relative pronoun

The relative pronoun **кото́рый** (*who, which*) gives some difficulty, for although it declines like an adjective and must agree in gender and number with the noun or pronoun to which it refers, its case is determined by its function within the subordinate clause in which it stands. Thus in all the following examples the relative pronoun is feminine and singular, like **маши́на**, *car*, but its case varies in accordance with its grammatical role as, respectively, subject, direct object, and word governed by **в**:

Маши́на, **кото́рая** стои́т пе́ред вокза́лом, слома́лась.
The car which is outside the station has broken down.

Маши́на, **кото́рую** я купи́л(а) вчера́, слома́лась.
The car which I bought yesterday has broken down.
Маши́на, **в кото́рой** е́хал президе́нт, слома́лась.
The car in which the president was travelling has broken down.

Note: **кто**, *who*, and **что**, *what, which*, may also function as relative pronouns, although they are more commonly used as interrogative pronouns. As relative pronouns they occur mainly in conjunction with some form of **тот** or **все/всё**, eg **Те, кто** чита́л рома́н «Преступле́ние и наказа́ние», по́мнят о́браз Свидрига́йлова, *Those who have read 'Crime and Punishment' remember the character of Svidrigailov*; Я не согласен/согла́сна **с тем, что** он говори́т, *I do not agree with what he says.*

10.2.2 Use of како́й and кото́рый as interrogative pronouns

These pronouns, which may be used in questions asking *what?* or *which?*, used to be more clearly distinguished than they are now. A question introduced by **како́й** anticipated an answer describing quality, eg **Кака́я сего́дня пого́да**? *What is the weather like today?*, whereas one introduced by **кото́рый** anticipated an answer selecting an item out of a number of things or indicating the position of sth in a numerical series, eg **Кото́рую из э́тих книг вы предпочита́ете**?, *Which of these books do you prefer?*

Nowadays almost all questions requiring the use of one of these pronouns may be put by using **како́й**, eg

Каки́е ви́на вы лю́бите?	*What wines do you like?*
Каки́х ру́сских а́второв чита́ли?	*Which Russian authors have you read?*
—**Како́й** у вас но́мер?	*'Which room are you in?'*
—Два́дцать шесто́й.	*'Twenty-six.'*

Кото́рый, as an interrogative pronoun, can only really be considered obligatory in expressions of time such as **Кото́рый час**? *What time is it?* and **В кото́ром часу́**? *At what time?*

10.2.3 Use of negative pronouns (никто́, etc)

It must be remembered that the negative particle **не** must precede any verb with which the negative pronouns (**никто́**, **ничто́**, **никогда́**, **нигде́**, **никуда́**, **никако́й**, **ника́к**) are combined, eg

Никто́ не ви́дел его́.	*Nobody saw him.*
Она́ **ничего́ не** ви́дела.	*She didn't see anything.*
Он **ни с ке́м не** говори́л.	*He didn't speak to anyone.*
Я **ни о чём не** ду́маю.	*I'm not thinking about anything.*
Мы **никогда́ не** говори́м об э́том.	*We never talk about that.*
Я **никуда́ не** ходи́л(а).	*I didn't go anywhere.*

Note: **никто́** and **ничто́** decline (see 8.2) and, if governed by a preposition, split into two components with the preposition between them. (See also 10.2.4.)

10.2.4 Use of не́кто, etc

The pronouns dealt with in 10.2.3 should not be confused with similar forms which are used in contexts where English has the expressions *to have no-one/nothing/no time/nowhere to* or *there is no-one/nothing/no time/nowhere to*, viz

не́чего	*to have nothing to*
не́кого	*to have no one to*
не́когда	*to have no time to*
не́где	*to have nowhere to* (position indicated)
не́куда	*to have nowhere to* (movement indicated)

Being impersonal, these expressions are invariably used with the neuter form **бы́ло**, if they are in the past tense, and the third-person singular form **бу́дет**, if they are in the future. Examples:

Нам **не́чего** де́лать.	*We have nothing to do/There is nothing for us to do.*
Ему́ **не́кого бы́ло** люби́ть.	*He had no one to love.*
Ей **не́когда бу́дет** ви́деть вас.	*She will have no time to see you.*
Я́блоку **не́где** упа́сть.	*There isn't room to swing a cat.* (lit *There is nowhere for an apple to fall.*)

Note: **не́чего** and **не́кого**, which are accusative/genitive forms, also have dative, instrumental and prepositional forms. When these words are governed by a preposition they are generally split to enable the preposition to be inserted between the particle **не** and the appropriate form of **кто** or **что**, eg

Мне **не́ на кого́** полага́ться.	*I have no one to rely on.*
Ей **не́кому** дать ли́шний биле́т.	*She has got no one to give the spare ticket to.*
Мне **не́чем** есть суп.	*I've got nothing to drink my soup with.*
Ему **не́ с кем** говори́ть об э́том.	*He's got nobody to talk to about this.*
Им **не́ о чем бы́ло** говори́ть.	*They had nothing to talk about.*

10.2.5 Use of the particles -то, -нибудь, -либо

Use of these particles, any of which may be added to **кто, что, когда́, где, куда́, како́й, как, отку́да, почему́**, to render *someone, something, some time, somewhere, (to) somewhere, some, somehow, from somewhere, for some reason*, respectively, gives the English-speaking student some difficulty. The fundamental distinction between them is that **-нибудь** is vaguer than **-то**, while the less common **-либо** is either a more bookish alternative to **-нибудь** or vaguer still.

- **-то** will translate into English as *some* and indicates a degree of certainty on a speaker's part about some event although precise information about it is lacking, eg Он сказа́л **что́-то**, но я не расслы́шал(а), *He said something but I didn't catch it* (ie sth definitely was said, but what exactly is not known).

- -**нибудь**, being vaguer than -**то**, may be translated, depending on the context, as either *some* or *any*. It occurs with the imperative, eg Поговори́те **с ке́м-нибудь** об э́том, *Have a talk with somebody about it.* It also tends to occur:

(a) more with the future, about which there is less certainty, than the present, eg Е́сли **кто́-нибудь** позвони́т, скажи́те им, что я заболе́л(а), *If anyone rings, tell them I'm ill*;

(b) in the past tense when there is a choice or range of possibilities. Compare eg

Ка́ждое у́тро он уходи́л **куда́-то**.
Every morning he went somewhere [always the same place].
Ка́ждое у́тро он уходи́л **куда́-нибудь**.
Every morning he went somewhere [different places on different mornings].

(c) in combination with expressions such as **вероя́тно**, *probably*; **наве́рно**, *probably, I expect*, which indicate uncertainty, eg Наве́рно он ку́пит **что́-нибудь**, *I expect he'll buy something* [but what exactly is not yet known].

- -**либо** may indicate even greater vagueness than -**нибудь**, eg Я не зна́ю **кого́-либо**, кто мог бы вам помо́чь с э́тим, *I don't know anyone at all who could help you with this.*

10.2.6 Use of свой

Use of this word gives much difficulty to the English-speaker. **Свой** declines like **мой** and agrees in gender, case and number with the noun it qualifies. It denotes possession by the person or thing which is the subject of the clause in which the possessive pronoun occurs irrespective of whether that subject is first, second or third person and singular or plural. It might therefore translate any of the English possessive pronouns in the following variations:

I/you/he/she/we/they have/has lost my/your/his/her/our/their money.
Я/ты/он/она́/мы/вы/они́ потеря́л(а/и) **свои́** де́ньги.

If any of the third-person possessives (*his/her/its/their*) are rendered by **его́/её/их** then those Russian pronouns indicate possession by somebody other than the subject of the clause. Compare eg

Он потеря́л **свои́** де́ньги.	*He has lost his (own) money.*
Он потеря́л **его́** де́ньги.	*He has lost his (sb else's) money.*

- It is not possible to use **свой**:

(a) to qualify the subject itself. In the statement *His money has been lost*, for example, in which *money* is the subject, *his* must be translated by **его́**;

(b) when the possessive pronoun indicates possession by a subject which stands in another clause. In the sentence *He knows that I have lost his money*, for example, *his* indicates possession by the person who is the subject of the sentence as a whole (*he*), but it is *I* that is the subject of the clause in which *his* occurs. The sentence must therefore be translated: Он знаёт, что я потеря́л(а) **его́** де́ньги.

- In certain circumstances the point made in (a) above is overruled, viz

(a) in set expressions in which **свой** does qualify the subject, eg **Своя́** руба́шка бли́же к те́лу, *Charity begins at home*;

(b) in impersonal constructions in which the subject appears in the dative or is understood, eg На́до служи́ть **свое́й** ро́дине, *One must serve one's country*;

(c) in constructions with **у** + gen which equate to the English verb *to have*, eg У ка́ждого студе́нта **свой** компью́тер, *Each student has his own computer*.

10.3 Use of short adjectives

The short forms of the adjective may only be used when the adjective is predicative, that is to say when in the English translation of the Russian some form of the verb *to be* stands between the subject and the adjective, as in the sentences Э́тот студе́нт **умён**, *This student is clever*; Де́вушка была́ **грустна́**, *The girl was sad*.

If the adjective is not separated from the noun in this way, then only a long form of the adjective may be used, irrespective of the word order employed, eg Он **у́мный** студе́нт/Он студе́нт **у́мный**/**У́мный** он студе́нт, *He is an intelligent student*; Она́ была́ **гру́стной** де́вушкой, *She was a sad girl*.

Even when the adjective is predicative the short form is not invariably used. Often the long form is preferred or possible, and when some form of **быть** is used an instrumental form of the adjective is also possible. The following guidance can be given, although this is an area of grammar in which usage is relatively fluid.

- Many common adjectives are found only in the short form when used predicatively, eg

винова́т, винова́та, винова́то, винова́ты	*guilty*
гото́в, гото́ва, гото́во, гото́вы	*ready*

далёк, далека́, далеко́, далеки́	*far, distant*
дово́лен, дово́льна, дово́льно, дово́льны	*satisfied with*
до́лжен, должна́, должно́, должны́	*bound to* (ie *must*)
досто́ин, досто́йна, досто́йно, досто́йны	*worthy of*
наме́рен, наме́рена, наме́рено, наме́рены	*intending to*
ну́жен, нужна́, ну́жно, нужны́	*necessary*
похо́ж, похо́жа, похо́же, похо́жи	*like, similar*
прав, права́, пра́во, пра́вы	*right*
свобо́ден, свобо́дна, свобо́дно, свобо́дны	*free*
скло́нен, склонна́, скло́нно, скло́нны	*inclined to*
согла́сен, согла́сна, согла́сно, согла́сны	*agreeable to*
спосо́бен, спосо́бна, спосо́бно, спосо́бны	*capable of*

- Short forms are preferred, provided that the adjective is predicative, in the following circumstances:

(a) when the adjective is followed by some sort of complement (as many of those in the list above almost invariably are), eg (with nature of complement defined in brackets):

Он **равноду́шен к му́зыке**. (preposition + noun)
He is indifferent to music.
Сау́довская Ара́вия **бога́та не́фтью**. (noun in oblique case)
Saudi Arabia is rich in oil.

(b) when the subject of the statement is one of the words **то**, *that*; **э́то**, *this, it*; **что**, in the sense of *which* or *what*; **всё**, *everything*; **друго́е**, *another thing*; **одно́**, *one thing*; **пе́рвое**, *the first thing*, eg

Всё бы́ло **споко́йно**.
Everything was peaceful.
Одно́ **я́сно**.
One thing is clear.

(c) when the subject is qualified by some word or phrase such as **вся́кий**, *any*; **ка́ждый**, *every*; **любо́й**, *any*; **подо́бный**, *such*; **тако́й**, *such*, which serves to generalise it, eg

Ка́ждое сло́во в рома́не **уме́стно**.
Every word in the novel is apt.
Подо́бные зада́чи **просты́**.
Such tasks are simple.

(d) if the adjective is derived from a present active participle (ending in **-щий**); a present passive participle (ending in **-мый**); or a past passive participle (ending in **-тый** or **-нный**), eg

Ва́ше поведе́ние **неприе́млемо**.
Your conduct is unacceptable.
Он **жена́т**.
He is married.

(e) with some adjectives when they denote excessive possession of a quality, especially:

большóй: вели́к, великá, великó, велики́	*too big*
мáленький: мал, малá, малó, малы́	*too small*
дорогóй: дóрог, дорогá, дóрого, дóроги	*too dear*
дешёвый: дёшев, дешевá, дёшево, дёшевы	*too cheap*
ширóкий: ширóк, широкá, широкó, широки́	*too wide*
ýзкий: ýзок, узкá, ýзко, ýзки	*too narrow*

eg Э́ти тýфли мне **малы́**, *These shoes are too small for me.*

(f) in general statements of a philosophical or scientific nature, eg

Душá человéка **бессмéртна**.
Man's soul is immortal.
Судьбá Росси́и **загáдочна**.
Russia's fate is enigmatic.

- The long form of an adjective is preferred, when the adjective is used predicatively, in the following circumstances:

(a) if it is intended to particularise, ie to draw attention to the fact that a particular subject possesses the quality denoted by the adjective or to pick out one object from among several or many, eg

Тéмза корóткая рекá, Вóлга—**дли́нная**.
The Thames is a short river, the Volga is a long one.

Note: the inclusion in English of the definite article and the pronoun *one* points to the singling out of the object.

(b) in statements incorporating a phrase with **у** + gen (in which the object in question is being particularised), eg

Глазá у неё **краси́вые**.
She has beautiful eyes [ie *her eyes are beautiful ones*].

(c) with some adjectives, to indicate that the quality is a permanent one, eg

Онá—**больнáя**.
She is an invalid.

Note: cf Онá **больнá**, *She is ill.*

10.4 Use of numerals

This is a particularly complex area for the foreign student of Russian. Much of the complexity arises from the fact that (a) usage of **два** and other numerals bears traces of the existence of the old dual category (see Glossary); and (b) numerals themselves are capable of declension. It is helpful to deal separately with the use of **оди́н** (10.4.1) and then to examine separately use of the other numerals when they are themselves in nominative or accusative form (10.4.2) and use of those numerals when they are themselves in an oblique case (10.4.3).

10.4.1 Use of оди́н

Оди́н, which declines like the demonstrative pronoun **э́тот** (8.2), is generally followed, when it means *one*, by a singular noun, even in higher numbers in which it is the last component, such as *twenty-one*. It agrees in gender and case with nouns and adjectives which follow it, eg

оди́н дом	*one house*
два́дцать одна́ кни́га	*twenty-one books*
в одно́й изве́стной статье́	*in one famous article*

Note: **оди́н** does have plural forms which are used with nouns which themselves exist only in a plural form (see 2.6.1; eg **одни́ су́тки**, *one twenty-four-hour period*) or when the word means *only* (eg **Я** чита́ю **одни́ ру́сские рома́ны**, *I read only Russian novels*).

10.4.2 Use of numerals above *one* in nominative/accusative

When a numeral above *one* is itself in the nominative or accusative case (ie when it is the subject of a clause or the direct object of a transitive verb), usage is as follows:

- **два/две, три, четы́ре, о́ба/о́бе, полтора́/полторы́**, and any number of which one of these numerals is the last component, govern a noun in the genitive singular, eg

два грузовика́	*two lorries*
две кни́ги	*two books*
три по́ля	*three fields*
четы́ре ме́сяца	*four months*
о́ба телефо́на	*both telephones*
полтора́ часа́	*one and a half hours*

Note: **две, о́бе, полторы́** are feminine forms.

- adjectives after any of the above numerals are genitive plural, if the noun is masculine or neuter, or nominative/accusative plural if the noun is feminine, eg

два **деревя́нных** стола́	*two wooden tables*
три **гря́зных** окна́	*three dirty windows*
четы́ре **чёрные** ко́шки	*four black cats*

Note: the use of genitive plural adjectives after these numerals with feminine nouns (eg две **но́вых** книги), as well as masculine and neuter nouns, is old-fashioned, but is widely encountered in classical literature.

- numerals from **пять** upwards (and also **ты́сяча**, which may be treated as either a noun or a numeral, and **миллио́н** and **миллиа́рд**, both of which are nouns) govern a noun in the genitive plural, and any adjectives are also genitive plural irrespective of the gender of the noun, eg

пять больши́х городо́в	*five large cities*
два́дцать шесть но́вых книг	*twenty-six new books*
шестьдеся́т де́вять золоты́х меда́лей	*sixty-nine gold medals*

- the above rules relating to adjectives apply also to substantivised adjectives, eg

три **портны́х**	*three tailors*
четы́ре **моро́женых**	*four ice-creams*
две **столо́вые**	*two dining-rooms*

10.4.3 Use of numerals in oblique cases

When the numeral itself is in an oblique case (eg if it is governed by a preposition or by a verb which governs the genitive, dative or instrumental), then all nouns and adjectives which follow it are, in R2/3 at least, in the same case and in the plural, eg

в двух вечёрних газе́тах	*in two evening newspapers*
по обе́им сторона́м доро́ги	*down both sides of the road*
Она́ позвони́ла **трём друзья́м**.	*She telephoned three friends.*
законопрое́кт, при́нятый **девяно́ста пятью́ голоса́ми** про́тив **четырёх**	*a bill accepted by ninety-five votes to four*

Note 1 All components of the numeral itself decline.

2 In R1 a speaker might put only key components of a compound number in the appropriate oblique case, eg с семьсо́т шестьдеся́т **девятью́** солда́тами, *with 769 soldiers*. Not that such an example is commonly encountered in ordinary speech: a speaker would most probably use an approximation or, if a precise number had to be given, use a construction in which the numerals did not have to be put in an oblique case.

3 If **ты́сяча** is treated as a numeral it is generally followed by plural nouns and adjectives in the same case as itself, eg в ты́сяче **сиби́рских деревня́х**, *in a thousand Siberian villages*. If on the other hand it is treated as a noun then it is followed, irrespective of its own case, by a noun and adjectives in the genitive plural, eg в ты́сяче **сиби́рских дереве́нь**. The latter usage is more common in R3a/b, eg расхо́ды, исчисля́емые не одно́й ты́сячей **до́лларов**, *expenses running to thousands of dollars*.

10.4.4 Use of numerals with animate direct object

Numerals have distinct accusative and genitive forms and the question therefore arises as to which case should be used when they introduce an animate direct object (see 10.1.3). However, in practice it is only with **два/две**, **три** and **четы́ре** that difficulty arises.

- It is felt more correct to use the genitive rather than the accusative forms of **два/две**, **три**, **четы́ре** when they are the direct object of a verb and are used with an animate noun denoting a person, particularly when the noun is masculine, eg

ЦРУ раскры́ло **четырёх аге́нтов**.	*The CIA discovered four agents.*
Он ви́дел **трёх де́вушек**.	*He saw three girls.*

Note: the use of a genitive form of the numeral entails the use of a plural form of the following noun.

- When the animate noun denotes an animal then a genitive form of the numeral is still considered more correct if the noun is masculine (though this usage is perhaps less clear-cut than with nouns denoting people), whilst with nouns which are feminine the use of the genitive may seem stilted, eg

Он ви́дел **двух слоно́в**.	*He saw two elephants.*
Он ви́дел **две коро́вы**.	*He saw two cows.*

- If the numerals **два/две**, **три**, **четы́ре** occur as the last component of a compound number, then they are likely to be used in the accusative form, esp in R1, eg Он ви́дел два́дцать **два** ма́льчика, *He saw twenty-two boys.*
- With the numerals **пять** and above only the accusative forms are used with animate direct objects, even in R3, eg Он ви́дел **пять** ма́льчиков, *He saw five boys.*

10.4.5 Use of collective numerals

The collective numerals are **дво́е**, **тро́е**, **че́тверо**, **пя́теро**, **ше́стеро**, **се́меро**. Higher numerals of this type (**во́сьмеро**, **де́вятеро**, **де́сятеро**) are no longer used; nor are **пя́теро**, **ше́стеро**, **се́меро** any longer commonly used in all the contexts in which **дво́е**, **тро́е**, **че́тверо** are possible. If these numerals are used in the nominative or accusative then, like cardinal numerals from **пять** upwards, they are followed by nouns and adjectives in the genitive plural. They have the following uses:

(a) to indicate the number of people in a group, especially when the people are denoted by a pronoun or when the numeral stands on its own as the subject, eg

Нас бы́ло **дво́е**.	*There were two of us.*
Вошли́ **тро́е**.	*Three people came in.*

(b) to indicate a number of male persons or the number in a family, eg

че́тверо рабо́чих	*four workers*
У нас **дво́е дете́й**.	*We've got two children.*

(c) with nouns which exist only in the plural (see 2.6.1), eg

дво́е но́вых джи́нсов	*two new pairs of jeans*

Note: the collective numerals decline like plural adjectives (see 8.3.1). They may be used in all cases with animate nouns (eg мать **тройх** детéй, *the mother of three children*), but with inanimate nouns only the nominative/accusative forms are used (eg **трóе** сýток, but óколо **трёх** (not тройх) сýток, *about three days*).

10.4.6 Approximation

Approximation may be expressed in the following ways:

(a) by reversal of order of numeral and noun, eg

недéли две	*about two weeks*
часá чéрез два пóсле э́того	*about two hours after that*

(b) by using **óколо** with a numeral in the genitive, eg

óколо ста километров от Москвы́
about 100 kilometres from Moscow

(c) by placing an appropriate adverb before the numeral, eg

приблизи́тельно сто фýнтов	*approximately £100*
примéрно три́дцать студéнтов	*roughly thirty students*

Note: see also **так** (c) in 4.4.

10.4.7 Agreement of predicate with a subject containing a cardinal numeral

When a numeral is the subject of a clause, or when it combines with a noun to form the subject, then the predicate may be in the 3rd person plural (or plural form of the past tense) or it may be in the 3rd person singular (or neuter form of the past tense). Usage is not clear-cut, but some guidance can be given.

- Plural verb forms tend to prevail when:

(a) the subject is animate and the verb denotes action (as opposed to state), eg За негó **проголосовáли** сто члéнов парлáмента, *A hundred members of parliament voted for him*;

(b) the numeral is qualified by a word which is itself in a plural form, eg **Поги́бли** все дéсять члéнов экипáжа, *All ten members of the crew were killed*.

- Singular/neuter forms are preferred when:

(a) the subject is a phrase defining a period of time, eg **Прошлó** пять мéсяцев, *Five months passed*;

(b) attention is being drawn to the number, perhaps because of its large or small size or because the context is a statistical one, eg

Всегó **пришлó** пять человéк.
(Only) five people in all came.

10.4.8 Translation of *years* and *people* after numerals

(a) After **оди́н** and numerals followed by a genitive singular noun the word **год** is used, in an appropriate form, to mean *year*, but after numerals requiring a genitive plural noun the form **лет** is used, eg

оди́н год	*one year*
два го́да	*two years*
сто лет	*100 years*
о́коло трёх лет	*about three years*

Note 1 gen pl **годо́в** does exist and is used in referring to decades, eg **му́зыка шестидеся́тых годо́в**, *the music of the sixties.*

2 When the numeral is in the dative/instrumental/prepositional case then an appropriate form of **год** is used, eg **пяти́ года́м, пятью́ года́ми, о пяти́ года́х**.

(b) After numerals, and also the word **не́сколько**, the word **челове́к** is used, in an appropriate form, in the meaning *person/people* (the form **челове́к** is genitive plural as well as nominative singular), eg

три́дцать четы́ре челове́ка	*thirty-four people*
де́сять челове́к	*ten people*
не́сколько челове́к	*several people*

After **ты́сяча** and **миллио́н** there is now a tendency to use **челове́к**, although **люде́й** may also be found.

After **мно́го** and **немно́го** both **челове́к** and **люде́й** may be used; with **люде́й** it may be felt that attention is being focused on the group rather than the individuals in it.

Note: *a lot of people/not many people* may also be translated by **мно́го/немно́го наро́да** (or **наро́ду**) if it is meant that a place is crowded/not crowded.

After **ско́лько** and **сто́лько** *people* should be rendered by **челове́к** unless the meaning is exclamatory, in which case **люде́й** is preferred, eg

Ско́лько челове́к там бы́ло?	*How many people were there?*
Ско́лько люде́й поги́бли на войне́!	*How many people died in the war!*

10.4.9 Distributive expressions

The preposition **по** may be used with numerals to indicate distribution of a certain number of things to each of a number of objects. Modern usage in such expressions is as follows.

(a) **Оди́н** and any nouns that follow it are put in the dative case; the nouns **ты́сяча**, **миллио́н**, **миллиа́рд** are also put in the dative case, but following nouns and adjectives are genitive plural, eg

Ма́ть дала́ де́тям **по одно́й сла́дкой ири́ске**.
The mother gave her children a sweet toffee each.

Он дал нам **по ты́сяче рубле́й**.
He gave us a thousand roubles each.

Note: if there is no accompanying adjective then **оди́н** is often omitted, eg О́бе кома́нды име́ют **по ма́тчу** в запа́се, *Each team has a game in hand.*

(b) All other numerals are nowadays put in the accusative case and the following nouns and adjectives conform to the normal rules applicable after the numeral in question (see 10.4.2), eg

Инопланетя́не име́ли **по три гла́за**.
The extra-terrestrials had three eyes each.
С ка́ждого гекта́ра—**по две́сти пятьдеся́т тонн** овоще́й.
From each hectare [you get] 250 tonnes of vegetables.

Note: the use of numerals from **пять** upwards in the dative followed by a noun in the genitive plural in such expressions (eg Он дал нам **по пяти́ до́лларов**, *He gave us five dollars each*) is now felt to be old-fashioned or bookish.

10.4.10 Time

(a) The neutral or formal way to ask the question *What time is it?* is **Кото́рый час**? Similarly **В кото́ром часу́**? *At what time?* Colloquially one may ask these questions with the phrases **Ско́лько вре́мени**? and **Во ско́лько**? respectively.

(b) *o'clock*: numeral + appropriate case (though **оди́н** is usually omitted). *At* with time on the hour: **в** + acc:

час	*one o'clock*
два часа́	*two o'clock*
пять часо́в	*five o'clock*
в четы́ре часа́	*at four o'clock*

(c) Time past the hour: numeral + **мину́та** in appropriate case + genitive singular form of ordinal number indicating the hour (first hour, second hour, etc). *A quarter past* the hour: **че́тверть** (f) + genitive singular form of ordinal. *At* with time past the hour: **в** + acc:

(в) два́дцать пять мину́т пе́рвого	*(at) twenty-five past twelve*
(в) че́тверть седьмо́го	*(at) a quarter past six*

(d) *half past* the hour: **полови́на** + genitive singular form of ordinal number indicating the hour. *At half past* the hour: **в полови́не** (ie **в** + prep):

полови́на двена́дцатого	*half past eleven*
в полови́не шесто́го	*at half past five*

(e) time *to* the hour: **без** + genitive of all components of the cardinal numeral or of **че́тверть** + the hour itself. *At* time to the hour is not expressed:

без двадцати́ пяти́ пять *(at) twenty-five to five*
без че́тверти во́семь *(at) a quarter to eight*

Note: if a time is followed by one of the phrases *in the morning, in the afternoon, in the evening, at night*, then the genitive case of the word for *morning*, etc must be used, eg в де́вять часо́в **утра́**, *at nine in the morning*; cf the use of the instrumental (**у́тром**, etc) when the phrases *in the morning*, etc stand on their own.

10.4.11 Dates

(a) *on* a day of the week: **в** + acc, eg **в сре́ду**, *on Wednesday*.

(b) *on* days of the week: **по** + dat, eg **по среда́м** (in R1, **по сре́дам**), *on Wednesdays*.

(c) *in* a month: **в** + prep, eg **в январе́**, *in January*.

(d) a date in a month: neuter nominative singular form of ordinal number (**число́** is understood) + genitive form of the month, eg **пе́рвое ма́я**, *1 May*.

(e) *on* a date: as in (d) above but with the ordinal in the genitive, eg **пе́рвого ма́я**, *on 1 May*.

(f) a year: a compound number with an ordinal as the last component, eg **ты́сяча девятьсо́т девяно́сто четвёртый год**, *1994*.

(g) *in* a year: as in (f) above but preceded by **в** and with the ordinal and **год** in the prepositional, eg **в ты́сяча девятьсо́т девяно́сто четвёртом году́**, *in 1994*.

Note: if the year is preceded by a more precise date, then the ordinal indicating the year must be in the genitive case and must be followed by **го́да**, eg пе́рвое ма́рта ты́сяча девятьсо́т восьмидеся́того **го́да**, *1 March 1980* (see also the note to 10.4.10 (e)).

(h) *in* a century: **в** + prep, eg **в** два́дцать **пе́рвом ве́ке**, *in the twenty-first century*.

Note: *AD* and *BC* are **на́шей э́ры** (or **н.э.**) and **до на́шей э́ры** (or **до н.э.**) respectively.

10.4.12 Distance

This may be expressed in the following ways:

(a) with the prepositions **от** and **до** + cardinal numeral in the nominative, eg

От це́нтра до стадио́на два киломе́тра.
It is 2 kilometres from the centre to the stadium.

(b) with **в** + cardinal numeral and following noun in the prepositional, eg

Стадио́н нахо́дится **в двух киломе́трах** от це́нтра.
The stadium is (situated) 2 kilometres from the centre.

(c) with the phrase **на расстоя́нии** + cardinal numeral in the genitive and a following noun in the genitive plural, eg

на расстоя́нии двух киломе́тров от це́нтра
at a distance of 2 kilometres from the centre/2 two kilometres away from the centre

Note: the expressions **на высоте́**, *at a height of*, and **на глубине́**, *at a depth of*, are analogous to the expression **на расстоя́нии**, but in ordinary speech a large numeral following them is likely to be left in the nominative case, eg Самолёт лети́т на высоте́ **де́сять** ты́сяч ме́тров, *The plane is flying at a height of 10,000 metres.*

10.4.13 Nouns expressing number

These nouns (viz **дво́йка, тро́йка, четвёрка, пятёрка, шестёрка, семёрка, восьмёрка, девя́тка, деся́тка**) decline like feminine nouns in **-ка**. They may denote the shape of the digit, the number of a bus or tram, a playing card (eg **пи́ковая** (in R1, **пико́вая**) **семёрка**, *the seven of spades*), or they may have some special use (eg **тро́йка**, *three-horse carriage*; **восьмёрка**, *an eight* (at rowing). In the case of **дво́йка, тро́йка, четвёрка, пятёрка**, they also represent, in ascending order, marks in the Russian educational system.

10.5 Use of aspects

Aspectual usage is an area of Russian grammar which gives particular difficulty to English-speakers, not least because aspectual distinctions cut across the distinctions of tense to which English-speakers are accustomed.

10.5.1 Basic distinction between the aspects

For practical purposes one can draw a basic distinction in usage between the two aspects which is quite straight-forward.

- The imperfective, broadly speaking, is used to denote past, present or future actions which are seen as incomplete or which are frequent or repeated. Imperfective verbs naturally refer to actions which take place concurrently with other actions or which are interrupted by other actions.
- The perfective verb has the function of presenting a single action in its totality. It is therefore used when the speaker is referring to an action that has been or will be successfully completed. The perfective will commonly be used where an action has some result or where the action belongs in a past or future sequence, because each action in a sequence is complete before the next action takes place, eg Она́ **вста́ла, умы́лась, оде́лась,** и **вы́шла**, *She got up, washed, got dressed, and went out.* The perfective does not as a rule

have present meaning, since actions in the present are by their nature incomplete.

Note: once the above distinction has been drawn, it is useful also to bear in mind the fact that whereas the perfective form has a clear or marked meaning, the imperfective is used to convey a whole range of meanings that fall outside the scope of the marked form.

10.5.2 Effect of adverbial modifiers

It is in keeping with the basic distinction made in 10.5.1 that certain adverbs or adverbial expressions should encourage, if they do not actually oblige, the use of one aspect or the other. Contrast the following sets of adverbial modifiers.

adverbs and adverbial expressions tending to dictate use of impf		adverbs or adverbial expressions which encourage use of pf	
всегда́	*always*	**вдруг**	*suddenly*
вре́мя от вре́мени	*from time to time*	**неожи́данно**	*unexpectedly*
иногда́	*sometimes*	**совсе́м**	*quite, completely*
ка́ждый год	*every year*	**сра́зу**	*immediately*
ка́ждый день	*every day*	**за** + acc	*over, in the space of*
мно́го раз	*many times*		
не раз	*more than once*		
пока́	*while*	**пока́ не**	*until*
постоя́нно	*constantly*		
ча́сто	*often*		

10.5.3 Use of aspect in the indicative

imperfective	perfective

present tense

- incomplete action

  Я **чита́ю**.
  I am reading.
  Он **пи́шет** письмо́.
  He is writing a letter.
  Она́ **идёт** по у́лице.
  She is walking down the street.

- repeated action

  По воскресе́ньям я **отдыха́ю**.
  I relax on Sundays.
  Почти́ ка́ждый день она́ **посеща́ет** теа́тр.
  She goes to the theatre almost every day.

future tense

- incomplete action

  Когда́ ты придёшь, мы **бу́дем у́жинать.**
  When you arrive we shall be having supper.

- repeated action

  По вечера́м я **бу́ду писа́ть** пи́сьма.
  I shall write letters in the evenings.

- action about to be begun

  Сейча́с мы **бу́дем выходи́ть.**
  We're going to go out now.

- single completed action or event

  Я напишу́ ему́ письмо́.
  I shall write him a letter.

past tense

- incomplete or prolonged action

  Я **у́жинал**, когда́ вошла́ жена́.
  I was having supper when my wife came in.
  Я всю неде́лю **рабо́тал(а).**
  I worked all week.

- repeated action

  Я не раз **объясня́л(а)** э́то.
  I have explained this more than once.

- annulled action
  Он **открыва́л** окно́.
  He opened the window.
  (but has now shut it again)
  Она́ **приходи́ла.**
  She came. (but has gone away again)

- statement of fact without stress on completion of action

  Ты **писа́л(а)** сочине́ние?
  Have you written the essay?
  Вы **чита́ли** пье́сы Че́хова?
  Have you read Chekhov's plays?
  По ра́дио **передава́ли**, что бу́дет снег.
  They said on the radio that there would be snow.
  Вы **зака́зывали**?
  Have you ordered?

- attempt but non-achievement

  У него́ бы́ло напряжённое лицо́: он **вспомина́л**, где он ви́дел её.
  He had a strained look on his face: he was trying to recall where he had seen her (before).

- single completed action or event, sequence of actions

  Я вы́пил(а) стака́н пи́ва.
  I drank a glass of beer.
  За одну́ неде́лю она́ **написа́ла** це́лую главу́.
  In the space of one week she wrote a whole chapter.

  Он **встал, поза́втракал,** и **вы́шел.**
  He got up, had breakfast and went out.
  Он **откры́л** окно́.
  He opened the window.
  (and it remained open)
  Она́ **пришла́.**
  She came. (and is still here)

Он **бил** и не забил пенальти.
He took the penalty but did not score.

сдава́ть or **держа́ть** экза́мен	cf **сдать** or **вы́держать** экза́мен
to sit/take an exam	*to pass an exam*
дока́зывать	cf **доказа́ть**
to try to prove, ie *to contend*	*to prove*

Note [1] The distinctions drawn in the last section above (attempt with reference to non-achievement or achievement) apply only in relation to a single instance. In frequentative contexts the imperfective may well convey achievement, eg Ка́ждый год он **сдава́л** экза́мены на «отли́чно», *Every year he passed his exams with commendation.*

[2] The imperfective forms **ви́деть** and **слы́шать** may mean *to be able to see* and *to be able to hear* respectively. The perfective forms of these verbs (**уви́деть** and **услы́шать**), on the other hand, are not necessarily used to render English tenses that an English-speaker would normally expect to be rendered by perfective verbs (eg *saw*, *have heard*, etc). The perfective forms tend to refer to the beginning of a perception, eg Снача́ла он ничего́ не **ви́дел** вдали́, но пото́м **уви́дел** ма́ленькую ло́дку, *At first he could not see anything in the distance, but then he caught sight of a tiny boat.* See also 3.3, *can* (d).

10.5.4 Use of aspect in the infinitive

After certain verbs an infinitive of one aspect or the other is obligatory, eg Он переста́л **петь** (impf), *He stopped singing*; Она́ забы́ла **посла́ть** письмо́ (pf), *She forgot to send the letter.*

- an imperfective infinitive is required after:

начина́ть/нача́ть	*to begin, to start*
стать (pf), in the meaning:	*to begin, to start*
принима́ться/приня́ться	*to set about*
научи́ться	*to learn to* (do sth)
полюби́ть	*to grow fond* (of doing sth)
привыка́ть/привы́кнуть	*to get used to* (doing sth)
продолжа́ть/продо́лжить	*to continue*
конча́ть/ко́нчить	*to finish*
броса́ть/бро́сить, in the meaning:	*to give up, abandon*
перестава́ть/переста́ть	*to stop* (doing sth)
надоеда́ть/надое́сть	*to grow tired of* (used impersonally)
отвыка́ть/отвы́кнуть	*to get out of the habit of* (doing sth)
устава́ть/уста́ть	*to tire* (of doing sth)

Note [1] The perfective form **продо́лжить** is rarely used except in the sense of *to prolong*, and may be followed by a verbal noun rather than an infinitive, eg Мы **продо́лжили** обсужде́ние, *We carried on the discussion.*

[2] All these verbs essentially indicate the stage an action has reached (eg *to begin*, *to continue*, *to stop*, *to finish*) and the action denoted by the infinitive therefore cannot in this context be seen in its totality.

- a perfective infinitive is required after:

забы́ть	*to forget* (to do sth)
оста́ться	*to remain* (to be done)
уда́ться	*to succeed in, manage to* (used impersonally)
успе́ть	*to have time to*

10.5.5 Use of aspect in negative constructions

- With negated verbs in the past tense an imperfective verb should be used to denote complete absence of a particular action, eg

Мы не **встреча́лись**.
We have not met.
Свою́ та́йну я **не открыва́л(а)** никому́.
I have not revealed my secret to anyone.

Note: a perfective verb should be used, on the other hand, to indicate that an action was not performed on a specific occasion, eg Мы не **встре́тились**, *We did not meet.*

- The negated perfective may also mean that the subject was not able to carry out an action or failed to do sth which it was intended to do, eg

Звоно́к буди́льника не **разбуди́л** его́, так кре́пко он спал.
The alarm-clock did not wake him, so soundly was he sleeping.
Он до́лжен был прийти́, но не **пришёл**.
He was due to come but he did not come.

- Many types of negative expression and types of verb, when negated, require a following infinitive to be imperfective, especially those which express:

(a) prohibition; modal constructions with the meaning *may not* or *should not*, eg Нельзя́ тут **переходи́ть** доро́гу, *One must not cross the road here* (because eg there is no crossing and one may be fined).

Note: constructions meaning *cannot*, on the other hand, are rendered by perfective forms, eg Нельзя́ тут **перейти́** доро́гу, *One cannot cross the road here* (because eg there is too much traffic or the road is up and it is dangerous).

(b) dissuasion:

Он уговори́л меня́ не **остава́ться**.
He persuaded me not to stay.

Note: the verb *to dissuade*, **отгова́ривать/отговори́ть**, also requires a following infinitive to be imperfective, eg Оте́ц отговори́л сы́на **меня́ть** профе́ссию, *The father dissuaded his son from/talked his son out of changing his profession.*

(c) advice or request that sth not be done:

Врач посове́товал больно́му не **выходи́ть**.
The doctor advised the patient not to go out.

Председа́тель предложи́л не **откла́дывать** реше́ние.
The chairman proposed that a decision not be delayed.

(d) a decision, promise or intention not to do sth:

А́рмия реши́ла не **наступа́ть** на столи́цу.
The army decided not to attack the capital.

Note: if on the other hand verbs such as **угова́ривать/уговори́ть**, **сове́товать/посове́товать**, **предлага́ть/предложи́ть**, **проси́ть/попроси́ть**, **реша́ть/реши́ть** are followed by a verb that is not negated, then the following infinitive may be of either aspect, depending on the usual considerations concerning prolongation or frequency of the action. Thus a perfective infinitive will be required if the action is performed on a single occasion, eg Врач посове́товал больно́му **приня́ть** [pf] снотво́рное, *The doctor advised the patient to take a sleeping tablet.*

(e) inexpediency:

Не сто́ит **смотре́ть** э́тот фильм.
It's not worth seeing this film.
Вре́дно **кури́ть**.
Smoking is bad for you.

10.5.6 Use of aspect in the imperative

imperfective	perfective
• commands relating to repeated action, eg По воскресе́ньям **звони́** ма́ме, *Phone mother on Sundays.*	
• invitation to do sth, eg **Сади́тесь**, пожа́луйста, *Sit down please*; По доро́ге домо́й **заходи́** ко мне, *Call in to see me on the way home.*	instruction* to do sth on single occasion, eg **Ся́дьте** побли́же к све́ту, *Sit nearer the light*; По доро́ге домо́й **зайди́** в апте́ку, *Call in at the chemist's on the way home.*
• instruction to do sth on single occasion expressed by transitive verb without direct object, eg **Чита́йте** ме́дленнее, *Read more slowly*; **Пиши́те** аккура́тнее, *Write more neatly.*	
• request to begin to do sth or to get on with sth, eg Ко́нчили смотре́ть телеви́зор? Тепе́рь **выключа́йте** его́, *Have you finished watching television? Now switch it off*; **Встава́й**, уже́ по́здно, *Get up, it's late.*	
• with **не**: prohibition, eg Бо́льше ко мне не **приходи́те**, *Don't come to me any more.*	with **не** (often with **смотри́(те)** or **осторо́жно**): warning, eg Смотри́ не **урони́** ва́зу, *Watch out, don't drop the vase*; Осторо́жно, не **упади́**, здесь ско́льзко, *Be careful, don't fall over, it's slippery here.*

- **не** + infin: formal prohibition (see 5.8), eg Не **прислоня́ться**, *Do not lean.* (on door of train)

  infin, not negated: formal instruction (see 5.8), eg При ава́рии **разби́ть** стекло́ молотко́м, *In the event of an accident break the glass with the hammer.*

* Because it expresses an instruction or request rather than an invitation the perfective imperative may seem less polite, but it may be softened – as may invitations – by the insertion of **пожа́луйста**, *please*, or some phrase such as **бу́дьте добры́**, *be so kind as to* (see also 6.12). In R1 the particle **-ка** (4.4 (a)) serves the same purpose, eg На́дя, **иди́-ка** сюда́, *Come over here, would you, Nadia.*

10.6 Problems in choice of tense

Russian in some contexts requires use of a tense which is unexpected to English-speakers.

(a) Reported speech, in which Russian verbs are put in the tense which would have been used in the original statement or question. Reported speech may be defined for this purpose as statements introduced by verbs of thinking, knowing, hoping and even verbs of perception such as hearing as well as verbs of saying, asking and replying. This usage differs from English usage. Compare for example the tenses used in the reported speech in the following Russian and English sentences:

Я сказа́л(а) ему́, что **живу́** в Ло́ндоне.
*I told him that I **lived** in London.*
Солда́ты убеди́лись, что ми́на не **взорвётся**.
*The soldiers made sure that the mine **would** not **explode**.*
Он спроси́л, **изуча́ю** ли я ру́сский язы́к.
*He asked whether I **was studying** Russian.*
Она́ спроси́ла, согла́сен ли я.
*She asked whether I **agreed**.*

Note: in reported questions *whether* is rendered by **ли** and the Russian word order, with inversion of subject and predicate, is an order possible in a question. The last two examples above illustrate the point.

(b) Present perfect continuous: a present tense is used in Russian to denote an action which began in the past and is still continuing, eg

Я пять лет **изуча́ю** ру́сский язы́к.
*I **have been studying** Russian for five years.*
Он три́дцать лет **рабо́тает** ди́ктором.
*He **has been working** as a newsreader for thirty years.*

(c) Logical future: the future tense, expressed by a perfective verb, is used in Russian subordinate clauses after conditional and temporal conjunctions such as **е́сли** and **когда́** if the action clearly is yet to take place (cf English use of present tense in these circumstances), eg

Éсли вы **прочитáете** э́ту кни́гу, вы всё поймёте.
*You will understand everything if you **read** this book.*
Когдá он **придёт**, мы поговори́м об э́том.
*We shall talk about this when he **arrives**.*

(d) Near future: the present tense is used, as in English, with verbs of motion indicating that an action is to take place in the near future, eg

Я **иду́** в кинó сегóдня вéчером.
*I **am going** to the cinema tonight.*

10.7 Use of verbs of motion

There are fourteen pairs of verbs of motion which give particular difficulty to the foreign student. There is perhaps no entirely satisfactory term to define the two categories: the terms abstract, indeterminate, multidirectional are all applied to the category including **ходи́ть**, whilst the terms concrete, determinate and unidirectional are applied to the category which includes **идти́**. The fourteen pairs are as follows:

ходи́ть	**идти́**	*to walk, go on foot*
éздить	**éхать**	*to travel, go by transport*
бéгать	**бежáть**	*to run*
летáть	**летéть**	*to fly*
плáвать	**плыть**	*to swim, float, sail*
пóлзать	**ползти́**	*to crawl*
носи́ть	**нести́**	*to take (by hand), carry*
води́ть	**вести́**	*to take, lead*
вози́ть	**везти́**	*to take (by transport), convey*
лáзить	**лезть**	*to climb*
гоня́ть	**гнать**	*to drive, pursue*
катáть	**кати́ть**	*to roll, push*
таскáть	**тащи́ть**	*to pull*
броди́ть	**брести́**	*to wander, amble*

Note 1 All the above verbs are imperfective.
2 The verbs **броди́ть** and **брести́** are not always included in such lists, since **броди́ть** cannot suggest movement in only one direction and differs in meaning from **брести́** which conveys a sense of slowness or difficulty.

Use of verbs like идти́

The easiest way to grasp the distinction between the verbs in the two categories is perhaps to treat those like **идти́** as having quite specific meaning and those like **ходи́ть**, on the contrary, as covering a broader range of meanings outside the scope of those like **идти́** (cf the similar distinction made in 10.5.1 between the perfective aspect of the verb and the broader imperfective).

Verbs like **идти́** indicate movement in one general direction.

The movement is not necessarily in a straight line, but progress is made from point A towards point B, eg

Она́ **идёт** по у́лице. *She is going down the street.*
Он **бежи́т** к авто́бусу. *He is running towards the bus.*

It may be clear that the movement described by the verb is repeated or even habitual, but a verb in the category of **идти́** may still be used if it is wished to emphasise the sense of progress in a certain direction or vividly to evoke one particular instance of such movement, eg

Что́бы отпра́вить письмо́ ну́жно **идти́** де́сять киломе́тров.
In order to send a letter one has to walk 10 kilometres.
Чёрные стра́усы **бегу́т** легко́, вы́прямив ше́ю, как балери́ны на пу́антах.
The black ostrich runs easily, straightening its neck like a ballerina on the tips of her toes.

Use of verbs like ходи́ть

One may list a number of meanings outside the scope of verbs in the category of **идти́**, and these meanings are all conveyed by verbs like **ходи́ть**.

(a) Repeated or habitual action, eg

По суббо́там мы **хо́дим** в кино́.
On Saturdays we go to the cinema.

(b) Round trip, eg

Я **ходи́л(а)** в те́атр.
I went to the theatre.

Note: it may be difficult to separate the sense of round trip from the sense of repetition, eg Ка́ждый день де́ти **хо́дят** в шко́лу, *Each day the children go to school* (and of course come home again).

(c) movement in various directions, eg

Де́вочки **бе́гали** по са́ду.
The little girls were running round the garden.

(d) non-contextual movement, ie a certain type of movement without reference to any specific example of it, eg

Ребёнок на́чал **ходи́ть**.
The child began to walk.
Я не уме́ю **пла́вать**.
I can't swim.
Пти́цы **лета́ют**, зме́и **по́лзают**.
Birds fly, snakes crawl.

10.8 Use of reflexive verbs

- Many common verbs exist only in a reflexive form but have no obvious reflexive meaning, eg

боя́ться (impf)	*to fear, be afraid of*
горди́ться (impf)	*to be proud of*
пыта́ться/попыта́ться	*to attempt*
смея́ться (impf)	*to laugh*
стара́ться/постара́ться	*to try*
улыба́ться/улыбну́ться	*to smile*

Note: in a few pairs the imperfective form is reflexive but the perfective form is not:

ложи́ться/лечь	*to lie down*
ло́паться/ло́пнуть	*to burst* (intrans)
сади́ться/сесть	*to sit down*
станови́ться/стать	*to become*

- In a very large number of verbs the reflexive particle renders a transitive verb intransitive, in other words it fulfils the function of a direct object, eg

возвраща́ть/возврати́ть or **верну́ть** *to return* (give back)	**возвраща́ться/возврати́ться** or **верну́ться** *to return* (go back)
конча́ть/ко́нчить *to finish* (complete)	**конча́ться/ко́нчиться** *to finish* (come to end)
начина́ть/нача́ть *to begin* (sth, to do sth)	**начина́ться/нача́ться** *to begin* (come into being)
одева́ть/оде́ть *to dress* (sb)	**одева́ться/оде́ться** *to dress, get dressed*
остана́вливать/останови́ть *to stop* (bring to halt)	**остана́вливаться/останови́ться** *to stop* (come to halt)
поднима́ть/подня́ть *to lift*	**поднима́ться/подня́ться** *to go up*
раздева́ть/разде́ть *to undress* (sb)	**раздева́ться/разде́ться** *to undress, get undressed*
увели́чивать/увели́чить *to increase* (make bigger)	**увели́чиваться/увели́читься** *to increase* (get bigger)
удивля́ть/удиви́ть *to surprise*	**удивля́ться/удиви́ться** *to be surprised*
улучша́ть/улу́чшить *to improve* (make better)	**улучша́ться/улу́чшиться** *to improve* (get better)
уменьша́ть/уме́ньшить *to decrease* (make smaller)	**уменьша́ться/уме́ньшиться** *to decrease* (get smaller)
ухудша́ть/уху́дшить *to make worse*	**ухудша́ться/уху́дшиться** *to get worse*

- reciprocal action, eg

встреча́ться/встре́титься	*to meet one another*

обнима́ться/обня́ться	*to embrace one another*
целова́ться/поцелова́ться	*to kiss one another*

- characteristic action: some verbs which are normally transitive and non-reflexive take the reflexive particle in contexts where they have no specific object but denote action characteristic of the subject, eg

Крапи́ва **жжётся**.	*Nettles sting.*
Соба́ка **куса́ется**.	*The dog bites.*
Ло́шадь **ляга́ется**.	*The horse kicks.*
Ко́шки **цара́паются**.	*Cats scratch.*

- impersonal verbs: with some common verbs a third-person reflexive form is used to indicate the physical condition or mood of a subject, eg

Мне **хо́чется** есть/пить.	*I am hungry/thirsty.*
Ему́ не **спи́тся**.	*He can't get to sleep.*
Ей не **чита́ется**.	*She doesn't feel like reading.*

- with passive sense: many imperfective verbs are used in a reflexive form with an inanimate subject to mean that sth has been/is being/will be done, eg

Э́тот вопро́с до́лго **обсужда́лся**.
This question was discussed for a long time.
Зна́ние—э́то то́же това́р, кото́рый **покупа́ется** и **продаётся**.
Knowledge too is a commodity that is bought and sold.
Ры́ночные отноше́ния бу́дут **стро́иться** в Росси́и ещё до́лгие го́ды.
Market relations will be built in Russia over many long years to come.

Note: this use of the reflexive belongs mainly to R2/3, as the flavour of the above examples shows.

- in combination with certain verbal prefixes (see also 7.3), eg

всма́триваться/всмотре́ться	*to peer at*
зачи́тываться/зачита́ться	*to get engrossed in reading*
наеда́ться/нае́сться	*to eat one's fill, stuff oneself (with food)*
расходи́ться/разойти́сь	*to disperse*
съезжа́ться/съе́хаться	*to gather, assemble*

10.9 The conditional mood

Conditional sentences in Russian are of two types, depending on whether the speaker means that in certain circumstances (a) sth will/will not happen or (b) sth might happen. Usage in the two clauses of a conditional sentence (ie the subordinate clause which contains the condition, usually introduced by **éсли**, *if*, and the main clause, which states the consequence) differs in the two types of conditional sentence.

Note: in both types of conditional sentence the clause stating the consequence may be introduced by **то** or **тогдá** (Eng *then*), provided that it follows the clause containing the condition.

- Real conditional sentences, in which the speaker is saying that given certain conditions a particular consequence definitely did/does/will or did not/does not/will not follow, a verb in the past, present or future tense (depending on the context) is used in each clause, eg

Éсли ты **дýмаешь** [impf pres], что он чéстен, **то** э́то оши́бка.
If you think he's honest then you're mistaken.
Éсли вы **перестáнете** [pf fut] кри́чать, я **отвéчу** на ваш вопрóс.
If you stop shouting I'll answer your question.

Note: a future must be used in the clause containing the condition (**перестáнете** in the second example above) when the verb denotes an event that has yet to take place (see also 10.6(c); cf English use of the present tense in such clauses).

- Hypothetical conditional sentences, in which the speaker is saying that given certain hypothetical conditions some consequence would/would not follow or would have/would not have followed, both clauses must have a verb in the conditional mood. This mood is rendered in Russian simply by the appropriate form of the past tense (masculine, feminine, neuter or plural) together with the invariable particle **бы**, eg

Éсли бы рабóты **нáчались** вóвремя, тогдá расхóды **бы́ли бы** горáздо ни́же.
If work had begun on time [but it did not], then the cost would have been much lower.
Как **бы** вы **отнесли́сь** к томý, **éсли** ваш четырёхлéтний ребёнок вдруг **пропéл бы** такýю пéсенку?
How would you react if your four-year-old child suddenly sang a song like that?

Note 1 Conditional sentences of this type may relate to past, present or future time, and only from the context will it be clear which meaning is intended.
2 In the clause containing the condition the particle **бы** generally follows **éсли** (and it may be contracted to **б**). In the clause describing the consequence **бы** generally follows the verb in the past tense. However, **бы** may also follow some other word in the clause to which it is intended to give emphasis.
3 The clause containing the condition may also be rendered with the use of a second-person singular imperative, eg **Живи́** онá в други́х услóвиях, из неё вы́шел бы прекрáсный худóжник, *Had she lived in other conditions, she would have made a fine artist.*
4 A clause containing a condition may be lacking altogether, eg **Я бы** э́того не сдéлал, ***I*** *would not have done that.*

10.10 The subjunctive mood

As well as forming the conditional mood, the past tense of the verb + the particle **бы** renders the subjunctive in Russian. There are no sets of distinctive verbal endings or different subjunctive tenses of the sort found in, for example, French, Italian and Spanish. As in these Western European languages, though, the subjunctive in Russian is used in concessive clauses and in subordinate clauses after verbs of wishing. It may also be used, but tends in R1 and R2 to be avoided, in subordinate clauses after verbs of ordering, permitting, fearing and doubting and after various negative antecedents.

- Concessive clauses: these are clauses introduced by *whoever, whatever, whichever, however, wherever, whenever,* etc, and they may be translated into Russian by the appropriate pronoun (**кто, что, како́й, как, где, куда́, когда́**, etc) in the form required by the context and followed by the particle **бы + ни** + verb in past tense, eg

Кем бы пото́м они́ **ни ста́ли**, а чу́вство благода́рности ва́м от них никогда́ не уйдёт.

Whoever they may become later on, the sense of gratitude to you will never leave them.

Я счита́ю, что про́шлое непреме́нно на́до бере́чь, **како́е бы** плохо́е оно́ **ни́ было**.

I think the past should definitely be preserved however bad it might have been.

Всем гра́жданам, **како́й бы** национа́льности они́ **ни́ были** и **где бы** они́ **ни прожива́ли**, гаранти́рованы ра́вные права́ и возмо́жности.

All citizens, of whatever nationality they may be and wherever they may reside, are guaranteed equal rights and opportunities.

Note 1 As with conditional sentences in which **бы** is used, so in such concessive clauses too a verb accompanied by this particle may refer to past, present or future actions.

2 Concessive clauses may also be translated by the use of the appropriate pronoun + **ни** + verb in the appropriate tense, eg Что **ни говори́те**, а прия́тно поро́й встре́тить для себя́ неожи́данное, *Whatever you say/Say what you will, it is nice sometimes to encounter the unexpected.*

3 *Whatever, whenever, wherever,* etc do not invariably introduce concessive clauses; they may merely impart emphasis, as in the question *Wherever have you been?*, which might be translated: **Где же** ты был(а́)? (See also 4.4, же (d).)

- Exhortation: the particle **бы** may also be used, with a verb in the past tense, to express an exhortation or gentle command or the desirability of some action, eg

Вы **бы помогли́** ему́.
You should help him/should have helped him.

- Wishing: after verbs of wishing the subordinate clause should be introduced by **чтóбы** (a coalescence of **что** + **бы**) and the verb in the subordinate clause should be in the past tense, eg

  Я хочý, **чтóбы** нáши дéти **знáли** наш роднóй язы́к.
  I want our children to know our native language.

- Commanding, permitting: after verbs of this type the subjunctive may also be used, eg

  Я сказáл(а), **чтóбы** дéвушка **принеслá** стакáн воды́.
  I told the waitress to bring a glass of water.

Note: subjunctive constructions in such sentences are only alternatives to the use of an object and verb in the infinitive, and indeed the latter, simpler, construction prevails in R1/R2. Thus the above English sentence might also have been rendered thus: Я сказáл(а) **дéвушке принести́** стакáн воды́.

- Fearing: verbs of fearing may be followed by (a) in R2/3, a negative subjunctive (eg Я бою́сь, **чтóбы** [or **как бы**] он **не пришёл**), or (b) in R1/2 by a verb in the future tense in a clause introduced by **что** (eg Я бою́сь, **что** он **придёт**). Both sentences mean *I am afraid he may come.* When it is feared that something may not happen, then only the second construction is possible. Thus the sentence *I was afraid he would not come* may only be rendered by Я боя́лся, **что** он не **придёт**.

- Negative antecedent: **бы** and a verb in the past tense may also be used in subordinate clauses after negated verbs such as **дýмать**, *to think*, and **знать**, *to know*, eg

  Я не дýмаю, **чтóбы** ктó-нибудь **мог** так вести́ себя́.
  I don't think anyone could behave like that.

10.11 Use of gerunds and participles

10.11.1 Use of gerunds

- The imperfective gerund describes action which is taking place at the same time as the action described by the main verb in the sentence (though the main verb itself may be in the past, present or future tense). It may translate English expressions such as *while doing, by doing, although they do*, as well as simply *doing*, eg

  Войскá нáчали осторóжное продвижéние к цéнтру, мéдленно **подавля́я** очаги́ сопротивлéния.
  The troops began a careful advance towards the centre, slowly suppressing centres of resistance.
  Слýшая рáдио, мóжно узнавáть, чтò происхóдит в ми́ре.
  One can find out what is going on in the world by listening to the radio.
  Обогревáя странý, рабóчие на электростáнциях не чýвствуют, что странá забóтится о них.

Although they heat the country, the power workers do not feel the country cares about them.

- The perfective gerund describes action that has taken place, and has been completed, before the action described by the main verb (which is not necessarily in the past). It translates an English expression of the sort *having done*, or, if it is negated, *without having done*, eg

Просидéв дéсять лет в тюрьмé, он поседéл.
Having been in prison for ten years, he had gone grey.
Сдéлав свой доклáд, онá сейчáс отвечáет на вопрóсы.
Having given her report she is now answering questions.
Нельзя́ уходи́ть, не **заплати́в**.
One mustn't go without paying [having paid].

Note 1 Gerunds may only be used when the subject performing the action in question is the same as the subject of the main clause, as is the case in all the above examples. A gerund cannot be used in a sentence of the type *While she reads the text I write out the words I don't know*, in which the two clauses have different subjects (*she* and *I*) and which must be translated thus: **Покá** онá **читáет** текст, я выпи́сываю незнакóмые словá.

2 Gerunds (mainly imperfective) have become established in set phrases, eg **прáвду говоря́**, *to tell the truth*; **сýдя по** (+ dat), *judging by*; **сидéть сложá рýки**, *to sit idly* (lit *with arms folded*). With the exception of such set phrases, though, the use of gerunds is largely confined to R3.

10.11.2 Use of active participles

Active participles correspond exactly, from a semantic point of view, to phrases containing **котóрый** + verb in the present tense (in the case of the present participles) or in the past tense, of either aspect (in the case of the past participles). The participle must agree in gender, case and number with the noun to which it relates (cf use of **котóрый**, 10.2.1), eg

Докумéнты, **подтверждáющие** [= котóрые подтверждáют] э́тот факт, бы́ли нáйдены в архи́вах.
Documents confirming this fact were found in archives.
Для пассажи́ров, **отправля́ющихся** [= котóрые отправля́ются] по сáмым популя́рным авиатрáссам, цéны тóже вы́росли.
Fares have also risen for passengers departing on the most popular air routes.
Автóбус, **вёзший** [= котóрый вёз] гостéй на свáдьбу, упáл с мостá.
A bus [which was] carrying guests to a wedding fell off a bridge.
Компáния нанимáет инострáнцев, специáльно **приéхавших** [= котóрые приéхали] для э́того в Росси́ю.
The company is employing foreigners who have come to Russia specially for the purpose.

Note: active participles differ from semantically identical phrases with **котóрый** in that their use is confined to R3, except insofar as some have become established in the language in set phrases (eg **пи́шущая маши́нка**, *typewriter*) or adjectives (eg **блестя́щий**, *brilliant*; **бы́вший**, *former*) or substantivised adjectives (eg **куря́щий**, *smoker*).

10.11.3 Use of present passive participles

These participles are rarely used predicatively, but used attributively they occur quite frequently in the modern written language. They must agree in gender, case and number with the noun to which they refer, eg

безрабо́тица и **порожда́емые** е́ю отча́яние и гнев
unemployment and the despair and anger generated by it
среди́ зало́жников, **уде́рживаемых** экстреми́стскими гру́ппами . . .
among the hostages held by extremist groups. . .

10.11.4 Use of past passive participles

These participles correspond to English participles of the type *read, written, washed.*

- Long forms of these participles decline like adjectives and must agree in gender, case and number with the noun to which they refer, eg

Маши́ны, **сде́ланные** в Япо́нии, сравни́тельно дёшевы.
Cars made in Japan are relatively cheap.
Здесь продаю́тся проду́кты, **пригото́вленные** без консерва́нтов.
Food-stuffs made without preservatives are sold here.
Я чита́ю кни́гу, **напи́санную** ва́шим отцо́м.
I am reading a book written by your father.

- Short forms of these participles, like short forms of adjectives, cannot be used unless the participle is used predicatively (ie unless some part of the verb *to be* comes between the noun and the participle which relates to it). However, when the participle is used predicatively then it must be in the short form, eg

Наш телефо́н давно́ был **отключён**.
Our telephone was cut off a long time ago.
В не́которых города́х **введена́** тало́нная систе́ма.
A system of rationing has been introduced in some cities.
Зда́ние **опеча́тано**.
The building has been sealed.
Э́ти дома́ бы́ли **постро́ены** в про́шлом году́.
These houses were built last year.

Note [1] Past passive participles are widely used in speech but in R1/R2 there is a tendency to avoid them by using instead a verb in the active voice (in the 3rd person plural without a pronoun; cf the unspecified English *they*, French *on*,

German *man*). Thus the above examples might be more colloquially rendered in the following way:

Наш телефо́н давно́ **отключи́ли**.
В не́которых города́х **ввели́** тало́нную систе́му.
Зда́ние **опеча́тали**.
Э́ти дома́ **постро́или** в про́шлом году́.

2 In many passive sentences the agent is named, eg Он был уби́т **партиза́нами**, *He was killed by guerrillas*; Она́ была́ арестóвана **мили́цией**, *She was arrested by the police*. Such sentences too may be rendered with an active verb, although Russian generally preserves the word order of the passive construction, with the named agent following the verb, eg

Его́ уби́ли партиза́ны.
Её арестова́ла мили́ция.

10.12 Conjunctions

10.12.1 Coordinating conjunctions

(a) The main coordinating conjunctions (**и**, **а**, **но**, **и́ли**) may be used in all registers. In R1, in which language tends to be spontaneous and less well organised, coordinating conjunctions are the principal means of linking the clauses of complex sentences and subordinating conjunctions (10.12.2) play a lesser role. The following points about these conjunctions should be particularly noted by the English-speaking student.

- Both **а** and **но** may be translated as *but*. However, **а** normally suggests a stronger opposition than **но**: it excludes one factor in favour of another, whereas **но** has only a sense of limitation. Contrast:

Сове́тую идти́ ме́дленно, **а** не бежа́ть.
I suggest you go slowly, don't run.
Сове́тую торопи́ться, **но** не бежа́ть.
I suggest you hurry, but don't run.

In the first example going slowly and running are presented as opposites and running is ruled out. In the second running is presented not as an opposite of hurrying but as an unnecessary intensification of it.

Note: **а** used in this contrastive sense may not be directly translated at all in English, eg «Лебеди́ное о́зеро» бале́т, **а** не о́пера, *'Swan Lake' is a ballet, not an opera* (see also the first example above).

- **а** may also translate English *and*, when that conjunction has contrastive meaning, eg

Сади́тесь, **а** я постою́.
You sit down and I shall stand.
Они́ оста́лись, **а** мы ушли́.
They stayed and we went home.

- in lists, in which in English *and* is placed as a rule before the last member, **и** may be omitted in Russian, particularly in sedate narrative style, eg

  Продавáли óбувь. Тýфли, кроссóвки, сапоги́, вáленки.
  They were selling footwear. Shoes, trainers, boots and felt boots.

  Inclusion of **и** in a list might give the list an exhaustive air and is therefore more probable in the precise language of R3a/b.

(b) There are in addition a few coordinating conjunctions which are not stylistically neutral but belong to R1, especially:

- **да** (esp in N dialects), eg

день **да** ночь	*day and night*
кóжа **да** кóсти	*skin and bone*
Я охóтно остáлся/остáлась бы, **да** порá уходи́ть.	*I'd willingly stay, but it's time to go.*
Бли́зок лóкоть, **да** не укýсишь.	*So near and yet so far.* (lit *One's elbow is near, but you can't bite it.*)

- **да и**, *and besides/and what is more*, eg

  Хóлодно бы́ло, **да и** дождь шёл.
  It was cold, and besides, it was raining.

- **а то**, *otherwise/or else*, eg

  Одевáйся потеплée, **а то** простýдишься.
  Put some more clothes on, otherwise you'll catch cold.
  Спеши́, **а то** опоздáем.
  Hurry or we'll be late.

- **ли́бо**, *or*, eg

Ли́бо пан, **ли́бо** пропáл.	*All or nothing.* (lit *Either a gentleman or I'm done for.*)

10.12.2 Subordinating conjunctions

The conjunctions given in the following examples are standard forms. They may all be used in all registers. It should be noted though that subordinating conjunctions tend to occur more in R3 (ie in formal language, where a speaker or writer is perhaps concerned to establish the logical connections which conjunctions indicate) than in R1, where language is more expressive and spontaneous and ideas less clearly organised, and where coordinating conjunctions therefore prevail.

Note: some English subordinating conjunctions (eg *after, before, since*) may also function as prepositions. When they are prepositions they are followed by a noun, pronoun or verbal noun, eg *after dinner, before us, since graduating*. When they are conjunctions they introduce a subordinate clause, eg *after I had had dinner*. In

Russian the two functions are distinguished. Thus **после** is a preposition, but the conjunction is **после того, как**.

causal

Де́вочка пла́кала, **потому́ что** она́ уста́ла.
*The little girl was crying **because** she was tired.*
Ле́кции не бу́дет, **так как** профе́ссор заболе́л.
*There won't be a lecture **since** the professor is ill.*

temporal

Я не зна́ю, **когда́** приду́.
*I don't know **when** I'll come.*
Он пришёл на остано́вку **по́сле того́, как** авто́бус ушёл.
*He arrived at the stop **after** the bus had gone.*
Нам на́до поговори́ть с ним об э́том, **пока́** он тут.
*We must have a word with him about that **while** he's here.*
Посмо́трим телеви́зор, **пока́** она́ **не** придёт.
*Let's watch television **until** she comes.*

Note: **пока́ не** is followed by a perfective verb.

Что он де́лал **с тех пор, как** око́нчил университе́т?
*What had he been doing **since** he left university?*
Она́ осозна́ла свою́ оши́бку, **как то́лько** вы́шла из ко́мнаты.
*She realised her mistake **as soon as** she left the room.*
Едва́ самолёт взлете́л, **как** пило́т обнару́жил непола́дку.
***No sooner** had the plane taken off **than** the pilot detected a fault.*
Ты до́лжен/должна́ дое́сть ры́бу, **пре́жде чем** взять моро́женое.
*You must eat up your fish **before** you have any ice-cream.*
Он пришёл **пе́ред тем, как** проби́ли часы́.
*He arrived **just before** the clock struck.*
Она́ рабо́тала перево́дчиком **до того́, как** ста́ла журнали́стом.
*She worked as translator **before** she became a journalist.*

Note: see 10.6(c) on use of tense after temporal and conditional conjunctions.

purposive

Она́ подошла́ к нему́, **что́бы** прошепта́ть ему́ что́-то на у́хо.
*She went up to him **so that** she could whisper something in his ear.*
Я говорю́ э́то **(для того́), что́бы** вы предста́вили себе́ все опа́сности.
*I am telling you this **so that/in order that** you should understand all the dangers.*

Note: **что́бы** + past tense is used when the subjects are different, as in the last example above, but when the subject of the verb in the subordinate clause is the same as that in the main clause **что́бы** is followed by the infinitive, eg **Я** э́то говорю́ **что́бы вы́разить** своё негодова́ние, *I am saying this in order to express my indignation.*

resultative

Маши́на слома́лась, **так что** мы опозда́ли.
*The car broke down **so that** we were late.*
Мы **до того́** уста́ли, **что** засну́ли в авто́бусе.
*We got **so** tired **that** we fell asleep on the bus.*

concessive

Я там бу́ду, **хотя́**, наве́рное, и опозда́ю.
*I'll be there, **although** I expect I'll be late.*

Note: see also modal particle **и** (4.4, и (c)).

На се́вере страны́ хо́лодно зимо́й, **тогда́ как** на ю́ге тепло́.
*It's cold in the north of the country in winter, **whereas** in the south it's warm.*

conditional

Е́сли вы не понима́ете, я объясню́.
***If** you don't understand I'll explain.*
Я уе́ду в командиро́вку, **е́сли то́лько** вы одо́брите мой план.
*I'll go on a business trip **provided** you approve my plan.*

Note: see 10.9 on conditional sentences and also 10.6(c) on use of tense in them.

10.12.3 Subordinating conjunctions used in R1 or R3

Some subordinating conjunctions that are not standard in R2 may also be encountered. These may be divided into (a) those which are still used but which belong mainly in R1 or R3 (including, in R3, many compound conjunctions), and (b) those which are considered obsolete in the modern literary language (although they will be found in classical literature and in some cases may persist in R1, especially in dialect).

restricted use

раз (R1)	*if*, eg **Раз** бу́ду в Москве́, загляну́ к тебе́, ***If** I'm in Moscow I'll call on you.*
благодаря́ тому́, что (R3)	*thanks to the fact that*
в связи́ с тем, что (R3)	*in connection with the fact that*
в си́лу того́, что (R3)	*by virtue of the fact that*
ввиду́ того́, что (R3)	*in view of the fact that*
вслéдствие того́, что (R3)	*owing to the fact that*
и́бо (R3)	*for*, eg Вся́кий труд ва́жен, **и́бо** облагора́живает челове́ка, *All labour is important, for it ennobles a man.* (Tolstoy)
невзира́я на то, что (R3)	*in spite of the fact that*
по ме́ре того́, как (R3)	*in proportion as*
посто́льку, поско́льку (R3)	*insofar as, to the extent that*
при усло́вии, что (R3)	*on condition that*
с тем что́бы + infin (R3)	*with a view to (doing)*

obsolete or colloquial

бу́де (N dialects)	*if, provided that*
дабы́	= что́бы
доко́ле (доко́ль)	*as long as, until*
е́жели	= е́сли (possible in R1)
ко́ли	*if* (possible in R1, esp dialect)
коль ско́ро	*so long as* (possible in R1)
пока́мест	= пока́ (possible in R1)

10.13 Syntactic features of colloquial speech

The language of R1 is characterised by a number of other syntactic features, as well as predominance of coordinating conjunctions over subordinating conjunctions and the use of some coordinating conjunctions not widely used in R2, eg

(a) ellipsis, which may be produced by omission of the verb (especially – but not exclusively – of a verb of motion) or of some other part of speech, eg

Вы ко мне?	*Are you coming to see me?*
Вдруг мне навстре́чу па́па.	*Suddenly dad was coming towards me.*
Мам, за до́ктором!	*Mum, get the doctor!*
Вы́стрел. Я че́рез забо́р.	*There was a shot. I was up and over the fence.*
Два на во́семь часо́в.	*Two [tickets] for eight o'clock.*
Мне пора́.	*It's time for me to go.*
Вы меня́?	*Is it me you're asking?*
Как дела́?	*How are things?*
Как жизнь?	*How is life?*
Всего́ хоро́шего!	*So long.*

(b) combination of a verb denoting condition or motion with another verb in the same form to indicate that the action is carried out in a certain state, eg

Она́ **сиде́ла ши́ла**.	*She was sitting sewing.*
Е́дем дре́млем.	*We were travelling along in a doze.*

(c) repetition of the verb to emphasise the protracted nature of an action, eg

Е́хали, е́хали, и наконе́ц прие́хали.	*We travelled and travelled, and eventually we arrived.*

(d) the combination of two verbs from the same root, separated by **не**, to indicate the fullness of an action, eg

Она́ **ра́дуется не нара́дуется** на сы́на.
She just dotes on her son.

(e) a construction containing a form of **взять** (often the imperative) and another verb in the same form, the two verbs being linked by **да** or **и** or **да и**; the construction expresses sudden volition on the part of the subject, eg

Он **взял да убежа́л**.	*He was up and off.*
Она́ **вдруг возьми́ да и разозли́сь** на меня́.	*She suddenly went and got angry with me.*

(f) the very colloquial construction **то́лько и де́лает, что/то́лько и**

зна́ет, что, together with another verb in the same form, indicating a single, exclusive action, eg

День-деньско́й **то́лько и зна́ет, что смо́трит** телеви́зор.
He's always watching TV all day long.
Мы с бра́том **то́лько и де́лали, что игра́ли** в ша́хматы.
My brother and I just played chess all the time.

(g) the use of **знай (себе́)** with a verb to indicate that the subject perseveres with the action in question in spite of unfavourable circumstances or obstacles, eg

Де́ти крича́ли. Ма́ма **знай себе́ чита́ла** газе́ту.
The children were shouting. Mum went on reading the paper quite unconcerned.

(h) the use of **смотри́(те)** and a negative imperative in the sense of *mind you don't*, eg

Ты **смотри́ не говори́** про меня́!
Mind you don't talk about me.

Note: see also 4.4 on modal particles (так (b) and -то (c)) and 4.5 on interjections.

10.14 Word order

Word order is much more flexible in Russian than in English, since it is primarily inflection that establishes the relationship between the words in a Russian utterance. Whereas the order of words in the English statement *John loves Mary* cannot be altered without a consequential change of meaning, in Russian one may say, depending on the context or emphasis, either **Ива́н лю́бит Мари́ю** (*Ivan loves Mariia*) or **Мари́ю лю́бит Ива́н** (*It's Ivan who loves Mariia*).

However, Russian word order, while being flexible, is not random, but conforms to certain principles and rules. Moreover, it may be affected, like other aspects of language, by register. The following guidance can be given.

(a) Neutral word order: as a general rule the same sequence of subject + verb + object/complement which characterises English statements is observed in matter-of-fact statements in Russian too, eg

Ма́ма пи́шет письмо́.	*Mum's writing a letter.*
Охо́тники пойма́ли льва.	*The hunters caught a lion.*
Са́ша ста́нет инжене́ром.	*Sasha will become an engineer.*

(b) New and known or given information (**но́вое и да́нное**): the point in an utterance on which the speaker or writer wishes to focus attention, the novel element in it, is placed at or towards the end of the Russian utterance, since it carries more weight there. The earlier part of the utterance, on the other hand, contains the information which leads up to the novel point, information that is already familiar or taken for granted or less important. Contrast eg

По́езд пришёл.	*The train arrived.*
Пришёл по́езд.	*A train arrived.*
Ко́шка сиде́ла на печи́.	*The cat was sitting on the stove.*
На печи́ сиде́ла ко́шка.	*A cat was sitting on the stove.*

Note 1 What is new in a statement varies of course according to the point in a conversation or narrative which has been reached.

2 If it is the subject of the statement that represents the new information then the order of subject and verb will be inverted.

3 The distinctions achieved in Russian by variations of word order may be achieved in English by choice between the definite article (introducing known information) and the indefinite article (introducing a new element).

(c) Other rules obtaining in specific circumstances: the following guidance can be given (note differences from English usage).

- Subject and verb are inverted in statements in which the verb denotes natural event, existence, process, state, becoming or occurrence, eg

Идёт снег.	*It's snowing.*
Существу́ет риск пожа́ра.	*There's a risk of fire.*
Прошли́ го́ды.	*The years went by.*
У меня́ боли́т голова́.	*I've got a headache.*
Наступи́ла зима́.	*Winter came.*
Произошёл взрыв.	*There was an explosion.*

Note: it will be seen that in all these sentences the word order is consistent with the point made in (b) above about known and new information: in each instance the weight of the utterance is contained in the subject, while the verb is a weak word with relatively inconsequential meaning.

- Inversion is also common when the place where an action occurred is indicated at the beginning of the statement, eg

С за́пада шли облака́.	*Clouds were coming from the west.*

- The order of subject and verb is also inverted in questions introduced by an interrogative word and after reported speech, eg

Где нахо́дится вокза́л?	*Where's the station?*
Когда́ начина́ется фильм?	*When does the film begin?*
Я уста́л,—сказа́л он.	*'I'm tired', he said.*

- Object pronouns are frequently placed before the verb, eg

Я **вас** слу́шаю.	*I'm listening to you.*
мы **вам** сказа́ли, что. . .	*we told you that. . .*
Тру́дности бы́ли, но мы с **ни́ми** спра́вились.	*There were difficulties, but we coped with them.*
Он **ничего́** не зна́ет.	*He doesn't know anything.*

- Objects indicating the person in impersonal expressions also tend to be placed before the predicate, eg

Мне на́до идти́.	*I must go.*
У нас не хвата́ет де́нег.	*We haven't got enough money.*

- Infinitives as a rule follow the verb or expression on which they are dependent, eg

Мы прие́хали **отдыха́ть**.	*We have come to rest.*
Собира́юсь **уе́хать**.	*I am about to go away.*
Ну́жно **рабо́тать**.	*It's necessary to work.*

- In the modern language attributive adjectives, as in English, normally precede the noun they qualify, but they may follow the noun in menus or catalogues, eg

хоро́шая пого́да	*fine weather*
ско́рый по́езд	*a fast train*
напи́тки **прохлади́тельные**	*soft drinks*
сала́т **столи́чный**	*'capital-city salad'*

Note: predicative adjectives, on the other hand, generally follow the noun irrespective of whether they are long or short, eg Кни́га **интере́сна**, *The book is interesting*; Зада́ча была́ **тру́дная**, *The task was a difficult one.*

- Adverbs tend immediately to precede the verb they modify, eg

Всегда́ сия́ет со́лнце.	*The sun always shines.*
Он **ещё** спит.	*He's still asleep.*
Она́ **хорошо́** вы́глядит.	*She looks good.*
И́скренно благодарю́ вас.	*I sincerely thank you.*

Note 1 Adverbs indicating language used, on the other hand, follow the verb, eg Она́ говори́т **по-ру́сски**, *She speaks Russian.*

2 Certain adverbs which are used with a limited number of verbs and most of which are derived from nouns also generally follow the verb, eg идти́ **пешко́м**, *to go on foot*; ходи́ть **босико́м**, *to go about barefoot.*

(d) In expressive registers, eg R1, R3c and the language of belles-lettres, emphasis or emotive effect is achieved by subversion of the rules given above. Consider the following examples which all embody some departure from neutral word order as it has been described in the preceding paragraphs:

Был **он** до́брый ма́лый.
He was a nice fellow.
Рома́ны чита́ете?
Do you read novels? (as opposed to eg plays)
Простоя́ли **мы** час в о́череди.
We stood in the queue for an hour.
Все **смея́ться** ста́ли.
Everybody started laughing.

Она́ **пла́вать** о́чень лю́бит.
She likes swimming very much.
Рабо́тать ну́жно.
One must work.
Я вам расскажу́ анекдо́т **смешно́й**.
I'll tell you a funny story.
Поэ́т земли́ **ру́сской**. (rhet; eg in newspaper headline)
A poet of the Russian land.
В степи́ **глухо́й**.
Deep in the steppe. (poet; eg in folk song)
Печа́льно э́то ме́сто в дождли́вый день.
This place is miserable on a rainy day.

10.15 Punctuation

Russian usage with regard to punctuation differs significantly from English usage, and since Russian usage is also more rigid the student aiming for a high degree of accuracy in the language needs to pay some attention to the Russian rules in this area.

- The full stop (**то́чка**), the question mark (**вопроси́тельный знак**) and the semi-colon (**то́чка с запято́й**), broadly speaking, are used as in English, to mark respectively: the end of a sentence, the end of a question, and a division within a sentence that is more marked than that indicated by a comma.
- The colon (**двоето́чие**) too is used in a similar way in both English and Russian, ie it may introduce:

(a) a clause that explains or expands on the preceding clause, eg

Она́ опозда́ла на ле́кцию**:** по́езд, на кото́ром она́ е́хала, был заде́ржан.
She was late for the lecture: the train she was travelling on was delayed.

(b) direct or reported speech, eg

Он провёл руко́й по лбу**:**
—Нет, я не бу́ду.
He passed his hand over his brow. 'No, I'm not going to.'
Все сказа́ли одно́ и то же**:** что́бы я рабо́тал(а) побо́льше.
Everybody said the same thing: that I should work a bit harder.

(c) a list, eg

Выра́щиваем вся́кого ро́да о́вощи на огоро́де**:** карто́фель, морко́вь, лук, капу́сту. . .
We grow all sorts of vegetables on the allotment: potatoes, carrots, onions, cabbages. . .

(d) a quotation, eg

Мо́жет быть, по́мнишь слова́ Пу́шкина: «Весна́, весна́, пора́ любви́!»
Perhaps you remember Pushkin's words: 'Spring, spring, the time of love!'

However, the remaining punctuation marks used in English (the comma, the dash, the exclamation mark, quotation marks, brackets, omission dots) require more attention.

- Comma (**запята́я**): this is used in Russian to serve many of the purposes of the comma in English, for example to indicate minor pauses as in lists, to separate adjectives qualifying the same noun or adverbs modifying the same verb, after **да** and **нет**, and so forth, eg

Она́ говори́т по-ру́сски, по-по́льски, по-неме́цки и по-да́тски.
She speaks Russian, Polish, German and Danish.
Э́то до́брый, весёлый, у́мный челове́к.
He's a kind, cheerful, intelligent man.
—Вы уме́ете пла́вать?
—Да, уме́ю.
'Can you swim?' 'Yes, I can.'

Use of the comma is also obligatory in Russian in the following circumstances in which its use may be optional in English or in which English usage tends to be lax:

(a) to separate clauses linked by coordinating conjunctions, eg

Са́ша гимна́ст, а Пе́тя штанги́ст.
Sasha's a gymnast and Petia's a weight-lifter.

Note: when the conjunction is **и** a comma is not used if the subject of the verb in the two clauses is the same, eg Она́ легла́ на дива́н **и** засну́ла, *She lay down on the sofa and went to sleep.*

(b) to mark the division (or divisions) between a main clause and any subordinate or relative clauses, eg

Он сказа́л, что э́того не забу́дет.
He said he would not forget this.
Э́то бы́ло два го́да тому́ наза́д, когда́ я рабо́тал(а) в Москве́.
It was two years ago, when I was working in Moscow.
Гости́ница, в кото́рой мы остана́вливались, была́ постро́ена в про́шлом году́.
The hotel in which we were staying was built last year.

(c) to mark off any phrases containing gerunds or participles, eg

Нача́в чита́ть, я сра́зу по́нял(а́) значе́ние э́того докуме́нта.
Having begun to read, I at once realised the importance of this document.
Лю́ди, нося́щие то же са́мое и́мя, называ́ются «тёзками».
People who have the same name are called namesakes.

(d) to mark off any parenthetical words, eg

Мой брат, наве́рное, ста́нет врачо́м.
My brother'll probably be a doctor.
Я всё могу́ прости́ть лю́дям, да́же преда́тельство, так как счита́ю э́то сла́бостью.
I can forgive people anything, even treachery, because I consider it a weakness.

(e) to mark off any comparative phrases, eg

Он говори́т быстре́е, чем я.
He speaks more quickly than I do.

- Dash (**тире́** [э́]; indecl): this punctuation mark, which is longer than an English dash, has several important uses, eg

(a) to indicate some sort of omission, either of a copula (as is the case when it is necessary to render in Russian the English verb *to be* in the present tense) or of some part of an utterance expressed elliptically, eg

Мой брат—студе́нт.
My brother is a student.
Серёжа—к воро́там, но вдруг из до́ма послы́шался крик.
Seriozha was off towards the gate, but suddenly from the house came a shout.

Note: the dash is not normally used to indicate a missing copula when the subject is a pronoun, eg **Он студе́нт**, *He is a student.*

(b) to introduce direct speech and (if the verb indicating that direct speech is being reproduced follows the speech itself) to close that speech, eg

Он спроси́л:
—Ско́лько про́сишь?
Ди́ма назва́л це́ну.
—Ого́!—вы́пучил он глаза́.—Тебе́ повезёт, е́сли найдёшь дурака́ на таку́ю це́ну.
He asked:
'How much are you asking?'
Dima named his price.
'Oho!' he opened his eyes wide. 'You'll be lucky if you find a fool prepared to pay that.'

Note: the direct speech introduced by the dash must begin on a fresh line.

(c) to draw attention to something unexpected, to mark a syntactic change of direction, or to give a sense of energy to an utterance, eg

Я ожида́л(а), что они́ приглася́т меня́—а они́ не приглаша́ли.
I expected them to invite me – but they haven't.
И́ре не приноси́ли посы́лок—то́лько пи́сьма шли в её а́дрес.
They didn't bring any parcels to Ira; she was just sent letters.

Безрабо́тица—э́то са́мая о́страя пробле́ма, стоя́щая пе́ред прави́тельством.
Unemployment is the most serious problem facing the government.

(d) a pair of dashes may mark off a parenthetical remark in a more emphatic way than a pair of commas, eg

Следы́ э́того пери́ода её жи́зни—боле́знь, преждевре́менная ста́рость—оста́лись у неё навсегда́.
The traces of this period of her life – illness and premature old age – remained with her for ever.

- Exclamation mark (**восклица́тельный знак**): this tends to be used more widely than in English. It is placed, for example, after instructions expressed by some part of speech other than an imperative and after greetings (6.6), congratulations and wishes (6.8–9) and forms of address at the beginning of letters (6.17), as well as after interjections (see 4.5) and other phrases that would be followed by an exclamation mark in English too, eg

Здра́вствуйте!	*Hello.*
Споко́йной но́чи!	*Good night.*
С днём рожде́ния!	*Happy birthday.*
Дорога́я Ири́на!	*Dear Irina,*
Многоуважа́емый Никола́й Петро́вич!	*Dear Nikolai Petrovich,*
тсс!	*Hush!*

- Quotation marks (**кавы́чки**): marks of the sort used in English (‘ ’ or “ ”) do not occur in Russian, but guillemets (« ») are used to enclose titles, quotations, unusual words, eg

Я чита́ю «Преступле́ние и наказа́ние».
I am reading ‘Crime and Punishment’.
Что тако́е «катра́н»?
What is a ‘katran’? (see 4.1.2)

Note: guillemets may also be used as an alternative to a dash as an introduction to direct speech if the verb which indicates that direct speech is being reproduced precedes the speech itself, eg Го́рка пи́сем нараста́ет, кто́-то се́рдится—«вы мне не отве́тили!», *The pile of letters grows and somebody gets angry: ‘You haven’t replied to me!’*

- Brackets (**ско́бки**): these indicate a parenthesis more marked than that indicated by commas or dashes.

- Omission dots (**многото́чие**): these are quite widely used to indicate that a thought is incomplete or that speech is hasty or awkward, eg

Он… вы не ду́маете… он не вор…
He… you don't think… He's not a thief…

10.16 Use of capital letters

Capital letters are used much more sparingly in Russian than in English. In particular the foreign student should note that:

- capital letters are not used in Russian at the beginning of words naming days of the week or months of the year, or indicating nationality or religion, place of origin or language, eg

понеде́льник	*Monday*
янва́рь (m)	*January*
англича́нин	*Englishman*
мусульма́нин	*Moslem*
москви́ч	*Muscovite*
ру́сский язы́к	*Russian (language)*

- in titles of organisations, institutions, posts, journals, newspapers, books and so forth, it is usual for only the first word in the title to begin with a capital letter (cf the English practice of beginning each noun and adjective with a capital), eg

Консервати́вная па́ртия	*the Conservative Party*
Ло́ндонский университе́т	*the University of London*
Мини́стр оборо́ны	*the Minister of Defence*
Аргуме́нты и фа́кты	*Arguments and Facts* (a contemporary journal)
Ра́ковый ко́рпус	*Cancer Ward* (Solzhenitsyn's novel)

- in place-names the generic name (eg **океа́н**, **мо́ре**, **о́стров**, **река́**, **о́зеро**, **пло́щадь**, **у́лица**) is usually written with a small letter and the proper noun and accompanying adjectives with capitals, eg

Ти́хий океа́н	*the Pacific Ocean*
Се́верный Ледови́тый океа́н	*the Arctic Ocean*
Каспи́йское мо́ре	*the Caspian Sea*
о́стров Сахали́н	*the Island of Sakhalin*
Гибралта́рский проли́в	*the Strait of Gibraltar*
Суэ́цкий кана́л	*the Suez Canal*
тро́пик Козеро́га	*the Tropic of Capricorn*
Се́верный по́люс	*the North Pole*
Кра́сная пло́щадь	*Red Square*
Зи́мний дворе́ц	*the Winter Palace*
Петропа́вловская кре́пость	*the Peter and Paul Fortress*

Note: in some names the above conventions are not observed, eg

Да́льний Восто́к	*the Far East*
Организа́ция Объединённых На́ций	*the United Nations Organisation*
Соединённые Шта́ты Аме́рики	*the United States of America*
Сою́з Сове́тских Социалисти́ческих Респу́блик	*the Union of Soviet Socialist Republics*

Russian words and affixes

This index contains words (including interjections and particles), phrases and affixes (ie prefixes, infixes, suffixes) on which specific information is given in Chapters 2–5 and 7–10 inclusive. Not included in this index are the alphabetically arranged loanwords in 4.1.1–2, obscenities (4.6), abbreviations (5.9), acronyms and alphabetisms (5.10), geographical names and words derived from them (5.11), words given as examples of various types of word-formation in Chapter 7, words given as examples of standard types of noun and adjectival inflection in Chapter 8 and verbs listed as examples of a given type of conjugation in Chapter 8.

Where more than one form of a noun, adjective or pronoun occurs it is generally the nominative singular form that is given here. Both aspects of a verb are usually given together, with the imperfective invariably first, although in many cases the point dealt with in the text relates to use of only one aspect. The perfective forms given are not all invariably used as the perfective of the imperfective in question. Where one aspectual form differs markedly from the other (eg брать/взять) it is also given separately.

For the purpose of arranging forms in alphabetical order phrases and hyphenated words are treated as indivisible.

Index